PRACTICAL
JUNK RIG

Jester *in 1960 before the start of the first singlehanded transatlantic race. She has taken part in every subsequent race and still carries this early type of Hasler sail design.* (Photo: Eileen Ramsay)

HG Hasler
JK McLeod

PRACTICAL JUNK RIG

Design, Aerodynamics and Handling

INTERNATIONAL MARINE PUBLISHING
Camden, Maine

International Marine Publishing
Route One, Box 220
Camden, Maine 04843

First published in Great Britain by
Adlard Coles 1988

Illustrations by Mike Collins

Typesetting and origination by
CG Graphic Services, Tring, Herts
Printed and bound in Great Britain by
Butler and Tanner Ltd, Frome

Contents

Foreword   ix
Preface   xi

PART I THE CHINESE RIG

Introduction   3

1 The Rig   **10**
   The mast   13
   Battens   13
   The sail   16
   Aerodynamics and the junk rig   18

2 The Geometry of the Sail   **19**
   Sail analysis   20
   Basic sail shapes   22
   Recommended sail form   30

3 The Rigging of the Sail   **32**
   Halyards   32
   Yard hauling parrel   37
   Mast line   39
   Mast rake   40
   Control of the boom   42
   Sailcloth creasing   42
   Batten downhauls   48
   Yard downhaul   49
   Topping-lifts   50

4 The Sheets   **56**
   Sheet power and sheet spans   56
   Reefing and furling   62
   Six-point sheeting system   66
   Positioning lower sheet blocks   70

5 Ghosters and Lightning Conductors   **78**
Ghosters   78
Lightning Conductors   82

PART II   DESIGNING A RIG

Introduction   87

6 Designing the Sailplan (1)   **90**
Position of the sailplan   90
The sailplan   94
Drawing the sail   103
Summary: drawing a standard Chinese sail   110

7 Designing the Sailplan (2)   **114**
Positioning a single-sailed rig   114
Positioning a multi-sailed rig   114
Unacceptable mast positions   115
Unacceptable sheet positions   116
Suggested solutions   116
Positioning the lower sheet blocks   119
Summary: designing a sailplan (2)   119

8 Masts   **120**
Timber masts   122
Species of timber   124
Hollow timber masts   124
Gluing   126
Preservation of a timber mast   127
Cable fastening   128
Designing and drawing a hollow mast   128
Designing a hollow staved timber mast   132
Designing a grown mast   132
Mast fittings   133
Masts of other materials   138

9 Partners and Mast Step   **141**
The partners   141
The mast step   145
Tabernacles   148

10 Yard, Battens, and Boom   **151**
The yard   151
The battens   154
The boom   159

11   The Sail   **163**
   The scale outline   163
   Detail drawing and specification   163

12   The Rigging   **171**
   The halyard   172
   The Sheets   176
   Topping-lifts   178
   Mast lift   179
   Parrels   179
   Tackline   180
   Lacings   180
   Optional rigging items   180

13   Cockpit and Deck Layout   **181**
   Boom gallows   181
   Lower sheet blocks   183
   Rope leads   183
   Cleats, hitches, and jammers   184
   Stowage of spare rope   185
   Integrated deck layouts   187

PART III   USING THE RIG

14   Setting up the Rig   **197**
   General points   197
   Stepping and unstepping the mast   197
   Dressing the mast   201
   Rigging the sail   202

15   Handling the Rig   **204**
   Sail-handling   204
   Maintenance   210
   Repairs and emergency procedures   210
   Correction of excessive lee/weather helm   215

16   Specimen Chinese-Rigged Vessels   **216**
   Jester (1960)   216
   Redlapper (1962)   216
   Galway Blazer II (1968)   218
   Ròn Glas (1970)   220
   Yeong (1972)   222
   Sumner (1972)   223

Design SSF/1 (1973)   225
Hum (1974)   227
Batwing (1974)   228
Pilmer (1975)   229

APPENDICES

A Imperial/metric equivalents   233
B Inches as decimals of a foot   233

Bibliography   235

Index   237

Foreword

Blondie Hasler died after completion of the present work but before its publication. The name Hasler is readily associated with a number of marine projects of which perhaps the most significant was the development of wind vane steering for yachts. However, it may be that his most enduring contribution will be seen to be the adaptation of the principles underlying the traditional Chinese rig to western sailing craft. He devoted his last twenty years to it.

Blondie was of course responsible for the first singlehanded transatlantic race in 1960, and shortly before it he altered the rig of his modified folkboat *Jester* from the experimental Lapwing to a single Chinese lugsail slung on an unstayed mast. The boat has used the same rig ever since on her many long voyages, which include thirteen transatlantic passages.

With his co-author Jock McLeod Blondie designed junk rigs for a number of vessels and, in addition to their own considerable experience, was able to profit by the seagoing experience of others such as Bill King whose junk-rigged *Galway Blazer II* completed a circumnavigation in 1973. This book is the result of all that work. But it is more.

There appears to be no comprehensive Chinese text on the rig and although a number of Western sources describe in detail the rigging of contemporary Chinese vessels, there is nothing that tells you how to design junk rigs or how to sail them. Neither is there any work on the geometry and aerodynamic theory that lie behind them. *Practical Junk Rig* admirably fills that need. It is both a handbook for the mariner and a work of reference for anyone who wants to study in detail this most appealing and seamanlike of rigs.

Michael Richey
Yacht *Jester*
Plymouth

Preface

Sail enthusiasts all over the world are showing an increasing interest in the Chinese, or 'junk', rig. This is because the rig is incomparably safe, seamanlike, and easy to handle. It is particularly suitable for small boats and for short-handed or family sailing, in open water and in unpredictable weather conditions.

This book is intended to provide a primer for those who want to study the rig in detail. It describes the process of designing a rig for any specific boat, rigging it, and sailing it. It is written equally for the amateur owner and for the professional designer who may be approaching the subject for the first time.

The authors' qualifications are simply that we have worked together on the development of the Chinese rig for 25 years, using it on our own boats and designing rigs for other yachtsmen in various parts of the world. Between us we have sailed at least 65,000 miles of open sea with it, including ten crossings of the North Atlantic. The more we sail with it the more we like it, and this is true both on ocean passages and when cruising in coastal waters.

Our most distinguished client is undoubtedly Bill King, whose 42 ft (12.8 m) *Galway Blazer II* (p 215 and Fig. 16.3) carried him across 40,000 miles of ocean singlehanded before he sold her to Peter Crowther for further voyaging. We believe that she may have been the first junk-rigged vessel in history to have sailed round the world or round the Horn.

We are not experts on the vessels of the China coast, nor in the history of the rig, but hope that some of the references in the Bibliography will help readers whose interest lies in that direction. Inevitably this list is incomplete, as is our knowledge of the work done by other Western designers.

The adaptation of this ancient rig to modern needs is still in an early stage, but we have tried to provide a starting point from which other enthusiasts will make further headway. We hope they enjoy working with the rig as much as we do.

We would like to take this opportunity to express our thanks to those who have provided advice and information from their own experiences or specialist knowledge. The most important of these is Michael Richey, the present owner of *Jester* and the editor of a number of publications. His ability as an author and his experience and knowledge of publishing with his helpful criticism and advice have been invaluable to us. We would also like to include Peter

Lucas of W. G. Lucas and Son, sailmakers; R. Mason of R. Mason and Son, the patentees of the 'Noble Mast' system; and David Hunt of Needlespar Ltd, Warsash; for their specialist advice and comments.

We also wish to thank Rear Admiral R. L. Fisher, the original owner of *Yeong*, Commander Bill King (*Galway Blazer II*), and Timothy Dunn of *Batwing*, for permission to use drawings and to mention their experiences. There are also other friends and acquaintances who have helped, encouraged or stimulated thought, and we extend our thanks to them too.

HGH
JKM
1987

PART I

THE CHINESE RIG

A large Chinese Junk running goosewinged. Note the huge mainsail and the different balance of the sails and their design. (Photo: South China Morning Post Ltd)

Introduction

The first Chinese lugsails, made of matting woven from thin strips of bamboo and stiffened by bamboo or pine battens, are believed to have appeared in China before AD 300. By 1430 the seagoing junks of the Ming dynasty seem to have been substantially larger than any ships of the Western world and to have voyaged in huge fleets at least as far as the Red Sea and East Africa.

The great junks of this time may have reached 500 ft (152 m) in overall length, which is far larger than any seen since and nearly twice as long as the *Cutty Sark*, but by the 16th century the Ming navy had all but vanished, a victim of political change. This left only the smaller coasters and river traders that have continued to develop in design, but not in size, into the 20th century. These include junks of 180 ft (55 m) in length with anything up to five masts, some of them over 6 ft (1.8 m) in diameter at the deck and carrying sails of over 3,000 sq ft (279 m²).

From Marco Polo onwards, Western observers on the China coast have become fascinated by junks in their endless variety of size and type, and have praised their efficiency as practical sailing craft while struggling to understand the thinking of Chinese shipwrights and sailors, which seemed so often to be the exact opposite of their own.

The junk rig is not a square rig but was one of the earliest of the true fore-and-aft rigs, that is to say rigs in which the wind blows against opposite sides of the sail on opposite tacks. For centuries it may have been the most efficient windward rig in the world, particularly in hard winds when the flat sail develops good drive while inducing minimum leeway.

The windward ability of Western rigs has been transformed in fairly recent times by the development of high-quality sailcloth and sophisticated sailmaking. Previously, all large Western sails tended to develop too much 'belly' for windward work, and seamen were continually trying to make them set flatter. The junk sail can be made to set very flat in all wind strengths regardless of whether it is made of good sailcloth, bamboo matting, or indeed old flour sacks.

Comparisons between rigs are difficult to make, particularly when mounted on different hulls, but nowadays the windward performance of a good junk rig seems to be comparable with that of a gaff rig – perhaps less good in light airs but better in a blow. Its worst point of sailing is ghosting to windward in a lop or swell. Off the wind, the sail is excellent for its area in all wind strengths. The

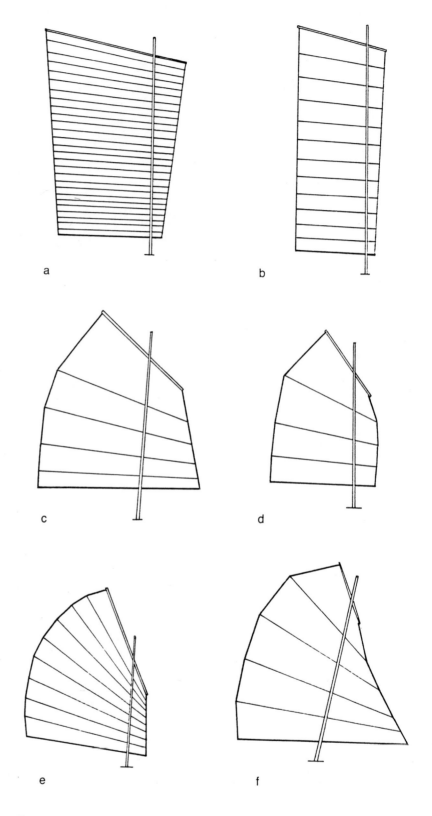

Fig. 1.1   Some sail shapes seen in China

ability to square the whole sail off at right angles to the boat is a considerable bonus. Conventional spinnakers are not efficient for their area; they are just an efficient way of setting a lot more area.

There is no standard type of sail in China, and every conceivable variation seems to exist. Fig. 1.1 shows some of the sail shapes recorded there in the past fifty years. The square-headed sail a seems to be the ancient shape and is still widely used, particularly on inland waters in the high-aspect-ratio form shown at b. The remaining sketches show forms in which the head is more steeply angled, that shown at f, which is the foresail of a three-master, having a head that is actually in line with the luff.

It will be seen that the number of battens, and hence the width of the sail panels, varies very considerably. It seems possible that the mat sails used in the past demanded narrow panels, a large number of battens, and square heads. The introduction of cotton sailcloth has probably contributed to the development of high-peaked sails with fewer battens and wider panels.

All native Chinese rigs share a number of features. They are constructed of cheap and readily available materials, with very few metal parts. The subdivision of the sail into a number of separate panels, each supported and controlled by its own system of sheets, battens, bolt ropes, and parrels, ensures that the stresses are shared between many load-carrying components and that no one part takes a heavy load except for the mast and halyard. Even on the mast, the lateral loads are distributed along it by the battens and parrels and not concentrated at the masthead as they are with the dipping lugsail favoured by British fishing boats in the last days of sail. The loads on sailcloth and sheets are vastly less than with the Western rig, and it is difficult to think of any other rig in which a huge seagoing sail could be made of bamboo matting and yet be able to sail through a gale without damage. In many ways it is valid to think of the junk sail as being a number of much smaller sails joined together.

The rig can be used on boats of widely different sizes and functions. A dinghy of 8 ft (2.4 m) overall length has given good service as a yacht's tender with a simplified and portable junk sail of 49 sq ft (4.6 m²). At the other end of the scale it would clearly be possible to emulate the Chinese with junk-rigged cargo-carrying coasters. The upper limit of size is imposed by the fact that all halyard loads must be carried by the masthead and cannot be distributed lower down the mast. An area of about 3,000 sq ft (279 m²) for a single sail would seem to be near the practical limit.

The 'twist' of a sail is defined as the variation in its incidence to the wind, taken at different heights above the deck. The junk sail commonly shows little or no twist whereas Western rigs, particularly the gaff rig, often develop far too much twist in a hard breeze, with the foot sheeted too flat and the head sagging too far off. Fig. 1.2 illustrates this difference as seen from the lee quarter.

The aerodynamicist may argue that a certain amount of twist is needed for efficiency when close-hauled with a tall sail, because the wind velocity increases with height. The Chinese sail and its sheeting system may be designed to give any such small amount of

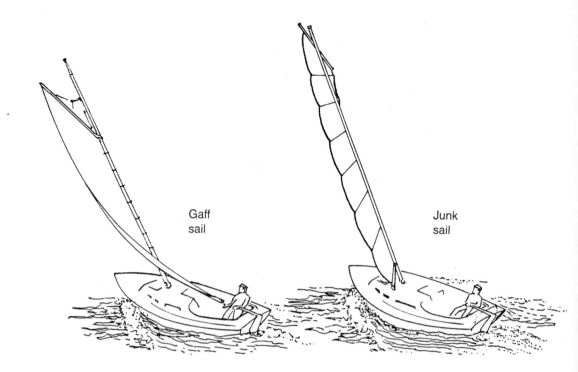

Gaff
sail

Junk
sail

Fig. 1.2 Twist

twist as may be required.

The hulls of many Chinese workboats have very little lateral resistance, and there is evidence that such hulls can get to windward better with the Chinese than with a Western rig. Joshua Slocum chose a three-masted junk rig for the 35 ft (11 m) canoe *Liberdade* which he built for himself after the wreck of the barque *Aquidneck*, and in which he and his family sailed 5,500 miles from Brazil to South Carolina in 1888, averaging 105 miles a day. He wrote: 'Her rig was the Chinese *sampan* style, which is, I consider, the most convenient boat rig in the whole world.'

The mainsail of a large Chinese junk may weigh five tons, with a yard over 65 ft (20 m) long and two or more separate halyards. It can take the whole crew over an hour to hoist such a sail, but reefing and furling is a matter of seconds and the rig is almost squall-proof. Unlike other rigs, the junk sail *wants* to reef and furl itself, and will do so as soon as it is given the opportunity.

The battens hold the sail stretched from luff to leech at all times so that it cannot thrash or flog when head to wind with a slack sheet, but will 'weathercock' quietly, even in a gale, by just swinging gently from side to side. The flogging of a soft sail is unnerving, noisy, and a quick way of wearing out sailcloth and stitching. In a conventional rig with a fresh breeze it happens every time you hoist sail, every time you tack, and every time you luff up to a mooring or a man overboard. It altogether inhibits the useful and safe operation of hulling with slack sheets, something that is second nature to the docile junk rig.

Two lesser degrees of sail shaking may be defined: 'flapping', in which only a part of the sail oscillates rhythmically (for example, a flapping leech on a conventional sail), and 'fluttering', in which small oscillations are confined to a very small area of sail. Flapping is seldom experienced in the junk rig, and should be cured by a sailmaker. Fluttering may sometimes be found near the luff or leech, and also in the loose folds of cloth lying in the lifts when reefed or furled. Narrow sail panels are the best insurance against an untidy bundle that flutters.

When a Chinese sail becomes torn or lets go a seam, the damage remains localised and the repair may be postponed indefinitely. The Western observer, laughing at the sight of a junk with her sails full of holes, may overlook the fact that she is working briskly to windward through a crowded anchorage.

In the past, Western seamen have used the junk rig in three different ways:

(a) by using genuine Chinese rigs, designed and built in the East, on either Chinese or Western hulls;
(b) by devising hybrid rigs, which combine certain features of the junk rig with other major features not found in China;
(c) by using rigs that are Chinese in all major characteristics, but which have been designed and built in the West to suit Western requirements.

Of these, group (a) is beyond the scope of this book. In group (b) many experimenters are still at work, mainly in the development of battened fabric aerofoils embracing the mast. Here the main problems seem to be complexity of batten construction, lack of 'topsail' area for light going, and reluctance of the sail to furl itself neatly. None of these 'improvements' has yet proved superior to the standard junk sail for serious ocean cruising, whether up or down wind. In this book we concentrate on group (c), in which the recommended rigs have already proved themselves to be fully seaworthy and widely acceptable.

In general, we are dealing with fully-rigged sailing vessels, i.e. vessels in which sail provides the main means of propulsion or has at least an equal importance with the power unit, but the junk sail has also proved effective as an auxiliary sail for fully-powered vessels. In this role the apparent complexity of gear can be more than offset by its freedom from flogging, its self-stowing facility, and the possibility of handling all running ropes from inside the wheelhouse. One such user also found that the inertia effect of the cantilever mast slowed down the boat's period of roll, even with no sail set, to such an extent that he was able to remove his bilge keels and thereby get an extra half-knot under power.

The requirements of Western seamen are different from those of the Chinese in a number of ways. Commercial sail is almost extinct, or at least dormant, in the West, and the demand so far has been for yachts. Many Western yachtsmen now want to make long open-sea passages in very small boats, an ambition that has never been evident in China. Many also want to sail singlehanded, or with a weak crew of family or friends that may not include any other competent seamen. The advent of wind-vane steering gear has made it possible for these short-handed boats to make long passages efficiently, provided that the rig can be easily handled. The junk rig offers this ease of handling, together with safety and sailing efficiency, with the help of some fresh development work that started in Britain in 1960 and is still continuing.

In recent years there has been a movement, started in the United States, to develop other forms of easily-handled cruising rigs set on unstayed masts. Gary Hoyt's original Freedom rig uses wrap-around jib-headed sails spread by wishbone booms, and there have been many later variations on this idea. These rigs demonstrate that cruising yachtsmen are willing to turn away from the labour-intensive rig of conventional ocean-racers and to accept the idea of unstayed masts. The rigs themselves have not so far been able to compete with the main handling virtues of the junk rig, namely freedom from flogging, absence of concentrated stresses, and instantaneous reefing right down to bare poles. Similar objections apply to various modern developments of roller headsails and roller mainsails on stayed masts.

Chinese vessels commonly carry large crews and have ample decks protected by bulwarks. There is no requirement for short-handed sailing and the crew is prepared to do a lot of 'fiddling' with the rig. For example, many Chinese sheet systems must be flipped round the leech when tacking or gybing. The lower sheet block sometimes has a rope tail that is belayed to the weather rail and has to be changed over when tacking or gybing. Sheet hauling spans are often used, and have to be readjusted when reefing or furling. The first reef is often taken upwards, by heaving in on the topping-lifts. By accepting this kind of deck work the Chinese are able to use a wide variety of sail shapes and layouts.

As developed in Britain, the rig is fully automatic in that all sail handling is done simply by veering or hauling ropes from a single position, and without ever touching the sail itself. Tacking and gybing are performed simply by steering the boat round on to the new course, without touching the sheets. Gybing is noticeably gentler than with a gaff or Bermudian sail. Unlike a conventional spinnaker, the junk sail will never induce rhythmic rolling on a run. A junk-rigged yacht of 50 ft (15 m) in length never demands more than a single watchkeeper for any sailing operation, including tacking, gybing, reefing, furling, and making sail. When furled the sail remains ready for use, and never has to be unbent or stowed below. For fishing and workboats the rig is unrivalled, being docile and controllable when set but held well above the deck while reefing or when furled.

An aesthetic attraction of the rig for many sailors lies in its use of seamanlike cordage and traditional fittings. Whereas with a normal Western rig traditional gear is less efficient than modern gear, with the junk rig it is more efficient and the traditionalist need make no excuses for using it. All the hauling ropes may be led to the steering position and there will be no need for the watchkeeper to move around the deck — a valuable safety feature in a small boat at sea, especially when a gale blows up in the middle of the night.

A number of notable ocean passages with junk rig have been made singlehanded by severely disabled yachtsmen who could not possibly have coped with a conventional rig. Almost any squall can be ridden out in peace by letting go the sheet and lying a-hull. It is quite difficult for the sail to get itself into a real mess. The ends of all running ropes may be secured to the ship, and if you let go everything within sight the sail furls itself without smothering the deck in loose canvas. The smaller the boat the more demanding the deck work in bad weather at sea, and the greater the advantage of the junk rig.

In *Jester* (Fig. 16.1) the watchkeeper is protected from rain and spray. In *Ròn Glas* (Fig. 16.4) the system of protection goes further, in that all running ropes are led inside the doghouse so that the whole rig can be handled without wearing oilskins. Protection of this sort is seamanlike, since it eliminates the physical exposure that is one of the most potent sources of exhaustion.

The area of a junk sail may be kept constantly adjusted to changing conditions without imposing any real strain on the crew. It is not necessary to worry about what the weather is going to do, but only about what it is actually doing. It is often convenient to use reefing as a way of 'easing the throttle', slowing down temporarily for reasons of comfort or safety, or for better control in narrow channels.

By making the sail more controllable the junk rig is improving the capabilities of small cruising yachts and setting new standards for short-handed seamanship. In demanding a fully-automatic sail the Western designer accepts more restrictions on the shape of the sail than his Chinese counterpart, but his work remains wholly based on 1,700 years of continuous development in China.

1 The Rig

The word 'rig' is used for the whole assembly of sails, masts, spars, fittings and cordage as used on any one boat. Only one junk sail is carried on each mast, but the number of masts may be varied. In any one rig the sails may be of different sizes and shapes, but each sail will be rigged in substantially the same way, as described in the following pages. A few junk-rigged boats set lightweight unbattened ghosting sails in light airs, but these are not part of the working rig and will not be discussed until Chapter 5.

It is convenient to establish Western names for the various different arrangements of the rig, and Fig. 1.3 shows the names adopted for this book. This seems to cover all the variations likely to be used in the West, but anyone wishing to use four or more masts could extend the nomenclature for himself. So far the majority of Western rigs have been single-masted, and most of the rest have been two-masted schooners with the mainsail about twice the size of the foresail. The considerations that affect the choice of rig are discussed on p 94.

The junk sail may be described as a fully-battened balanced lugsail. Fig. 1.4 shows its essential features and the names of its parts.

The sail is spread between a yard and a boom and is stiffened by a number of full-length battens that divide the sail into panels. The battens are attached to the sail along most of their length as well as at either end, and are numbered upwards as shown. The yard is hoisted by a halyard leading from the masthead.

The sail remains always on the same side of the mast, and when sailing is therefore sometimes to windward and sometimes to leeward of it. A proportion of the sail, varying between 5 and 30 per cent of its area, lies forward of the mast, and this percentage is known as the 'balance'. Balance may also be measured in linear terms: e.g. a batten may have 10 per cent of its *length* forward of the mast.

The sail is sheeted by a system of ropes that pull on the after ends of all, or nearly all, the battens. Normal single sheets are shown, in which a single system is attached to the leech and controls the sail on either tack. The alternative, but rarely used, double sheets will be considered in Chapter 4. We use the word 'sheet' for the running part, and 'sheet spans' for the standing parts attached to the battens. Many Chinese and some Western variations interpose adjustable spans (not shown) between sheet and sheet spans, and we call these 'sheet hauling spans'.

When on a broad reach or run the sheets are paid out until the sail is square to the boat.

A system of topping-lifts, or lazy-jacks, leads from the masthead down one side of the sail and passes through eyes on the underside of the boom to a similar system on the other side of the sail. These lifts are slack when under full sail, but as soon as the sail is lowered for reefing or furling they automatically go taut and gather the furled panels into a bundle. The forward end of the bundle is supported by a 'mast lift' that leads from the masthead down the outside of the sail and finishes in a loose loop around the mast, holding the bundle in against the mast.

Each batten is held close to the mast by a batten parrel which permits it to slide freely up or down the mast.

Various secondary ropes, commonly used, are not shown here but will be described in Chapters 2 and 3.

In this simple form of the sail, reefing is achieved by paying out the halyard until one or more of the lowest panels of the sail have stowed themselves in the topping-lifts. As soon as the halyard is started the pressure on the sail is relieved because the sheet goes slack. After the halyard is belayed the slack sheet is taken in until the sail is correctly trimmed. Fig. 1.5 shows the same sail reefed down to two panels. It will be seen that the sheet spans hold the leech of the sail, including the furled part, down, and it is not normally necessary to pass any lashings, pendants, or reef points to hold it down.

If the remainder of the halyard is paid out the sail will furl itself into the lifts and the sheets may be set up to hold the furled bundle fore-and-aft.

Making sail, or shaking out reefs, is done by letting go the sheet, preferably until the sail is weathercocking, then hoisting on the halyard until the required amount of sail is spread. The slack of the sheet may then be taken in to trim the sail.

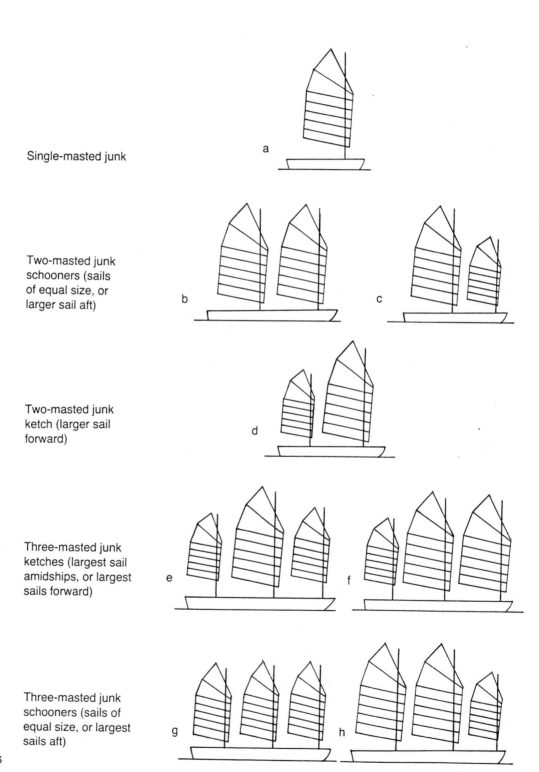

Single-masted junk

Two-masted junk
schooners (sails
of equal size, or
larger sail aft)

Two-masted junk
ketch (larger sail
forward)

Three-masted junk
ketches (largest sail
amidships, or largest
sails forward)

Three-masted junk
schooners (sails of
equal size, or largest
sails aft)

Fig. 1.3   Rig arrangements

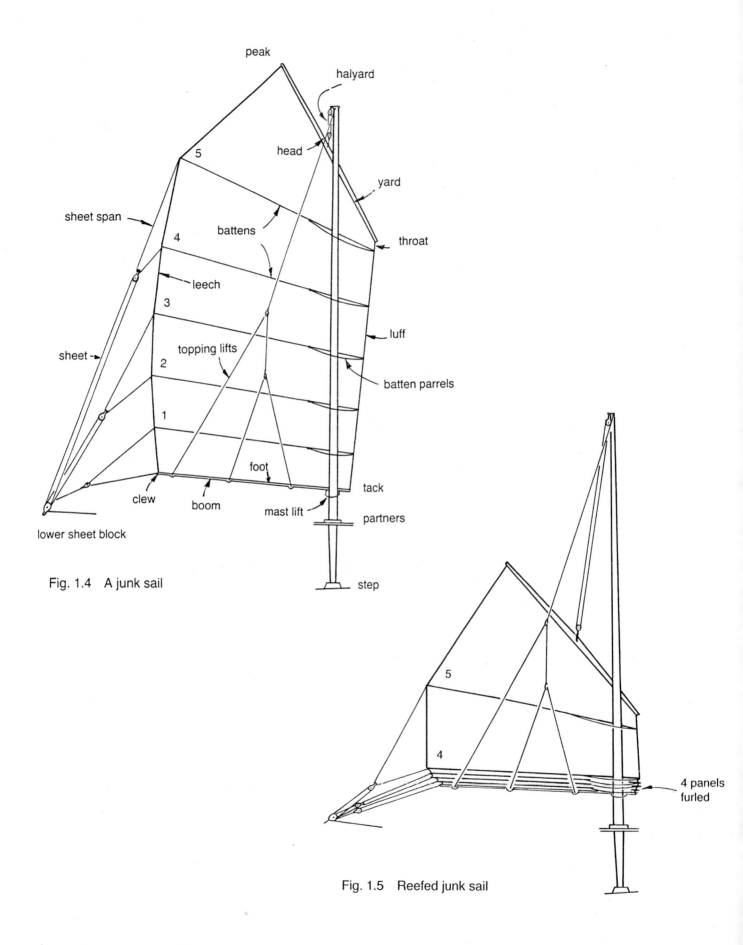

Fig. 1.4   A junk sail

Fig. 1.5   Reefed junk sail

Although simple in concept, the geometry of the rig is fairly subtle, as discussed in Chapter 2, and imposes a number of limitations on the shape and battening of the sail if it is to reef and furl neatly.

The Mast

In China, this sail has usually in the past been carried on an unstayed (cantilever) mast, even in very large ocean-going junks. Such a mast stands up like a tree and bends like a tree under load, being stepped on the keelson and supported at the partners. There should be nothing in this to alarm the Western seaman, since many sizeable working vessels on both sides of the Atlantic were rigged with unstayed masts in the days of sail. For example, the Scottish Fifies and Zulus carried their huge dipping lugs, sometimes of 1,600 sq ft (149 m²), on masts that were innocent of any standing rigging.

An unstayed mast naturally needs to be strongly connected to the hull at the partners and step, but the stresses transmitted to the hull are much lighter than those imposed by standing rigging, and much less likely to strain the hull.

In recent years some Chinese vessels have fitted shrouds to the masthead, perhaps in imitation of Western practice, and some Western users of the junk rig have done likewise. The disadvantages of using shrouds are:

1. On a run or broad reach the sail chafes against them.
2. The sail cannot be squared fully off at right angles to the hull. Weathercocking is restricted and running becomes less efficient and more prone to accidental gybes.
3. Since it is impossible to use lower shrouds, or to fit effective spreaders, the angle between shroud and mast is nearly always too small, giving poor lateral support, heavy shroud tensions, and severe compression loads that may actually break the mast instead of supporting it. It is considered that 15° is the minimum permissible angle between a masthead shroud and the mast, and this can seldom be achieved without spreaders on a mono-hulled boat, although possible with a multi-hull.

The authors have always used unstayed masts on all types of hull, and these have proved fully seaworthy if correctly designed and built. *Jester*'s original unstayed mast, of glued hollow spruce, survived 33 years of annual cruising and Atlantic crossings before it broke during a capsize in a storm at the end of her thirteenth crossing.

Unstayed masts cannot be used to carry conventional headsails or spinnakers except in the lightest of weather, as discussed in Chapter 5. Junk rigs carry one sail only on each mast. There is no sail changing, but only reefing and furling of this sail.

Junk sails may be designed to lie either on the port or starboard side of the mast, and both may be found in China, with some multi-masted junks setting some of their sails on one side and some on the other. There is no clear-cut difference in efficiency between sailing with the sail to windward or to leeward of the mast, and different users form different opinions. This is of course quite different from the soft Western lug, which performs much better when to leeward of the mast. The battens of a junk sail lie between the sail and the mast, and tend to hold the sail off the mast when on the windward side.

All the sails in this book are designed to lie on the port side of the mast for a practical reason: if anything should go wrong aloft it is then convenient to heave-to on the starboard tack, with right of way over other sailing vessels and with all the parrels and most of the other ropes on the windward side. This makes it easier to see what is wrong, and if necessary to get aloft and attend to the trouble. In this book it will be assumed, for convenience in description, that all Chinese sails are set on the port side of the mast.

Battens

The bending (arching) of the battens plays a vital part in the boat's performance and also affects her steering. From an aerodynamic point of view, with the wind on or forward of the beam the battens should be well arched in ghosting weather and should get progressively flatter as the wind speed increases. This is the exact opposite of the natural behaviour of battens, and we have as yet no way of achieving it. It is possible to make ingenious suggestions for compound or fabricated battens which incorporate some positive means of controlling the arching to suit the aerodynamic requirements, but none of these has yet looked like meeting the practical need for a batten that is very strong, light, unbreakable, and cheap. We are therefore stuck with battens that do the opposite of what we want, giving a flat sail in ghosting weather and a well-arched sail in a hard breeze. It is important that battens should not bend too much, particularly when close-hauled or reaching, since this gives less drive, more lateral force inducing heeling and leeway, and more weather helm. It has been found that fitting stiffer battens will reduce weather helm.

Luckily, as soon as the sail is reefed the topping lifts go taut and the sail leans against the leeward lifts, which then help to prevent the battens from bending too far. Battens are therefore designed to reach their maximum bend when running before the wind in a hard puff under full sail.

A batten acts partly as a beam and partly as a strut, having to deal with bending loads and longitudinal compression. The bending loads are caused by the wind

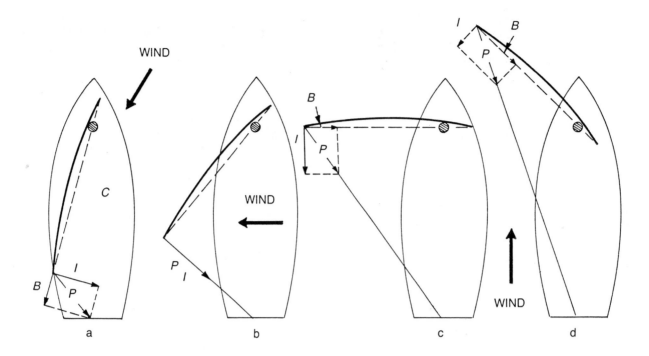

Fig. 1.6   Compression of battens

pressing the batten to leeward. The compression loads are more complex, and arise from a number of sources.

Viewed from above (Fig. 1.6), the sheet parts exert a pull P which may be resolved into a force I controlling the incidence of the sail by acting at 90° to its chord C, and a force B in line with the chord of the sail. Force B is trying to stretch and straighten the battens if it points away from the mast, or to compress and bend the battens if it points towards the mast. With the sheet anchorage well abaft the leech of the sail, situation a shows that the sheets are trying to straighten the battens when close-hauled. On a reach b, P and I may coincide so that there is no force B. In c the sail is squared off for a run and the pull of the sheets is increasing the compression of the battens. The final attitude d shows a situation that should never be allowed to develop; with the wind astern the sheets have been paid out until the leech of the sail is well forward of the mast, developing a very heavy compression B on the battens while the drive of the sail makes the boat heel to starboard.

In the above paragraph force P is the horizontal component of the pull of the sheet. There is also a vertical component acting downwards, but this is not relevant to the present discussion. The downward pull is transmitted through the leech to the yard, and thence to the halyard.

The attitude c shows why, in smooth water, the most severe batten-bending occurs when running hard-

pressed under full sail, but (as with the mast) it is the snatch loadings induced by steep waves and swell that may momentarily produce heavy additional loads, and these may arise on any point of sailing. Even if the waves are running true to the wind, the wash of a passing ship may hit you straight on the nose.

The battens must be strong and stiff enough to withstand such accumulative loading, and this inevitably means that the sail will set very flat in light airs. The sails in China seem to do the same, giving a rig that reaches its full efficiency in a hard breeze, the harder the better.

Another source of batten compression is leech tension, but only if the leech changes direction at that batten. In Fig. 1.7, the leech at A is exerting no compression, whereas that at B is. Any unsheeted battens, such as the top battens on many sails, take less bending load than a sheeted batten but throw additional loads on to their neighbours. When close-reefed in a gale, however, unsheeted top battens may tend to bend the wrong way when off the wind. Fig. 1.8 shows such a batten supported in its middle by the topping-lifts but bent to leeward at its leech end. This may be described as 'S-bending'. A similar effect could be induced by double sheets (see p 72), if these sheets were attached to the battens at points well forward of the leech.

S-bending may also be detectable at the luff of the sail if there is a large amount of balance forward of the mast.

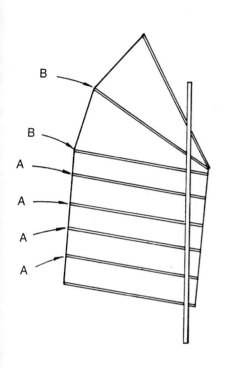

Fig. 1.7   Leech tension

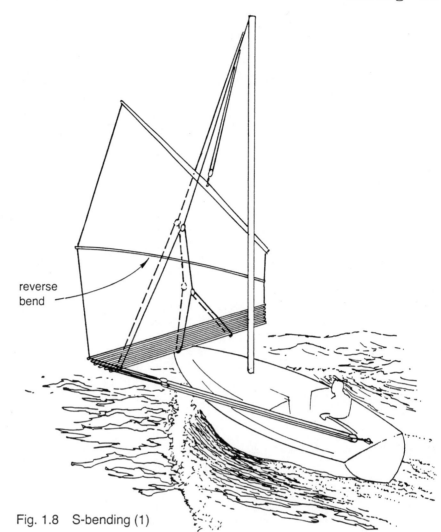

reverse
bend

Fig. 1.8   S-bending (1)

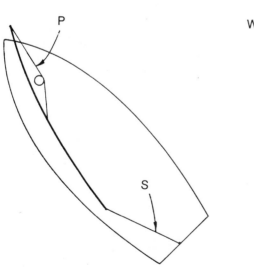

WIND

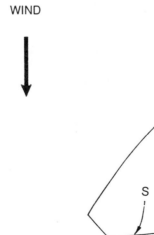

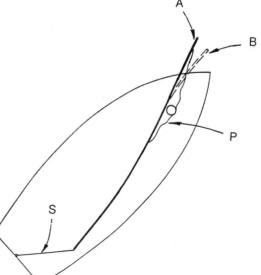

Fig. 1.9   S-bending (2)

Fig. 1.9 shows one batten of such a sail with its curvature exaggerated. On the starboard tack it hangs clear of the mast on a taut batten parrel P and the sheet S, and will take up a fair continuous curve. On the port tack the batten presses against the mast and the batten parrel is slack. There is no external force capable of curving the forward end of the batten to windward. Normally, with stiff battens and a moderate amount of balance, the forward end of the batten will appear to be straight, as at A, but with a soft batten and/or too much balance it can show an S-bend as at B. Quite apart from any aerodynamic objections, S-bending when close-hauled is undesirable because the sail becomes unstable and the boat will no longer carry a steady amount of helm. If she luffs a little the batten snaps back to line A and the luff of the sail is relieved of wind pressure, whereupon the boat develops more weather helm and tries to luff further. If she is made to pay off again, the batten snaps back to line B and the luff of the sail catches more wind, whereupon she loses weather helm and tries to pay off further. This can be even more perplexing to a vane steering gear than it is to a human helmsman, but luckily no S-bending is normally detectable in rigs designed to the guidelines laid down in this book.

The Sail

So far the curvature of the sail has been discussed only in relation to the bending of the battens, i.e. curvature along the line of the batten. The sail also curves in a plane at right angles to the battens, i.e. by 'scalloping' between battens as shown diagrammatically in Fig. 1.10. Scalloping becomes more significant in a sail with relatively few battens and wide panels. It is reduced by any vertical tension in the sailcloth, and therefore tends to be greatest in the lowest panel, which is supporting less weight. It will be least in the top panel, which is supporting the weight of all the panels below it.

Scalloping may be reduced by pulling downwards on the sail, by means of a tackline when under full sail or by batten downhauls when reefed, as discussed in Chapter 3, but in fact it does not seem to do much harm to the boat's performance if allowed to develop naturally without any such restriction, as in China. A possible exception is the situation mentioned earlier as being the rig's worst point, namely ghosting to windward in a lop. Here it may be that the scalloped sail disturbs the smooth airflow when pitching, in which case reducing the scalloping could be beneficial.

On the port tack the sail presses against the batten, and if the sail's scalloping is greater than the thickness of the batten it will press lightly against the mast in the middle part of each panel. This effect is presumably undesirable, but does not seem to cause any detectable inefficiency. Indeed, several owners feel that their boats

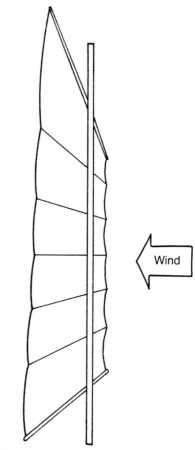

Fig. 1.10   Scalloping (1)

sail to windward better on the port tack, particularly in fresh winds. If true, this may be an effect of having the windage of the mast on the lee side.

Much could no doubt be learned by 'tufting' Chinese sails in order to study the airflow near the surfaces. Tufting consists in passing pieces of wool about 8 in (20 cm) long through the sail with a sail needle, middling them and tying an overhand knot each side of the cloth so as to retain them in position with about 3½ in (9 cm) hanging free each side. Tufts could be placed about 12 in (30 cm) apart right along the middle of each panel.

A sail stretches somewhat with use, and the bunt of the sail stretches more than the luff or leech, particularly if these edges are taped or roped. The effect of this stretch is that the luff and leech scallop less than the middle of the sail, so that a plan view of one panel would show that the middle of the panel has greater fore-and-aft arching than that of the battens above and below it, as shown diagrammatically in Fig. 1.11. It would be possible to cut a sail with this fullness built into each panel, thus achieving more arching in ghosting weather without requiring the battens to bend at all, but the implications

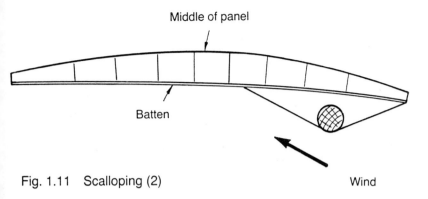

Fig. 1.11   Scalloping (2)   Wind

of this would have to be studied empirically on a
full-sized boat.

The Chinese construct a sail by laying out the yard,
battens, and boom correctly positioned on a piece of flat
ground and joining them all together with boltropes
along the luff and leech. On large sails one or more
'batten lifts' may be added, i.e. ropes joining yard,
battens, and boom up the middle part of the sail. The
resulting strong framework does not require any support
from the sailcloth, which is then cut to fit the framework
and secured to it. The cloths are arranged more or less
vertically, but may change direction at one or more
battens to stay parallel with the leech.

The edges of the cloths are usually sewn together to
make a single sail, but there are variations on this. Some
large square-headed sails have a vertical gap right down
the sail, dividing it into two vertical bonnets whose
edges are then laced together across the gap as in Fig.
1.12 (after Worcester), which shows an 18-batten sail. It
seems probable that these laced gaps provide a convenient means of tensioning the sail along the battens
without requiring the battens to protrude beyond the luff
or leech, but one Western writer has suggested that they
serve an aerodynamic purpose, producing some sort of
slot effect. This seems unlikely, but the gap will undoubtedly permit the battens to take on more stagger
when reefed, as discussed in Chapter 2.

Where such gaps exist it is common to take some of the
battens through the gap and along the other side of the
after part of the sail, as shown by dotted lines in Fig. 1.12.
The forward part of the sail always has all its battens
between sail and mast.

In another Chinese variation, the after bonnet consists
of separate vertical cloths, or groups of cloths, whose
edges are not sewn together but are held together by
stops at intervals of about a foot (0.3 m). Adjacent cloths
then weave in and out of the battens in opposite
directions, giving a basket-weave effect. The reason for
this is not known, unless it is to save sewing.

Large Chinese sails are often fitted with lighter auxiliary battens on the opposite side of the sail to the main
battens, so that the sail is held between pairs of battens.

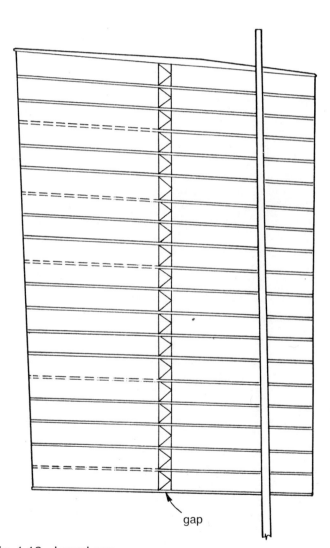

Fig. 1.12   Laced gap

gap

The purpose of the auxiliary battens is believed to be to reduce the chafing of the sail by the topping-lifts, even though the junk rig seems to suffer less from chafe than many Western rigs. The batten of a large junk sail often consists of two shorter spars or bamboos fished together with a considerable overlap in the middle and with their butts outwards. Such a batten offers easy adjustment for length.

Aerodynamics and the junk rig

Any study of the sailing efficiency of the rig leads into the field of aerodynamics, but here it is best to tread with caution. More hot air has been talked about the aerodynamics of yacht sails than ever came out of a wind tunnel, and attempts to apply undiluted aircraft theory to sailing boats have often done more harm than good. Nearly all progress in rig design has been made by practical skippers and yacht designers who have declined to believe any theory until it has been confirmed by comparative testing, preferably on full-sized boats racing against other similar boats. We need much more of this process to continue to improve the junk rig.

Anyone who insists on trying to relate the behaviour of a junk sail to aerodynamic theory might well start by looking at the theory of thin-plate aerofoils of different curvatures; but there may be more profitable ways of spending his time. In the following discussion the reader must distinguish between what is conjecture and what is fact.

In the design of a single-masted rig, the first decisions to be taken are the sail's area and its profile shape. Since we cannot use additional working sails such as jibs or spinnakers without nullifying some of the main advantages of the rig, and since the sail is so easily reefed, it is best to give it a large area and accept early reefing. Some successful junk-rigged yachts take down their first panel somewhere between Force 3 and Force 4 when going to windward.

The profile shape is related to area because there is a maximum permissible capsizing moment for every hull. A tall, narrow sail will have a greater capsizing moment than a lower, broader sail of the same area, for three reasons: its centre of area will be higher; its centre of gravity will be higher; and its head will be working in somewhat stronger wind because of the 'wind gradient', i.e. the fact that wind near the surface of the sea is slowed down by friction. A sail that is broadest at the foot will obviously generate less capsizing moment than one which is broadest at the head.

Aerodynamicists often advocate the use of a very tall, narrow sail for efficiency to windward, and although there is evidence to support this the practical disadvantages may be decisive. The choice of shape will often be influenced by considerations of mast position and helm effects, as discussed in Chapter 6.

Most Western seamen feel instinctively that a 'fanned' sail, with the yard at a steep angle, should be more efficient than a square-headed sail (compare Figs. 16.2 and 16.4), but this is not yet established very firmly. The square head is used in China on a number of junks of apparently advanced design, both seagoing and inland, and is perhaps best suited to tall, narrow sails.

In aircraft, 'slot effect' is a means of preventing the breakdown of airflow over a wing when it would otherwise stall due to low speed and high incidence, conditions that normally arise only during landing and take-off. It is achieved by extending 'slats' (small auxiliary aerofoil surfaces) close ahead of the wing, and also by extending slotted flaps at the trailing edge. In Bermudian sloops it is held that slot effect is developed between headsail and mainsail, and that this is responsible for increases in windward efficiency. Whether or not this is the whole truth is beyond the scope of this book.

If beneficial slot effect can be induced in multi-masted Chinese rigs it should be possible to demonstrate, by tufting, that the turbulence in the airflow is reduced by it. It is possible that a small junk foresail can be made to improve the efficiency of a junk mainsail, and that the sail plans shown in Fig. 1.3 c, e and h benefit from this effect, but we have as yet no evidence of it. The single-masted rig seems to be at least as efficient to windward as the multi-masted rigs, and sometimes more efficient downwind in light or moderate going, but there has been no opportunity for direct comparison on identical hulls. In our present state of knowledge the choice of rig should be based on considerations of size, mast position, and steering effects, rather than on half-digested aerodynamics. To be preoccupied by theory is often a sign of inexperience, and a reason for not gaining more experience.

2 The Geometry of the Sail

The ways in which a Chinese sail may be reefed and furled are severely restricted by the battens and by the diagonal tensions in the sailcloth. Fig. 2.1 shows a rectangular sail panel with battens AB and CD. If there were no sailcloth and they were simply joined together by boltropes AD and BC, the top batten could furl to A_1B_1 if it were forced fully to the right, or to A_2B_2 if forced fully to the left, or to any intermediate position between these two. The limits are defined by the radii DA and CB. For clarity, the two positions of the furled batten are shown one above the other, whereas in practice they would both come right down to the lower batten.

If the same panel is now filled with a polyester sailcloth that is inelastic and cannot be distorted diagonally, the limits become much narrower since they are now imposed by the unstretchable diagonals CA and DB (Fig. 2.2), giving new limiting positions A_1B_1 and A_2B_2, with possible furled positions anywhere between these two. The limits are defined by the radii DB and CA.

If, as is usual, the shape of the sail panel is some form of quadrilateral other than a rectangle, the diagonals will still control the limits of the furled positions as shown in Fig. 2.3a, b, and c, while the near-triangular panel (d) has in effect only one furled attitude.

The narrower the panel (i.e. the smaller AD and BC

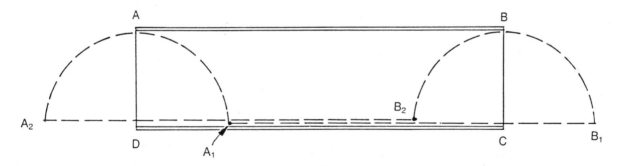

Fig. 2.1 Rectangular panel furling – boltropes only

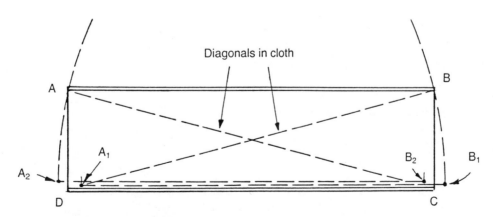

Diagonals in cloth

Fig. 2.2 Rectangular panel furling – with sailcloth

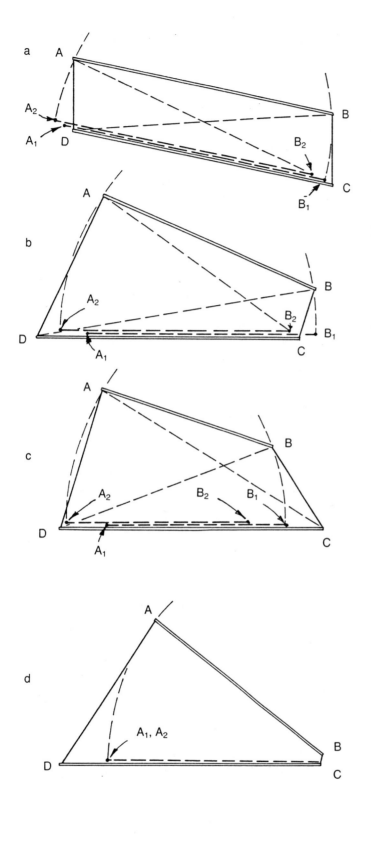

Fig. 2.3   Furling of non-rectangular panels

are, in relation to AB and DC) the narrower will be the limits of the furled attitudes.

When a panel is furled the folded sailcloth would, if not supported by topping lifts, be free to hang below the lower batten in a shape that would depend partly on the attitude of the upper batten. If the latter were midway between its limits the cloth would often hang in a single uncreased fold, but if near its limit the fold would become complex and heavily creased along the controlling diagonal. Obviously, the wider the panel the greater the amount of loose cloth that would hang down when furled and the greater the need for a multiple topping-lift system to gather and hold it.

Sail analysis

When drawing a complete sail it is necessary to analyse its reefing and furling characteristics by taking each panel in turn and superimposing it on the furled attitude of the panel below it. Fig. 2.4 shows an analysis of a sail whose outlines were originally sketched at random to form what the draughtsman regarded as an aesthetically pleasing shape, and shows how it would furl if each batten and the yard were forced fully forward. Fig. 2.5 shows how a pair of compasses and a straight edge were

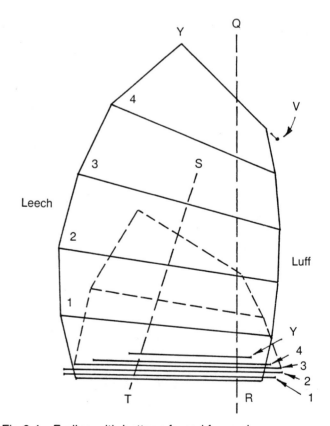

Fig.2.4   Furling with battens forced forward

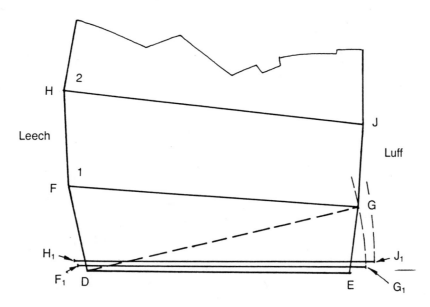

Fig. 2.5   Construction – battens forced forward

used to construct the position of the furled battens, as follows:

1. With centre D and radius DG, strike an arc down to a level just above the boom and mark G_1, which is the furthest forward position of the forward end of batten 1 when furled.
2. With centre G_1 and radius GF mark F_1, which is the after end of batten 1 when furled.
3. With centre F_1 and radius FJ, strike an arc down to a level just above G_1 and mark J_1, which is the furthest forward position of the forward end of batten 2 when furled.
4. With centre J_1 and radius JH, mark H_1 which is the after end of batten 2 when furled.
5. Continue with remaining battens and yard.

The position of the reefed sail is drawn by superimposing the required number of panels on top of the furled position of the lowest operational batten. Thus in Fig. 2.4 the top two panels of the close-reefed sail are shown, dotted, superimposed on the furled batten 3.

Fig. 2.6 shows an analysis of the same sail with each batten and the yard forced as far aft as it could go. Fig. 2.7 shows the method of construction which is the same as for Fig. 2.5 but reversed, using the other diagonals.

The positions of the furled battens in Fig. 2.4 and 2.6 show the extreme limits that can be obtained in that sail using modern synthetic sailcloth which will not distort diagonally. If the battens do not come down to one of these limits, then they must finish somewhere in between them. It will be shown in Chapter 3 that in fact the battens of all normal Chinese sails are trying to move forward, and can only be prevented from doing so by

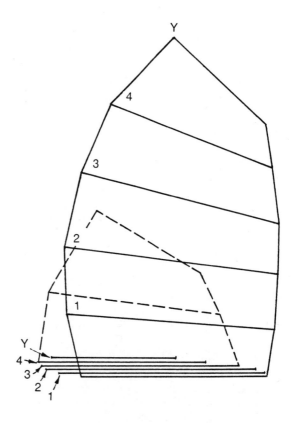

Fig. 2.6   Furling sail 2-4 with battens forced aft

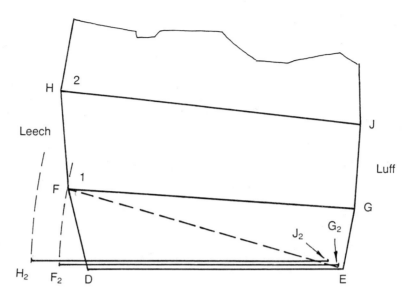

Fig. 2.7   Construction – battens forced aft

physical restraint. These restraints are not normally operative while the sail is being reefed or furled and for practical purposes the situation shown in Fig. 2.6 can be ignored, and it can be assumed that Fig. 2.4 shows the actual situation we have to deal with, namely with all battens lying as far forward as the diagonals of the sail panels will permit.

STAGGER. The amount by which the ends of furled battens overlap each other is called the 'stagger', and is positive when the upper batten projects further and negative when the lower batten projects further. In Fig. 2.4 it will be seen that batten 1 (in relation to the boom) has positive stagger at both ends; batten 2 has very slight positive stagger at the leech and more positive stagger at the luff; batten 3 has negative stagger at the leech and very slight positive stagger at the luff; batten 4 and the yard both have negative stagger at both ends.

A 'fully automatic' sail with a single sheet system requires positive stagger on all sheeted battens at the leech, so that the sheet spans will hang clear when furled and the sail can be rehoisted without fouling them. The sail shown in Fig. 2.4 would not meet this requirement on battens 3 and 4. Any unsheeted battens, and the peak of the yard, need not have positive stagger at the leech but must come far enough aft to remain well abaft the topping-lifts at all times. On Fig. 2.4 the topping-lifts would have to lie forward of the line ST to achieve this.

The forward ends of all battens, and of the yard, may be designed with either positive or negative stagger provided that they reach far enough forward to keep a reasonable overlap on the mast at all times. On Fig. 2.4, a mast line QR would achieve this, but the yard has very little overlap when close-reefed and it could be safer to

extend it beyond the throat as at V. This expedient is used on *Jester* (Fig. 16.1).

The amount of batten stagger should be designed into the sail, and should be constant at the leech for each sheeted batten of a fully automatic sail.

Fig. 2.8 shows a panel of sail with adjacent battens A and B and controlling diagonal C. The positive stagger PS at the leech is B − C, and the negative stagger NS at the luff is A − C.

The foregoing analysis of the sail drawn in Fig. 2.4 has shown that there was more to it than met the eye when this random shape was first sketched. The sail shape is not very suitable for Western needs, and it is now appropriate to make a fresh start by considering some very basic sail shapes.

Basic sail shapes

Fig. 2.9 shows a rectangular sail in three attitudes: full sail, close reefed to two panels, and furled. The battens are all of the same length, an obvious practical advantage if spare battens have to be carried. In this and all subsequent examples the battens will be shown furled according to the principle already stated, i.e. each pushed forward as far as the diagonal tension in the panel below it will permit. In this case the mast line (broken line) would present no problems, but all the battens have negative stagger at the leech and are therefore unsuited to single sheets. The amount of negative stagger would be reduced if the sail had more, and hence narrower, panels, but the same objection would apply.

Fig. 2.10 shows this sail made broader in the head,

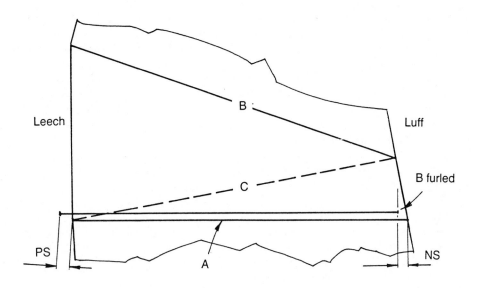

Fig. 2.8   Positive and negative stagger

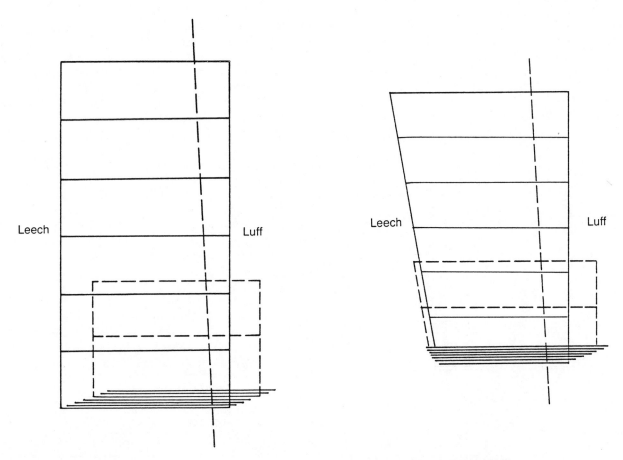

Fig. 2.9   Rectangular sail

Fig. 2.10   Broad-headed sail

forming a trapezium with right angles at the tack and throat. The after ends of the furled battens now have enough positive stagger for single sheets, but the battens are all of different lengths and it may be felt that the great width of the head of the sail is unattractive and perhaps unseamanlike, giving a close-reefed sail (dotted outline) of very low aspect ratio.

Fig. 2.11 shows a parallelogram sail in which the angle between battens and luff has been chosen so as to give good positive stagger to the furled battens at the leech. This is achieved when the length AB of the batten is greater than the length CB of the shorter diagonal below it. The difference between these two measurements is the amount of positive stagger (Fig. 2.8). For the first time, we now have a sail with equal-length battens which can all be controlled by a system of single sheets. This would be a perfectly serviceable sail, and in fact sails similar to Fig. 2.10 and 2.11 are common in China.

Western seamen tend to dislike parallel battens for aesthetic reasons. It is often thought that fanning (i.e. each batten having a steeper slope than the one below it) produces a more attractive and, by inference, more efficient sail, although it is difficult to find any evidence for the latter assumption. Fig. 2.12 shows a regular fan shape ABC which may be described as a 40° fan with ribs spaced every 5°. If everything pivoted about the centre B, as in a fan, it would of course fold so that A and the whole curved edge between A and C came down immediately on top of C.

If the wide end were cut off along an arc DE (struck from centre B), the shape ADEC could be suggested as the shape of a Chinese sail with equal-length battens, but when furled its battens would stagger unacceptably forward, as shown, being controlled by the sailcloth diagonals and no longer pivoting about centre B. To achieve positive stagger on the leech of this sail it would be necessary to alter the line of the luff and leech. These lines may be *constructed* so as to give the required stagger by the method shown in Fig. 2.13. Having drawn the regular 40° × 5° fan shape (broken lines) from centre B, mark the boom CE as in Fig. 2.12. Take two pairs of compasses and set one of them to the length (X) of the boom CE and the other to the diagonal length Y which may be 0.99 X. With centre C and radius Y, cut the first rib of the fan at F, which will be the forward end of batten 1. With centre F and radius X, mark the after end of batten 1 at G. With centre G and radius Y, mark the forward end of batten 2 at H. With centre H and radius X, mark the after end of that batten at J.

Continue this process up the sail to derive the shape shown in Fig. 2.13, with the new yard position at $A_2 D_2$ as compared with the previous yard at (AD) (Fig. 2.12). The ends of the battens are joined together by straight lines to give the luff and leech, as shown. This shape may be described as a 'staggered regular fan'. It has slightly more area than the previous sail and the sail panels get slightly wider as they go up.

It is found that the batten ends of this sail lie very nearly, but not precisely, along arcs struck from a new centre B_2 which is vertically above the fan centre B. There is a geometrical relationship between distance BB_2, distance BE, and the amount of batten stagger, but this will not be explored here. It is better to rely on the direct construction using lengths X and Y, which is applicable to all shapes of sail.

There are other ways of looking at Fig. 2.12 and 2.13 and their close relationship with Fig. 2.9 and 2.11. By taking liberties with the language we could describe Fig. 2.12 as a 'bent rectangle', and Fig. 2.13 as a 'bent parallelogram'. Each has constant angles at both ends of each of its battens, as shown in Fig. 2.14 and 2.15. These angles provide another clue to the different furling characteristics of the two sails.

The sail shown in Fig. 2.13 would be usable, although its concave luff would need to be held firmly aft by luff hauling parrels as discussed in Chapter 3. In China, most fanned sails have a straight luff, and this certainly simplifies the design if unequal batten lengths can be accepted.

Fig. 2.16, 2.17, and 2.18 show the sail from Fig. 2.13 modified in this way, with a choice of three different straight luffs. In this and all subsequent sails the positive stagger at the leech has been maintained, leaving only the problem of keeping the yard and battens on the mast when furled. Fig. 2.16 was drawn by joining D_2 and E

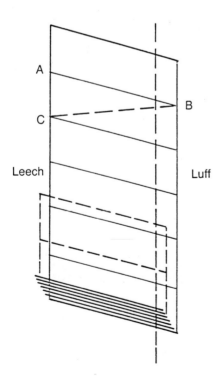

Fig. 2.11   Parallelogram sail

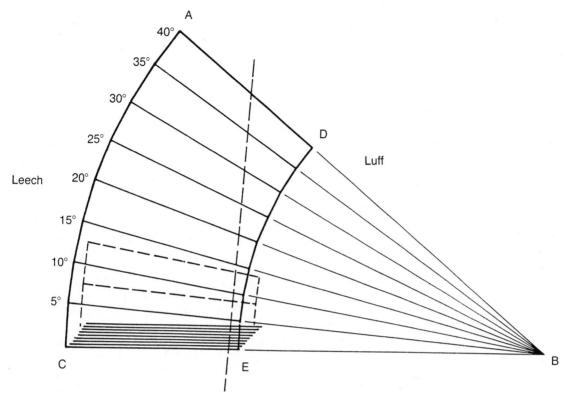

Fig. 2.12   Regular fan sail (1)

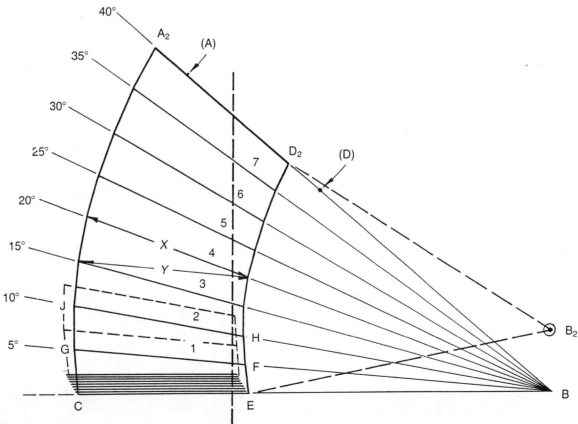

Fig. 2.13   Regular fan sail (2)

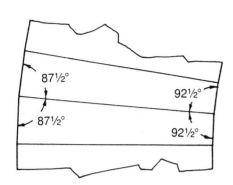

Fig. 2.14　Angles for Fig. 2.12

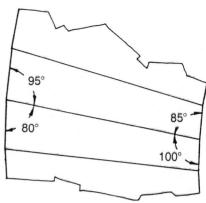

Fig. 2.15　Approximate angles for Fig. 2.13

from Fig. 2.13 with a straight line, so that the boom and yard remain the same length while the battens get progressively longer towards the middle of the sail. This sail could be satisfactory, but the yard would come off the mast when close-reefed or furled unless extended to T, or unless the boom and furled bundle were allowed to move forward on the mast by one of the means described in Chapter 3. This latter expedient is often used in China and is applicable to all cases where the battens and yard

tend to come off the mast when furled.

Fig. 2.17 is similar, but with the yard somewhat shorter and the boom somewhat longer. The longest batten is now 3, and the increased negative stagger of the forward ends of the battens aggravates the problem of keeping the furled yard on the mast.

Fig. 2.18 shows a larger, low aspect-ratio sail with the original yard length A_2D_2 and a much longer boom, with the battens getting progressively longer from head to

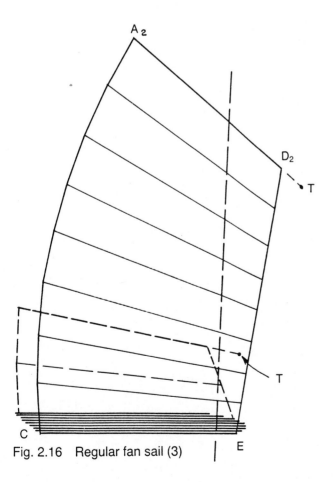

Fig. 2.16　Regular fan sail (3)

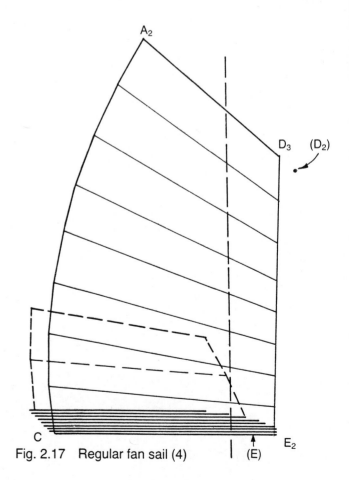

Fig. 2.17　Regular fan sail (4)

foot. The amount of negative stagger at the luff is now so great that it would hardly be possible to keep the furled yard on the mast by any expedient.

Fig. 2.19 shows a sail that is identical with Fig. 2.13 except for the luff, which is now bowed forward into a strong convex curve, with the battens getting much longer towards the centre of the sail. The forward ends of the furled lower battens have positive stagger, becoming strongly negative on the upper battens, with the furled yard finishing in roughly the same place as in Fig. 2.13, but it is difficult to draw a mast line that will not give the sail too much balance.

Convex luffs are often found in China, and may suit any sail in which unequal batten lengths can be accepted. The tension in a convex luff will help to counter the natural tendency of the battens to drift forward when sail is set. The sail of *Jester* (Fig. 16.1) is slightly convex in the luff.

This concludes a brief investigation into a number of different sails all based on a regular 40° fan with 5° ribs. Having established in Fig. 2.13 a line of leech that furls with a small amount of positive stagger, we have retained this leech while varying the line of the luff. These luff changes have scarcely affected the stagger of the leech but have had a marked effect on the stagger of

the furled luff. The main problem has been to keep the furled yard on the mast without drawing a mast line that is too far aft, and it is self-evident from Figs. 2.17 and 2.18 that this cannot be achieved unless the yard is about as long as the boom, or longer.

The stagger of the battens is affected by changes in the width of the panels. Fig. 2.20 shows the sail from Fig. 2.17 redrawn with only three battens instead of seven, by omitting every other batten. A comparison of its furled attitude with that of Fig. 2.17 shows that all the battens have gone forward, losing the positive stagger at the leech. For use with single sheets the battens would have to be lengthened to F at the leech (dotted lines) to bring back this positive stagger. The throat of this sail behaves in a rather unexpected manner, falling abaft the hypothetical mast line when reefed to one panel but going forward across it again when furled. Unforeseen effects of this sort serve to underline the need for analysing every Chinese sail geometrically before starting to make it.

Wide panels simplify the rig by reducing the number of battens, sheet parts, and parrels, but at the expense of increasing the loading on all these parts. They also increase the load on the halyard, and hence the compression load on the mast, because of the increased

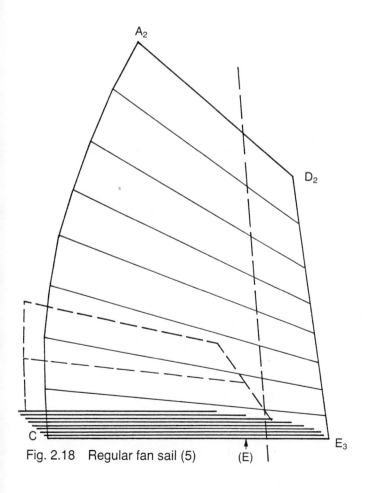

Fig. 2.18   Regular fan sail (5)

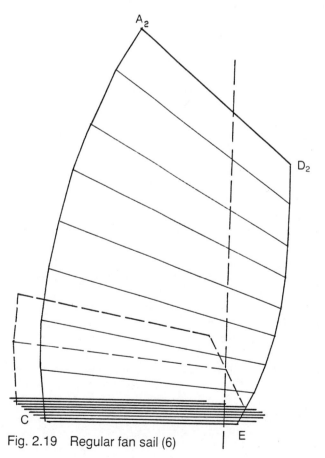

Fig. 2.19   Regular fan sail (6)

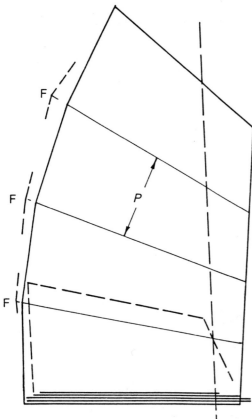

Fig. 2.20   Regular fan sail (7)

account, notably wind velocity, pitching, and heeling. Heeling reduces the effective slope of any battens whose after ends slope upwards.

In our present state of knowledge we do not know how the slope of the battens affects the efficiency of the sail, nor even whether Fig. 2.11 shows a more efficient sail than Fig. 2.16. The answer cannot be reached by theoretical reasoning.

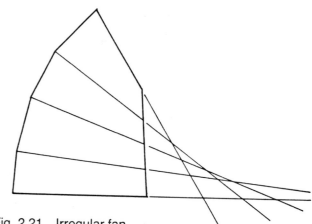

Fig. 2.21   Irregular fan

vertical tension needed to prevent the wide panels from scalloping too much. When furled, wide panels do not stow as well in the topping-lifts and are more likely to show a bit of slack sailcloth that can flap in a gale. To enjoy the full virtues of the junk sail the mean panel width P (Fig. 2.20) should not be greater than one-third of the batten length, preferably between a quarter and one-fifth.

Since all Chinese sails 'scallop' between the battens (Fig. 1.10) it may be assumed that for maximum efficiency the airflow over both sides of the sail should follow the lines of the battens when close-hauled. If it does not, then the ridges and valleys formed by the battens will presumably cause undesirable turbulence near the sail's surface. But aerodynamic theory suggests that the lines of flow on the windward surface are trying to diverge while those on the leeward surface are trying to converge, this being the cause of trailing vortices beyond the leech. If this can be shown to occur in a junk sail then part, at least, of the flow lines must lie diagonally across the battens whatever the batten angles. With a fanned sail it might perhaps be expected that the windward side could develop a beneficial divergent airflow while the leeward side could become more turbulent. It would be interesting to investigate this by tufting (see p 16) but many different variables would have to be taken into

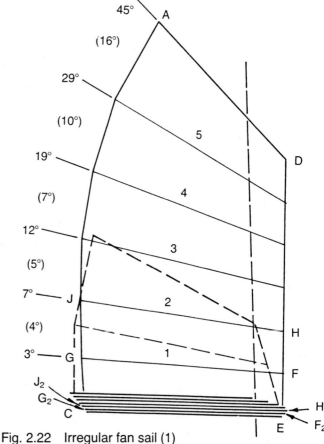

Fig. 2.22   Irregular fan sail (1)

IRREGULAR FAN SAILS. The fanned sails so far examined in this chapter were all based on a regular fan whose ribs radiate from a common centre (B in Fig. 2.12) while their slope increases in regular 5° steps. In practice, most junk sails in China are based on an irregular fan whose ribs have no common centre, as in Fig. 2.21, and the angular difference between the slope of adjacent battens usually increases as you go up the sail, with the greatest difference between the top batten and the yard. This usually improves the furling characteristics of the fanned sail.

Fig. 2.22 shows a sail of this sort, constructed on a base line CE representing the boom. The straight luff DE has been drawn at right angles to the boom and divided into six equal parts marking the forward ends of the battens and yard. From these points the ribs of the irregular fan have been drawn at angles to the horizontal of 3°, 7°, 12°, 19°, 29°, and 45°. The angles between adjacent battens are shown in brackets.

The line of the leech has been constructed with a pair of compasses so as to give a regular amount of positive stagger to the after ends of the furled battens, using a variation of the process described on p 24 since we are now forced to use battens of unequal length. With centre

C and radius CF strike an arc downwards to mark F_2, the forward end of batten 1 when furled. Draw this furled batten extending to G_2 so as to give the required amount of stagger. Transfer this length up to the working position of batten 1, to give point G. With centre G_2 and radius GH mark H_2, the forward end of batten 2 when furled. Draw this furled batten extending to J_2 to give the required stagger, then transfer its length up to the 7° rib to mark point J. Continue this process up to the yard. Trace the top two panels of the sail and transfer them to sit on the furled batten 4, as shown dotted.

This is a fairly good sail, better than its first cousin in Fig. 2.17, but the yard has too little overlap on the hypothetical mast line when close-reefed or furled. A very Chinese way out of this difficulty is shown in Fig. 2.23, where the sail is identical with that in Fig. 2.22 except that battens 4 and 5 and the yard have been extended forward by the amount necessary to enable their forward ends to furl more or less vertically above those of the other battens. This makes no perceptible difference to the line of the leech and the sail is good geometrically although (as before) the concave luff would need to be held firmly aft as shown in Chapter 3.

The sail in Fig. 2.24 has battens of unequal length and

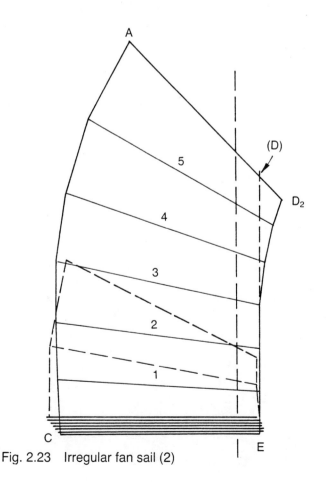

Fig. 2.23   Irregular fan sail (2)

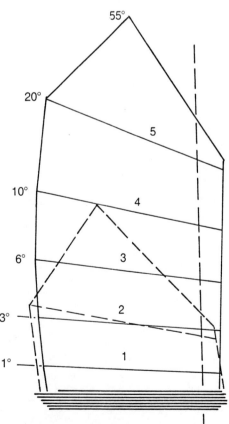

Fig. 2.24   Irregular fan sail (3)

is based on an even less regular fan shape than that of Fig. 2.22, since the intervals between battens at the luff are themselves irregular (increasing from the boom up to batten 5), while the batten angles increase less rapidly up to batten 5 but show a large change of angle between this batten and the yard. The head panel is 'near-triangular', with the shortest possible luff. Triangular head panels permit the yard to be peaked up to a much higher angle than the top batten without making the head panel too big, and in this case the peak of the yard has also been shortened to reduce the head panel and the length and weight of the yard. This creates a sharper angle in the leech at batten 5, which will put a bit of extra compression on that batten. It would no doubt be possible to make a genuinely triangular head panel, with the throat of the yard actually pivoted to the forward end of the top batten, but we have so far preferred the Chinese system, in which the two spars are brought as close together as practical sailmaking will permit but are still separated by a few inches of luff, as described in Chapter 11. It will be seen that the mast line in Fig. 2.24 may be well forward on the sail. The sail shape is good but the battens are all of different lengths and the sail is broader at the head than at the foot.

It is highly preferable to sling the yard at or near its centre, and this point must be close abaft the mast when under full sail. Fig. 2.25 shows that the amount of overlap (balance) at the head of the sail will then automatically be greatest with the flattest head and will

become less and less as the angle of the yard is increased. The amount of balance that the sail should have will be discussed in Chapter 3.

If the slope of the yard is too steep there may be difficulty in keeping the peak of the reefed sail from getting forward of the topping-lifts, and this is one reason for drawing the close-reefed sail on all sail drawings. This also helps the designer to assess the probable efficiency of the sail when close-hauled under gale conditions.

It would be conventional to believe that the close-reefed sail will go to windward better with a long leading edge, as in Fig. 2.24 where the yard acts to some extent as a leading edge, rather than with the squat shape of Fig. 2.19, but this has not yet been established by trial. All junk sails seem to perform unexpectedly well to windward when close-reefed, and the furled bundle itself acts as part of the sail.

Recommended sail form

The above lengthy examination of the geometry of the sail is intended to help any reader who wants to design his own shape of sail from first principles, or to analyse the characteristics of other Chinese sails.

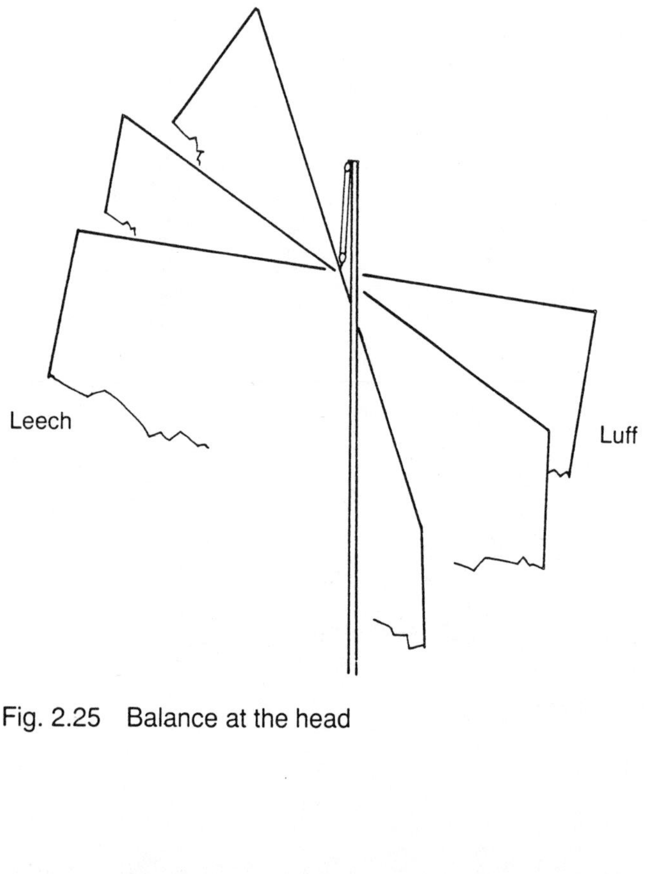

Fig. 2.25   Balance at the head

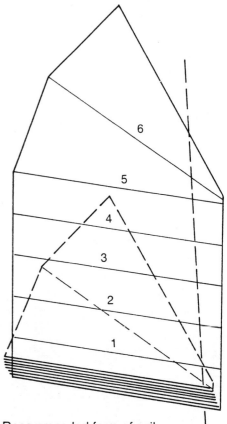

Fig. 2.26   Recommended form of sail

For those who simply want to be told how to design the recommended form of sail, Fig. 2.26 shows the form that we are currently using, as on *Pilmer* (Fig. 16.10). It is simple to design and make, handles easily, and performs well. It is a combination of two of the basic shapes already described, having a double triangular head on top of a parallelogram lower part whose battens are equally spaced. It is designed to use single sheets but the top batten is usually left unsheeted.

The yard, battens, and boom are all of the same length, or to be precise the net lengths of the *sail* along these different lines are the same. The yard and boom project slightly beyond the sail, whereas the battens need not project. Unbreakable battens have yet to be developed, and if it is necessary to replace a broken batten at sea it is convenient to be able to shift a lower batten up into its place, or better still to bring out a spare batten that will fit in any position. A secondary advantage lies in simplifying the construction of the battens and the cutting of the sail.

When furled, battens 1–5 show regular positive stagger at the leech, while the top batten and yard have little or no stagger.

In Fig. 2.26, as in the preceding ones, the furled battens and yard are shown diagrammatically, lying on top of one another. In practice they tend to lie at random and partly alongside each other in the lifts so that the bundle will be less than half the height shown. The method of drawing this sail is described in detail in Chapter 6.

3 The Rigging of the Sail

This chapter examines in more detail the mechanics of the Chinese sail and the individual ropes that control it, with the exception of the sheets which are the subject of Chapter 4. Ropes are referred to as 'running' if they are hauled in and paid out during the ordinary processes of sailing, and as 'standing' if they require nothing more than very occasional adjustment for rope stretch or twist.

Halyards

The most important running rope is the halyard, which may take a number of forms. Fig. 3.1 shows the simplest form, a single whip or single-part halyard which may pass through a hole in the masthead over a sheave (a) or through a dumb hole with a hardwood insert (b), or alternatively through a single block at the masthead (c).

In plan view, halyards should not lie in a fore-and-aft plane but in a vertical plane that passes through the yard sling plate (S) and the centre of the mast when the yard is fore-and-aft (line LM in Fig. 3.1d). This will assist the yard to hang fore-and-aft when under the influence of gravity alone. The yard has to swing 90° either way (clockwise and anti-clockwise) from this position and it calls for a fair amount of 'drift' above the sling plate in order to avoid wringing the masthead. Design rules for ensuring this will be given in Chapter 6.

A single-part rope halyard should be adequate for any sail of up to about 100 sq ft (9.3 m²). On larger sails, a single whip is often used in China with a purchase on the running end as in Fig. 3.2. In this case the halyard itself may be of wire rope.

With any single-part halyard, if the weight of the sail assembly is W then (neglecting friction) the downward pull on the masthead cannot be less than $2W$. When the sail is full of wind the compression load on the mast will rise well above this, since the halyard must exert a substantial additional force to prevent the sail from scalloping excessively between the battens, and to counter the downward pull of the sheets.

With the arrangement shown in Fig. 3.2 the length of

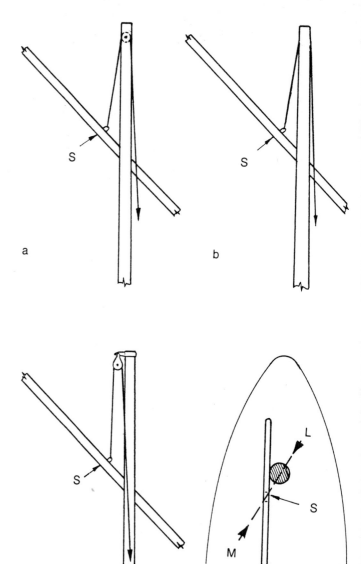

Fig. 3.1 Single-part halyards

the whip is critical. It must be short enough to allow the sail to reach its fully-hoisted position before the purchase comes 'two blocks', and yet must be long enough to allow the yard to be lowered into its furled attitude before the upper purchase block jams at the masthead. There will be very little tolerance in its length, and it will not be possible to lower the yard beyond its furled attitude (for example, down on to the deck for repair work) without unshackling it from the halyard.

A better arrangement for a single whip on a heavy sail is to wind the running end of the wire on to a drum winch as in Fig. 3.3 or, if it is cordage rather than wire, to lead it to a capstan type of winch as in Fig. 3.4.

A drum winch is defined as one that has a barrel, normally cylindrical, of sufficient capacity to wind on all the wire needed for its working range, the tail of the wire being permanently secured to the drum. A crab winch (Fig. 3.3) is a large drum winch mounted on deck. It may have a geared drive, sometimes with a choice of two speeds. A winch of this sort would be suitable for the halyard of a very large Chinese sail. The type of mast-mounted drum winch often fitted to the wire halyards of Bermudian-rigged yachts could be used for the wire halyard of a smallish Chinese sail.

It is doubtful whether a drum winch can be used effectively with fibre rope under heavy tension unless the drum is so large that not more than one layer of rope is needed. Otherwise the outer turns of rope tend to pull down and jam between the inner turns.

A capstan winch is defined as one whose waisted barrel is designed to take only a few turns of rope and to hold it by friction, the rope tail being led away from the barrel and kept lightly tensioned. When heaving in, the turns of rope surge (i.e. skid), often imperceptibly, sideways towards the centre of the barrel, thus preventing the rope from piling up against the base. This is referred to as 'axial surging'. One end of the barrel is normally left open, so that turns may easily be thrown on or off it, and it works equally well with the barrel vertical or horizontal. The number of turns may have to be varied according to the load: too few will fail to grip the drum; too many will prevent axial surging and cause the rope to pile up at the base.

A self-tailing capstan winch incorporates a rope-gripping device on the top of the barrel which makes it unnecessary to keep manual tension on the rope tail when heaving in. The rope is automatically pulled in on one side and pushed out on the other. This permits continuous hauling by one man, using either one or two hands on the handle, and is of great advantage on a Chinese halyard or sheet with above a certain size of sail. In order to pay out rope it is first pulled out of the gripping assembly and then veered by surging as for a plain capstan winch. It is usual for a capstan winch to have a removable top handle, often incorporating its own ratchet.

A capstan winch may be used on the fall of any purchase just as well as with a single whip, and will

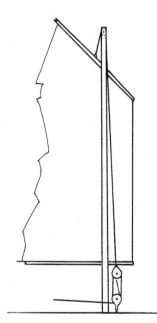

Fig. 3.2
Single-part halyard and purchase

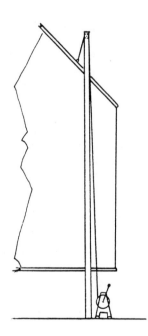

Fig. 3.3
Single-part halyard and crab winch

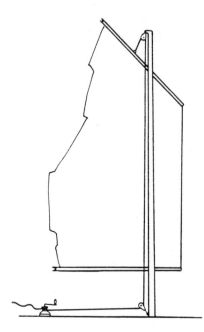

Fig. 3.4
Single-part halyard and capstan winch

often make it possible to reduce the number of parts needed in the purchase, and hence the length of rope needed, but at the expense of using larger rope. Whether a winch is more efficient than the equivalent purchase will depend on the design and condition of the two systems. With ordinary yacht equipment a capstan winch may be slightly more efficient, but its full advantage will be gained only if it is self-tailing with a ratcheted top handle capable of 360° rotation. It is usually possible, and quicker, to haul by hand in the early stages, transferring to the winch only for the final stages. With junk rig the winch loadings are generally very light compared with those of conventional genoa sheets, or headsail halyards.

The systems shown in Fig. 3.3 and 3.4 both permit the yard to be lowered to the deck, but neither does anything to reduce the high mast-compression loadings inherent in the single whip arrangement. Taking the halyard through the mast gives a fairer compression loading than offset blocks at the masthead, but it may not be necessary to worry too much about these differences. Experience so far seems to suggest that any mast stiff enough to take the bending loads is certain to stand up to the fairly modest compression loads, even with a single-part halyard, always provided that it is led down close to the mast.

Wire halyards are not recommended for sails of less than about 700 sq ft (65 m²). Rope halyards, ideally of polyester fibre, are nicer to handle and last longer, and for sails of more than about 100 sq ft (9.3 m²) it is usual to arrange them in a purchase between masthead and yard, giving enough mechanical advantage for the sail to be at least partly hoisted by one man without the help of a winch. Hoisting by hand is quicker, and if the sail is weathercocking relatively little power is needed to hoist the first few panels. The heaviest pull is needed in the final stages of hoisting, when the halyard must lift the full weight of the sail assembly and sheets against the total friction of all the parrels.

The halyard purchase may be described by the number of parts of rope at the moving block, and Fig. 3.5 shows a two-part halyard suitable for sails of between 100 and 180 sq ft (9.3 and 16.7 m²). This uses a single block on the yard and a single block with becket at the masthead. If the weight of the sail assembly is W, then (neglecting friction) the static tension in the hauling part will be $0.5\,W$, giving a minimum compression loading on the mast of $W + 0.5\,W = 1.5\,W$. Compared with a single-part halyard, it will need nearly twice as much rope but the rope may be smaller, having only half the loading.

Fig. 3.6 is a simplified plan view of a boat with her junk sail set and with the diameter of the mast exaggerated. The sail is assumed to hang vertically below the yard and is shown in four sailing positions:

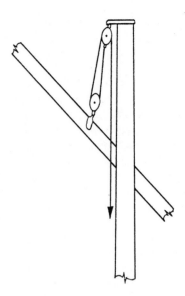

Fig. 3.5   Two-part halyard

S_1 Close-hauled on the starboard tack
S_2 Close-hauled on the port tack
S_3 Running on the starboard gybe
S_4 Running on the port gybe

The two latter are the limiting positions of the sail's swing around the mast. The arcs swept by the luff and leech of the sail are shown by solid lines, and the centre of these arcs is the centre of the mast even though the sail itself is offset.

The diagram shows the asymmetry of the two close-hauled attitudes, with the leech of the sail slightly further forward and further over the side on the starboard tack (S_1) than on the port tack (S_2). In practice this difference is made somewhat greater by the fact that the sail hangs a few inches away from the mast on the starboard tack.

Ropes leading down to the deck from the upper part of the mast should if possible lie in the 'chimney', the narrow space on the starboard side of the mast which is never swept by the sail.

Fig. 3.7 shows a similar plan view but with the sail (S) lying fore-and-aft. P is the sling point on the yard and this defines the line LM (see Fig. 3.1d) on which the upper block (Q) of the halyard should lie. The fall (F) has to lead down the chimney to the deck block (Y) and thereby presses lightly against the mast in order to turn through rather more than 90°. Because of the distance between masthead and deck this pressure is very light and quite acceptable. The fall passes outside the batten parrels (T) and all other parrels in order to avoid getting jammed between them and the mast.

If the *sheave* of the upper block is arranged to lie along the line LM, as in Fig. 3.8, the crane (A) must have a

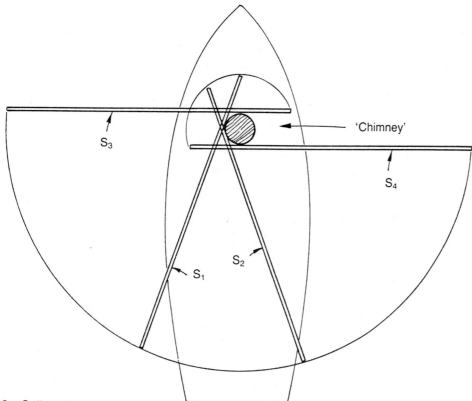

Fig. 3.6   Sail positions

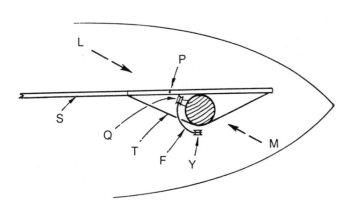

Fig. 3.7   Fall of halyard

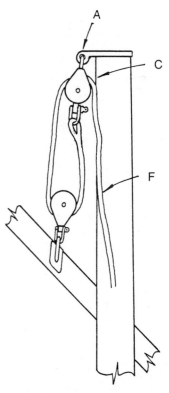

Fig. 3.8   Sheave on line LM

considerable throw, i.e. must stand out a long way from the mast, so that the fall (F) may avoid rubbing against the mast at C. Failure to ensure this has often induced an unacceptable amount of friction, quite apart from chafing of the rope and the mast. It is better to use a shorter crane with the upper block arranged so that the *pin* of its sheave lies along the line LM and points at the centre of the mast, as in Fig. 3.9. Now the cheek of the block may press lightly against the mast without doing much harm, while the rope remains entirely free. The sheave of the lower block, which is of course shackled to the yard sling plate, may be arranged either fore-and-aft, as shown, or athwartships, since a 90° twist between the blocks will be immaterial if the recommended amount of drift has been provided.

Fig. 3.10 shows a three-part halyard, suitable for sails of between 180 and 250 sq ft (16.7 to 23.2 m²). This uses a double block at the masthead and a single block with becket at the yard. The weight on the hauling part may be thought of as $0.33\,W$, and the minimum mast compression as $1.33\,W$. Again, the block at the masthead should be arranged with its sheave pin pointing to the centre of the mast, as shown. Otherwise there could be a great deal of friction, with two parts of the rope pressed between block and mast. The lower block is shown with its sheave athwartships, but it may equally well be arranged with its sheave fore-and-aft, i.e. in line with the yard. In

this case it is reasonable, but not essential, to reeve it slightly differently as in Fig. 3.11.

Fig. 3.12 shows a four-part halyard, suitable for sails of between 250 and 400 sq ft (23.2 and 37.2 m²). This uses a double block on the yard and a double block with becket at the masthead. The weight on the hauling part may be thought of as $0.25\,W$ and the minimum mast compression as $1.25\,W$. Again the upper block is arranged with its sheave pin pointing to the centre of the mast, while the lower block has its sheaves in line with the yard. Fig. 3.13 shows the method of reeving the purchase so that the parts are not twisted. As a matter of interest, the sheaves within each block will then rotate in opposite directions.

Fig. 3.14 shows the method of reeving a five-part purchase to be arranged in a similar manner, using a treble block at the masthead with the hauling part leading off the centre sheave and a double block with becket at the yard. The tension on the hauling part may now be thought of as $0.2\,W$ and the minimum mast compression as $1.2\,W$. This halyard would be suitable for sails of over 400 sq ft (37.2 m²).

It would be possible to continue this series upwards with a six-part or even a seven-part halyard, but this is not recommended. As the number of parts in a purchase is increased the cumulative effects of friction are also increased, resulting in a disappointing gain in hauling

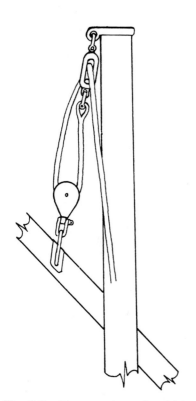

Fig. 3.9   Sheave pin on line LM

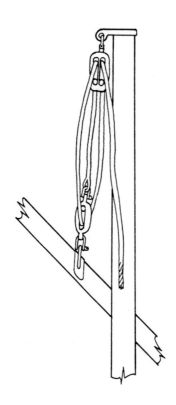

Fig. 3.10   Three-part halyard (1)

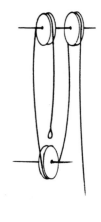

Fig. 3.11   Three-part halyard (2)

power coupled with an increased reluctance of the purchase to overhaul, i.e. to run out when the hauling end is released. One manufacturer of ordinary yacht blocks suggests a figure of 10 per cent frictional loss for each sheave, so that a pull of 100 lb would become 90 lb after passing round the first sheave, 81 lb after the second sheave, and so on. For a very large sail it is best to use not more than five halyard parts in conjunction with an adequate winch.

In all halyards with an even number of parts the standing end, where the rope is shackled or spliced to a block, is at the masthead. With an odd number of parts the standing end is on the lower block, and comes down with the yard. The latter arrangement has practical advantages when it comes to inspecting and, perhaps, renewing or end-for-ending the rope, and for this reason halyards with odd numbers of parts may be preferred.

In this book we limit ourselves to one halyard per sail, but in China, with much larger and heavier sails, it is common to use two halyards, as in Fig. 3.15 (after Worcester). It is not known whether the masthead halyard has a function in peaking up the sail, as in the peak halyard of a gaff mainsail, or whether it is simply to spread the load and provide more hoisting power. As many as four halyards have been reported on the mainsail of a Foochow Pole Junk.

Yard hauling parrel

The attitude of the sail on the mast is influenced in the first place by gravity. It is necessary for the halyard to have a fair amount of drift between the sling plate (B) of the fully-hoisted yard and the masthead crane (A) (Fig. 3.16), in order to avoid wringing the masthead when the sail is squared off for running. The halyard can pull only in direction (H), radial to the masthead, and exerts no restraint on the movement of B along the arc XY.

The weight (W) of the sail assembly acts through its centre of gravity (CG) which will be close to the geometrical centre of the sail. Treating the sail for a moment as a rigid sheet of plywood, if it were to be hoisted by the halyard with no other restraint it would hang as in Fig. 3.17, with A, B, and CG all in the same vertical line.

If its tack were now to be hauled aft into its designed position by a horizontal tack parrel (6) (Fig. 3.18) the head of the sail would also move aft as shown, until the moment $W \times d$ was countered by an equal and opposite moment $H_2 \times e$, where H_2 is the horizontal component of the pull of the halyard H.

It is not acceptable for the halyard to pull the masthead aft, nor for the yard to be able to swing fore-and-aft, in a seaway. Point (B) is therefore hauled

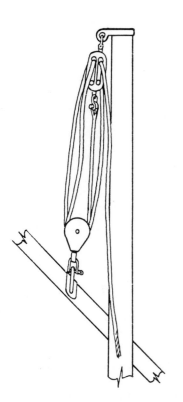

Fig. 3.12   Four-part halyard (1)

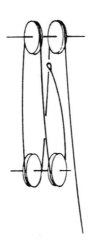

Fig. 3.13   Four-part halyard (2)

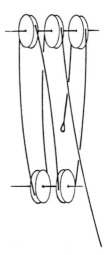

Fig. 3.14   Five-part halyard

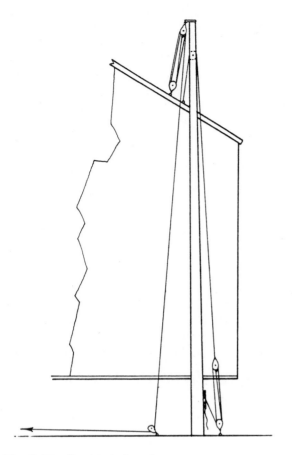

Fig. 3.15   Double halyards

close to the mast by a yard hauling parrel (3) (Fig. 3.19) until the halyard is again almost vertical and the sail is in its designed attitude (Fig. 3.20).

The yard hauling parrel has its standing end secured at or near the sling plate on the yard, then passes round the mast and back through a block or eye on the starboard side of the yard near the sling plate, then down to the deck. It performs a function similar to that of the mast traveller (Fig. 5.5) used in traditional Western lug rigs, but with two differences: it is adjustable, permitting a certain amount of variation in the fore-and-aft position of the yard on the mast, and it automatically goes slack as the sail is lowered and must be left slack as the sail is hoisted, thereby reducing friction during these operations.

If a Chinese sail were designed so that the yard did not need to move aft on reefing, it would be possible to use a traveller in place of a yard hauling parrel, and this was done on both sails of *Redlapper* (Fig. 16.2), but if there is much angle on the yard it would be necessary to unhook the traveller before the yard could be fully lowered into the furled position, thus introducing an unnecessary piece of deck work that might have to be performed in a gale at sea.

A yard hauling parrel is better than a traveller, and well worth the penalty of an extra running rope. It can be

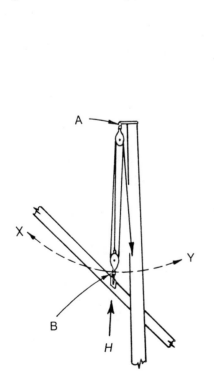

Fig. 3.16   Halyard drift

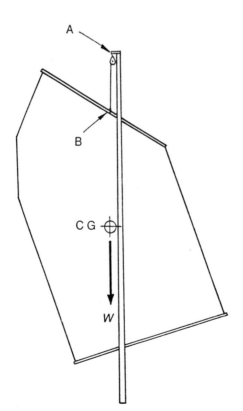

Fig. 3.17 Rigid sail hanging under gravity

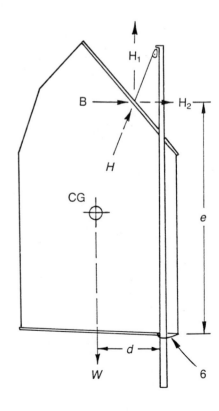

Fig. 3.18   Effect of tack parrel

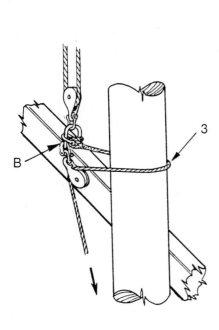

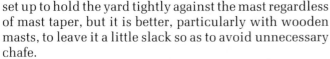

Fig. 3.19   Yard hauling parrel

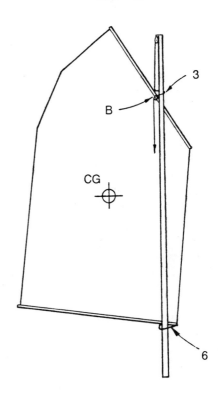

Fig. 3.20   Effect of yard-hauling parrel

set up to hold the yard tightly against the mast regardless of mast taper, but it is better, particularly with wooden masts, to leave it a little slack so as to avoid unnecessary chafe.

Fig. 3.19 shows the standing end of the yard hauling parrel secured to the starboard side of the sling plate. It would hold the yard even more firmly against the mast if it were secured to the port side of the sling plate, and this is often done, but it is rather more likely to twist the yard and cause chafe by pulling its top edge against the mast. Fig. 3.19 is the preferred arrangement. Both parts of the yard hauling parrel should lie clear of each other, and of the lower halyard block.

Mast line

The position of the mast line on the sail has been discussed in Chapter 2 in relation to the stagger of the battens and yard when reefed and furled, but there are other considerations. The proportion of the sail lying forward of the centreline of mast (the balance) may be between 5 and 30 per cent of its area. A fairly small amount of balance, say about 10 per cent of the area, is generally preferred, since this ensures that the sail weathercocks freely and that the battens take up a fair continuous curve without S-bending (Fig. 1.9). Reducing the amount of balance brings the mast further forward in the boat but reduces its bending loads while

increasing the load on the sheets and making it more necessary to 'peak up' the yard by pulling back on the upper luff, as discussed later.

In China it is common for multi-masted rigs to have a lot of balance on the foresail, less on the mainsail, and less still on the mizzen. It is possible to perceive aerodynamic advantages in this, but it also enables the foremast and mizzen mast to be stepped further into the boat for a given length of sailplan. This latter effect may be augmented by raking the foremast forward and the mizzen mast aft.

The distribution of balance up the luff is also subject to wide variations. It is satisfactory to have the luff parallel with the mast, as in *Ròn Glas* (Fig. 16.4). If it is possible to have more balance at the throat than at the tack, as in *Pilmer* (Fig. 16.10), this can reduce or eliminate the twist developed under full sail, particularly if combined with anti-twist sheets (see Chapter 4). Conversely, there are many sails, both in China and the West, which have more balance at the tack than at the throat, a feature that may be difficult to avoid with a forward-raking mast, as in *Batwing*'s foresail (Fig. 16.9).

It is preferable to have the yard sling plate at or near the middle of the head of the sail, but it is often well forward of this point as in *Redlapper* (Fig. 16.2) and *Galway Blazer II* (Fig. 16.3), at the expense of greater loads on the halyard and on the parrels that keep the sail peaked up. It must lie close abaft the centreline of the mast when under full sail. A few boats have had sling plates abaft the middle of the head of the sail. This gives low halyard loading and a sail that is easy to keep peaked up, but requires a taller mast.

The position of the mast line on the sail does not in itself affect the geometry of reefing, which is governed by the panel diagonals as discussed in Chapter 2, but the mast line must be compatible with the reefed and furled attitudes of the sail.

Mast rake

If a mast is raked aft, gravity effects will tend to swing the sail inboard in a calm. If this effect is pronounced it can be annoying in light weather, particularly on a dead run when it may be necessary to rig a boom guy and a yard guy to the lee side of the bow to prevent the sail from falling in.

If a mast is raked forward, gravity effects will tend to swing the sail outboard on one side or the other, depending on which way it starts to fall or which way the boat is heeled. This effect is not necessarily objectionable, since it can be fully controlled by the sheet. In ghosting weather it may be advantageous, helping the sheet to overhaul freely when it is eased and holding the sail out in its working attitude when it might otherwise fall in.

As a general rule it is suggested that Chinese masts should be plumb, but that it is permissible for them to rake aft not more than about 3°, or forward not more than about 10°.

It is sometimes argued that forward-raking masts produce 'pressing' sails, that tend to press the bow down in hard weather, but a study of the fore-and-aft moments of the driving forces would suggest that this effect cannot be very marked. Nearly all working sails in any rig are pressing sails in that they are trying to press the bow downwards, but luckily all normal hulls tend to lift their bows at speed, a fact that is evident if they are towed too fast. Forward-raking masts, particularly foremasts, have been commonplace for centuries in the seagoing vessels of both East and West. The sail plans of *Yeong* (Fig. 16.5) and *Batwing* (Fig. 16.9) show foremasts which have been raked forward in order to get the centre of the effort of the sail well forward whilst stepping the mast well into the boat.

Another effect of mast rake is to alter the 'roll angle'. When broad-reaching or running in a seaway, the clew of the sail and the after end of the boom may get plunged into a wave-top as the boat rolls. This is obviously undesirable and could be dangerous under gale conditions, and it is worth considering the point when designing a rig. 'Roll angle' is defined as the angle of roll at which the clew touches the water, assuming that the sail is fully squared-off, that the boat rolls about the centre of her waterline, and that the water is smooth. It may be plotted as shown in Fig. 3.21, where P_1 is the clew with sail amidships and P_2 the clew when squared

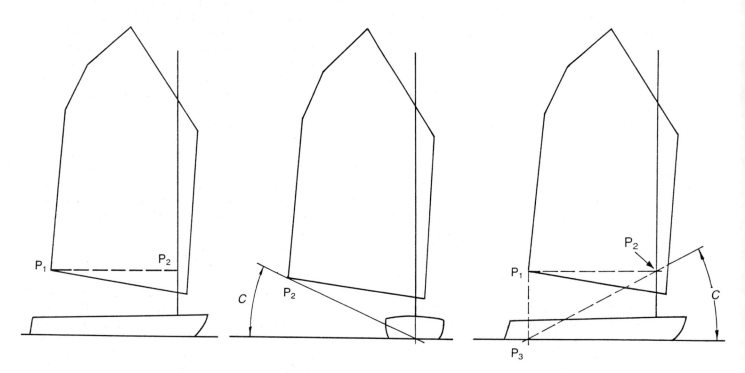

Fig. 3.21   Roll angle (1)   Fig. 3.22   Roll angle (2)

right off. The line $P_1 P_2$ is perpendicular to the centreline of the mast, which is of course the axis about which the sail swings. Here the mast is plumb and the line is horizontal. The roll angle (C), in this case 24°, is found from the end elevation by drawing a line through P_2 and the point where the centreline of the mast cuts the waterline. It is not in fact necessary to draw two views. Fig. 3.22 shows how Fig. 3.21 may be drawn as one diagram, dropping a vertical line from P_1 to cut the waterline at P_3 and drawing a line through P_3 and P_2. The reason for introducing a notional position of the mast at $P_1 P_3$ will be apparent when dealing with raked masts as in Fig. 3.23. This shows (a) that raking the mast aft while keeping the sail in the same position causes the clew to lift higher when squared off and increases the roll angle, whereas (b) raking it forward does the reverse, although in this case the effect is partly masked by the fact that the clew does not swing so far outboard.

It is believed that the roll angle should not be much less than 30° for open-sea work, bearing in mind that wave crests will often rise up on the lee side. With running topping-lifts it is possible to top up the boom, whether reefed or not, if it starts hitting the sea, at the expense of making the lowest operative panel of the sail look rather untidy.

Yeong in Howth harbour in 1979. Note the forward rake of the foremast and the different sail shapes. *(Photo: W. M. Nixon)*

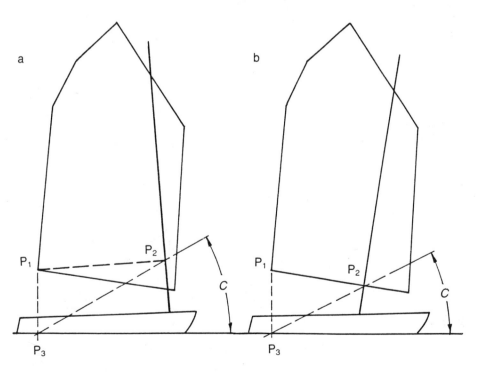

Fig. 3.23   Roll angle (3)

Control of the boom

Figs. 3.18 and 3.20 have shown the use of a horizontal tack parrel, whose function is to limit the forward movement of the tack. It may be either standing or running. Fig. 3.24 shows a running tack parrel as used extensively in China, with a loose strop (S) round the mast, but the principles of sail design recommended in this book normally enable this extra running rope to be eliminated in favour of either a standing tack parrel (Fig. 3.25) or the standing lower luff parrel shown in Fig. 3.26. The latter automatically permits the tack and lower luff to move forward by a small amount, as shown by the dotted line, when the first panel is reefed, and automatically hauls them aft again as full sail is spread. This action helps to keep the yard on the mast when close-reefed, but adds to the halyard load when setting full sail. The tackline (T) prevents the lowest sail panel from scalloping excessively when under full sail and also restricts the aft movement of the boom.

The standard type of mast lift shown in Fig. 3.49 supports any of the above parrels when the sail is reefed or furled, and prevents them from sliding too far down the mast.

Sailcloth creasing

The 'plywood sail' analogy (p 37) is valid, up to a point, for a complete Chinese sail, but the behaviour of each panel of an actual sail is governed by the behaviour of soft sailcloth. The way in which this affects the reefing and furling of the sail has been discussed in Chapter 2.

We now consider the creasing of sail panels when fully set.

Fig. 3.27a shows a rectangular sail panel which is stretched along battens at AB and CD. If CD is held and AB moved to the right, creases will form as in b, with the cloth very taut along the diagonal BD and very slack along the diagonal AC. Conversely, if AB is moved to the left, creases will form in the opposite direction as shown in c.

If the cloth has a slack weave these creases will be slow to form, but with polyester sailcloth, particularly when new, the creases will form as soon as any diagonal distortion is apparent.

Fig. 3.28 shows a complete sail hoisted as in Fig. 3.20, in that the yard is held forward by a yard hauling parrel (A) and the tack is held aft by a tack parrel (B), but instead of the notional plywood sail we now have a soft sail whose six panels are separated by battens. The weight (W) of the sail acting through the CG is supported by tension in the sailcloth which may be regarded as acting in direction (T) through the yard sling plate. This force has a component trying to pull the CG forward, and in effect causes each batten to try to slide forward. Fig. 3.29 shows the result, exaggerated. The luff and leech have both bowed forward while the yard and boom remain fixed, causing diagonal creases along the tension lines. In the upper panels the forward ends of the creases point downwards, while those of the lower panels point upwards.

In practice, the creases may be more noticeable than the bowing of the luff and leech, and one tends to look at the sail and say, 'It isn't setting very well, but I can't see why.' Creases develop much more strongly on a large

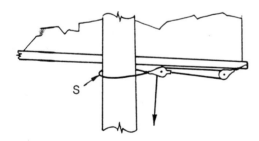

Fig. 3.24   Running tack parrel

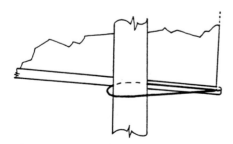

Fig. 3.25   Standing tack parrel

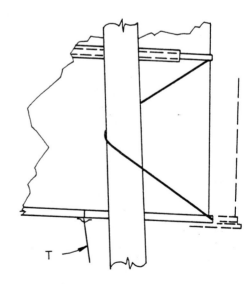

Fig. 3.26   Standing lower luff parrel

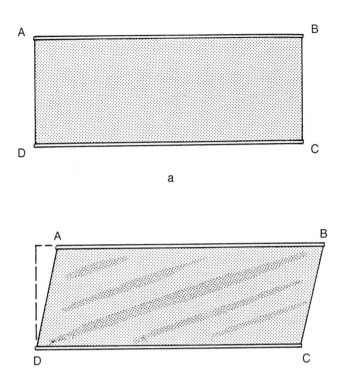

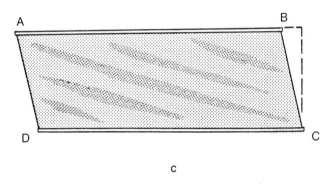

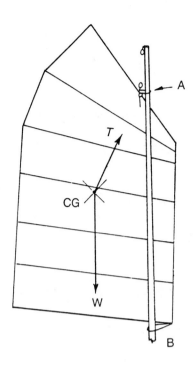

Fig. 3.28   Sail about to crease

Fig. 3.27   Creasing of sail panel

sail than on a small one, and on sails that have only a little balance rather than on those with a lot of balance, but no sail will set perfectly unless the forward ends of its battens are held aft so as to hold it to its designed shape. This can be achieved in the following ways.

SHORT BATTEN PARRELS. The normal (long) batten parrels as shown in Fig. 1.4 do nothing to prevent the battens from moving forward and aft on the mast, but if the after end of the parrel is shortened and secured to the batten at a point level with the after side of the mast it will prevent the batten from drifting forward, as shown in horizontal section in Fig. 3.30. This simple system has

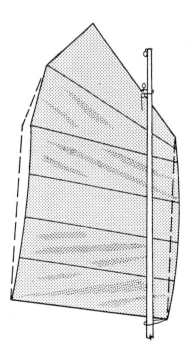

Fig. 3.29   Creased sail

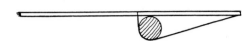

Fig. 3.30   Short batten parrel

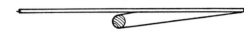

Fig. 3.31   Short batten parrel near masthead

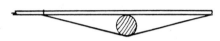

Fig. 3.32   Long batten parrel

Fig. 3.33   Long batten parrel set in from luff

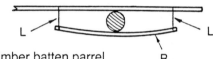

Fig. 3.34   Timber batten parrel

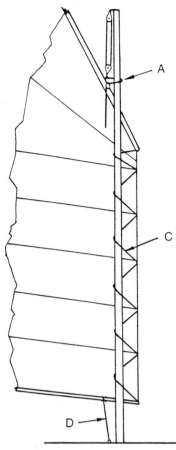

Fig. 3.35   Standing luff parrels

been used with reasonable success in *Jester* (Fig. 16.1) and other small craft, but is difficult to set up accurately and causes unnecessary friction when hoisting and lowering sail. With larger sails it becomes more difficult to control creases, and short batten parrels are unsatisfactory. In order not to stick on the mast, the parrels must have a little slack when fully lowered. If the mast is tapered, as it should be, the upper parrels will then get progressively slacker as the sail is hoisted, allowing that part of the sail to drift forward on the mast, as in Fig. 3.31. Because of these difficulties, short batten parrels cannot really be recommended, and do not seem to be used in China.

The normal (long) batten parrel is attached to the batten well forward and well aft of the mast (Fig. 3.32), thus allowing the batten considerable fore-and-aft movement and developing the minimum amount of friction when hoisting and lowering. Its function is to hold the batten in to the mast on the starboard tack, and to prevent it from sliding aft off the mast when hoisting or lowering sail in a seaway. On sails with a large amount of balance, the forward end of the parrel need not reach to the luff (Fig. 3.33). It is usual for the parrel to extend about equal distances forward and aft of the mast under full sail.

Batten parrels are normally made of rope, but occasionally in China they consist of a short bamboo or rattan spar (R) (Fig. 3.34) held to the batten by a slack lashing (L) at either end.

Since long batten parrels do nothing towards holding the battens aft, they must be used in conjunction with one of the following systems.

STANDING LUFF PARRELS. These, again, are not found in China. They consist of rope parrels that are hitched to the forward ends of the battens and zig-zag down the luff, passing round the mast between each pair of battens. Fig. 3.35 shows the luff of a sail whose yard is held forward by a yard hauling parrel (A). A continuous standing luff parrel (C) is hitched to the forward end of each batten, and to the tack and throat. It by-passes the top batten, since the batten ends are close together at the head of the luff. It would be easier to adjust, but less neat, if it were made up of separate parrels between each pair of battens. No tack parrel is needed.

Standing luff parrels work automatically. When the sail is set they hold the battens back to their designed position. As the sail is reefed and furled they allow the furled part of the luff to move forward somewhat on the mast, as in Fig. 3.26. If it cannot move forward, e.g. because the furled battens are staggered strongly aft, the parrel will go slack.

The top end of the parrel has a tendency to pull the

throat downwards, which helps to peak up the yard. The bottom end of the parrel tends to pull the tack upwards, and so increases the scalloping of the bottom panel unless the boom is held down by a tackline (D) (Fig. 3.35).

The tackline is a short standing rope hitched to the boom just abaft the mast and running down to a deck eye close to the mast. In this position it also acts to some extent as a kicking strap to discourage the boom from lifting and prevents the foot of the sail from swinging aft as the boat pitches. If the upper end of the tackline were taken to the tack itself it would not perform either of these functions. A tackline is also useful to show when to stop hoisting sail. If there is a reasonable amount of drift below the boom, the tackline may alternatively be anchored to an eye on the mast. Neither deck eye nor mast eye should lie on the centreline, but vertically below a line (R–S) joining the top of the tackline to the centre of the mast when the sail is fore-and-aft (Fig. 3.36). The tackline tends to tauten slightly when the sail is squared off on to either gybe, and should not be set up bar taut with the sail fore-and-aft.

It is slightly preferable for standing luff parrels to spiral round the mast in an anti-clockwise direction, as shown in Fig. 3.35. These standing luff parrels will not

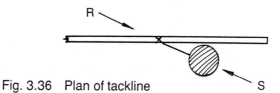

Fig. 3.36   Plan of tackline

work properly unless the luff is more or less parallel with the mast, but the taper on the mast affects them in the same way as it does the short batten parrels (Fig. 3.31). If they are to remain taut at all stages of setting sail, the battens must move forward on the mast as the sail is hoisted. If the mast has a straight (conical) taper, this need not induce any diagonal distortion in the panels. In the ideal arrangement the designed line of the luff will be sloped slightly more than the *after* side of the mast, as shown much exaggerated in Fig. 3.37, in which line X–Y is parallel with the after face of the mast. The amount by which the slope U–Y of the luff should exceed this may be derived geometrically, or by measurement with a flexible tape. All parrels (A) have the same length.

In Fig. 3.37 all the standing luff parrels are taken to the luff, but Fig. 3.38 shows that it would also be possible for any of them to be secured to its batten at a point that is short of the luff. The line U–Y remains identical with

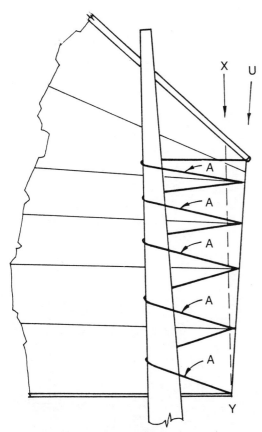

Fig. 3.37   Standing luff parrels on tapered mast

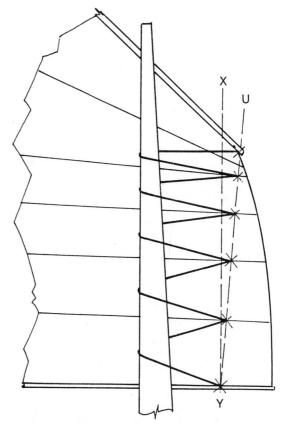

Fig. 3.38   Standing luff parrels set in from luff

that of Fig. 3.37 and the reefing and furling characteristics of the parrels are the same whilst permitting any shape of luff in relation to the line of the mast. The reefing and furling action is, however, always subject to the constraints imposed by the diagonal tensions in the sailcloth, as discussed in Chapter 2, and it would be necessary to consider which of these different constraints would be dominant, thereby introducing rather more theory than many owners would be prepared to stomach.

Apart from this, the main objections to standing luff parrels are, first, the difficulty of setting them up accurately, and, second, the amount of friction induced when hoisting and lowering, since all the parrels on the exposed part of the sail tend to remain taut, or nearly so, during these operations. Standing luff parrels are therefore no longer recommended as a means of holding the sail in shape, but may be used as a single span at the tack (Fig. 3.26) in place of a tack parrel. The top span may also be used by itself (Fig. 3.39) as a throat parrel (A), whose function is to limit the amount by which the yard can swing forward when hauling parrels are slack, e.g. when raising or lowering sail with the boat rolling and pitching. When the yard hauling parrel (B) is set up to pull the sling plate forward, a throat parrel holds the throat back and so helps to peak up the yard, but it may later go slack if a luff hauling parrel (see p 47) is used. A

throat parrel will not be effective unless the luff is more or less parallel to the mast.

A variation which is sometimes suggested, although unknown in China, would be to lash the battens to mast hoops similar to the wooden hoops often used on the luff of a gaff sail. They would combine the duties of luff parrels and batten parrels, but would be a slack fit on the upper part of a tapered mast and would not furl into such a neat bundle as conventional parrels. In any case, the upper battens will usually need to drift aft on the mast when reefing (Fig. 2.26). Mast hoops would interfere with the essential flexibility of attitude of a Chinese sail, and are not considered to be worth further investigation.

Another type of standing luff parrel is the Hong Kong parrel, so called because it has appeared in recent photographs of Hong Kong junks although not found in earlier works of reference. Hong Kong parrels (Fig. 3.40) comprise a separate rope parrel (A) for each panel, each secured at F to the forward end of a batten and running diagonally downwards between the sail and the mast and secured to a point (E) on the batten below it. Normal batten parrels (C) and yard hauling parrel (D) are fitted, and a stout tack parrel (B) holds the tack aft. When the sail is hoisted the forward end of each batten is held aft and down by the batten below it, and these tensions are transferred progressively down the sail until the accumulated load is taken by the tack parrel (B).

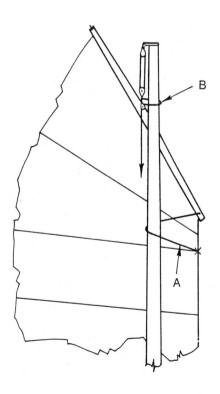

Fig. 3.39   Standing throat parrel

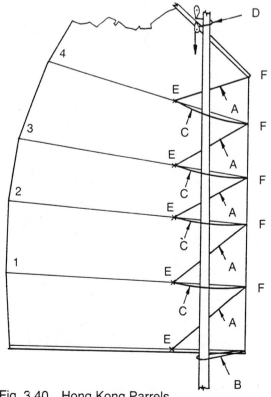

Fig. 3.40   Hong Kong Parrels

Setting up the system is not easy. For example, if it were necessary to adjust batten 2 further aft it would involve easing out rope at 2E and taking rope in at 2F. It might be thought logical to take each parrel from E to F round the starboard side of the mast, with the idea of holding the battens in to the mast and so doing away with the batten parrels (C), but in Hong Kong they seem to be rigged as shown.

The points (F) are sometimes arranged a little way abaft the luff, and the points (E) may vary from level with the mast to more than halfway along the batten. When a panel is furled, as shown in Fig. 3.41, the parrel will

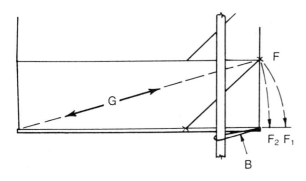

Fig. 3.41 Furling with Hong Kong parrel

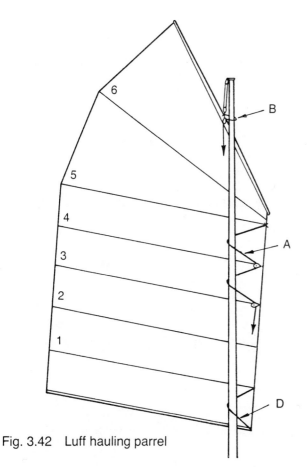

Fig. 3.42   Luff hauling parrel

remain taut only if point F can come down to F_1, but this could only be achieved by stretching the sailcloth along its diagonal (G). If the sailcloth could not be stretched, point F could not come down any further forward than F_2, and the parrel would go slack. With polyester sailcloth it must be assumed that furled Hong Kong parrels will go slack, and that the fore-and-aft loadings from the exposed part of a reefed sail will be transferred to the tack parrel (B) via the diagonal tension in the cloth of the reefed panels.

We have experimented with Hong Kong parrels on a dinghy, but did not like them. They seemed difficult to set up accurately, and on the port tack the sail was girt by the parrels and did not scallop nicely. The boom tended to lift under the pull of the lowest parrel, as did the lowest operative batten when the sail was reefed. In any case, it seems retrograde to concentrate the loadings from one parrel to another in this way, when a prime virtue of the junk rig is the distribution of loads between many parts.

LUFF HAULING PARREL. The final method of controlling the set of the sail, which is standard in China, is the luff hauling parrel, a running rope whose purpose is to provide rapid adjustment, from the deck, of the fore-and-aft position of the battens on the mast. Fig. 3.42 shows a simple form used on many of our recent designs. The sail has normal batten parrels (not shown), a yard hauling parrel (B), and a standing lower luff parrel (D) in place of a tack parrel. The luff hauling parrel (A) is secured to the forward end of batten 5, descends anti-clockwise round the mast and through a small block shackled to the forward end of batten 4, again round the mast anti-clockwise and through a block on batten 3, and thence down to the control position on deck. The parrel thus controls battens 3, 4, and 5, and in practice this is found to be enough to control the set of a sail of up to about 500 sq ft (46 m²).

This arrangement can be regarded as having four parts, since if it were bunched together it would resemble a four-part purchase. It would be possible to take in another batten, making a six-part luff hauling parrel, but this would tend to have too much friction to be fully effective at the top end. When reefed, a luff hauling parrel continues to do useful work but becomes difficult to operate when its lowest span gets furled into the bundle of sailcloth. This is an additional reason for not taking the system any lower down the luff.

In China, particularly on very large and heavy sails, the luff hauling parrel is commonly divided into two separate systems, so that the upper system remains fully operational after the lower system has been furled into the sail. Fig. 3.43 (after Worcester) shows such a system used on a junk mainsail of about 1,500 sq ft (139 m²) divided into 11 panels. The standing end of the upper luff hauling parrel is bent to the throat, no doubt as an aid

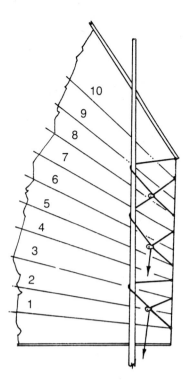

Fig. 3.43   Separate luff hauling parrels in China

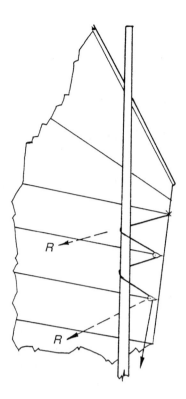

Fig. 3.44   Downward pull of luff hauling parrel

to peaking up the 40 ft (12 m) yard, and this parrel uses four hauling parts to control six panels, by spanning two pairs of battens together and missing out a batten in the middle of each span. The lower parrel uses two hauling parts to control three panels, again missing out a batten in the middle of the span. For clarity, Fig. 3.43 omits all the batten parrels, which in this case start from a point about half-way between mast and luff and extend for a similar distance abaft the mast.

A luff hauling parrel, like the yard hauling parrel, must be allowed to run out freely while sail is being hoisted. When the sail is being lowered it automatically goes slack, and must be set up taut again when the sail has been lowered by the required amount. The fact that the parrel is quite slack during hoisting and lowering ensures the minimum of friction during these operations.

For many years we managed without luff hauling parrels, using short batten parrels or standing luff parrels in order to eliminate a Chinese running rope whose purpose was not clearly understood, but further experience has shown that the luff hauling parrel provides a delicate and subtle control that is well worth its place even on a dinghy. With large and heavy sails it becomes almost essential if they are to set properly.

Any luff parrel exerts a compressive force on its batten, or at least provides the equal and opposite reaction when compression is applied to its after end.

Hauling in on a luff hauling parrel increases the compression loads on those battens to which it is attached, and thereby encourages them to bend. Provided that the battens are stiff, as they should be, this effect is beneficial.

On sails of less than about 500 sq ft (46 m²), luff hauling parrels are needed only on the upper half of the luff as in Fig. 3.42, and it is not necessary to take them as high as the throat. The lower part of the sail tends to hang without creasing once the upper luff has been set up, even if it is set up so hard that the whole sail swings aft a little, pivoting about the yard hauling parrel and causing the tack to swing aft a little. When reefed, a luff hauling parrel may to some extent be used to stagger the exposed battens aft in order to discourage their sheet spans from fouling the after ends of the furled battens below.

It has been reported that Chinese junks sometimes adjust the whole sail forward or aft on the mast so as to achieve the right balance of the helm, using luff hauling parrels plus a running tack parrel (Fig. 3.24), but this has rarely proved necessary with Western versions of the rig.

Batten downhauls

A luff hauling parrel exerts a pull (R) that is partially downward on the highest and lowest battens to which it is attached (Fig. 3.44), and to this extent tends to tension the luff above it, but if there is a need to pull the battens down more firmly it will be necessary to use batten downhauls whenever the sail is reefed. Under full sail these are not needed, since the sail may be tensioned vertically by setting up the halyard against a tackline (see p 45).

It is possible to rig batten downhauls to the forward ends of the battens, but better to attach them just abaft the mast, where they exert a mild kicking strap effect and help to tension the leech as well as the luff, in effect replacing the tackline. One of the simplest forms of batten downhaul would be a single hook-rope which could be hooked to the lowest operative batten when reefed, and then tensioned, but this would require the watchkeeper to get to the mast.

Other forms of batten downhaul use ropes that are permanently hitched to the battens and whose standing ends go aloft as the sail is hoisted. These can be handled from aft, but if each batten had a separate downhaul there would be an excessive number of running ropes. The number is halved by spanning each downhaul between two battens, as in Fig. 3.45. Each span passes through a thimble on the end of the downhaul, and its ends may be hitched at the after ends of the batten parrels, as shown. Downhaul spans require a drift (D) between the boom and the deck which is at least 0.8 of the panel width (P). When reefed it is necessary only to set up the downhaul that pulls on the lowest operative batten. The other downhauls should merely have the slack taken in before belaying.

Another use for batten downhauls is to haul the sail down when reefing or furling in conditions that prevent it from coming down under gravity: for example, reefing on a dead run with the sail full of wind and pressing against the lee topping lifts. This is just about possible, although not easy, with good downhauls. As already stated, the normal and best way of hoisting, reefing, or furling sail when under way is with the boat lying a-hull, beam-on to the wind and sea, and with the sheet right off so that the sail is weathercocking. The sail should then drop down easily under its own weight.

There are, however, situations in which lying a-hull is either awkward or impossible. A boat hit by a squall while running up a narrow channel may have no room to luff up. Even in open water she may not be able to luff without risking collision with other vessels, or getting a steep breaking sea across her deck. It is then convenient to be able to drag the sail down, panel by panel, while she continues to run before the wind with the sail kept correctly sheeted athwartships. In doing this, there will be slightly less friction on the starboard gybe, with the sail to leeward of the mast, than on the port gybe when both sail and battens are pressing against the mast, but downwind reefing is possible on either gybe.

Batten downhauls do not seem to be used in China, and have been eliminated from many of our recent

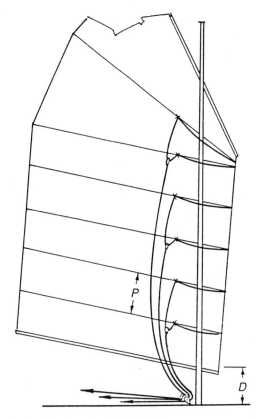

Fig. 3.45   Batten downhaul

designs without regrets. If it is accepted that a certain amount of scalloping is harmless, and if the sail is designed with fairly narrow panels as in Fig. 2.26, and if the battens are of normal weight, then batten downhauls need not be fitted. If, however, the boat is designed to run singlehanded down the Roaring Forties, they would probably be worth fitting. In marginal cases they could be fitted to the upper battens only.

Yard downhaul

Another non-Chinese rope that may earn its keep in heavy weather is a yard downhaul (Fig. 3.46), whose purpose is to haul the head of the sail down to the furled bundle and hold it there, at the cost of adding another running rope that must be tended every time sail is made or shortened. It might be thought that this rope could simply be made fast to the yard sling plate, but this is found to haul the yard down past the top batten, instead of gathering up all the head of the sail. The recommended way of rigging it is as shown, with the rope permanently hitched or spliced to the after end of the top sheeted batten, then passing up the port side of the sail, through the eye of the yard sling plate, and thence down the starboard side of the sail to a block near the mast.

To sum up, most of our recent designs manage very well under all conditions without ever fitting either batten downhauls or a yard downhaul, but we have described these extra running ropes for the benefit of those owners who find that they need them.

Topping-lifts

We now turn to the topping-lifts, which may be either standing or running. Their function is to support the boom as soon as the halyard is eased and to gather and hold the bundle of sail, battens, and yard as the sail is reefed and furled. The junk sail needs far less gathering than a soft sail because the battens hold it stretched fore-and-aft at all times and the amount of slack sailcloth is very limited, particularly if the sail has been designed with narrow panels.

The topping-lift system starts from the masthead, passes down one side of the sail, under the boom, and up the other side of the sail back to the masthead. The layout is commonly, but not always, the same on both sides of the sail. The lifts are located along the underside of the boom by thumb-cleats or eyeplates and it is usual for them to pass straight through at least one of these, so that the system can render from one side to the other.

STANDING TOPPING-LIFTS are those which end in one or more hitches on, or near, the boom. These provide the means of adjustment, e.g. for rope stretch, but once they have been set up the lifts need not be touched again

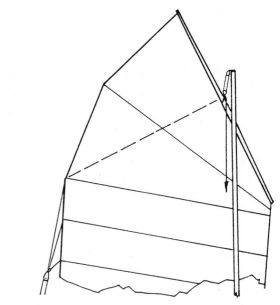

Fig. 3.46   Yard downhaul

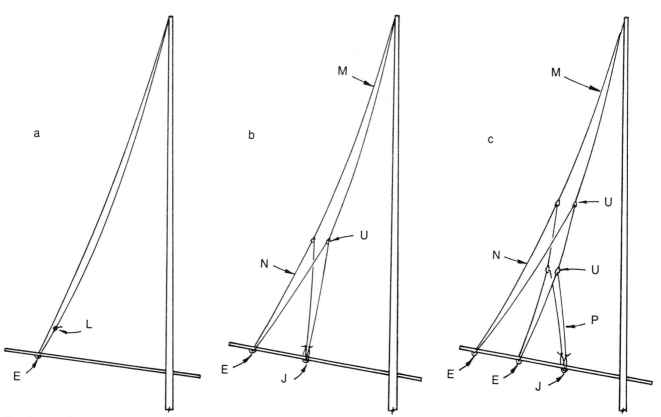

Fig. 3.47   Standing topping-lifts

during any normal sailing operation. They should have a few inches of slack when the sail is fully hoisted, taking the weight as soon as the halyard is eased a little. If a gallows or crutch is to be used to support the furled bundle, it must be hinged or portable so that it can be raised to support the bundle a little higher than its hung position.

Fig. 3.47 shows three possible systems, each of which has eyes (E) on the underside of the boom through which the rope may render freely. Systems b and c have other eyes or stops (J) which locate the bowline hitches that provide the adjustment. L is a sheet bend or similar knot that provides the adjustment for system a, which would not be suitable for anything much larger than a dinghy.

The systems may be divided into upper spans (M) which are attached to the masthead, after spans (N), and middle spans (P). Thimbles (U) spliced into the ends of the appropriate spans allow the rope to run freely through them. Although yard, sail, and battens are omitted for clarity, it will be understood that these lie above the boom, between the two sides of the topping-lifts, and on the port side of the mast. All three systems are free to render from side to side under the boom. In the case of b and c this involves rope rendering through thimbles (U) as well as through eyes (E). This lateral rendering is a desirable feature, since the lifts on the lee side of the sail are pressed outwards by the sail into a curve, whereas those on the windward side hang straight.

When the sail is well reefed there is often a tendency for the leeward side of the lifts to pull the boom round to the leeward side of the bundle of furled battens, instead of rendering through the eye. This canting of the boom is somewhat irritating to a tidy mind, but does not seem to do much harm.

If it is ever necessary to lower the furled sail on to the deck or coach roof for repairs, it will be necessary to let go the adjusting hitches and bend temporary tails to the ends of these ropes.

Fig. 3.48 shows how to draw a multiple lift system to scale, with construction points (T) on the boom.

MAST LIFT. In addition to rendering from side to side, the systems shown in Fig. 3.47 will also allow the furled bundle to find its own angle in profile, since it can tilt up and down like a see-saw without causing any part of the lifts to go slack. To prevent this it is necessary to fit a mast lift to support the forward end of the sail bundle and to hold it gathered together. Fig. 3.49 shows our normal form, in which a single lift is attached to the port side of the masthead and is formed at the bottom into a long bowline eye passing under the boom and embracing the mast. The sail lies between the lift and the mast and the bowline provides the adjustment. The boom rests on the two parts of the bowline as soon as the halyard is eased, and as successive reefs are taken in the

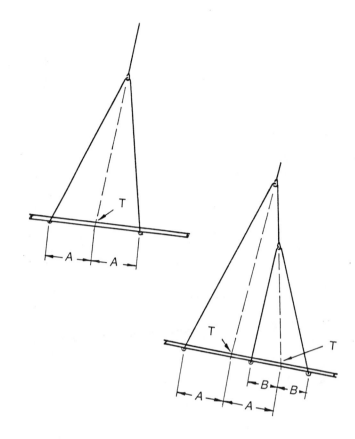

Fig. 3.48   Designing topping-lifts

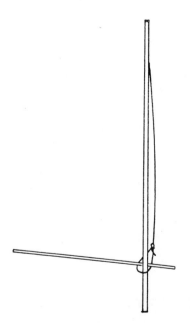

Fig. 3.49   Standard mast lift

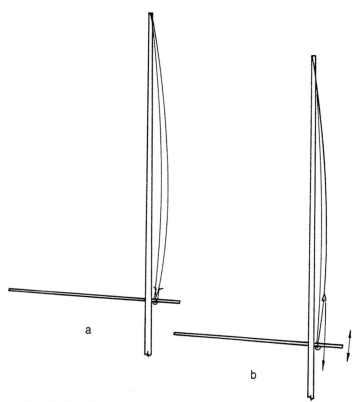

bundle of furled battens is automatically gathered and held hard in to the mast. In an alternative form (Fig. 3.50a) two lifts are attached to the forward side of the masthead, and each is hitched to the boom through a single locating eye just forward of the mast. The sail lies between the two lifts.

Of these systems, the first is simple and effective but with a very large sail tends to clamp the furled bundle too tightly against the mast, causing unnecessary chafe when it works against the mast in a seaway. With the system in Fig. 3.50, if it is found that the forward ends of the reefed battens tend to get the wrong side of the lifts it is possible to take the lifts to the boom immediately abaft the mast, and it may be desirable to fit a boom parrel (similar to a batten parrel) to help in holding the furled bundle in to the mast.

RUNNING MAST LIFT. On large sails in China it is common to find running mast lifts, in which a whip or purchase worked from the deck enables the forward end of the furled sail to be adjusted up and down as in Fig. 3.50b, in which the block is on the starboard side and the lift runs freely through the eye fitting on the boom. The

Fig. 3.50   Alternative mast lifts

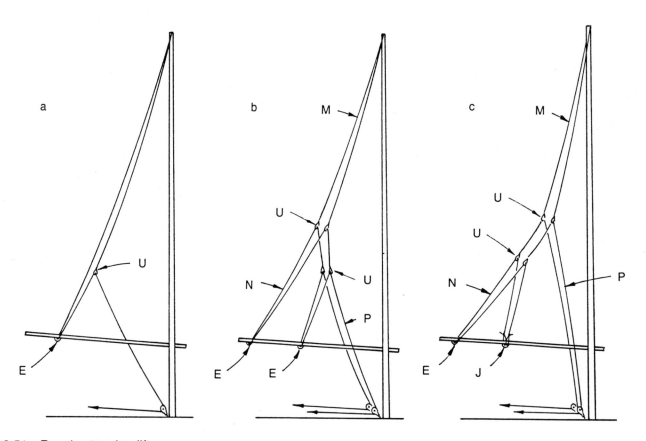

Fig. 3.51   Running topping-lifts

Chinese often take their first reef upwards in this way, by heaving in on a running mast lift and running topping-lifts, but this practice has not been adopted in the West.

RUNNING TOPPING-LIFTS, on the other hand, are recommended for all Western sails of over about 250 sq ft (23 m²), and also for smaller sails if they are to be stowed in a fixed gallows. At sea, it is convenient to be able to lower the furled sail to within easy reach if any work has to be done on it, and this can be done alongside a fixed gallows if necessary.

Fig. 3.51 shows three different layouts for running topping-lifts, with upper spans (M), after spans (N), and middle spans (P). Small blocks or thimbles (U) permit the ropes to render through them, as do eyes (E) on the underside of the boom. The eye (J) locates two bowline hitches in system c. All the hauling ends are taken through deck blocks and led aft to the control position. System a could be used for a dinghy sail with narrow panels, whereas the other two systems are suitable for sails of all sizes. Their twin hauling parts may be worked singly or (preferably) together. System b resembles a Spanish Burton and its mechanical advantage makes it easier to hoist a heavy sail bundle. System c brings the upper spans slightly further forward and is less likely to get foul of the peak (see below) but has no mechanical advantage. With this system, if the sail is more than about 200 sq ft (19 m²) it is desirable to rig a purchase on each of the hauling parts, either 2:1 or 3:1, as shown at A and B in Fig. 3.52. Alternatively, the two parts may be led directly through deck blocks as in Fig. 3.51 c and may each have a purchase along the deck, or may be married together to a single purchase. A similar purchase system will be needed with larger sails even with the more powerful system shown in Fig. 3.51 b.

SAIL-GATHERER. It is sometimes found, particularly with wide sail panels, that a fold of the leech may escape from the after spans of the topping-lifts when all or part of the sail is furled. This is irritating rather than serious, but may be cured by bringing the aftermost eye further forward along the boom, or by using a (non-Chinese) sail-gatherer, as shown in Fig. 3.53. This consists of a piece of light rope (A) seized at either end to the after spans and passing through its own eye (E) on the underside of the boom. It may be rigged either forward or aft of the after spans, as shown.

REEFING AND FURLING. The way in which the sail will reef and furl has been examined in Chapter 2, and all the specimen sails have been shown (by dotted lines) reefed down to two panels as well as unreefed, in order to assess the problem of keeping the throat and the upper battens with enough overlap on the mast. It is also necessary to provide the peak of the yard with enough overlap abaft the topping-lifts. In checking these over-

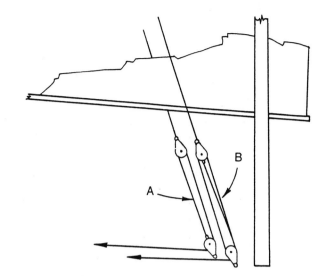

Fig. 3.52 Topping-lift purchases

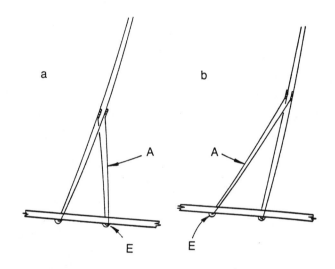

Fig. 3.53 Sail-gatherers

laps it is wrong to assume that the sail will remain static in the close-reefed position.

The risk of fouling the ends of the yard around the mast, mast lift, and topping-lifts is much aggravated by the motion of the boat in a seaway. Fig. 3.54 shows the sail from Fig. 2.23 reefed down to two panels, and it is assumed that it has just been 'crash reefed' from full sail simply by letting go the halyard. The yard hauling parrel, sheet, and any luff hauling parrel will automatically have gone slack. In calm water, the sail will settle peacefully to the position shown by the solid line, but if the motion of the boat causes the masthead to swing vigorously in the same direction as the plane of the sail, the yard can pitch bodily to and fro over quite a wide arc as shown by dotted lines, limited ultimately only by the batten parrel (A) of the top batten. This pitching may cause alternate ends of the lowest operative batten to lift up from the furled bundle, as shown. On the backswing it is possible for the throat to get the wrong side of the mast or the mast lift, although with the recommended form of sail (Fig. 2.28) this is unlikely because the throat is very close to the constraint of the top batten parrel. On the forward swing it is easy for the peak to get the wrong side of the topping lifts, although this swing will not normally be nearly as severe as the wind-induced 'fan-up' described on p 208.

The first way of preventing these snarl-ups is to avoid letting the pitching of the yard develop. If the yard hauling parrel is hauled in as the sail is lowered, the backswing will be prevented and the forward swing much reduced. Secondly, it is necessary to have designed the rig so that the yard has at all times a reasonable overlap on the mast and a good overlap on the aftermost parts of the topping-lifts. As a working approximation, when reefed to two panels (Fig. 3.55) the

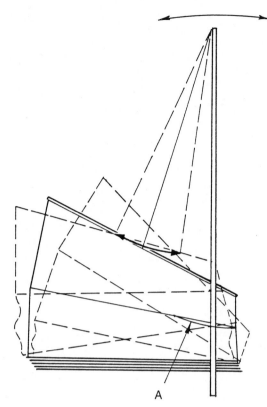

Fig. 3.54   Yard pitching

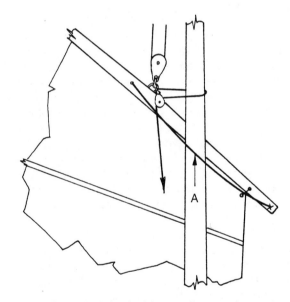

Fig. 3.56   Extended yard with standing yard parrel

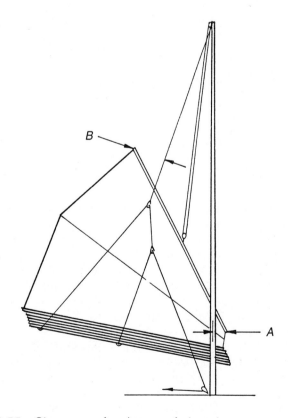

Fig. 3.55   Clearances for close-reefed yard

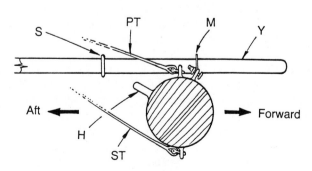

Fig. 3.57   Plan of normal masthead

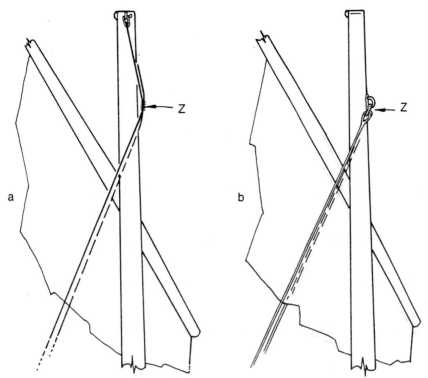

Fig. 3.58   Bringing upper topping-lift spans forward

forward end of the yard should overlap the centreline of the mast by a distance (A) equal to at least $Y/16$ ($0.06Y$), where Y is the length of the yard, and the peak should overlap the topping-lifts by a distance (B) equal to at least $Y/7$ ($0.14Y$).

If there is insufficient overlap at the throat the whole reefed luff may be allowed to move forward somewhat by using a standing lower luff parrel (Fig. 3.26), and/or the yard may be extended forward at the throat as in Fig. 3.56, which also shows a standing yard parrel (A) which may be fitted as a further reassurance to the single-hander. Both these precautions have been used in *Jester* (Fig. 16.1).

Another way of keeping the yard on the mast when reefed is to top up the after end of the boom and furled bundle with a running topping-lift, thus tilting the whole base line of the sail. A similar, but less tidy, effect is achieved by simply tilting the yard and head of the sail forward with the yard hauling parrel, at the expense of lifting the after end of the lowest operative batten away from the furled bundle while its forward end remains down. Neither of these expedients is desirable.

If there is insufficient overlap at the peak, it will be necessary to redraw the topping-lifts. The aftermost eye on the boom may be brought forward, perhaps adding a sail-gatherer as in Fig. 3.53b. The length of the upper span may be increased, or the top of the upper span may be brought forward at the masthead.

Normally the port and starboard lifts are shackled to tangs on either side of a masthead fitting as shown in plan view in Fig. 3.57, in which Y is the yard, PT and ST the upper spans of the topping-lifts, H the crane for the halyard and M the mast lift. The halyard (not shown) points directly from its crane to the yard sling plate (S) and so lies fairly between the lifts at all times.

There are two simple ways of bringing the top of the topping-lift spans further forward. Fig. 3.58a shows the same masthead arrangement as in Fig. 3.57 except that the topping-lift spans are brought forward round the mast and crossed over at Z, where they are seized together to avoid chafe. In the alternative shown in Fig. 3.58b, which is particularly suited to a metal mast, a single tang or eyeplate at Z carries both spans on a single bow shackle. Point Z may be positioned not more than halfway from the masthead to the highest position of the yard, as in *Pilmer* (Fig. 16.10).

The methods of attaching the yard, battens, boom, and sheets to the sail are dealt with in Chapters 10 and 11. This completes our examination of the ropes that control a Chinese sail with the exception of the sheets, which are the subject of the next chapter.

4 The Sheets

The sheets of a Chinese sail control the whole leech, not merely the clew or foot as in Western rigs. In China it is normal for the sheet system to be connected to the boom and to every batten, even on sails that have 20 or more battens, but it is hardly ever connected to the yard. It will be seen later that the sheeting systems of our 'fully-automatic' sails often omit the top batten as well as the yard, without any serious disadvantage.

The sheets perform three functions: they control the incidence of the sail to the centreline of the boat; they control the twist of the sail, i.e. the difference in incidence between boom, battens, and yard; and they pull downwards on the leech, holding down the after ends of any furled battens when the sail is reefed.

It would be easy to spend years studying all the possible permutations of sheeting systems, but in this chapter only those that seem significant will be described. The reader who is content simply to be told what to do may skip this discussion and turn to pp 110–11 for the recommended sheet systems.

The subject of sheet power and sheet spans will be considered first, followed by a discussion of the ways in which the sheets may get foul of the leech or other parts of the rig.

Sheet power and sheet spans

Fig. 4.1 shows a simple sheet system in which the sheet has its standing end made fast to the boom and is then led alternately through deck blocks (Q), which may be combined into multiple blocks, and blocks or thimbles

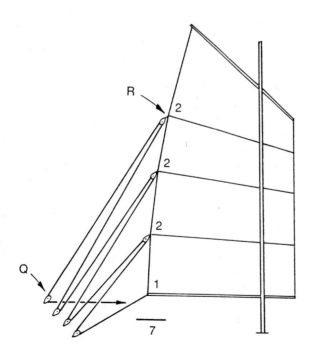

Fig. 4.1   Simple sheet system (1)

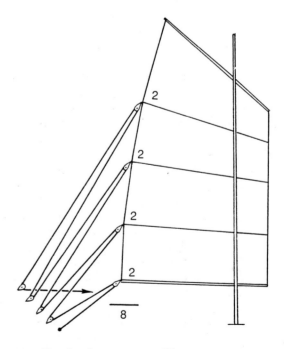

Fig. 4.2   Simple sheet system (2)

(R) on the ends of the battens. There are seven parts of sheet between deck and leech and this is referred to as a 'seven-part sheet'. As it is connected to the leech at four points it is also a four-point sheet. This seven-part sheet would give very light sheet loadings and be easy to heave in, but it would not be at all efficient because the accumulated friction in seven parts would prevent it from overhauling (paying out) or heaving in freely, and would demand a great length of rope in order to allow the full sail to be squared off at right angles to the boat. Furthermore, nearly all Chinese sails demand more than four sheeting points, which would aggravate the problems.

The power of a sheet is described by assuming that there is no friction and that each hauling part has a tension of one unit. The sheet in Fig. 4.1 would be described as pulling 1, 2, 2, 2, working from the boom upwards, and these figures are marked near the leech. They add up to 7 which is the power of the sheet and the same as the number of hauling parts between deck and leech.

In this case the boom is sheeted with only half as much power as the battens. This is not necessarily objectionable, but the power could be made the same as that of the battens by fitting a block or thimble to the boom and securing the standing end of the sheet on deck, as in Fig. 4.2. This would give powers of 2, 2, 2, 2, and an

eight-part sheet, which would further aggravate the problems of friction and length of sheet.

These two impracticable layouts have been shown merely to illustrate the concept of sheet power. They are simple only in the sense of needing no sheet spans. In practice we invariably use sheet spans in order to reduce the number of hauling parts.

Fig. 4.3 shows a practicable arrangement for a five-point sheet with two two-point sheet spans (A), each comprising a short length of rope whose ends are permanently attached to adjacent battens, and each rove through the eye of a block (B) which is free to run up and down the span. The sheet may be rove as shown, giving a five-part five-point sheet with power 1 on each of the five points.

If the sheet spans are unduly short they will tend to pull their two ends together, scalloping the leech. They should be made as long as possible, but the furled sail must sheet hard amidships without getting blocks B jammed against the deck blocks (Q). Long sheet spans give a further advantage in reducing the length of the sheet itself.

Even when the sheet spans are relatively long, the lower end of any span pulls the leech in somewhat harder than its upper end, and may cause a perceptible zig-zag in the leech as shown exaggerated in Fig. 4.4. This is explained diagrammatically in Fig. 4.5, where identical tensions (T) in the two ends of the span are resolved into horizontal components H_1 and H_2 and vertical components V_1 and V_2. It is evident that H_2 will pull the leech horizontally more than H_1 and that V_1 will pull downwards more than V_2. These differences will become less as the length of span is increased in relation to the width of the panel.

The vertical components may be ignored, and we do

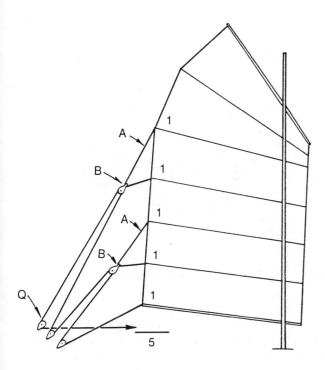

Fig. 4.3   Five-point five-part sheet

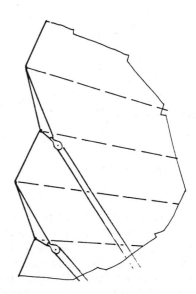

Fig. 4.4   Zig-zag leech

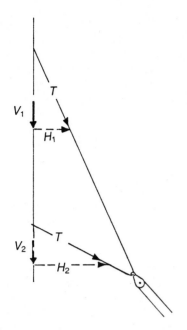

Fig. 4.5 Components of span tension

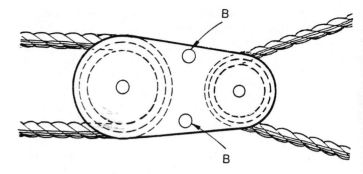

Fig. 4.7 Sister block

Fig. 4.8 Makeshift sister block

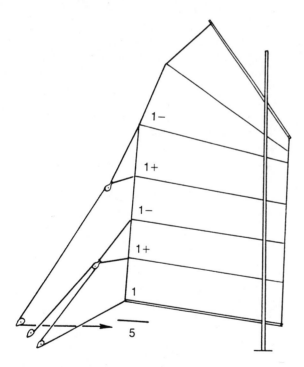

Fig. 4.6 Sheet power analysis

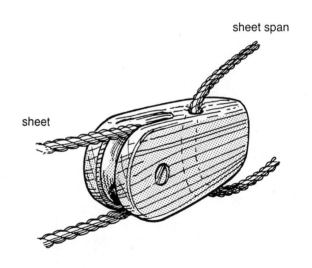

Fig. 4.9 Sheaved single-hole euphroe

not try to quantify the differences in the horizontal components, but sometimes use the notations + and − as in Fig. 4.6, which gives a more significant assessment of the power of the sheet shown in Fig. 4.3. These differences have nothing to do with friction, and the total power still adds up to 5. There is a further parameter to be kept in mind although not appearing in

this sheet power analysis. The angle of the sheets themselves is steeper at the top than at the bottom of the leech, so that for any given sheet power the horizontal component becomes progressively less as you move up the leech, while the vertical component becomes greater. This tends to allow the sail to twist, and if this twist is considered to be excessive it must be countered, either by using an anti-twist sheet arrangement as described later, or by using a sail that has more balance at the head than at the foot, as in Fig. 2.26, or is tapered at the head so as to require smaller horizontal components in its upper part.

A sheet span will work quite satisfactorily through the eye of a sheet block, or through a thimble, provided that these are really smooth. On some early designs we used sister blocks (Fig. 4.7) to reduce the friction in the spans, but these are no longer thought necessary. Sister blocks have to be made up specially for the job, and must be fitted with bushes (B) as shown to prevent them from capsizing endways and jamming the ropes. A makeshift alternative is to find two stock single blocks that can be riveted together with their bases outwards (Fig. 4.8).

There is perhaps more to be said for the 'euphroe', which is almost universally used in China. A 'euphroe' is defined as a separate piece of hardwood or plastic pierced with a hole or holes through which ropes may freely run. It may or may not incorporate a sheave in its base. Fig. 4.9 shows a type of sheaved euphroe suitable for connecting the sheet to a single sheet span. Euphroes made with smooth, curved surfaces are most unlikely to get foul of other ropes.

Two-point sheet spans will normally be controlled by either one or two parts of the sheet, the power exerted varying accordingly as shown in Fig. 4.10. The power in the lower span may easily be doubled, as in Fig. 4.11.

Fig. 4.12 shows an anti-twist two-point span that does not seem to be used in China but was devised in 1975 by

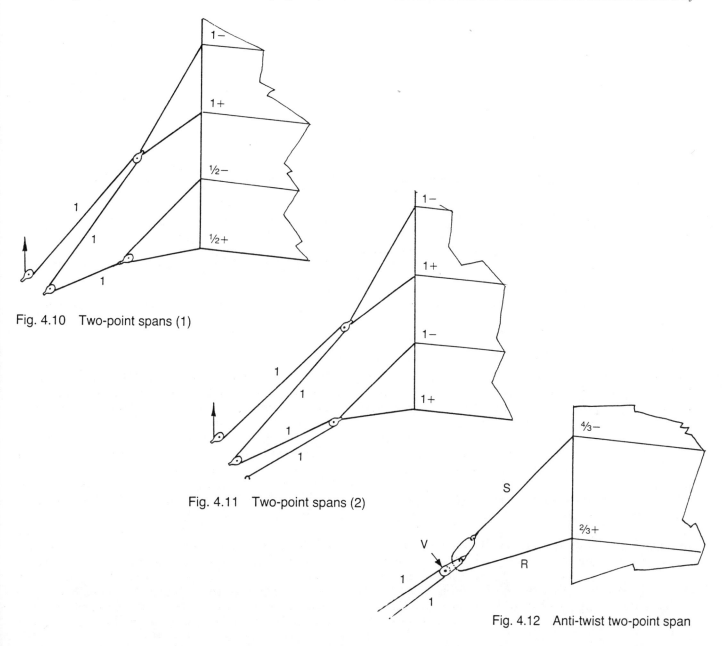

Fig. 4.10   Two-point spans (1)

Fig. 4.11   Two-point spans (2)

Fig. 4.12   Anti-twist two-point span

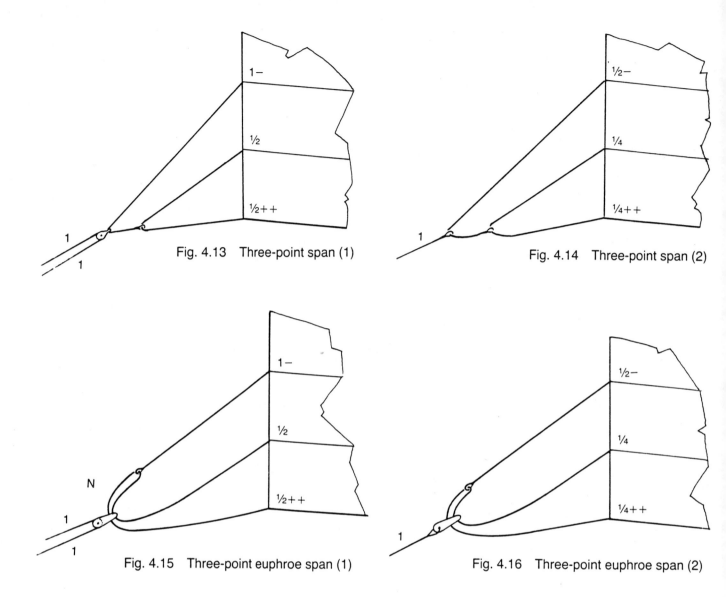

Fig. 4.13   Three-point span (1)

Fig. 4.14   Three-point span (2)

Fig. 4.15   Three-point euphroe span (1)

Fig. 4.16   Three-point euphroe span (2)

Admiral Fisher for the upper leech of the mainsail of *Yeong* (Fig. 16.5). The upper part (S) has nearly twice the power of the lower part (R), but the whole span requires slightly more drift when furled, as shown in Fig. 4.24. The part (V) may be either a euphroe as shown, similar to Fig. 4.9 but with an additional hole for the becket, or two single blocks similar to those of Fig. 4.8 but with a becket on the upper block.

When the use of two-point spans would require too many sheet parts, the next stage is to use three-point spans as in Fig. 4.13, where the upper part passes through the eye of the sheet block and finishes in a spliced thimble through which the lower part is rove. Fig. 4.14 shows a similar arrangement but with a single part of the sheet finishing in a spliced thimble.

The power analysis of three-point spans is a little more complicated, since the two lower parts both start

from a + part and then superimpose their own + and − as before, the signs of the middle part cancelling out.

Fig 4.15 shows a three-point euphroe span, which is the form of three-point span most commonly used in China. The sheet block (N) is now part of a euphroe with two vertical holes, and the thimble through which the lower part of the span is rove is now above the sheet block instead of below it. Fig. 4.16 shows the same arrangement used with a single-part sheet, requiring no sheave in the base of the euphroe.

The power analyses of Figs. 4.15 and 4.16 are identical with those of Figs. 4.13 and 4.14 respectively, but the euphroe arrangements have the advantage in offering greater tolerance of the different sheeting angles that arise from trimming sheets and from reefing. If the span shown in Fig. 4.13 were to be used at a very steep angle, the thimble would jam against the block and the lower parts of the span would go slack unless the lengths of the two spans were readjusted, whereas the arrangement shown in Fig. 4.15 will tolerate the full range of sheeting angles without any readjustment. At flat sheeting angles its lower parts form a long V with minimum pinching effect, whereas the V of Fig. 4.13 would be unnecessarily short.

These disadvantages in Fig. 4.13 and 4.14 tend to disappear if the rig layout permits the spans to be made longer than the minimum dimensions laid down later in this chapter.

The main reason for not using euphroe spans is simply that euphroes cannot be bought off the shelf, although they are easy enough to make up out of hardwood or strong plastic. If a euphroe has two or more rope holes for the spans, these may with advantage be bored in slightly

different planes, to prevent the spans from rubbing against each other.

It is inherent in all the above three-point spans that the upper batten is pulled with about twice the power of each of the two lower battens. If the whole assembly were inverted this situation would be reversed, but the inverted attitude would induce twist and seems to be rare in China.

It is possible to design a three-point span that will exert approximately equal power on all three battens. Fig. 4.17 (after Worcester) shows a span from the middle of the leech of a Foochow Pole Junk which could be used with advantage on some Western sails. It could equally well be controlled by a single part of sheet, in which case the powers would be halved.

Two other three-point spans recorded in China by Worcester (Fig. 4.18) seem to be inferior. Arrangement a gives very uneven powers and uses an awkward treble sister block (W) with a double sheave at its upper end. Arrangement b seems to require adjustment at point S if tension is to be maintained when reefed or furled, or when varying the sheet angle under full sail. Neither of these arrangements will be considered further.

As the number of battens in the sail is increased, it may become desirable to use one or more four-point spans, such as those shown in Fig. 4.19 and 4.20, but these are indifferent arrangements that have a poor tolerance for major changes in sheeting angle. The related four-point euphroe span shown in Fig. 4.21 is preferable. The fitting (U) may be either a ring or a two-hole euphroe.

In China, the arrangement shown in Fig. 4.21 seems to be the common form of four-point span, but Worcester has recorded at least five variations. However, many of them seem to show curious distributions of power which may, perhaps, have suited the sails on which they

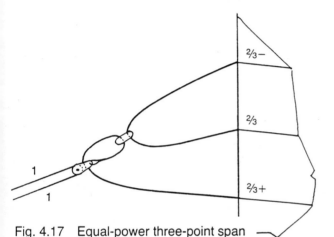

Fig. 4.17   Equal-power three-point span

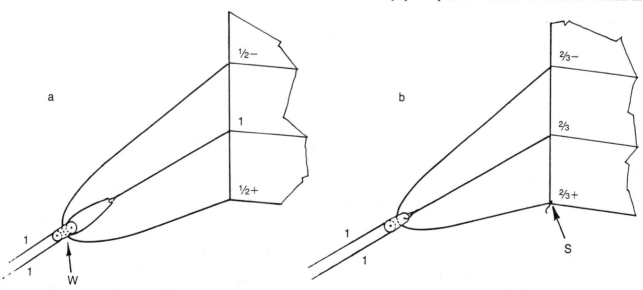

Fig. 4.18   Inferior three-point spans

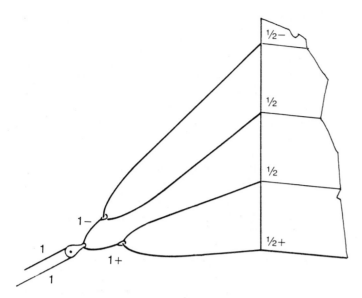

Fig. 4.19   Indifferent four-point span (1)

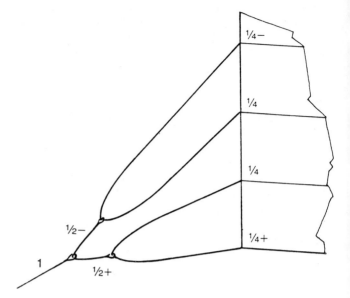

Fig. 4.20   Indifferent four-point span (2)

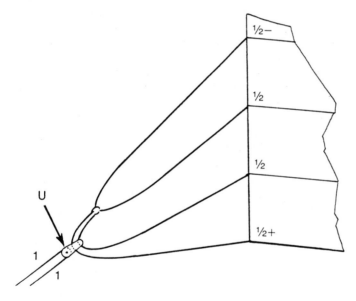

Fig. 4.21   Four-point euphroe span

were carried but for various reasons will not be considered further here.

Many interesting arrangements of sheet spans are possible, and any reader with an inventive mind may amuse himself by devising variations and studying their characteristics.

Reefing and furling

The implications of reefing and furling these spans will now be considered. In Fig. 4.22, C is the position of the clew as seen in profile when the sail is fully hoisted and aligned fore-and-aft. As soon as the halyard is eased the boom settles into the topping-lifts and the clew drops a short distance to a position such as C_1 or C_2, depending upon whether the boom is held aft by a standing tack parrel (Fig. 3.25) or a standing lower luff parrel (Fig. 3.26).

If the furled bundle is then lowered by running topping-lifts into a gallows or crutch the clew will finish up somewhat lower still, for example at C_3 or C_4, with the after ends of the battens staggered aft above it as shown in Fig. 2.26. It must be possible to harden the sheets in this attitude, with all the spans taut, so as to hold the bundle amidships. However, for practical purposes it is not necessary to work to the nearest inch, and it is usual to assume, when working out a sheet system, that the furled clew and the ends of the furled battens coincide at a point C on the sailplan, positioned to represent the furled position of the leech, possibly in crutch.

All sheet spans have a minimum acceptable length, which is the shortest length that will control the sail without distorting it and (in the case of multiple spans) that will reef and furl without any thimbles or blocks or euphroes becoming 'two blocks', i.e. jamming against each other. These minimum lengths are specified in relation to the panel width (P) (Fig. 4.22).

The total net length of rope in a two-point span, excluding any knots or splices at the ends, should not be less than $2P$. This applies also to any two-point span forming part of a multiple span. Beyond this minimum, all two-point spans should be as long as possible. If a span is too short it will try to pull its two ends together when sail is set and so cause the leech to scallop.

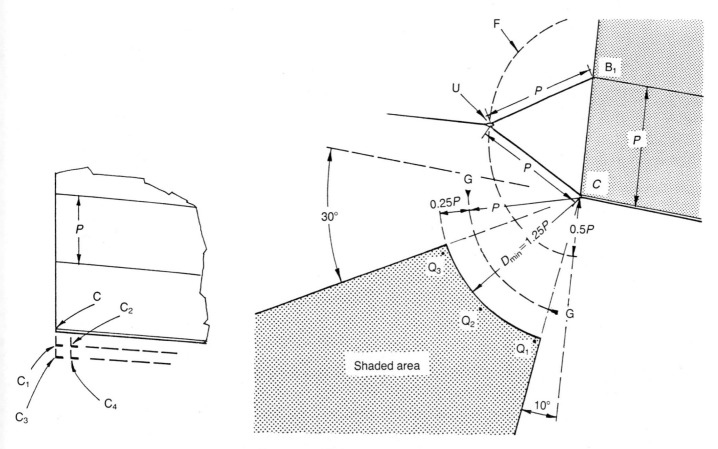

Fig. 4.22 Positions of clew

Fig. 4.23 Minimum two-point span

Furthermore, the tendency for its lower arm to pull sideways more strongly than its upper arm (Fig. 4.5) will be aggravated.

Fig. 4.23 shows the lower leech of a sail that is fully set. A minimum-length two-point span is fitted between the boom and batten 1, and controlled by a single part of the sheet. When extended at right angles to the leech the span forms an equilateral triangle as shown. When extended in any other direction the thimble (U) will lie somewhere along an ellipse (F) whose foci are C and B_1. When pulled downwards in line with the leech it will be distant 0.5 P from point C, as shown.

When the first panel is reefed, B_1 is regarded for our purposes as being superimposed on C, and the thimble U when extended will lie somewhere along the arc G at a radius P from point C.

When the furled sail is sheeted hard in the thimble of the span must lie clear of the lower sheet block. This block may be anchored on deck, on the rail of a strong pulpit, or on a bumkin. The minimum amount of drift between the clew C and the *anchorage* of the lower block (D_{min}) is found by adding to the length of the furled minimum span an arbitrary distance of 0.25P to allow for the dimensions of the span thimble and of the lower

sheet block with its shackle. Thus in Fig. 4.23, $D_{min} = P + 0.25P = 1.25P$ and is drawn as a radius from clew C, as shown.

The lower block anchorage may lie on or beyond this arc, but with two further limitations: in order to keep the sheets clear of the leech it must lie abaft a line drawn from C at 10° to the extension of the line of the leech; and in order to exert a downward pull it must lie below a line drawn from C at 30° to the extension of the line of the boom. The resulting segment of a circle (shaded in Fig. 4.23) gives in profile the area within which the lower block anchorage must lie. For example, Q_1, Q_2 or Q_3 would be possible positions for the lower block anchorage, but if the layout permits this anchorage should be placed further away than D_{min} and the spans lengthened accordingly.

The method of constructing the 'shaded area' remains the same for all junk sails. The only variable is D_{min}, which will change for different types of sheet span, as discussed below.

Although it might appear that the sheets from position Q_1 are too vertical, this is deceptive. Whenever the boat is sailing the leech is well out from the centreline and the true sheeting angle is much less steep than the angle

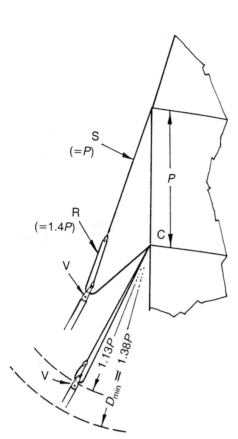

Fig. 4.24
Minimum anti-twist two-point span

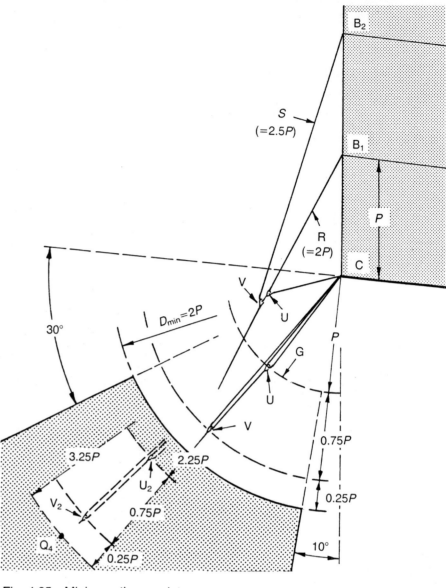

Fig. 4.25   Minimum three-point span

shown. Nevertheless, it would be better to sheet from further aft if possible.

Fig. 4.24 shows the reefing characteristics of the anti-twist two-point span from Fig. 4.12. Although this system will normally be used well up the leech, its critical lengths for reefing and furling apply when its two ends are brought down to clew C, as marked. The ellipse from Fig. 4.23 is no longer applicable. A mean sheeting angle has been assumed near the middle of the permissible sector and a position for the euphroe (V) under full sail corresponding with that of the thimble (U) in Fig. 4.23. If the net length of the upper part (S) is made equal to P, as here, then it is found that the length

of the lower part (R) is about $1.4P$ and the furled radius of V is about $1.13P$, giving a $D_{\min}$ of $(1.13 + 0.25)P = 1.38P$. This $D_{\min}$ lies between that of the simple two-point span and that of the nearest three-point span (Fig. 4.28).

The dimension $D_{\min}$ will increase relative to P as the number of points in the sheet span increases. With a three-point span such as those in Fig. 4.13 and 4.14, the minimum span dimensions are as shown in Fig. 4.25. The lower part (R) is a two-point span whose minimum length is therefore fixed at $2P$ and whose thimble (U), when reefed, will lie on an arc (G) of radius P from centre C. When the full sail is sheeted flat amidships, as in this figure, it is acceptable for the sheet thimble or block V to

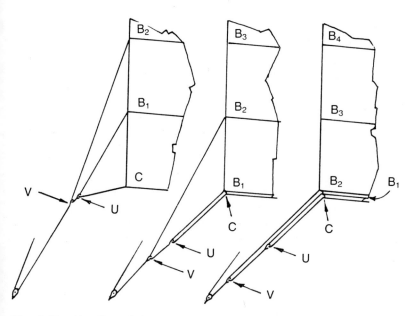

Fig. 4.26   Reefing of three-point span

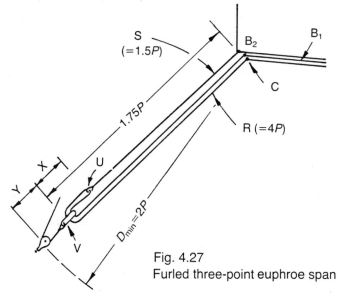

Fig. 4.27
Furled three-point euphroe span

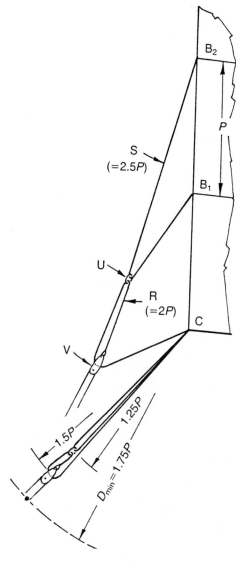

Fig. 4.28
Furling of equal-power three-point span

be touching U, observing that in all sailing attitudes the sheeting angle becomes less steep, causing V to move slightly away from U. The net length of the upper part (S) would vary slightly according to the basic sheeting angle, e.g. whether the sheet anchorage was further forward or further aft, but this variation is slight and for our purposes we can assume a mean sheeting angle as shown, giving a net length of S equal to about $2.5P$; it is seen that V has now pulled away from U by a distance of half $1.5P$, i.e. $0.75P$. The D_{min} is therefore $P + 0.75P + 0.25P = 2P$, and the 'shaded area' will be as shown.

If the sheet block anchorage can be further away from C than D_{min}, the length of both parts of the span should be increased, using the following procedure. The distance between U and V when furled can remain at $0.75P$ and the allowance for lower sheet blocks can remain at $0.25P$. Now if, say, it were possible to place the sheet anchorage at Q_4, a distance of $3.25P$ from clew C, the situation would be as shown dotted. The radius of V_2 would be $3P$, and the radius of U_2 would be $2.25P$. The net length of the lower part (R) would be $4.5P$, and of the upper part (S) would be $3.75P$. The accuracy of such length figures is adequate for planning and cutting the rope, after adding allowances for hitches and splices, but final adjustments will be made to the hitches after setting up the rig on the boat.

Fig. 4.26 shows, to scale, the three stages of reefing the minimum span from Fig. 4.25. By rendering through both thimbles between stages 1 and 2, and through thimble V between stages 2 and 3, all parts of the span can maintain their respective tensions at all times.

Fig. 4.27 shows stage 3 of reefing the related three-point euphroe span shown in Fig. 4.15, which is identical in its reefing characteristics with that of Fig. 4.25. D_{min} is unchanged, but the thimble (U), being now *above* euphroe V, must be positioned so as to avoid coming two blocks with V as the sail is furled. To achieve this, the net length of the upper span (S) is made 1.5P. The furled radius of V remains at 1.75P and the net length of the lower part (R) is therefore (1.75P + 0.25P) × 2 = 4P. Again, if it is possible for the sheet anchorage to be more than 2P away from C, then the furled distances X and Y may remain constant at 0.25P each, and parts S and R lengthened to suit the longer drift.

Where, as in this span, two parts of the same rope run parallel with each other and work through a thimble hung from a *single* part of rope, there is a danger that the single part will twist under load, or when the load is released, and thereby twist up the two parallel parts until they bind together and will not run. To obviate this, either the single span is made as long as possible so that the parallel parts are short and held untwisted by the euphroe or block, or the single part is eliminated and its thimble fastened directly to the leech in such a way that it cannot twist. The former method is used in all the spans in this book.

Fig. 4.28 shows the first and third stages of reefing the 'equal-power' three-point span shown in Fig. 4.17. In planning the full-sail attitude the position of the euphroe (V) has been made the same as that of the thimble (V) in Fig. 4.25, since the span will not take up efficient angles if V is any closer to the sail. The net length of the upper part S could be as little as 2P, being a simple two-point span, but it may be lengthened to 2.5P, as shown, without affecting D_{min}. The resulting net length of the lower part (R) may be measured off as about 2P.

When this span is reefed to stage 3 it will be seen that the radius of V is only 1.5P, giving 1.5P + 0.25P = 1.75P for D_{min} of the sheet anchorage, as compared with the figure of 2P for all the preceding types of three-point span. It is evident that this is a very good form of span, requiring the minimum of drift and giving roughly equal power on all three points. It also shares with the other euphroe spans (Fig. 4.15 and 4.16) the ability to tolerate the full range of permissible sheeting angles without coming two blocks.

The complete sheet system for any sail will include one or more of the different types of span described above. If more than one type of span is used the minimum drift (D_{min}) between clew and sheet block anchorage must be taken as that of whichever span

requires the longer drift. For example, a system including the spans from Fig. 4.23 and 4.24 would have a D_{min} of 1.38P, not 1.25P. It follows that the length of the two-point span could be increased above its minimum, to suit the longer drift.

Six-point sheeting system

For any particular sail there will be many possible sheet arrangements. We now consider some of the variations that might be used to provide a six-point sheeting system, for example on the recommended form of sail shown in Fig. 2.26. Various points of design will emerge from the comments on these variations. A number of other possible variations have been discarded as having obvious shortcomings. The diagrams are not to scale, and the D_{min} values are taken from the preceding figures. The sheaves of the deck block(s) are shown spaced out, for clarity.

Fig. 4.29 gives roughly equal power on all six points, but a six-part sheet involves rather a lot of friction and demands a lot of rope. There is no anti-twist effect, but this may not matter under full sail, particularly if the sail itself has more balance at the head than at the foot. As is reefed down the sail develops more and more twist. For example, with three panels down there will be a total

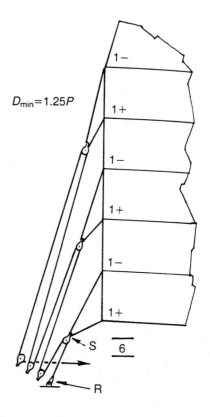

Fig. 4.29   Six-part sheet

power of 4 pulling on the reefed bundle and only 2 on the sail exposed above it.

Reefed twist may be reduced or even eliminated at the expense of extra deck work. A possible step is to use a snap shackle at R (Fig. 4.29) with a stopper knot above it. As soon as the first panel is reefed the snap shackle is let go and allowed to run up and jam against the span block (S), thus removing the lowest part of the sheet and reducing the number of sheet parts to five and halving the sheet power on the boom and no. 1 batten. However, this will not do a lot towards reducing the twist under close-reefed conditions, and may be a nuisance to recover when reverting to full sail.

It might be thought that this lower part of the sheet could be permanently dispensed with, as in Fig. 4.30, giving a slight anti-twist effect under full sail, but this would contravene the 'leech-kink rule' that must now be stated: *Under full sail, the power on any one batten should not be more than twice that of the batten below it.* In this layout batten 2 has more than twice the power of batten 1, and when sailing the leech will develop a kink, with batten 2 too far in and batten 1 too far out, an effect that is irritating although not very serious. It can be obviated by using an anti-twist two-point span at the bottom of the leech, as shown in Fig. 4.31, at the cost of a slight increase in D_{min}.

If more deck work can be tolerated, a more potent way of reducing the reefed twist would be to grab a bight of the sheet and belay it in such a way as to take all the weight off the lower parts of the sheet. For example, Fig. 4.32 shows the sail from Fig. 4.29 with four panels reefed. The bight of the sheet has been grabbed at point T and pulled forward to a deck cleat (A) in such a way that all the sheet below it is slack. This gives a two-part sheet controlling the exposed part of the sail only. When easing sheets to sail further off the wind, more slack would be pulled forward to the deck cleat and eased out into the lower (slack) part of the system at the same time as, or before, the upper sheet is eased out. This sort of deck work is not recommended. It is better to start with a sheet that is as anti-twist as possible without contravening the leech-kink rule, and to accept some twist when close-reefed. Any penalty is largely offset by the inherent efficiency of the flat sail in hard winds.

Fig. 4.33 shows a reasonable sheet, but one that can only be rigged as shown with the hauling part leading from the bottom span – 'first-pull-at-the-bottom-of-the-leech' as it is sometimes called. This feature is frequently found in China. Worcester noted: '. . . It would appear, however, that in the case of the mainsail the primary pull more often than not is on the lower part of the sail, and in the case of the foresail rather more often on the upper part of the sail, whereas with the mizzen it is almost invariably on the lower part of the sail. As there

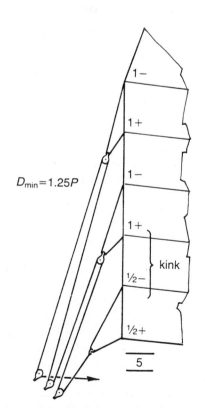

Fig. 4.30   Inferior five-part sheet

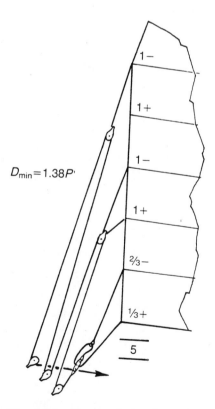

Fig. 4.31   Five-part sheet

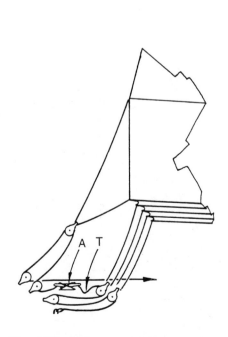

Fig. 4.32   Using upper sheets only

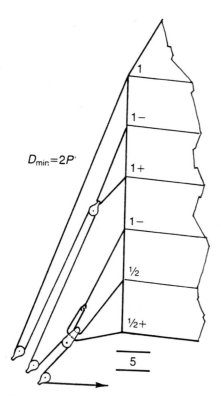

$D_{min} = 2P'$

1

1−

1+

1−

½

½+

5

Fig. 4.33　Five-part sheet

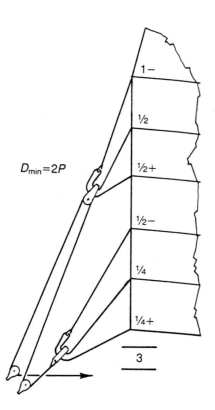

$D_{min} = 2P$

1−

½

½+

½−

¼

¼+

3

Fig. 4.35　Three-part sheet

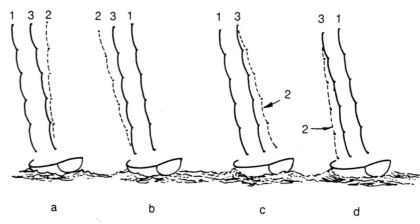

Fig. 4.34　Sheet friction

is always some practical reason for all Chinese customs it would be interesting to know what prompted them in this matter.' We have not yet been able to see any reason for these tendencies.

Owing to the friction in the sheet blocks, the first-pull part of the leech comes in further than the rest when the sheet is hauled in, and goes out further when the sheet is paid out. This effect increases with the number of hauling parts in the sheet, and so is much more marked with a six-part than with a three-part sheet. In a seaway, the pitching and rolling of the hull will soon shake the sheet into a state of even tension in each part, but even in calm water sheet friction need not affect the final attitude of the sail. When hauling or veering the sheet the watchkeeper can easily take it too far in the first place and then take some of it back to reach the correct attitude.

Fig. 4.34 a is an attempt to illustrate this process for a single sail whose first pull is at the top of the leech, as seen from the lee quarter. Only the leech of the sail is shown, in three stages of trim. Stage 1 shows the correct position for a close reach. To come up close-hauled, the leech is first pulled up to the position in stage 2 (shown exaggerated) and then eased back to the correct position at stage 3. Fig. 4.34 b shows the reverse process, in which stage 1 is the correct close-hauled attitude. When paying off on to a close reach the leech is first eased to the position in stage 2, then hauled back to the correct position at stage 3.

Figs 4.34 c and 4.34 d show the same processes for a sail whose first pull is at the bottom of the leech. Although it is thus possible, in calm water, to use sheet friction to increase or decrease the amount of twist in the sail, this technique is not much use at sea. The amount of twist should be controlled by the power of the different sheet parts and the balance characteristics of the sail.

Although it might appear from the above that there is nothing to choose between first-pull-at-the-top and first-pull-at-the-bottom, the former somehow seems right to the Western mind, and all our recommended sheet systems are so arranged.

Fig. 4.35 shows a very good form of six-point sheet which has a strong anti-twist effect without kinking the leech and has only three sheet parts, which may conveniently be of fairly large-diameter rope. With sails of more than about 350 sq ft (33 m²) it may be desirable to provide a self-tailing winch. Otherwise it will sometimes be necessary to luff up in order to get the sheet in, with the sail partly weathercocking, or to use the roll of the boat to help.

Fig. 4.36 shows a variation which would give a slightly stronger anti-twist effect at the cost of an increase in D_{min}, but which must be ruled out because the power of batten 4 is more than four times that of batten 3, giving rise to a severe kink in the leech. The addition of another sheet part as in Fig. 4.37 would reduce this kink, but not by enough to be admissible under our rule.

The sheet in Fig. 4.38 gives roughly equal power on all battens. When compared with Fig. 4.29 it shows half the number of sheet parts but nearly twice the D_{min}. Fig. 4.39 shows a strongly anti-twist sheet which we must disqualify for the kink between battens 4 and 5, but which is of interest in having the first pull in the middle of the leech. This is perfectly acceptable, and will respond to the same calm-water technique (hauling or veering the sheet too far, then taking some of it back) that has been described above.

Fig. 4.40 shows an arrangement in which a six-point span is controlled by a two-part sheet. The power of this sheet could of course be increased as desired by making it a three-, four-, or even five-part purchase, but the arrangement has several disadvantages: it has no anti-twist effect, a very large D_{min}, and the directions of pull of the spans are pinched in towards the euphroe instead of converging more gently towards the lower sheet blocks. If used with double sheets, however, as discussed on p 72–3, this system would obviate the problem caused by the lee sheets lying against the leeward side of the sail (see Fig. 4.50), provided that the D_{min} would fit inside the half-beam of the boat.

Fig. 4.41 shows a split sheet variation of Fig. 4.35. This provides some positive control of twist without requiring the watchkeeper to do any awkward deck work, but at the cost of handling two sheets instead of one. Since the purchase on the upper and lower sheets is the same the two hauling parts may be married (gripped together) when making small changes of sail trim but the pull will be rather heavy, with a mechanical advantage of 2:1

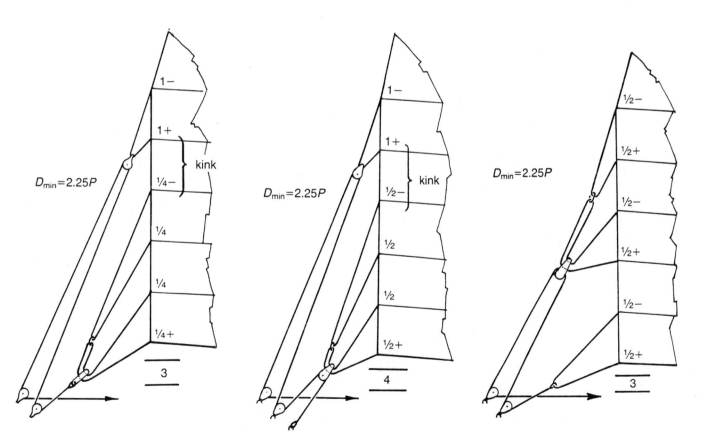

Fig. 4.36 Inferior three-part sheet   Fig. 4.37 Inferior four-part sheet   Fig. 4.38 Equal-power three-part sheet

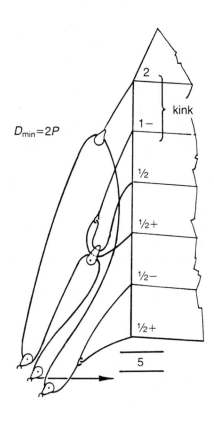

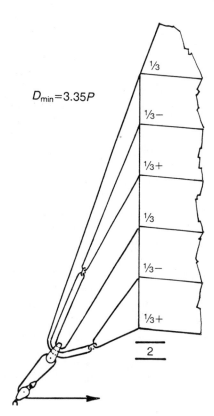

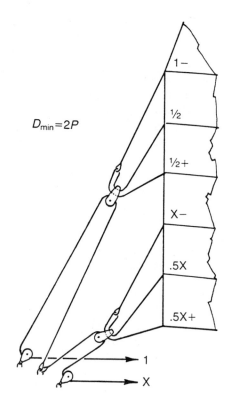

Fig. 4.39 Inferior five-part sheet   Fig. 4.40 Two-part sheet   Fig. 4.41   Split sheet (1)

only. When making large changes in sail trim or when reefing or unreefing, the two hauling parts will have to be separated and readjusted relative to each other.

Whether married or not the tension in the two sheets will normally be different, with the upper sheet having the greater tension. When married it would be convenient to make up the two parts together on to a single large cleat, but it is not possible to work the married parts round a single winch barrel without getting riding turns. With three or more panels reefed it is not necessary to take any weight on the lower sheet, simply taking in any slack by hand. The upper sheet may then be worked round a winch if necessary. For convenience, the two standing ends may share a common deck anchorage, as shown.

With sails of more than about 300 sq ft (28 m²) it would be best to abandon any idea of marrying the two parts and to give the upper sheet a three- or four-part purchase, as in Fig. 4.42 and 4.43. When working sheets in fresh winds with a single watchkeeper it would then be necessary to work the upper and lower sheet alternately in short steps. With still larger sails, the lower sheet could also be given more purchase.

Split sheets offer interesting possibilities of controlling twist in a seamanlike way at the expense of deman-

ding a bit more skilled work from the watchkeeper. Under full sail it is important, in a fresh breeze, not to allow the full weight of the sail to come on one half of the sheet only, since this may overload the battens. Split sheets do not seem to be used in China, but have found a place in a few Western yachts.

This survey of selected six-point sheeting arrangements has been made in some detail for the benefit of readers who want to master the underlying theory. Sheets with less than six points will offer fewer variations than this, while sheets with more than six points will offer more.

Positioning lower sheet blocks

In all the foregoing sheet diagrams, the lower sheet blocks and any deck anchorages for the standing parts have been drawn spaced out, for clarity. In practice, separate sheaves may be combined into one or more multiple-sheaved blocks if desired, and the standing parts may finish at beckets on the tails of such blocks, but it is slightly preferable to use closely spaced single blocks, each of which will take up the exact alignment to suit its own sheet parts.

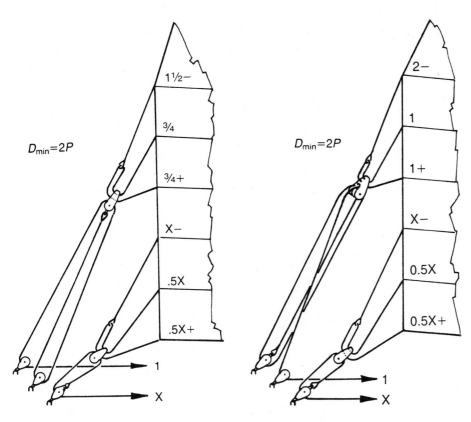

Fig. 4.42   Split sheet (2)   Fig. 4.43   Split sheet (3)

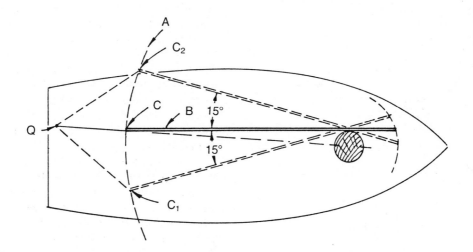

Fig. 4.44   Offset lower sheet blocks

Fig. 4.23 has shown the shaded area within which the lower sheet blocks should lie when seen in profile. In plan view, if these blocks are to be in a fixed position it should lie just to port of the boat's centreline so as to give the sail an equal angle of incidence on either tack without readjustment of sheets. Fig. 4.44 shows the boom (B) lying fore-and-aft alongside the mast, whose diameter has been exaggerated. The clew (C) moves along an arc (A) whose centre is the centre of the mast. The lower sheet blocks (Q) should lie on a line drawn through C and the centre of the mast, as shown. For any sheet setting the boom will then take up the same incidence (in this case 15°) on either tack, as shown at C_1 and C_2, but the clew will lie further outboard on the starboard tack.

The fact that the mast is tapered down above the boom will tend to cause the upper part of the sail to have less incidence on the port tack than on starboard, but this is offset by the reduction of incidence on starboard tack caused by the slack in the batten parrels allowing the battens to hang slightly away from the mast. It seems reasonable to assume that these effects cancel out.

The position of the lower sheet blocks (Q) shown in Fig. 4.44 is dictated solely by the convenience of tacking and gybing without readjustment of the sheet. From the point of view of controlling the set of a Chinese sail it is better to have point Q further to *windward* when close-hauled or reaching. This is another point of difference from conventional Western practice. Some Chinese vessels use tailed sheets in which a multiple

lower sheet block is anchored by a long rope tail that is commonly hitched to the weather rail, and has to be changed over to the opposite rail when tacking. This is obviously unacceptable in a short-handed yacht, but a similar effect can be obtained with a horsed sheet, which is not apparently used in China. Fig. 4.45 shows the arrangement used experimentally in *Jester*, in which the sheet (2) works through lower sheet blocks (Q) mounted on a traveller (T) that runs along an athwartships horse on track (H), and may be triced either way along the horse by tricing lines (W).

With Western rigs a boat is commonly sailed with the traveller at the leeward end of a horse, but with the Chinese sail the traveller is triced to windward when close-hauled in order to reduce the downward pull on the leech and the tension in the sheet. When bearing away onto a broad reach or run the tricing line should be eased right out before easing the sheet, allowing the traveller to run right down to leeward and achieving the best sheeting angle for downwind work. When short-tacking, both tricing lines may be set up so as to hold the traveller amidships, or slightly over to port as described above. Preferably the traveller is designed so that it cannot rotate about the horse, thus keeping the blocks more or less upright when sheets are slack.

The disadvantage of horsed sheets, apart from obstructing the deck and adding more running ropes, is that the sheet has to be led to a centreline cleat or fairlead (C) (Fig. 4.45) that is at least as far away from the horse as the length of the horse. The running part (3) then sweeps a lot of deck. The remedy would be to belay the sheet on the traveller (T) if it can be reached. Otherwise it would be necessary to accept the clumsy arrangement shown in Fig. 4.46, from which the tricing lines have been omitted for clarity. This sheet would have to have an even number of parts. The cleat (C) could now be placed anywhere on deck, but as the sheet would have to render through all its blocks when tricing the traveller, there would be great frictional resistance.

A more usual way of sheeting a sail from the windward side is to fit it with double sheets, a system that is sometimes used both in China and in the West. These consist of a complete set of sheets on either side of the sail, commonly secured to the boom and battens at points some way forward of the leech. The port sheets pass through small 'windows' in the sail in order to reach the battens. Fig. 4.47 shows the same sheet system as Fig. 4.3, but duplicated in this way.

The lower sheet blocks are normally secured to the rail either side abreast of, or slightly abaft, the sheeting points, as in Fig. 4.48. When sailing, the weight is taken on the windward set of sheets, the leeward sheets hanging slack. When beating to windward there is no need to touch the sheets, once both sides have been adjusted correctly so as to give the same incidence on either tack.

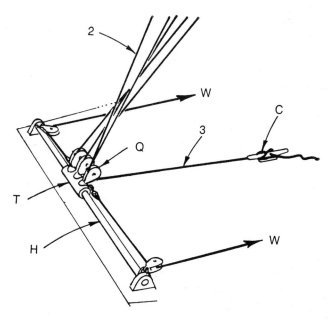

Fig. 4.45   Horsed sheet (1)

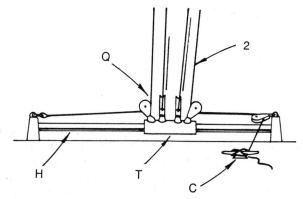

Fig. 4.46   Horsed sheet (2)

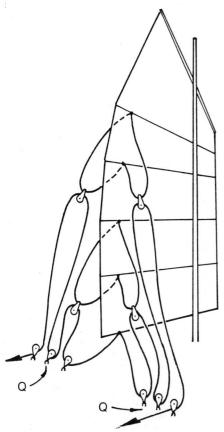

Fig. 4.47   Double sheets

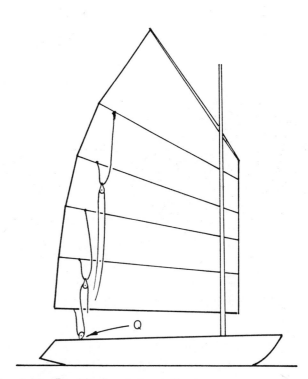

Fig. 4.48   Double sheets in profile

Double sheets offer several advantages. Since the sheets do not have to hang clear abaft the after ends of the battens, the sail may be made fully automatic without any of the restrictions on its shape that have been discussed in Chapter 2. It is not necessary for the after ends of the battens to furl with positive stagger and there is never any need to omit the top batten from the sheeting system. The leech of a mainsail or mizzen may be well aft on the boat without requiring a bumkin for the lower sheet blocks and without fouling a vane steering gear. With multi-masted rigs the gap between sails may be reduced to the point where the actual batten ends only just clear each other. These features enable a large sail area to be set on a short hull without having to use a very tall rig, as in *Batwing* (Fig. 16.9).

Sails with double sheets may be backed to a limited extent by setting up the windward sheet with the leeward sheet slack. This can be useful on the foresail of a multi-masted rig if the boat tends to hang in irons (i.e. head to wind) when tacking. Another advantage is that the double sheets can hold the furled sail firmly amidships. Single sheets, even if set up very taut, permit the furled bundle to swing slightly from side to side as it hangs in the lifts. This causes the lifts to snatch the

masthead aft and creates chafe between the bundle and the mast.

If double sheets are to be able to hold the furled sail firmly amidships in this way, the sheet system must be designed to conform with the rules already laid down, but with the shaded areas 'turned' athwartships so as to pass through the position of the lower sheet blocks on the rail each side. Fig. 4.49 shows a transverse section of the boat and at C the position of the clew when the sail is amidships. In this example the D_{min} of the sheet system would just permit the lower sheet blocks (Q) to be positioned on the rail as shown. If the shaded area were found to lie wholly outside the rail it would be necessary to raise the sail on the mast, and so to raise point C by the required amount.

The main disadvantage of double sheets, apart from the extra gear, is that when the sail is squared off for a run or broad reach the windward set of sheets has a poor lead that causes excessive tension on the sheet and undue compression of the battens. Fig. 4.50 shows this in plan view, with sheets S taking the load while sheets P hang slack around the forward side of the sail. D is the line of a single sheet system, which would give a better lead on this point of sailing. Most fully automatic sheet systems,

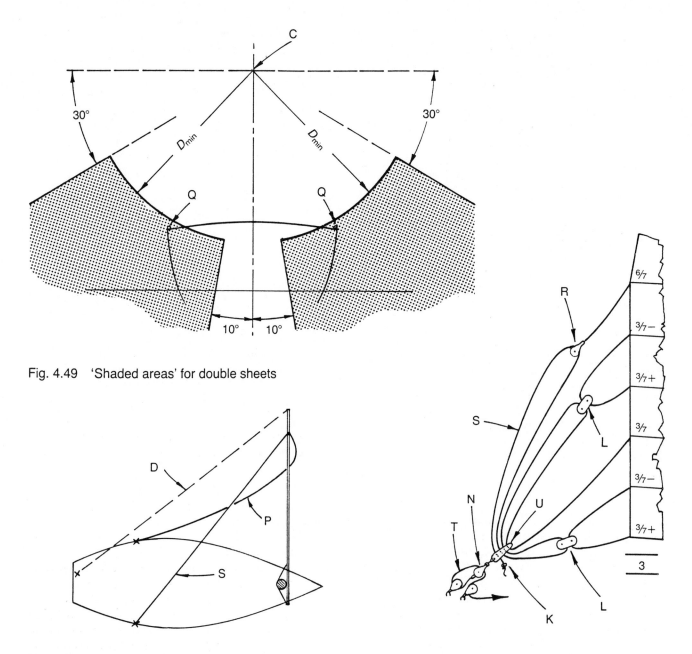

Fig. 4.49   'Shaded areas' for double sheets

Fig. 4.50   Running with double sheets

Fig. 4.51   Running spanline (1)

such as those in Fig. 4.47, are not very suitable for double sheets since the running parts will not overhaul freely when lying against the leeward side of the sail, for example as at P in Fig. 4.50. To remedy this it is necessary to use a system in which all hauling parts of the sheet are below boom level. Fig. 4.40 has shown one way of achieving this, but at the expense of a large $D_{\min}$ that would often be difficult to fit into the half-beam of the boat.

A more flexible scheme, often used in China, involves a 'running spanline', which is defined as an adjustable line connecting the sheet to the standing sheet spans.

Fig. 4.51 shows a six-point sheet layout used by Tom Colvin, who has been developing and using Chinese rig in the United States since the early 1960s. The three-part sheet (T) has its lower blocks fixed to a deck anchorage. Its upper block (N) is joined by a short strop to a euphroe (U) (in China, these are commonly combined by fitting a sheave into the base of the euphroe). At the leech, two two-point spans pass through the upper sheaves of sister blocks (L). From batten 5 a single-part sheet span terminates in a block (R).

The running spanline (S) has its standing end bent to batten 2 and is then rove between the euphroe (U) and blocks L and R as shown, finishing with a stopper knot (K) in the lowest hole of the euphroe. While under full sail it is not necessary to touch this knot but it is said to be possible to adjust sail twist as desired, presumably by pulling the parts of the running spanline to and fro through the euphroe and relying on friction to hold them there.

Sail incidence, from close-hauled to running, may be adjusted on sheet T only, but for a perfectly-setting sail it will be necessary for the running spanline to render through the euphroe in order to take up the best line of tension whenever sheets are hardened or eased. Whether this happens automatically, or whether it must be assisted by hand, will depend on the wind strength, the motion of the boat, and the amount of friction in the euphroe. It may be noted that the sheet power on batten 5 is slightly more than double that on batten 4, mildly contravening our leech-kink rule. When reefing with the wind forward of the beam it may be necessary to shorten the running spanline (S) in order to keep the upper and lower blocks of the sheet apart. This will involve tying a fresh stopper knot and hanging the coil of spare line, but the euphroe (U) will be within easy reach of the deck at this time.

With a running spanline it is easy to arrange for a small number of sheet parts to control a large number of points on the leech without requiring an excessive D_{min}, since the running spanline may be shortened right in when the sail is close-reefed or furled. The sheet may be short and of ample size, with the spanline of much smaller rope. With double sheets there is no difficulty in overhauling the slack leeward sheet, which hangs below the boom.

The main disadvantage lies in having to reach the euphroe in order to adjust the running spanline when reefing and unreefing. However, it is possible to imagine this line being led along the deck, provided that the euphroe has low friction and is thus self-adjusting. Fig. 4.52 shows a seven-point sheet with the running end of the spanline led down to a block alongside the lower sheet block, and thence to a cleat alongside the sheet cleat. If the load on the spanline is now taken as 1 unit, the total load on the sheet will be 6, reduced to 3 by the 2-part purchase. This purchase may be increased as necessary. It would not be necessary to work the two hauling ends simultaneously, and it would often be sufficient to work the sheet without touching the spanline. It would be interesting to develop a sheet system of this sort with either double or single sheets.

Double sheets, even though bent to the battens some way forward of the leech, may get foul in a number of ways, particularly if the boat is being thrown around in a seaway. Writing from Samoa of his ocean cruising in *Batwing* (Fig. 16.9), Timothy Dunn reported: 'The double sheets have proven acceptable on the foresail, but had to be scrapped on the mainsail. As you foresaw, there was some reluctance of the sheets to overhaul but

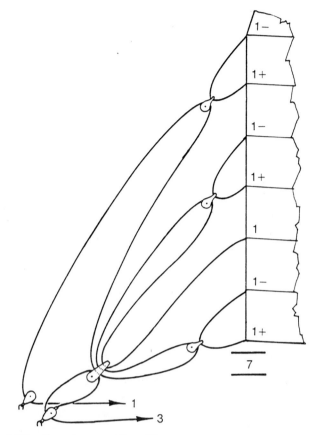

Fig. 4.52   Running spanline (2)

this was not insupportable. The main problem was the numerous ways the sheets and spans found to foul on the battens and each other. When the sail was being raised in a swell the spans sometimes caught underneath the battens. Being so high and so far aft, it was difficult to reach the bundle to extricate the span. Also the sheets had to be slackened, so the bundle would bang around out of control. The second type of fouling occurred when the sail was up and in use. The sheets would get caught behind various battens and under the boom. Sometimes they would get around the battens, boom, and each other, and become so tangled that the sheets would be reluctant to reeve through their blocks. The third kind of fouling occurred when the sail was being reefed or furled. The spans would sometimes be caught in a fold of the sail bundle, block and all. The sheet would not reeve through until it was freed, which was attended by the same difficulties as freeing the first type of fouling. We solved these problems by converting the mainsail to a single sheet. This was made possible by the addition of a bumpkin for the sheet blocks. They are about one and a half feet aft of the stern. The foresail sheets are as designed. They are subject to the same problems to a lesser extent, but the smaller size and more accessible position of the sail render them more tolerable.'

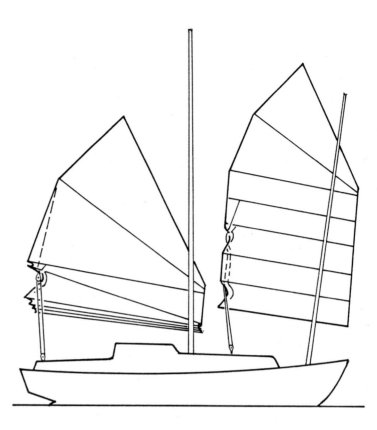

Fig. 4.53   Double sheets fouling

Two of the types of foul-up he experienced are shown in Fig. 4.53, which is made from his sketches and shows only the offending parts, for clarity. These problems would be less severe with a leech that sloped strongly forwards, but double sheets remain much more likely to get foul than single sheets, and we much prefer the latter.

The fore-and-aft position of the lower sheet blocks has been considered in relation to the boom and the lower leech (Fig. 4.23). It remains to consider the lie of the sheets in relation to the upper leech. In our recommended form of sail the leech is straight from the clew to batten 5. It then turns through a fairly sharp angle towards batten 6. With single sheets, batten 6 is usually omitted from the sheeting system as shown in Fig. 4.54, which shows the sheet from Fig. 4.35 arranged with its anchorage (Q_1) at the forward end of the shaded area. The upper sheet span then lies very close to the leech but will usually go clear of it when tacking, when the wind tends to blow it aft a little. It is helped to keep clear by having no protrusion of the battens beyond the leech, and by attaching the sheet spans to protrude aft. The means of achieving this are considered in Chapter 11.

When gybing, part of this sheeting system will sometimes remain on the wrong side of the sail, i.e. on the new leeward side. This is not particularly harmful, and it is not necessary to correct it for short periods of sailing, such as when manoeuvring in harbour. At sea, it will usually clear itself if the boat is brought up into the close-reaching attitude but with the sheet out and the sail weathercocking.

The only disadvantages of not sheeting the top batten are a slight increase in the twist of the sail, and the need for passing a reef pendant before sailing under one panel only. Neither of these is at all serious, but if the deck layout permits it is better to put the lower sheet blocks further aft. If they could be as far aft as Q_2, it would be possible to sheet the top batten, as shown dotted, but the seven-point sheet would then demand a larger D_{min}.

For a sail with a strongly curved leech the lower sheet blocks should be placed well aft in the shaded area. Fig. 4.55 shows a 'staggered regular fan' sail similar to that of Fig. 2.13 but with fewer panels. If the lower blocks were anchored at Q_1, the sheet would foul the leech unacceptably, whereas position Q_2 would be a possible anchorage for a six-point sheet that included the top batten. Leaving the top batten unsheeted would enable a five-point sheet to be anchored further forward, as at Q_3.

With all shapes of sail, the upper sheets will naturally lie further away from the leech as the sail is reefed.

It will be realised from this discussion that the Chinese sheeting systems vary from the simple single span, which is easy to design and rig, to the variations of multiple spans which can provide better control of the sail's twist, but require a greater understanding to design and rig. There is great scope for experiment and trial.

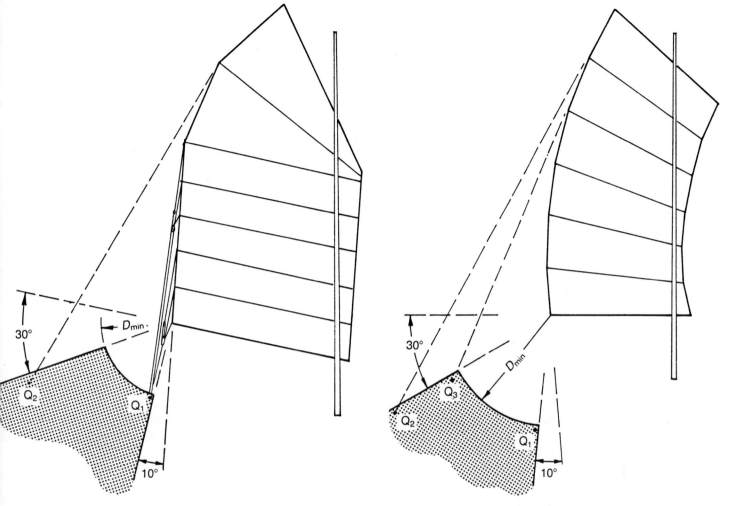

Fig. 4.54   Sheet clearances on leech   Fig. 4.55   Sheet clearances on curved leech

5 Ghosters and Lightning Conductors

Ghosters

Most users of the junk rig are content to use fully-battened Chinese lugsails only, enjoying their safety and seaworthiness and rejecting any modifications that call for the crew to get out of the cockpit and work around the deck. There remains a minority of sailing fanatics who are prepared to accept some optional deck work in light weather in order to improve their sailing performance still further by the use of 'ghosters', i.e. soft feather-weight sails that should not be carried in winds of more than Force 3 at the most.

Ghosters may be planned for two different purposes:

(a) To eliminate the slatting of a Chinese sail when rolling or pitching in a heavy swell and light airs. In this case the Chinese sail is furled and secured and the ghoster set in its place.
(b) To augment the performance of the flat Chinese sail when close-hauled or reaching in light airs, and perhaps to act as a spinnaker when running. In this case the Chinese sail is kept set and drawing and the ghoster works in harmony with it.

The use of any form of ghoster reduces the all-round visibility and involves extra gear, extra deck work, complications if caught aback, and a risk of carrying something away in a squall. Whereas with the junk sail the bending loads are fairly evenly distributed up the mast, with a ghoster they are concentrated at the masthead. Nevertheless, these disadvantages may be accepted by owners who want to race their boats, or who sail with an active crew who need employment, or who cruise without an engine.

Three forms of ghoster will be considered: the ghosting genoa, the ghosting dipping-lug, and the 'extra-foremast ghoster'.

GHOSTING GENOA. The genoa is the simplest of these, but will inevitably have its CE (see p 93) well forward of that of the Chinese sail on the same mast. This may induce some lee helm, but in practice this seems to be minimal, and in any case a bit of lee helm is acceptable in light going.

Fig. 5.1 shows a ghosting genoa set on a boat with a single junk sail. If the junk sail is furled, the genoa may be handled in the usual way when tacking or gybing, simply by working its sheets. If the junk sail is kept set, there will be a problem with its throat fouling the upper luff of the genoa. When tacking or gybing the genoa would have to be at least partly lowered while a man on the foredeck gathered it forward to allow the throat to swing past it. To make it handle like a normal headsail the head of the genoa would have to be brought further forward, perhaps by tacking it to a temporary bowsprit, but this would bring its CE even further forward. If it

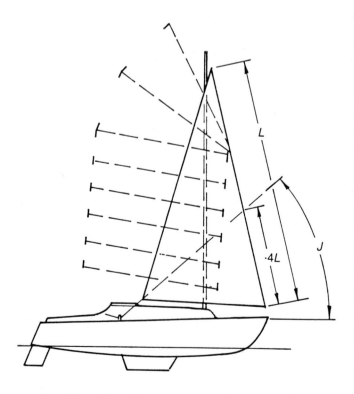

Fig. 5.1 Ghosting genoa

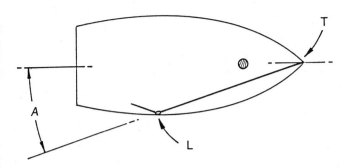

Fig. 5.2   Horizontal sheeting angle

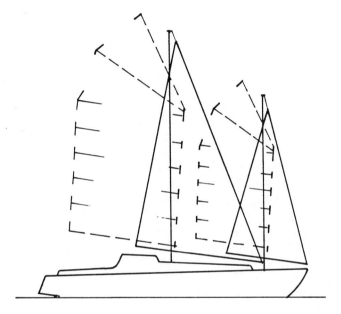

Fig. 5.3   Ghosting genoas

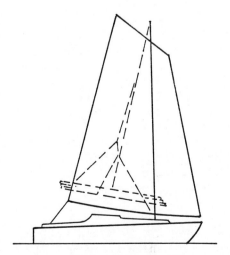

Fig. 5.4   Dipping lug ghoster

were then found that the *leech* of the genoa got foul of the throat, it might be necessary to reduce the height of the genoa until its head stood below the level of the throat.

If the boat is narrow and the genoa long in the foot it is necessary to consider the horizontal sheeting angle (A) (Fig. 5.2) which is defined as the angle, in plan view, between a fore-and-aft line through the tack (T) and a line joining T with the sheet lead (L). This angle is unlikely to be too great for efficient sailing but may well be too small. In general terms it should be about 20°, with 15° as the minimum. This consideration may limit the length of foot that can be used on a genoa.

The vertical sheeting angle (J) (Fig. 5.1) is also critical. As a simple guide, a line from the sheet lead through the clew should cut the luff at a point about 40 per cent up it, as shown.

Having arranged for the genoa to be efficiently sheeted, common sense and experiment may be needed to keep it clear of the furled Chinese bundle, or to get it working compatibly with a Chinese sail that is kept set.

The genoa will presumably be set flying, i.e. not hanked to a stay, and may be given modern handling aids such as a spinnaker sock. Alternatively it may be fitted with a roller furling system that can be operated from the cockpit, but it must be easy to lower and stow, i.e. its luff must be flexible and not of the rod type. It should always be handed when not in use in order to allow the mast to flex naturally. The single-part ghoster halyard will pass through a block on the forward side of the masthead fitting, which will need an extra tang for the purpose, as in Fig. 8.19 and 8.29.

The tensions in the genoa halyard and sheet are much greater than anything in a comparable Chinese sail in the same wind strength. Even in Force 1 the unstayed masthead will be pulled strongly towards the lee bow, thereby slackening the genoa luff and altering the set of the sail. The sailmaker should be asked to allow for this slack luff when cutting the *leech*. At the expense of more deck work it is best to set up the hauling end of the halyard to a point on the weather rail abaft the mast, where it will have a staying effect but will have to be watched for chafe in the masthead block caused by the mast flexing.

On a two-masted junk schooner it is possible to set two ghosting genoas as shown in Fig. 5.3, but difficult to use the main genoa without handing the junk foresail. Alternatively, a larger single genoa could be set from the head of the mainmast to the stemhead, or a quadrilateral 'fisherman's staysail' could be set between the masts.

DIPPING-LUG GHOSTER. The dipping-lug ghoster (Fig. 5.4) cannot be used without furling the Chinese sail on that mast, and cannot be tacked or gybed without a lot of deck work, since the yard must be dipped so as to remain on the leeward side of the mast when sailing. There are at least three ways of dipping a lug, but one of these is

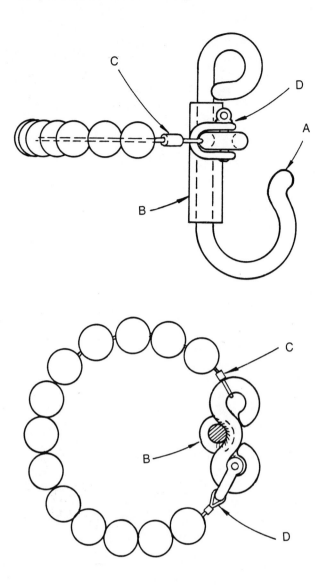

Fig. 5.5   Removable traveller

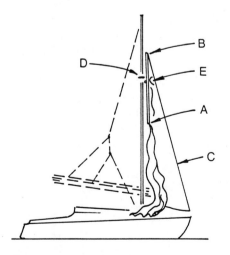

Fig. 5.6   Dipping the lug

obstructed by the topping lifts of the furled Chinese sail. For our purposes the West Cornish method is the best, and is achieved as follows.

Both parts of the halyard lie on the forward side of the masthead, where they pass through a swivel block. The hauling part may be set up to the weather rail if desired. The yard is held close to the mast by a removable traveller (Fig. 5.5) consisting of a steel hook (A) with a rawhide sleeve (B), held to the mast by a swaged wire rope (C) threaded through plastic parrel balls and secured by a shackle (D). Instead of a sling plate the yard has a rope or wire sling forming an eye for the hook of the traveller and sufficiently flexible to tolerate all the movements of the yard when tacking.

The tack is hooked to the centreline of the deck, or to the stemhead. The sheet is either a single rope spliced into the clew, or a separate sheet either side of the mast as with a normal headsail. With a sail of over 200 sq ft (19 m²) a small sheet winch may be needed.

To tack, the boat is brought as slowly as possible through the wind while the halyard is lowered to a predetermined mark, such as a piece of twine through the rope, which will just enable the *peak* of the yard to swing down round the mast with a taut luff. This attitude is shown in Fig. 5.6 with the peak (A), throat (B), taut luff (C), traveller (D) and yard sling (E). The sheet is let go and a crew member just forward of the mast hauls the leech and foot of the sail forward round the mast to the other side, taking the upside-down peak with it. Meanwhile the taut luff is helping to blow her head off on to the new tack. If the halyard is to be set up to windward its hauling end must now be passed round forward of the ghoster luff. The sheet is then set up on the new leeward side and the sail rehoisted.

To work this system, the luff of the sail must be a good deal longer than its yard, otherwise the tack will have to be unhooked when dipping. Gybing the sail requires a similar process to tacking.

The advantages of a dipping-lug ghoster are that even with a short yard it can spread a lot of sail on a given length of mast; it has plenty of area high up where the wind is, and its CE can be close to the CE of the Chinese sail that it replaces. Contrary to common belief, a well-set dipping lug is a very efficient sail to windward, but its horizontal sheet angle (Fig. 5.2) should be similar to that of a genoa, i.e. not less than 15°, preferably about 20°.

Its disadvantages, which are fairly daunting, are that it can only be used with the Chinese sail furled, that it puts even more load on the masthead than a genoa, that it needs skilled deck work to tack or gybe, and that the yard is an extra thing to stow.

EXTRA-FOREMAST GHOSTER. The 'extra-foremast ghoster' (Fig. 5.7) was evolved in the summer of 1981 for the boat shown in Fig. 16.10, which was racing every

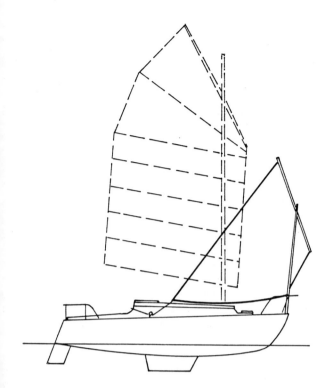

Fig. 5.7   *Pilmer* ghoster

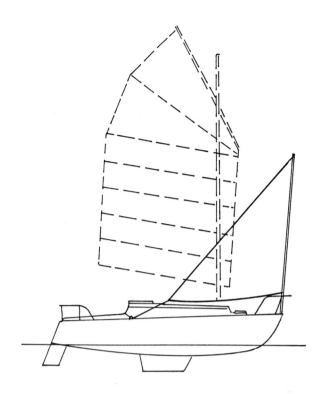

Fig. 5.8   'Topper' ghoster

Sunday in a menagerie class at Tayvallich, Argyll. Sometimes called a 'pilmer', it consists of a long-clewed boomless lightweight standing lug without battens but with double sheets like a conventional jib. It is carried on a small unstayed foremast raked forward 5° and stepped on top of the stemhead fitting, supported by partners bolted to the pulpit rail.

The train of thought behind the development of this sail was as follows:

1   It was not feasible to use a ghosting genoa in conjunction with the junk sail on this boat without getting foul at the throat, as discussed on p 78.
2   A large ghosting dipping-lug, similar to that shown in Fig. 5.4, had already been tried and discarded because of the severe loading at the masthead.
3   The separate unstayed foremast obviates any risk of overloading the mainmast if struck by a squall. A lightweight foremast can carry away without endangering the working rig.
4   The pilmer ghoster can be tacked or gybed from the cockpit simply by working the sheets, but it is necessary to rig an anti-snarl device to prevent the ghoster from fouling the forward end of the boom. A workable system consists of a horizontal length of shock cord stretching from the tack of the junk sail to the pulpit, but this may have to be slackened when running in light weather.

5   The shape of this ghoster, together with its arching and twist, seem to complement the attitude of the Chinese sail so that the two form a well-matched pair. The ghoster holds its arching in the lightest breath and pours air along the lee side of the mainsail when close-hauled or reaching, while its luff provides a sensitive indicator for close-hauled work.
6   In stronger winds the short foremast may be left standing without undue windage while the yard and sail are handed and stowed along the side deck. With a long halyard and tackline the pilmer can be set and handed from the cockpit, without having to go forward.

An alternative to this sail would be a 'Topper' ghoster (Fig. 5.8), i.e. a boomless triangular sail whose luff is attached to a taller unstayed mast stepped right forward. This mast could be in two parts sleeved together, as in a Topper dinghy, but the rig demands rather a tall foremast to achieve a reasonable ghoster area. It seems doubtful whether this sail would make such a good aerodynamic match with the mainsail and it would be more difficult to hand and stow.

Pilmer's ghoster adds 36 per cent to her working sail area and has proved to be successful. It can be used for engineless cruising as well as racing. Setting the ghoster moves the combined CE (see p 107) forward by no less than 2 ft (0.6 m), giving a 'lead' of 21 per cent, which we had expected to give an unpleasant amount of lee helm, but this is not found to be the case. The amount of lee helm is negligible. It is possible to dream up aerodynamic and hydrodynamic reasons for this, but the result serves once again to demonstrate that the balance of a boat under sail is a complicated matter that cannot be fully predicted from simple geometrical concepts. Guesswork and experiment may often be needed to reach the right answer.

To windward, *Pilmer*'s ghoster enables her to point higher with the junk mainsail sheeted flatter than usual and with a marked improvement in light airs. Off the wind it pulls well, and is goosewinged on a run with a light bearing-out pole (spinnaker boom) hooked into the clew and with jaws bearing against the mast. Round about the top of Force 3 the foremast and the pulpit begin to get overloaded and the ghoster is handed, leaving the junk sail by itself to give an excellent performance on all points of sailing.

Extra-foremast ghosters will be at their most effective with single-masted junk rigs. On multi-masters the area of the ghoster in relation to the total sail area will be less, and its slot effect will apply to the junk foresail only.

Lightning conductors

Some parts of the world have a higher frequency of lightning strikes than others. In most parts, including Britain, it is fairly rare for lightning to strike a small sailing boat but it does happen several times a year, and can sometimes result in the death of crew members and sinking of the boat. The taller the mast the more likely it is to be struck.

Many sailing people look askance at lightning conductors, particularly if led internally through the hull of the boat, feeling instinctively that this will encourage the lightning to destroy the boat. This is faulty thinking. One of the authors of this book once stood spellbound in a small boat in the East River, New York, watching a thunderstorm over Manhattan. The lightning was continuously striking the tops of the skyscrapers, but with efficient lightning conduction it is doubtful whether the people inside them even knew it.

In a vessel at sea, if a good enough electrical path exists between masthead and sea the high-voltage discharge can pass along it without damaging anything. This was established early in the 19th century by Sir William Snow Harris, who analysed all the logs of British sailing warships for the 16 years between 1799 and 1815 and found 150 cases of lightning damage, an average of 10 per year. One out of eight strikes set fire to rigging and sails. 70 men had been killed by lightning and 130 wounded. Ten ships had been completely disabled. In addition, HMS *Resistance* (unfortunate name) was known to have been blown up by a lightning flash in 1798. Harris then introduced a system of overlapping copper strips nailed all the way down each mast and connected by bands of copper to keel, keelson, and metal parts of the hull. In the later days of wooden-masted sailing ships this system was insisted upon by marine insurance companies. Nowadays, the United States Coast Guard requires yachts to be fitted with a proper lightning conductor system.

Unstayed masts are more vulnerable to lightning strikes than conventional stayed masts, whose steel shrouds often (but by no means always) provide a path for the lightning from masthead to chainplates. It is then capable of blasting a distance of several feet (over a metre) either through the air or along the surface of a non-conducting material to reach the sea, but it is not safe to assume that this will happen and all standing rigging should in fact be properly earthed to the sea.

Boats with unstayed metal masts do not need separate lightning conductors but do need a proper electrical path from the heel of the mast to the sea. Boats with wooden or other non-conducting masts need a copper conductor from the masthead to the sea.

Opinions differ about the minimum section for this conductor. Lloyd's Register of Shipping, London, calls for a minimum of 0.15 sq in (97 mm^2), which is the equivalent of a square-sectioned rod of about ⅜ in (10 mm) sides, or a strip of ¼ in × ⅝ in (6 mm × 16 mm) section, or a round rod of ⁷⁄₁₆ in diameter (11 mm). This is rather heavy metal, and we have never felt able to accept it in a small sailing yacht, preferring to follow the recommendations of the American Boat and Yacht Council (ABYC), which call for a copper conductor weighing at least 50 lb per 1,000 ft (1 kg per 13 m). This gives a cross-section of about 0.013 sq in (8.45 mm^2), less than a tenth of the Lloyd's figures. This would suggest a rod or solid wire of roughly ⅛ in diameter (3.3 mm), or strip ¹⁄₁₆ in × ¼ in (1.6 mm × 5.25 mm) or ¹⁄₃₂ in × ½ in (0.7 mm × 12 mm). We do not dispute that the Lloyd's section would be safer, but it seems to be too much solid copper to put up a small boat's mast. Nevertheless, any increase on the ABYC section will do nothing but good.

Ideally the top of the conductor should project several inches above the top of a wooden mast and finish in a point, but this inhibits using a masthead burgee and it is acceptable simply to bond it electrically to the metal masthead fitting. From there it should lead in as straight a path as possible to the earth, which may be any metal surface that is normally submerged in the surrounding water and has an area of at least 1 sq ft (0.1 m^2). For boats with metal keels it is sufficient to bond the conductor to the top of a keel bolt, but a propeller shaft or metal rudder may be used instead. The ground plate of a radio transmitter should also be adequate, after taking advice on isolating the radio from it when not transmitting. With a steel or aluminium hull it is only necessary to bond the conductor to the hull.

It is possible to provide a temporary lightning conduc-

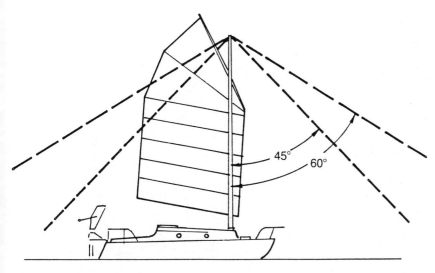

Fig. 5.9   Cones of protection

tor, to be rigged on the approach of an electrical storm, consisting of a metal spike sent up on the burgee halyard with the conductor wire bonded to its bottom end. From here it hangs down to a position on the boat's rail where it is lashed in such a way as to leave a long length of bare wire trailing in the sea. The surface area of ⅛ in diameter (3.2 mm) wire is 4.7 sq in per foot of length, and to get the required 1 sq ft of area you would need 31 ft (9.4 m) of bare wire actually underwater, which could be awkward. It might be better to have a short length of wire towing a short length of lightweight copper tube giving the required surface area.

However, this temporary system cannot be regarded as satisfactory. There is often little or no warning of a lightning strike, and it would be unfortunate if the skipper were in the middle of rigging the conductor when it got struck. To be effective, the system must be permanent.

A good lightning conductor will protect a cone-shaped space beneath its tip as in Fig. 5.9, which shows two alternative cones. The 60° cone is said to give a 99 per cent probability of protection for everything inside it, while the 45° cone is said to give 99.9 per cent. Any part of the boat that projects beyond the cone is liable to be struck in preference to the masthead, and this boat would need to reef two or three panels of sail to make the peak of the yard safe. A multi-masted junk rig will normally need a lightning conductor on each mast, but they may lead to a common earth.

It is inevitable that the conductor path will have to turn corners inside the boat to reach the earth, but it should lead as straight as possible, with provision for disconnecting it when unstepping the mast. Fig. 5.10 shows the system installed in *Pilmer* (Fig. 16.10). A bare copper strip (A) is held by three stainless machine

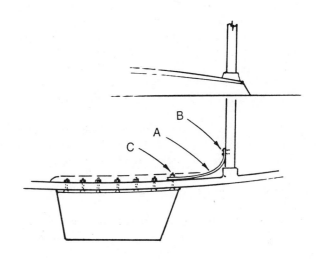

Fig. 5.10   Earthing mast to keel bolt

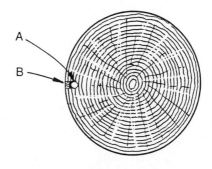

Fig. 5.11   Conductor in solid mast

screws (B) screwed into tapped holes near the heel of the light-alloy mast. Its other end (C) is bonded to the forward keel bolt of one of the twin cast-iron keels and then glassed over for protection. Copper and aluminium in contact with each other develop a strong electrolytic action when wet with salt water. To prevent rapid corrosion, the joint with the mast should be kept clean and well greased.

Having established the main conductor line or lines, it is necessary to consider 'side flashes'. Lightning tends to explore alternative paths on its way to earth and may blast sideways through air (and bulkheads) to reach a large metal object such as an engine or heating stove. All such objects should be separately bonded to the main conductor. A pile of chain in the cable locker presents a problem that could perhaps be solved by fitting a permanent metal plate or liner inside the locker, and earthing this to the conductor.

With a solid wooden mast the conductor may take the form of a round wire or rod (A) sunk into a groove and covered with a glued spline (B) (Fig. 5.11). Any insulated flex for masthead lights or instruments may be similarly glued into the opposite side of the mast. These splines must be well glued and regularly inspected; if the top of a length of spline were to become unstuck and project from the mast it could prevent the lowering of the sail.

With a hollow wooden mast (Fig. 5.12) the conductor (A) may be secured at frequent intervals to the inside surface before the final gluing up, leading out at a gentle angle somewhere below the partners. It will usually be on the after side of the mast, taking the shortest route to a keel bolt.

With a hollow mast of other non-conducting material,

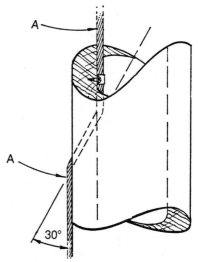

Fig. 5.12   Conductor in hollow mast

such as GRP, it may not be possible to secure the conductor to the inside surface or to encase it in the mast wall. In that case it may be left loose inside the mast and restrained in the way suggested for masthead flexes on p 139.

Finally, at the risk of stating the obvious: if a lightning strike seems possible everybody should try to remain below decks and well away from the conductor system and any large piece of metal. Radio and other instruments should be isolated and their aerials earthed. If in harbour, nobody should be in the water.

PART II

DESIGNING A RIG

Introduction

Part I of this book has dealt with the general theory of the junk rig and some of the different ways in which it may be arranged. Here in Part II we give instructions for fitting any given hull with our recommended form of the rig. Part I discussed a large number of options, many of them untried, but we now concentrate on layouts and specifications that have been used and tested in the West over the past 25 years, together with a few pointers towards possible future development.

There is no clear-cut division between the information given in Part I and that in Part II. To get full information on any particular aspect of the rig the reader should check all the references given in the index.

The information given is fairly comprehensive, to suit yacht designers and other enthusiasts who want to go deeply into the subject. Many others will prefer to take the theory for granted and will ask simply to be told the easiest way of designing a rig. For their benefit we have given short-cut methods where possible.

It is possible to buy a stock boat already fitted with a proven Chinese rig. Otherwise there are three ways in which a boat may acquire a Chinese rig:

1. Integrated design. The hull and rig may be designed from the outset to suit each other.
2. Rig conversion. The rig may be designed to suit an existing hull, which may be either a new hull or an older boat whose rig is to be changed. Conversion to junk rig will normally involve some modifications to the hull, and possibly to the accommodation.
3. Stock Chinese rig on different hull. A stock rig may be bought as a unit and installed in a hull for which it was not designed. Again, modifications may be needed to hull and accommodation.

Any of these three processes calls for some of the design work discussed on the following pages. Designing a rig involves at least a small amount of simple scale drawing and calculation, even if the amateur is going to make and fit everything with his own hands, and rather more so if he is going to get some of the work done professionally.

Nobody need be alarmed at the idea of starting scale drawing from scratch. Our experience has been that anyone can pick up the technique in a few hours, and will then enjoy doing it. No *artistic* talent is needed, only a little common sense and patience. In spite of this, there are always a few yacht owners who resolutely refuse to have anything to do with design work. These unfortunates should hand the book to their chosen designer or helper.

It is best to draw on draughtsman's tracing paper, which is sold in rolls or individual sheets and may be either real paper or plastic film with a matt surface. The latter is more expensive but superior, being stronger, waterproof, and more stable. The minimum size of sheet would be about 18 in × 18 in (45 cm × 45 cm), but we often use sheets up to 30 in × 22 in (75 cm × 55 cm). It is convenient to have some spare space all round the actual drawing.

A backing sheet of white paper (cartridge paper is ideal) will make the drawing more visible. It is handy, but not essential, to pin or tape both trace and backing sheet to a drawing board, which may be a piece of plywood. Adhesive drafting tape is the ideal means of temporarily locating any drawing or trace.

Some people like to draw on squared tracing paper or to use squared graph paper as a backing sheet, but this is not normal practice. It may be difficult to get the sheets big enough, and the printed squares are sometimes found to be inaccurate.

It is not necessary to draw in ink. Use a sharp pencil with a moderately hard lead, and a soft rubber (eraser).

Drawing on tracing paper permits one drawing to be laid on top of another for comparison, and enables copies to be made by dyeline printing. Such printing can usually be done quite cheaply by any commercial drawing office, or by a specialist photo-copying and printing shop.

The master drawing of the rig design will be a scale drawing of the boat in profile, including the underwater parts. The chosen scale should be such that the hull and its rig are shown at a reasonable size whilst fitting easily on to your drawing paper. Choose a scale that will make the hull as drawn somewhere between 9 in and 18 in (23 cm and 46 cm) long overall. For example, if drawing a 10 ft (3 m) dinghy the chosen scale could lie between 1/13 and 1/6.5, whereas for a 60 ft (18 m) yacht you would look for a scale between 1/80 and 1/40.

Within these limits you will naturally choose a standard scale. The standard imperial and metric scales are shown in Table 1.

Drawings of individual components will be made at a scale appropriate to their size, sometimes at full size.

It is best to use proper scale rules made of hardwood or plastic, but it is possible to construct a scale along the edge of a piece of paper or thin cardboard, marking it from an ordinary foot rule or 30 cm rule. Such a scale rule will not remain accurate with variations in humidity. Some further aspects of constructing a scale are discussed below.

Amateurs often use the edge of a scale as a straight-edge, but it is better to have a separate straight-edge, preferably at least 18 in (45 cm) long.

For measuring angles, an ordinary school protractor of about 2 in (5 cm) radius will do at a pinch, but a larger one is better and can be

**Table 1. Standard scales for
scale drawings**

Imperial

$\frac{1}{96}$	($\frac{1}{8}$ in = 1 ft)	very small scale
$\frac{1}{64}$	($\frac{3}{16}$ in = 1 ft)	
$\frac{1}{48}$	($\frac{1}{4}$ in = 1 ft)	
$\frac{1}{32}$	($\frac{3}{8}$ in = 1 ft)	
$\frac{1}{24}$	($\frac{1}{2}$ in = 1 ft)	usual choices
$\frac{1}{16}$	($\frac{3}{4}$ in = 1 ft)	
$\frac{1}{12}$	(1 in = 1 ft)	
$\frac{1}{8}$	(1$\frac{1}{2}$ in = 1 ft)	large scale

Metric

$\frac{1}{100}$	very small scale
$\frac{1}{50}$	
$\frac{1}{25}$	
$\frac{1}{20}$	
$\frac{1}{15}$	
$\frac{1}{10}$	
$\frac{1}{5}$	large scale

made to serve as a square for drawing right angles. Otherwise, a plastic square is handy. If using a T-square against the edges of the drawing board, check carefully that the edges are straight, and square to each other.

A pair of compasses will be needed and this may pose problems because ordinary school compasses will often not reach to the required radius unless the scale of the drawing is rather small. They may sometimes be extended by clamping two pairs together as in Fig. 6.1, but it is better to acquire a pair of beam compasses, which can draw accurate arcs up to at least 20 in (50 cm) radius.

A slide rule or calculator will help to speed up the few simple calculations needed. If using imperial measurements, all calculations should be made with figures that have been converted to feet and decimals, or inches and decimals, using the conversion tables in Appendix B. When transferring final measurements to a drawing they should be converted back to feet, inches, and fractions of an inch, except in large-scale drawings of small components to be made by a precision engineer, which are usually marked in inches and decimals.

Finally, a universal rule for all scale drawings: do not expect the man who has to read the drawing to take any measurements off it. All the measurements he could possibly need must be written in figures on the drawing. He can then use the print to stand his coffee on in the usual way.

6 Designing the Sailplan (1)

Position of the sailplan

HULL PROFILE. There are two ways of obtaining a scale profile of the hull: either by finding existing scale drawings, or by taking measurements off the actual hull. The perfect way is to get hold of a print of the designer's scale drawings, but it is then necessary to check that the boat has in fact been built to these drawings. It is quite common for a boat's underwater profile to be altered after sailing trials, and for the original drawings to be used in publicity material long after the change has been made.

With great luck you may find a drawing at an appropriate scale (see p 88) so that you can trace it straight on to the bottom of your own sheet. Failing this, you may find one at too small a scale (perhaps a drawing in a sales brochure) or at too large a scale. Such drawings must be scaled up or down to the required size.

To do this, it is first necessary to establish the scale of the drawing that you are confronted with. If it is a print of the designer's drawing it should be some standard scale, that is usually marked on it. If it is a reproduction in a brochure or yachting magazine it may have been photographically reduced without attempting to finish up at any particular scale. Sometimes the reproduction will incorporate a scale line that can be used. If not, it is necessary to construct a scale for it, usually based on the overall length of the hull, if that dimension is supplied.

A scale may then be constructed as shown in Fig. 6.2, in which AB is the overall length of the hull as it appears on the reproduction. From information given, you know that this length is (say) 27 ft 10 in in real life, and you therefore want to construct a 'brochure scale' that makes AB 27 ft 10 in long. To do this, draw a line from A at about 30° to AB and find a standard imperial scale that will enable you to mark off 27 ft 10 in along it, as shown, to give point C. AC will be either a bit longer or a bit shorter than AB. Join BC.

Now draw lines parallel to BC from each mark on AC down to cut AB, as shown. A simple method of drawing these parallel lines is to slide a square (D) along a

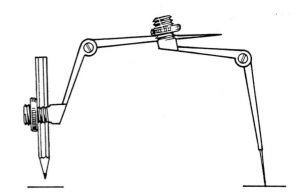

Fig. 6.1 Extending compasses

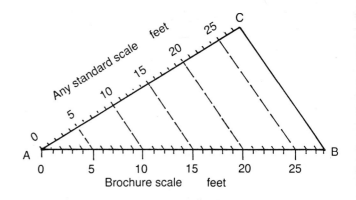

Fig. 6.2 Constructing a brochure scale

straight-edge (E) as in Fig. 6.3, the straight-edge being held firmly fixed throughout.

AB now provides the scale with which all dimensions on the brochure drawing should be measured, either with dividers or by cutting carefully along AB to provide a measuring edge.

An alternative, and rather elegant, way of transferring from one scale to another is to use proportional dividers, but these are an expensive item and need to be of large size to be useful.

Now select the standard scale that you want to use for your drawing (see p 89) which is not necessarily the same as the scale on AC, and you are ready to start drawing the hull profile as in Fig. 6.4, using the brochure scale for all measurements taken off the brochure drawing and the selected standard scale for all measurements on your drawing.

Measure the draught (D), add about an inch (25 mm) of actual spare space, and draw the load waterline (LWL) at this height above the bottom of your sheet. Draw vertical lines A and B, 27 ft 10 in apart, to define the overall length. These three datum lines are used for fixing all other points on the profile and must also be drawn on the brochure drawing. For example, the lower trailing corner of the rudder could be 3 ft 9 in below LWL and 10 in forward of A. The forward end of the coach roof might join the deck 3 ft 3 in above LWL and 5 ft 1 in abaft B. By plotting a great number of points in this way you could get an exact transfer of the brochure drawing to your profile drawing, but in practice it will be sufficient to plot 12 to 24 points and to join them up by eye as in Fig. 6.4, where the plotted points are shown emphasised. A yacht designer would use a set of standard curves or battens (splines) held down by weights, to help in drawing fair curves between the points, but these are not really necessary.

It is often suggested that drawings should be scaled up or down by purely photographic means, but there seems to be some doubt as to whether this is accurate enough, or very easily done.

If no drawings can be found, as may well be the case with an elderly boat, it will be necessary to construct a profile of the hull from measurements, perhaps augmented by profile photographs. The latter should be taken from a long way off and dead abeam, possibly with a telephoto lens, to reduce perspective distortion.

Measurements of the above-water hull may best be taken with the boat afloat in smooth water. The surface of the water may then be used as the horizontal datum, while plumblines at bow and stern will provide datums A and B (Fig. 6.4). Measuring the underwater profile is more difficult unless the boat can be out of the water, shored up with her waterline level, and standing on a level horizontal surface. Otherwise, the measurer will have to use his ingenuity to establish a datum and a way of taking measurements from it. Alternatively, in clear calm water and with the boat afloat, it would be possible to devise ways of plotting the underwater profile with the help of a diver. If this seems too difficult, ignore the underwater body and work from the existing rig as suggested on p 94.

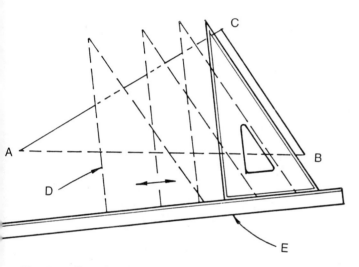

Fig. 6.3   Drawing lines parallel to BC

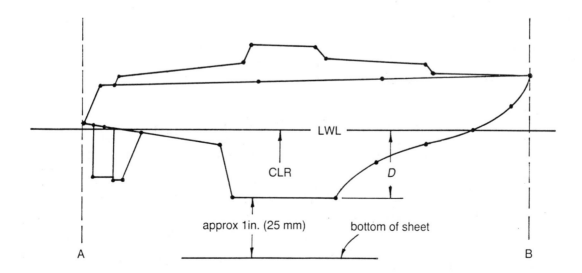

Fig. 6.4   Plotting the profile

CENTRE OF LATERAL RESISTANCE. Having now by one means or another produced a scale profile of the hull, keel, and rudder, we have to establish the point on it that will enable us to position the rig in its correct fore-and-aft position so that the boat is properly balanced under sail. The logical way would be to locate the position of the hull's centre of pressure (CP) or hydrodynamic centre, which is the point through which the side pressures on the underwater hull actually work when she is moving forwards through the water at a small angle of leeway. However, on any given hull the CP in fact wanders forward and aft with different boat speeds and different angles of heel, so we must reluctantly abandon trying to plot an accurate CP of the hull by geometrical means.

Instead, we use the centre of lateral resistance (CLR), avoiding a complex problem in order to get a rough-and-ready answer from a simple process. 'CLR' is used here with its common meaning, i.e. the geometrical centre (centroid) of the profile of the underwater part of the hull. We include in this the whole of the rudder, although some authorities exclude it, or include only part of it. When using somebody else's working of the CLR it is necessary to know whether or not he included the rudder. We feel that a rudder is indisputably a part of the hull's lateral resistance, although its effect on the hull's centre of pressure will vary according to whether she carries weather, lee, or neutral helm when sailing on a straight course.

We ignore any propeller aperture in the profile and treat twin keels or twin rudders as if they were single. Any centreboard should be shown lowered to its close-hauled sailing position. The underwater profile of a catamaran, trimaran, or proa may be taken as the outline of what you would see looking at it sideways, but here we are on rather thin ice and would prefer you to talk to its designer. The balance of multi-hulls is affected by two special factors: they heel very little, but when they do heel the leeward hull or float develops increased drag at a point well to leeward of the whole rig, and may tend to produce lee helm.

To find the CLR of any hull, trace its underwater profile onto a piece of stiff tracing paper with the LWL forming its upper boundary. Cut accurately round this outline with a pair of scissors and balance it on a sharp edge. Traditionally an open razor is the thing, but a carving knife will do if it has a straight cutting edge.

We do not need to know the vertical position of the CLR, but only its fore-and-aft position projected upwards to the waterline. It is therefore enough to balance the trace on a blade held at right angles to the waterline, as in Fig. 6.5a. Unless the scale is very small it is unlikely that the tracing paper will be stiff enough to do this without drooping, which will invalidate the result. The usual way of overcoming this is to stiffen the trace by folding it in narrow concertina pleats parallel to

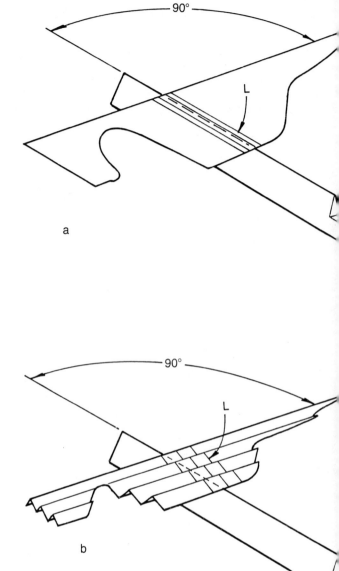

Fig. 6.5　Finding the CLR

the *waterline* as in Fig. 6.5b. It will be easier to keep the blade square to the waterline if you first draw two or three guide lines at right angles to the LWL, as at L in Fig. 6.5.

When a good balance is obtained, mark the point where the blade crosses the LWL, or imprint it directly by gently pressing the trace down on to the sharp edge. This point may then be transferred to your scale profile and marked as in Fig. 6.4.

A common problem when trying to balance a trace of the underwater profile of a modern type of hull is that the piece of immersed hull in front of the rudder or skeg is too slender to support the after part of the trace, and too narrow to be pleated. This can be dealt with by using good-quality thin cardboard instead of tracing paper, and not using concertina pleats. The profile may be transferred from the trace to the cardboard via a piece of carbon paper.

CENTRE OF EFFORT. Having established the position of the CLR on the waterline, there is no further need to consider the underwater profile of the hull, and this may be omitted from any subsequent drawings. The next stage is to draw the sail plan and to work out its centre of effort (CE), which is defined as the geometrical centre (centroid) of the area of the sail(s) when under full sail and with the sail(s) held fore-and-aft. With a single sail the CE of the sailplan is, of course, the same as the CE of the single sail, but with two or more sails the CE of the individual sails must be combined to give the CE of the sailplan. The method of doing this is given on p 107.

LEAD. The sailplan must be positioned on the profile so that a plumbline from its CE cuts the waterline at a point some way *forward* of the CLR. The distance between the two points on the waterline is known as the 'lead' (pronounced to rhyme with 'creed'). If the CE of the sailplan is placed too far aft the boat will develop too much weather helm when close-hauled, i.e. will have a strong tendency to turn into the wind. If it is placed too far forward she will develop too much lee helm, i.e. will have a strong tendency to turn away from the wind. For maximum efficiency close-hauled it is usually considered desirable to carry a small amount of weather helm, say between 1° and 5° of rudder, but this can be expected to vary in different wind strengths.

The immersed volume of a normal hull becomes asymmetrical when she is heeled. Most hulls have an increasing tendency to turn towards their high side (i.e. to windward) as the angle of heel increases, so that they develop more weather helm on heeling. This trait is most marked in beamy hulls with fine bows and full sterns, and is aggravated by the leeward shift of the centre of pressure of the sailplan on heeling.

The fore-and-aft position of the CE of the sailplan should be a compromise that gives acceptable control in all wind strengths. This often involves carrying a bit of lee helm when close-hauled in ghosting weather, changing progressively to strong weather helm when hard pressed by a squall, but she should remain under control in a squall and not gripe remorselessly up to windward against the full power of the rudder. It is sometimes held that uncontrollable griping is a safety factor, since the boat automatically luffs in a squall until her sails start lifting, but this presupposes that you have unlimited sea room. Such griping is obviously dangerous when close to other vessels, or when sailing through a narrow channel.

Chinese rigs commonly develop less weather helm when reefed, perhaps because the windage of the boat's bow and mast(s) begins to have a greater effect. Single-masted junk rigs of low aspect ratio sometimes develop more weather helm when reaching or broad-reaching than they do when close-hauled. It is possible to reduce this by paying out on a running tack parrel (Fig. 3.24) and so increasing the balance of the sail.

There is no foolproof way of calculating the correct 'lead' for any given hull, but there are two alternative systems that give an approximate answer. If both systems are applied to the same boat you are certain to get two different answers, which illustrates the inexact nature of the processes.

Our normal rule is to give a single-masted Chinese rig a lead of 9 per cent of the length of the waterline, and a multiple-masted rig a lead of 5 per cent, as shown in Fig. 6.6. Alternatively, if the hull has been designed with a conventional rig, the CE of the junk sailplan may be related to the CE of the conventional sailplan. The junk's CE is put slightly further aft because it has been found that the flatter junk sail develops its centre of pressure further forward than that of a soft, arched sail.

The CE of the conventional rig may be calculated from a scale profile as described on p 109. If the hull and rig exist but no scale drawing is available it is possible to construct one from measurements, ignoring the underwater body. This CE is then transferred down to the

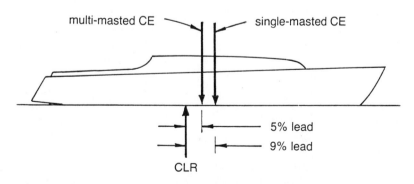

Fig. 6.6   Standard lead for Chinese CE

LWL. The position of the CE for a Chinese rig may then be worked out from Table 2 in which the measurements are expressed as a percentage of the boat's waterline length.

Table 2. Position of centre of effort of Chinese rigs relative to conventional rigs

Conventional rig	Chinese rig	Position of CE of Chinese rig relative to conventional CE
sloop or cutter	single-masted	6 per cent abaft
sloop or cutter	multiple-masted	10 per cent abaft
multiple-masted	single-masted	3 per cent forward
multiple-masted	multiple-masted	1 per cent abaft

Table 2 reflects the fact that a single-masted rig develops its true centre of pressure rather further forward than a multi-masted rig. The position of the junk's CE may be modified in the light of any reports about the balance of the boat under her conventional rig. For example, if she were reported to carry severe weather helm the Chinese CE could be moved further forward by a distance of 1 to 5 per cent of the LWL. Conversely, if she had been carrying lee helm in a good sailing breeze the Chinese CE could be moved aft by a similar amount.

As an extreme case, *Sumner*'s single-masted junk rig (Fig. 16.6) was designed with zero lead (CE vertically over CLR) because her hull is very narrow and symmetrical, because the windage of the long overhanging bow tends to hold her head off, and because she has a powerful skeg rudder a long way aft. She does not in practice develop excessive weather helm, although with hindsight the rig could ideally have been stepped a little further forward, say with 3 per cent lead.

In the light of the above discussion, mark a point along the LWL of your master drawing for the position of the CE of single-masted Chinese rig or multiple-masted Chinese rig as appropriate. If undecided between the two, mark both points.

The sailplan

TOTAL AREA. If the hull in question has been designed or used with a conventional Bermudian or gaff rig, the area of the Chinese sail may be related to that rig. If not, the Chinese sail's area will have to be an informed guess.

In order to give good light-weather performance, the Chinese area may be about 10 per cent more than that of a yacht's conventional working rig, which is here defined as the rig under which the yacht will sail to windward in Force 4 under cruising conditions. In a small boat with a single-masted junk rig it is quite normal to reef the first panel at the top of Force 4 when going to windward, but a multi-masted rig will probably permit full sail to be carried a bit longer.

We regard the conventional working rig as being the full sail area carried close-hauled and including an intermediate genoa, i.e. a genoa whose clew overlaps the mast by about 25 per cent of the length of the base of the fore-triangle.

The areas of the sails in a conventional rig may be calculated as shown in Fig. 6.8. If using imperial units, work in decimals of a foot for the calculations, not in feet and inches (see Appendix B). Fig. 6.7a shows a Bermudian mainsail with a curved leech. Draw a construction line AC, adjusting it by eye until the area of sail cut off by the middle of the line is equal to the sum of the areas of 'air' at either end. The sail area is now (AC × BD)/2. Fig. 6.7b shows a gaff mainsail whose area is (AC × BE)/2 + (AC × DF)/2. Fig. 6.7c shows a staysail or headsail whose area is (AB × CD)/2.

Published areas of sails as worked out for purposes of handicap rating, or for sales brochures, often do not give the true areas, and should not be used without checking.

Having added the individual sail areas together to get the total area of the working rig, enquire whether the hull seems to be over- or under-canvassed with this area. If so, apply an estimated correction to get the area of the 'ideal' working rig.

Choose the total area of the Chinese sailplan in the light of what you have discovered. For example, if the conventional working rig has an ideal area of 360 sq ft (33 m²), the junk rig might be 360 × 1.1 = 396 sq ft (37 m²). A single-masted junk rig will have more heeling effect than a multi-master of the same area, and this may slightly influence your choice of area.

If there is no standard rig for the hull it will be necessary to guess a suitable area. The advice of a yacht designer would help, but failing that your own informed guess will be good enough. There are various formulae that purport to calculate a suitable sail area for any size of hull, but none is of much use when applied to widely differing types of hull. The reader will do as well by sketching a tentative rig on his scale profile and then comparing it visually with an example on a similar hull in this book.

Having decided the total area, the next step is to decide the form of the rig.

SINGLE-MASTED OR MULTIPLE RIG? This choice is not dictated entirely by the size of the boat, although in practice it is rather difficult to design a sensible two-masted rig on a boat of less than about 32 ft (9.5 m) overall. It is often a good plan to draw alternative rigs before making the decision. For ordinary cruising and day-sailing yachts Table 3 may serve as a guide.

The single sail appears to be at least as good on all

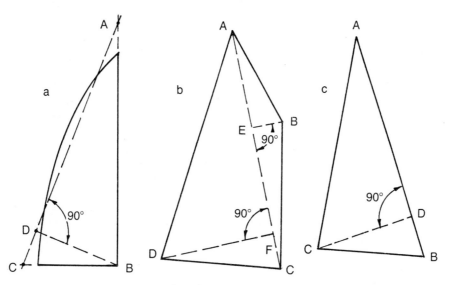

Fig. 6.7 Measuring sail areas

Table 3. Recommended rigs for different sail areas

Total sail area		
(sq ft)	(m²)	Recommended rig
up to 300	up to 28	Single-masted
300–450	28–42	Optional. Single-masted, or two-masted if LOA over 32 ft (9.5 m)
450–800	42–75	Two-masted if LOA over 32 ft (9.5 m)
800–1400	75–130	Optional. Two- or three-masted
over 1400	over 130	Three-masted

points of sailing as the multiple rig, so the choice remains a question of size, stability, convenience, accommodation layout, and appearance, as discussed later.

Of the eight arrangements shown in Fig. 1.3, three are recommended: (a) single sail, (c) two-masted schooner with larger sail aft, and (e) three-masted ketch, with largest sail amidships. The two-masted ketch, which is often suggested, is less desirable because the heavy mainmast has to be a long way forward. An exception was made for the design shown in Fig. 16.7, where the straight-stemmed 'Fifie' hull is of a type that traditionally carried a heavy unstaged mast well forward.

We prefer a foresail to be about half the area of the main, and a mizzen to be about one-third the area of the main. Expressed in percentages of the total area, this gives the two-masted schooner a foresail of 33 per cent and a main of 67 per cent, and the three-masted ketch a foresail 27 per cent, mainsail 55 per cent, and mizzen 18

per cent. With large yachts these proportions may have to be varied in order to keep the size of the mainsail within the limit, right up to the point where all sails are of the same area. Alternatively, the size limit for the mainsail will have to be exceeded, with special provision for handling it (see below).

The advantages of a single-masted rig are its simplicity; the ability to see your whole sailplan from the steering position; the absence of any blanketing effect downwind, and extra speed of furling, reefing, and trimming sheets. Being higher than a multiple-sailed rig, it may be of benefit when ghosting, particularly under the lee of the land.

The advantages of a multiple-sailed rig are the reduction in size and weight of individual masts, spars, and sails; avoidance of a heavy mainmast near the bows of the boat; less capsizing moment owing to lower centre of gravity and centre of effort; less strength needed to hoist sail and get the sheet in; and the extra insurance of having two or more masts and sails if something should happen to one of them. The ability to goosewing the foresail when running is an advantage insofar as it reduces the amount of weather helm, but it is often difficult to get the foresail to stay goosewinged, as discussed on p 206. Even without goosewinging, the multi-sail rig will develop less weather helm, and so have less tendency to broach when sailing downwind, because the CE of the sailplan is not so far outboard. The multiple rig also offers the ability to vary the distribution of sail area fore-and-aft, e.g. by reefing the aftermost sail to reduce weather helm, or running downwind under foresail only to achieve steadier steering. For trade wind sailing it may be an advantage to design a foresail whose area is rather more than half that of the mainsail.

If fitting junk rig to an existing design of hull, your

choice may be strongly influenced by the positions in which the mast(s) would have to be stepped in relation to the existing accommodation or deck layout.

MAXIMUM SIZE OF SAIL. This is entirely a question of weight. It is possible to raise and lower an enormous Chinese sail, as witness some of the larger junks in China, but it requires either a lot of men or a powerful winch and in either case the last part of hoisting is a very slow process. It has been reported that hoisting the mainsail of a large junk may give the whole crew an hour's hard work. If we were designing the largest possible junk-rigged vessel it would be necessary to use very large sails and to tackle the problem of handling them, probably by using wire halyards leading to a heavy crab winch as in Fig. 3.3. Such sails could well go to 2,000 sq ft (186 m²) or more. Any advance that could be made in reducing the weight of the sail assembly

would permit the use of larger sails, but in this book we are more concerned with sails that can be handled by one person from a cockpit or wheelhouse, using rope halyards and (if necessary) the type of capstan winch used for headsail sheets in conventional rigs. Such winches have only one direction of rotation, and the rope is paid out by surging it around the drum, or by taking the turns off the drum and paying out by hand.

In our present state of development the maximum area that can be recommended for such a sail is about 700 sq ft (65 m²), but a more normal limit would be about 600 sq ft (56 m²).

SHAPE OF SAILS. Enough has been said in Chapter 2 to encourage technically minded sailors to experiment with a variety of sail shapes. Here we concentrate on the recommended shape of sail shown in Fig. 2.26, whose features may be summarised as follows (Fig. 6.8). The

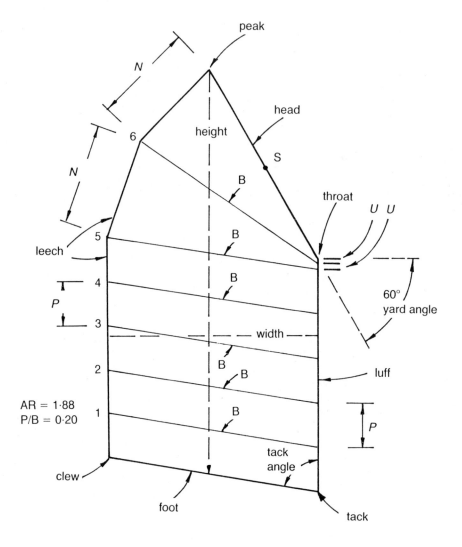

Fig. 6.8   Features of a standard sail

lower part of the sail is a parallelogram whose tack angle will vary slightly from one sail to another. The head, foot, and batten lines (B) are all of the same length. The sail is slung from the mid point (S) of the head and has a yard angle of 60° measured against a line perpendicular to the luff. The upper part of the sail consists of two near-triangular panels whose luff measurements (U) are very short and of equal length, and whose leech measurements (N) are also equal to each other.

The standard sail has five identical parallelogram panels, the panel width (P) being measured along the luff or leech. The total number of panels in the standard sail is therefore seven, requiring six battens which are numbered upwards as shown.

ASPECT RATIO. The proportions of this sail may be defined by its aspect ratio (AR), which is the ratio of height/width. A high-aspect-ratio sail is tall and narrow; a low-aspect-ratio sail is low and wide. In measuring aspect ratio, the height of any Chinese sail is taken as a vertical line from the peak to the boom, and the width as the horizontal distance from luff to leech at a point ⅓ of the way up this line. On the standard shape of sail the vertical line is taken as being parallel to the luff, regardless of how the sail may be canted on the mast when set, and the horizontal line is taken at right angles to it, as shown at the broken line in Fig. 6.8.

Measured in this way, and choosing convenient units, the AR of the sail in Fig. 6.8 works out at 1.88. The AR of the standard sail may be varied anywhere between arbitrary limits of 2.8 and 1.4. Figs. 6.9 and 6.10 show sails that approach these limits while having roughly the same areas as that of Fig. 6.8.

One important effect of altering the aspect ratio is that the proportion of the sail's area that is contained in the head panels increases as the aspect ratio decreases, as shown in Table 4.

Table 4. Effect of decrease in aspect ratio on proportion of sail area in head panels

Aspect ratio	Percentage of sail in head panels (%)	Ratio P/B	
2.78	19	0.38	(Fig. 6.9)
1.88	32	0.20	(Fig. 6.8)
1.46	43	0.12	(Fig. 6.10)

On the parallelogram part of the sail the relative width of the panels may conveniently be expressed as ratio P/B, and these ratios are also shown in the table.

A high-aspect-ratio sail is supposed to be better to windward, is lighter for a given area since yard, battens, and boom are all lighter, and gives less weather helm when reaching or running. Against this, it requires a longer and heavier mast and has a higher CE, reduced stability, and less favourable sheeting angles for the upper battens.

For single-masted rigs an aspect ratio of about 2.0 is a good starting point. For multi-masted rigs the aspect ratio of the individual sails can with advantage be a bit higher, and indeed may have to be in order to get adequate sail area on to a given length of hull. The height of the whole sail plan, however, will normally be much less than that of a single-master of the same area. An aspect ratio of about 2.1 is a good starting point for all sails of a multiple rig.

PANEL WIDTH VERSUS NUMBER OF PANELS. Table 4 shows how the panel width (ratio P/B) on the parallelogram part of the sail decreases steadily as the sail gets lower and broader. Fig. 6.8, 6.9, and 6.10 show that the maximum width of the head panels (dimension N) does the opposite, and is greatest in the low-aspect-ratio sail.

Very wide panels, whether in the parallelogram or the head, do not stow as neatly in the lifts and are subject to greater scalloping when set, but panel width may always be reduced by increasing the number of panels. For example, in a high-aspect-ratio sail another batten may be added to the parallelogram as in Fig. 6.11, which is otherwise similar to Fig. 6.9, giving an eight-panel sail with seven battens. Ratio P/B is thereby reduced from 0.38 to 0.31, giving a sail that will reef and furl more tidily. Conversely, with a low-aspect-ratio sail one batten may be transferred from the parallelogram to the head as in Fig. 6.12, which is otherwise similar to Fig. 6.10. This gives a three-panel head and the possibility of including the lower head batten in the sheeting system if the sheet anchorage can be on or abaft line Q. If the head is not modified in this way, these very low-aspect-ratio sails are rather unattractive because of the large area of head panel that is not dirctly controlled by the sheets and may therefore be expected to twist, particularly when reefed. With double sheets (see p 72) all battens may be sheeted and this objection does not apply.

Even if neither of the two head battens in Fig. 6.12 can be sheeted, there are clear advantages in dividing the large head area into three panels: neater stowage when furled, lighter batten loadings, lighter sailcloth loadings, and finer adjustment of sail area when very close-reefed and using reef gaskets or pendants (see p 207) – a situation that is more likely to arise with a low-aspect-ratio sail because of the large area of the head. Many of our existing sails have a yard angle of 70° instead of the 60° now recommended, and this adds further to the area of the head panels. Sumner (Fig. 16.6) is an example of such a boat, in which the head is divided into three panels even though neither of the head battens can be sheeted.

Another reason for varying the number of panels may

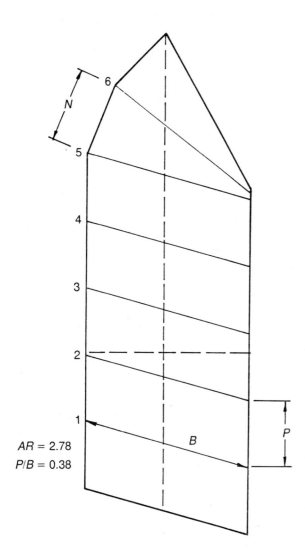

Fig. 6.9   High-aspect-ratio sail

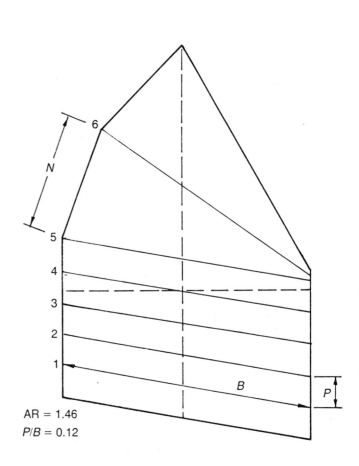

Fig. 6.10   Low-aspect-ratio sail

arise with very small or very large sails. Unless you are deliberately creating a scale model of a larger sail, there is little reason to use panel widths of less than about 18 in (0.46 m). On one sail of 49 sq ft (4.5 m²) for a small yacht's tender the parallelogram part of the sail was given only four panels, each having a width (P) of 17 in (0.43 m). This simplified the rig while giving enough stages of reefing for practical purposes.

On very large sails, increasing the number of panels gives a very controllable sail with lightly-loaded sail-cloth and battens at the expense of extra gear and more complicated sheeting. A panel width (P) of 4 ft 6 in (1.4 m) can be regarded as the maximum that is desirable in the parallelogram, and a length of 10 ft (3 m) as the maximum for the leech of a head panel (N) (Fig. 6.8). Extra panels may be added where necessary to keep within these limits, as has been done on both the head and the parallelogram of the mainsail of the fishing boat

design in Fig. 16.7, while her mizzen has a standard five-panel parallelogram but shows an extra panel in the head.

Altering the number of battens in the parallelogram will produce minor alterations in the tack angle and sail area, as discussed later. Adding another batten in the head will slightly increase the area of the sail for two reasons: there is an additional dimension U (Fig. 6.12), and the leech approaches more nearly to the arc of a circle.

LUFF OF HEAD PANELS. Regardless of the number of head panels, dimension U may be taken from Fig. 6.13, which shows U varying with the length of the batten. The measurement is not critical, and should be selected to the nearest inch (2 cm). It is designed to be as short as possible without cramping the sailmaking work at the forward ends of the top battens and the throat.

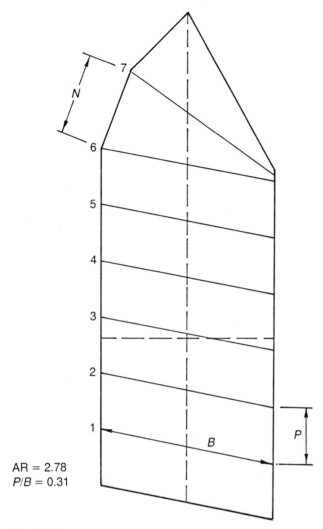

Fig 6.11
High-aspect-ratio sail with extra parallelogram panel

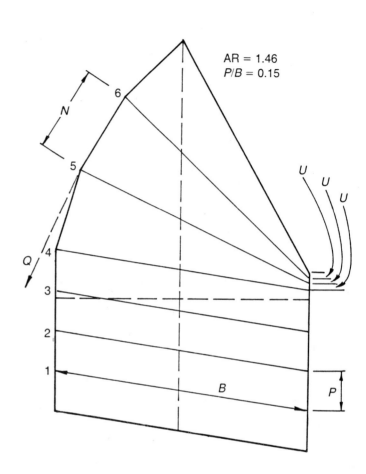

Fig. 6.12   Low-aspect-ratio sail with modified panels

SLOPE OF BATTENS. The exact slope of the battens in the parallelogram has a critical effect on reefing and furling. The theory governing the stagger of furled battens has been discussed in Chapter 2. In the parallelogram the battens are arranged to furl as in Fig. 6.14, each furled batten being held aft by the tension in the sailcloth along the shorter diagonal (D) of the panel below it. The tack angle is adjusted so that the length D is less than the length B, the difference $(B-D)$ being the amount of theoretical stagger (S), which is positive at the leech and negative at the luff, and is here shown exaggerated.

This stagger is not needed for sails that have double sheets (see p 73), but it is best to use the same geometry for all sails, since it gives neat furling and the practical advantage of a standard length of batten. Furthermore, it is not unknown for an owner who starts with double sheets to change to single sheets later.

It is suggested that the designed stagger should in all

cases be 1 per cent of the batten length. This of course refers only to the parallelogram part of the sail. Battens dividing the triangular head panels are unlikely to furl with any positive stagger.

Having decided on a batten length B and a panel width P, as described later, it would be possible to construct the lowest panel, and hence derive the slope of the battens, as in Fig. 6.15. This could be done by first drawing the luff (L) vertical and marking up it the width of the bottom panel (P), then striking an arc of radius B from the tack and another from the forward end of no.1 batten with radius $0.99\,B$. This would have to be done accurately, preferably with beam compasses. Where the two arcs intersected would be the position of the clew, and the foot of the sail could then be drawn. If desired, the tack angle and rise could also be measured, as shown.

If this were done with a variety of shapes of parallelo-

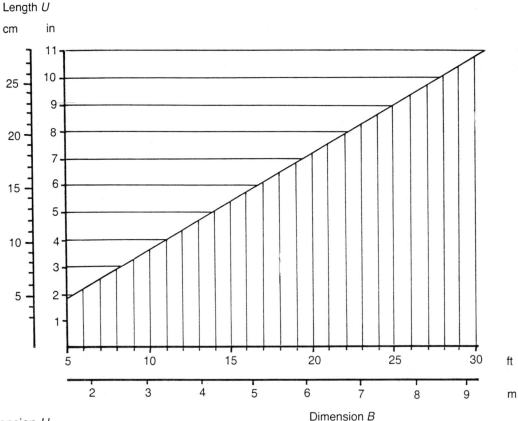

Fig. 6.13   Dimension U

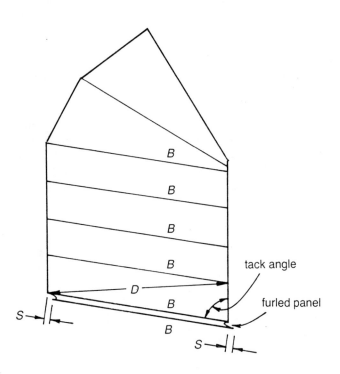

Fig. 6.14   Batten stagger

gram it would be found that the tack angle and rise varied appreciably as the ratio P/B varied, i.e. according to whether the sail panels were wide or narrow. It would also be found that for narrow panels, where ratio P/B was small, it would be difficult to construct Fig. 6.15 accurately because the two arcs would not cut at a large enough angle to give a positive point for the clew. We therefore do not use this method when drawing the sail, but define the slope of the battens by other means. Three possible ways of defining this slope are shown in Fig. 6.16:

1. Tack angle. This may be defined in degrees and minutes, or preferably in degrees and decimals (e.g. 80.6°), but this is of little use to the sailmaker, who will not want to use a giant protractor on the loft floor. Using the tack angle on the drawing board is possible, but calls for accurate reading of a large protractor and is not recommended. As a matter of interest for the technically-minded, Fig. 6.17 shows how the tack angle varies with different ratios of P/B, but this graph should not be used for drawing a sail. It will be seen that the tack angle reaches a maximum of nearly 82° when P/B is about 0.14. At this point the rise is equal to P. As the panels get even narrower the rise becomes greater than

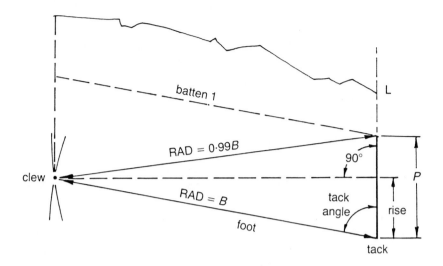

Fig. 6.15   Theory of clew position

P, but the curve begins to go wild when *P/B* becomes less than 0.1 and this may be taken as the narrowest permissible panel – somewhat narrower than those of Fig. 6.10. If narrower panels than this are used the tack angle becomes too acute and our theory of positive stagger is no longer applicable. Using any reasonable tack angle the battens would furl with less than 1 per cent stagger, or perhaps with negative stagger, unless positive stagger were introduced by other means, such as luff hauling parrels.

The widest permissible panel is considered to be with *P/B* equal to 0.5, i.e. considerably wider than those of Fig. 6.9. Within these two extremes, the recommended range of *P/B* is from 0.15 to 0.35, as shown on Fig. 6.17.
2. Master diagonal (*Dm*). This may be stated as a linear measurement in conjunction with the lengths of *B*, *L*, and *U*. It then provides an excellent way of defining the slope of the battens, and is the one that will be used by the sailmaker, having been marked on the sail drawing for that purpose. After marking the length *L* on the loft floor and adding the correct number of lengths *U* (usually two), he will strike arcs from the throat and tack (Fig. 6.18) that will intersect cleanly to give the exact position of the clew. Note that we use the whole luff, and not just the luff of the parallelogram. It is possible to use *Dm* for constructing the sail on the drawing board but we do not recommend it and do not show the necessary graphs.
3. Rise (*R*). This is the height of the clew above the tack assuming that the luff is vertical, and this is the preferred way of defining the slope of the battens on the drawing board. Like the tack angle, it varies with the ratio *P/B*, and for a stagger of 1 per cent may be calculated precisely from the formula $R = (0.0199B^2 + P^2)/2P$, where *R* is the

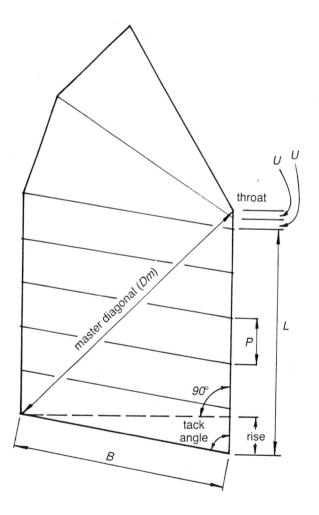

Fig. 6.16   Defining the batten slope

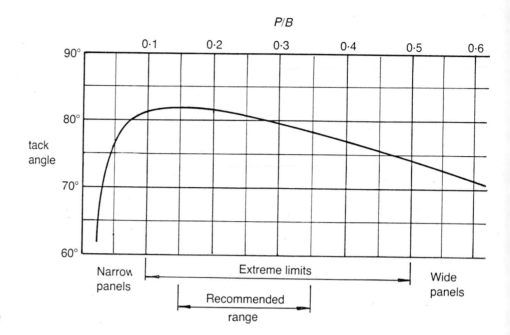

Fig. 6.17   Variation of tack angle

rise, *B* is the batten length, and *P* is the panel width. This remains valid regardless of the number of panels in the parallelogram.

For practical use the formula is rewritten in a simpler form,

$$R = (B/P \times B/100) + P/2,$$

which gives results well within the limits of accuracy required. Obviously, *R*, *B*, and *P* must all be expressed in the same decimal units.

Having marked the rise on the luff of your drawing it is necessary to draw an *accurate* perpendicular from this point past the clew. The accuracy of the 90° angle should be checked more than once with a large square or protractor, or alternatively it may be constructed geometrically.

An arc of radius B, struck from the tack, will cut this perpendicular at the correct position of the clew (Fig. 6.19).

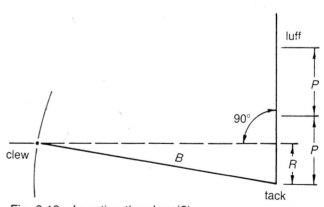

Fig. 6.18   Locating the clew (1)

Fig. 6.19   Locating the clew (2)

Drawing the sail

SAIL AREA AND ASPECT RATIO DIAGRAM. We now get down to the very first stage of planning an individual sail: deciding on the length of luff (L) and of battens (B), the latter of course being the same as the length of both the foot of the sail and its head. The use of Fig. 6.20 enables lengths of L and B to be selected that will give, with reasonable accuracy, a sail of the required area and aspect ratio. Fig. 6.21 is a similar diagram using metric measurements.

> Example: To draw the foresail of a two-masted junk schooner whose total sail area is to be 770 sq ft we select, as our first choice, an aspect ratio of 2.1 and an area of 34 per cent of 770 = 262 sq ft. Enter Fig. 6.20 with this aspect ratio and follow down the sloping line marked 2.1 until it meets the curve of the required sail area. In this case we interpolate an imaginary curve that is about ¼ of the way from the 250 curve towards the 300 curve. The point of intersection gives approximate values of B = 12.4 ft, L = 15.5 ft.

These figures should give the correct sail area to within 1 per cent, using the standard seven-panel sail with a five-panel parallelogram. Using more than five panels in the parallelogram, or more than two panels in the head, should result in a sail that is very slightly over 262 sq ft. Using less than five panels in the parallelogram should result in a sail that is very slightly under 262 sq ft.

To use Fig. 6.20 or 6.21 for a sail whose area X is larger than 700 sq ft or 65 m², first note what the measurements B_1 and L_1 would be for a sail of 700 sq ft or 65 m² of the required aspect ratio, then calculate the required lengths B_2 and L_2 as follows:

K (the required constant) = $\sqrt{(X \text{ sq ft}/700)}$ or $\sqrt{(X \text{ m}^2/65)}$. Then $B_2 = K \times B_1$ and $L_2 = K \times L_1$.

> Example: To plan a sail of 1,400 sq ft and aspect ratio 1.8 using Fig. 6.20, first read off the point of intersection of 1.8 and 700, which gives B_1 = 22.4 ft and L_1 = 20.8 ft. Calculate K = $\sqrt{(1400/700)}$ = $\sqrt{2}$ = 1.414. Then B_2 = 1.414 × 22.4 = 31.67, and L_2 = 1.414 × 20.8 = 29.41.

Although we have doubled the sail area, the linear increase in B and L is of course much less than double.

RATIONALISING B AND L, AND DETERMINING P. It is usual to make any necessary small adjustment to length (L) in order to make it easily divisible into the required number of panel lengths (P). For example, if L were read from the graph as 22.4 ft and you wanted five panels in the parallelogram, this would give P = 22.4/5 = 4.48 ft. This is about 4 ft 5¼ in (Appendix B), but it would be better to make L = 22.5 ft, giving a panel width of 4 ft 6 in. Similarly, if B were found from the graph to be

11.8 ft, which is roughly 11 ft 9⅝ in it should be rationalised to 11 ft 10 in, i.e. to the nearest inch.

The whole sail should be drawn with measurements that have been 'cleaned up' so as to avoid small fractions of inches. Sailmakers (and boatbuilders) have been known to dissolve into hysterical laughter when presented with infinitely precise measurements: 'Pull a bit harder on the tape, Charlie. The designer says this ought to be thirty-three feet seven and fifteen-sixteenth inches.'

When the dimensions B, L and P have been calculated and rationalised, the sail drawing may be completed as in the summary on p 110.

CHECKING THE SAIL AREA. A Chinese sail is bounded by straight edges and divided by straight battens, and its exact area may easily be worked out by adding the areas of triangles, rectangles, parallelograms, trapeziums, or trapezoids, calculated as in Fig. 6.22. If measuring from the drawing in feet and inches convert these to feet and decimals, or work wholly in inches and tenths, to simplify the multiplication.

Fig. 6.23 shows a simple way of calculating the area of our standard Chinese sail with two head panels. There may be any number of parallelogram panels without affecting the result. This simplified method assumes that the two head panels are of identical area, which is accurate enough for normal purposes. If there are three or more head panels, the area of each should be calculated separately as 'near-triangles'.

If a planimeter is available, the area of any sail, including Bermudian mainsails with curved leeches, may be measured very quickly and accurately.

There is not normally any reason for finishing *exactly* at the chosen area, but in some cases it may be necessary to alter the sail drawing, or redraw the sail, to obtain greater precision. *Small* alterations of area may be made by increasing or decreasing the length of the battens (B), and the head and foot, at their leech ends, without altering the geometry of the sail.

> Example: If the length of the whole leech of a sail, including the leech at the head panels, is, say, 24 ft 7 in, take it as 24.5 ft. To increase the sail area by 4 sq ft, length B should be increased by 4/24.5 = 0.16 ft or near enough 2 in. In other words, adding a strip 2 in wide along the whole leech will add 4 sq ft to that sail's area.

Conversely, reducing the sail area by 5 sq ft would entail shortening length B by 5/24.5 = 0.2 ft or near enough 2½ in.

Large alterations in sail area require the sail to be redrawn completely, using significantly altered values for the dimensions B and L, and hence U, P, and rise.

FINDING THE CENTRE OF EFFORT. The CE is a fixed

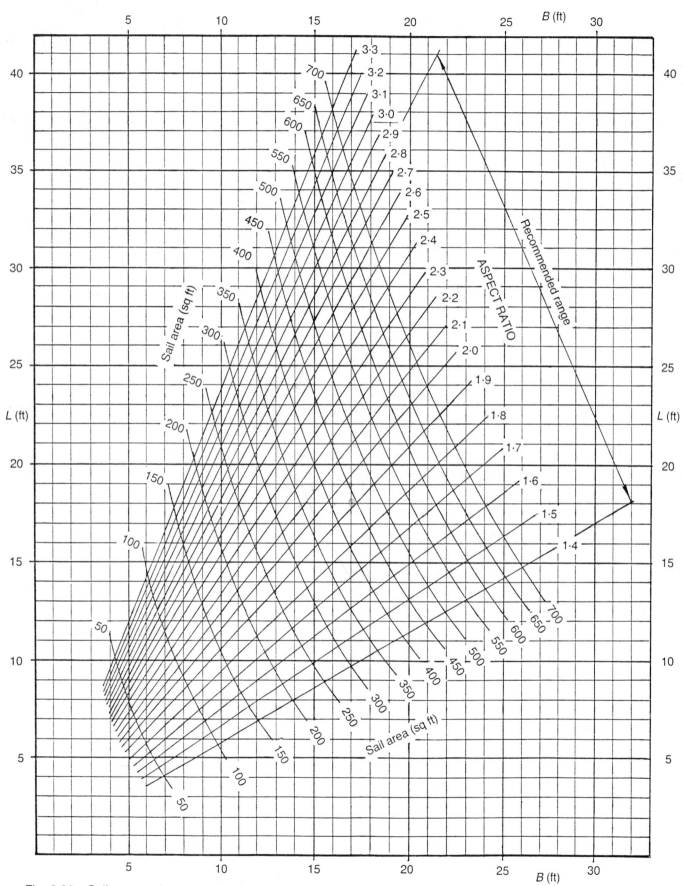

Fig. 6.20   Sail area and aspect ratio diagram (imperial)

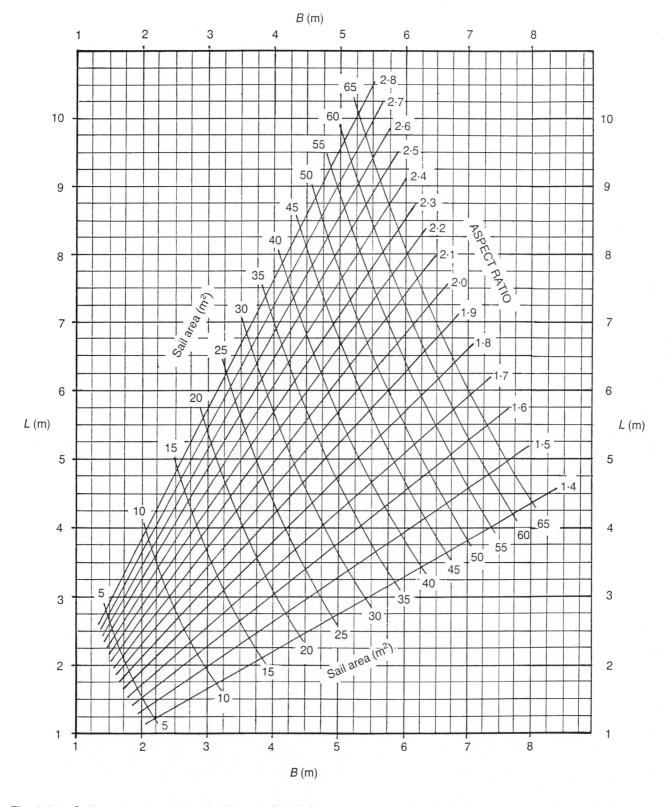

Fig. 6.21   Sail area and aspect ratio diagram (metric)

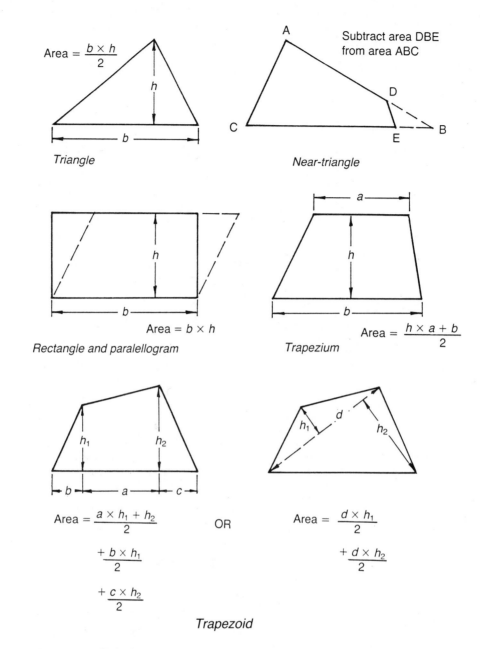

Fig. 6.22   Calculating areas

point on the sail's surface, and is the geometrical centre (centroid) of its area. It provides a convenient point of reference, but it would be wrong to assume that it is the same as the centre of pressure (CP), which is the point through which the total force developed by the sail acts. The CP moves around the sail on different points of sailing and with different amounts of arching. We do not attempt to plot its movements, but work instead from the CE in the light of results gained by practical experience.

To find the CE of a sail, trace its outline on to a piece of tracing paper that is reasonably stiff and quite flat, then cut accurately round the edge of the sail. Make pin holes near three of the corners, such as at X, Y, and Z in Fig. 6.24. Tie one end of a length of cotton to a large pin and the other to a small object that will act as a weight. The pin should be a loose fit in the holes in the paper.

Put the pin through hole X and into a vertical wooden surface. Make sure that both the tracing and the weight are swinging freely and not affected by air currents. Allow them to settle and mark point P where the cotton crosses the lower edge of the tracing. Repeat with the pin through hole Y to obtain point Q, and through hole Z to obtain point R. Place the tracing on the drawing board and join X–P, Y–Q, and Z–R. The three lines should

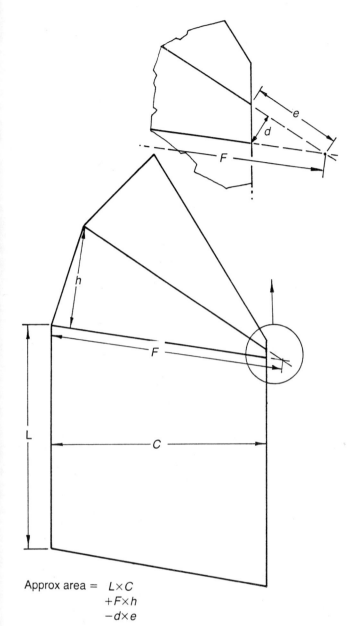

Approx area = $L \times C$
$+ F \times h$
$- d \times e$

Fig. 6.23
Calculating the area of a standard Chinese sail

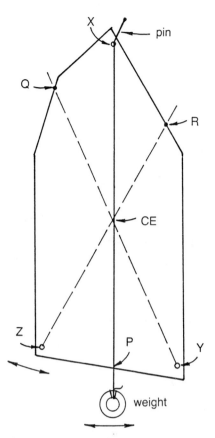

Fig. 6.24   Plotting the CE of a Chinese sail

intersect at a point, or at least in a very small 'cocked hat' whose centre may be taken as the CE. A large cocked hat indicates that you have been inaccurate, and should try again.

CE OF MULTIPLE RIGS. With a rig consisting of two or more sails it is necessary to work out the combined CE of the whole sailplan, as in Fig. 6.25. First obtain the CE and area of each sail, as at A and B. Join A–B with a straight line and draw a perpendicular upwards from B and downwards from A. Choosing an appropriate linear scale to suit the areas, mark off on each perpendicular a

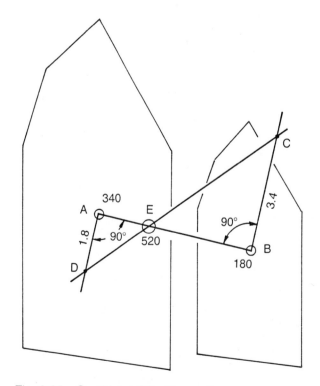

Fig. 6.25   Combined CE of two sails

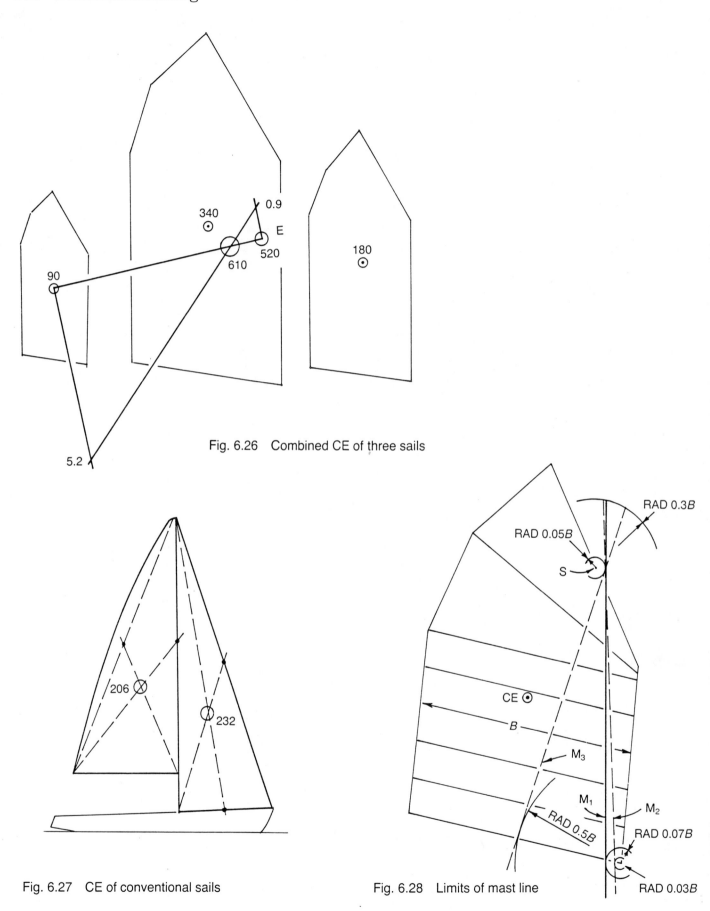

Fig. 6.26   Combined CE of three sails

Fig. 6.27   CE of conventional sails

Fig. 6.28   Limits of mast line

distance equivalent to the area of the *other* sail, as shown. Join C and D to cut AB at E, which is the combined CE of the two sails and is marked with the combined area.

With three-masted rigs, first work out the combined CE of main and foresail as above, then combine this with the mizzen as in Fig. 6.26, which shows a mizzen added to the rig in Fig. 6.25.

FINDING THE CE OF A CONVENTIONAL SAILPLAN. This will be needed if you are relating the lead of a junk rig to that of a conventional sailplan (see p 93). Here it is usual to ignore the roach (convex curvature) on the leech of a Bermudan mainsail and to treat it as a triangle. Many designers also disregard the size, shape, and overlap of the actual headsails and simply treat the fore-triangle between mast, deck, and forestay as being a single headsail. The areas of these triangles may be calculated as in Fig. 6.22. The CE of a triangle is found by joining any two corners to the centres of the opposite sides and taking the point (the centroid) where these lines (the medians) intersect (Fig. 6.27). The two CEs in Fig. 6.27 are then combined as in Fig. 6.25. With two or more masts the combined CE is then found as in Fig. 6.26.

The CE of a gaff mainsail is best determined by hanging up a trace of it as in Fig. 6.24.

DRAWING THE MAST LINE. Having drawn the recommended form of junk sail, the recommended mast line (M_1) may be drawn across it, as in Fig. 6.28. This is the centreline of the mast and is found from dimension *B* which is the length of the sail along the lines of the battens, head, and foot. The mast line is drawn as a tangent to the forward side of an arc whose radius is $0.05B$ and whose centre is the centre of the head (S). Its lower part is a tangent to the after side of an arc of radius $0.07B$ whose centre is the tack of the sail. This mast is normally stepped plumb in the boat.

If there are later found to be reasons for using a different mast line with the same sling point (S), the line may be anywhere between the extreme limits (M_2 and M_3) (Fig. 6.28). The implications of changing the mast line, and of raking the mast, and of slinging the sail from a different point on its head, are all discussed in Chapter 7.

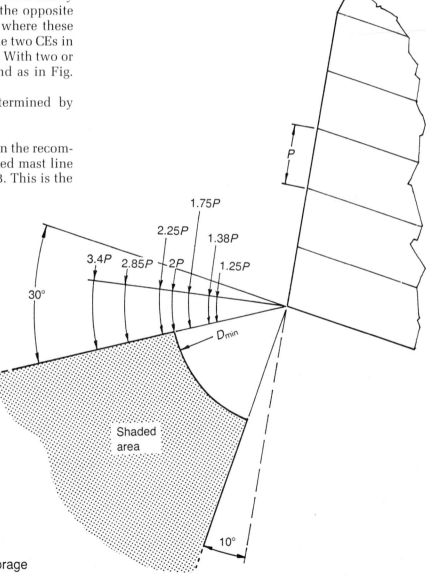

Fig. 6.29   Limits of lower sheet block anchorage

A suitable height for the masthead may be established for any mast line by striking an arc of length 0.3B from the sling point (S), as shown in Fig. 6.28.

POSITION OF DECK BLOCKS FOR SHEETS. As discussed in Chapter 4, the deck block anchorage should lie within the shaded area shown in profile in Fig. 6.29. Using the sheet spans described in this book, the D_{min} may vary from 1.25P to 3.4P, as marked, but in this example it has been taken as 2P. If the sail is canted either clockwise or anti-clockwise, the shaded area will of course move with it.

SHEET ARRANGEMENT. With the recommended form of seven-panel sail, single sheets will normally be arranged in a six-point system, connected to the boom and to battens 1, 2, 3, 4, and 5. A number of alternative six-point layouts have been examined in Chapter 4. The simplest is shown in Fig. 4.29 and has a sheet power of 6 and a short D_{min} of 1.25P but no anti-twist effect. Fig. 4.31 has a lower sheet power of 5 and a slightly higher D_{min} of 1.38P, but some anti-twist effect. Both these systems have been used successfully for many years and are suited to larger sails using small winches. However, for most sails we would recommend a system using multiple spans and giving an anti-twist effect, provided there is space for the longer D_{min} requirement, and the lower sheet power can be accepted by making more use of suitable winches.

The recommended systems are shown in Fig. 6.30 to 6.33. It will be realised that these sheet systems are devised by combining two of the different span systems discussed in Chapter 4 to produce a suitable sheet for six, seven or five points with an anti-twist effect. In each case the a arrangement, using euphroes, is preferable,

but if you cannot make or obtain euphroes use the b arrangement. These sketches are diagrammatic and do not show the correct lengths of spans or positions of sheet blocks.

A sheet power of 3 will make a self-tailing winch desirable for sails of over about 250 sq ft (23 m²). With a sheet power of 5 or 6 a winch will be desirable for sails of more than about 350 sq ft (33 m²).

These sheet systems are, of course, devised by combining two of the different span systems discussed in Chapter 4 to produce a suitable sheet for six, seven, or five points with an anti-twist effect.

It might at first sight appear that increasing the number of sail panels would, by shortening dimension P, reduce D_{min} for a sail of any given area. However, this alteration commonly involves introducing a sheet span with a greater number of points and this, with its larger D_{min}, may more than offset the gain found from reducing P. Each case should be calculated individually if a comparison is needed.

Summary: drawing a standard Chinese sail

It is now possible to summarise the complete process of drawing a trace of a Chinese sail, ready for offering up to the hull profile:

1. Decide on the total area of the Chinese sailplan (p 94).
2. Decide whether it is to be a single- or multi-masted rig (p 94).
3. If multi-masted, decide on the areas of the individual sails (p 95).

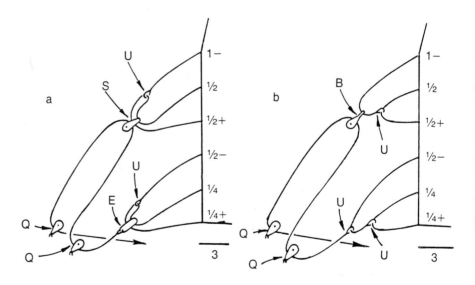

Key   B = block   E = plain euphroe
      R = ring   S = sheaved euphroe
      U = thimble   Q = deck block

Fig. 6.30   6-point sheets (D_{min}=2P, sheet power=3)

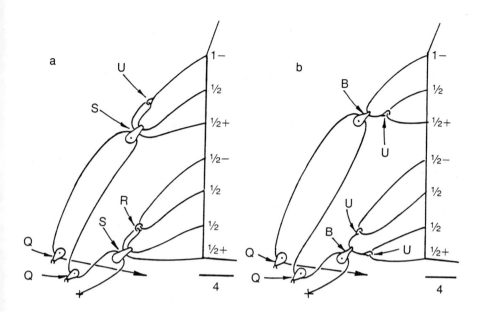

Fig. 6.31   7-point sheets ($D_{min}=2.25P$, sheet power=4)

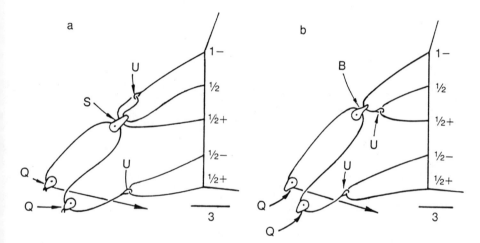

Fig. 6.32   5-point sheets ($D_{min}=2P$, sheet power=3)

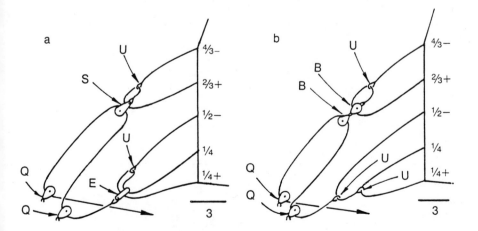

Fig. 6.33   Alternative 5-point sheets ($D_{min}=2P$, sheet power=3)

4. Check that the largest sail is within the suggested limit (p 96).

5. Choose the aspect ratio of the sail you wish to draw (p 97).

6. If the aspect ratio is very high or very low, decide on whether to vary the standard number of panels for that reason (p 97).

7. If the sail's area is very large or very small, decide on whether to vary the standard number of panels for that reason (p 97–8).

8. Enter Fig. 6.20 or 6.21 with the area and aspect ratio, and find values for L and B. Rationalise these (p 103).

9. Decide on dimension U (p 98).

10. Divide L by the number of parallelogram panels to obtain P. Check that P is within the recommended limits (p 97).

11. Calculate the rise (p 101).

12. Choose the scale for the sail drawing, to be the same as that of the profile drawing on which you have already marked the CLR.

13. Take a piece of tracing paper large enough for the sail including its sheets down to the deck blocks, and with a margin of at least $0.3B$ all round. Then proceed as in Fig. 6.34: draw the luff (L) vertically, divide it into the required number of panels (P), and extend it upwards by the required number of lengths U.

14. Place a protractor on the throat and mark the 60° yard angle; the simplest way is to take 90° + 60° = 150°

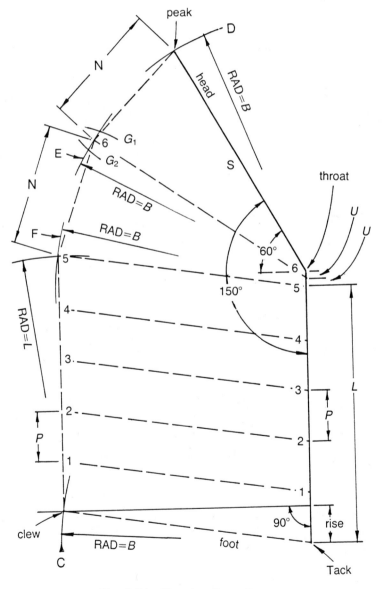

Fig. 6.34   Drawing the sail

from the luff. Draw the line of the head.

15. With compasses set to radius B and centred at the tack, strike an arc C on which the clew will lie.

16. With the same radius, strike an arc D from the throat to cut the line of the head, and so mark the peak.

17. Again with the same radius, strike a short arc E with centre at the forward end of the top batten, and another arc F from the forward end of the top parallelogram batten.

18. Mark the rise up the luff from the tack, and from this point lightly draw an accurate line perpendicular to the luff to cut arc C at the clew.

19. Check that batten 1 will furl with the correct amount of negative stagger at the luff (Fig. 6.35): with the point of

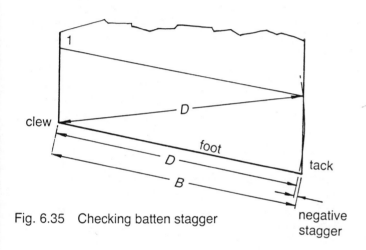

clew

Fig. 6.35   Checking batten stagger

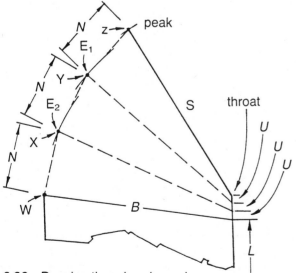

Fig. 6.36   Drawing three head panels

the compasses at the clew and radius D, strike an accurate arc downwards to cut the foot; measure the stagger and check that it is negative and roughly 0.01 B. If it is less than this the clew must be raised a little higher along the arc C, and vice versa. The error will have occurred either in calculating the rise or in marking it off on the drawing. Check that the amount of stagger is now correct.

20. Mark the final position of the clew. Draw the foot. Set the compasses with radius L and with centre at the clew strike an arc to cut the previous arc F and so fix the top after corner of the parallelogram. Draw the leech and divide it into the required number of panels (P). Draw the batten lines of the parallelogram. Number the battens upwards.

21. By measurement, check that head, foot, and all battens are the same length (B), that the two vertical sides of the parallelogram are the same length (L), and that the panel widths (P) along these two sides are the same.

22. With the standard two head panels, fix the after end of the top batten as follows (Fig. 6.34): set the compasses to an estimated length N and strike an arc (G_1) from the top after corner of the parallelogram to cut arc E; with the same radius strike an arc (G_2) from the peak. The point on E that is midway between the two points of intersection is the after end of the top batten, regardless of whether your estimated distance N was too long (as shown) or too short. Check that the two lengths N are equal, and draw in the top batten and upper leech.

With three head panels (p 97) it is best to establish length N by trial and error, as in Fig. 6.36. Strike arcs E_1 and E_2 with radius B from the forward ends of the two head battens and experiment with the setting of compasses or dividers until they will 'walk' exactly in three steps W–X–Y–Z. Check that the three lengths N are equal.

23. Check the area of the sail (p 103) and confirm that it is acceptable. If not, make any small adjustment to the area as described on p 103 and again check the amount of stagger. The outline of the sail with its batten lines has now been finalised. Mark the centre of the head at S.

24. Cut out a separate piece of tracing paper and find the CE of the sail (p 103–7). Transfer this point to the first trace and mark the area against it.

25. Draw the normal mast line (M_1) across the sail (p 109), extending upwards to the masthead and downwards to the edge of the trace.

26. Decide on the arrangement of sheets and sheet spans (p 110) and hence what D_{min} is applicable. Draw the shaded area for the deck block anchorage (Fig. 6.29) on the individual sail trace, which is now ready to be offered up to the master trace of the sailplan.

7 Designing the Sailplan (2)

The individual sail or sails for the proposed sail plan have now been drawn on separate pieces of tracing paper, each showing its normal mast line (M₁), its CE and area, and the 'shaded area' for the sheet block anchorage. These traces are now laid on the master profile trace whose waterline has already been marked (see p 94) with the chosen position for the CE of the Chinese rig. If both single- and two-masted rigs are being considered, two separate CEs will have been marked, as in Fig. 6.6. On the master trace, draw a faint line vertically upwards from each CE.

Positioning a single-sailed rig

Place the sail trace over the profile trace with its CE on the vertical line. Cant it as necessary to bring the mast line M₁ vertical. Slide it up or down until it is as low as possible while giving the following clearances.

BOOM CLEARANCES. The underside of the boom should be at a height that is at least $0.4P$ above any part of the deck, coachroof, doghouse, bulwark, or guardrail when under full sail, and at least $0.2P$ above any fixed boom gallows, where P is the panel width of the sail in question. When reefed, these clearances will be reduced somewhat as the boom settles down into the topping-lifts. Remember that the deck, coachroof, and doghouse are normally cambered, i.e. higher on the centreline than at the sides. If it is decided to fit batten downhauls (see p 49) there should be a clearance of at least $0.8P$ between boom and deck at a point about 1 ft (0.3 m) abaft the mast.

All-round visibility for the watchkeeper is an important safety feature of the junk rig, and it is sometimes worth arranging the sail a little higher on the mast to achieve it. On all points of sailing the boom will of course swing lower against the horizon as the boat heels or rolls. There is seldom any reason to squeeze the sail right down to the minimum clearances; it can be high enough to look right and to permit a man to scramble under the boom from one side of the deck to the other.

ROLL ANGLE. (See p 40) With the sail trace held in position on the profile drawing, preferably with two small pieces of drafting tape, construct the roll angle as shown in Fig. 3.22 and check that it is not less than about 30° if the boat is to sail in open water. If necessary, raise the sail further up the mast.

Having now provisionally positioned the sail, look at the implications of the mast position and sheet layout, as on p 115–19. If there are no problems, the sail plan may be finalised. Otherwise, start readjusting it along the lines suggested.

Positioning a multi-sailed rig

If you are considering either a two-masted schooner or a three-masted ketch, as recommended on p 95, start by trying the mainsail with its normal mast line (M₁) vertical and cutting the centre of the waterline. Adjust its height so as to give the required boom clearances (see above) and roll angle (see above). Tape it temporarily to the master trace in this position.

Now offer up the trace of the foresail, again with its mast line M₁ vertical and with the minimum gap between its leech and the luff of the mainsail. This minimum gap is the space needed to allow a sheet system to work between two sails without fouling the luff of the aftermost sail. Since the leech of the forward sail may not be exactly parallel with the luff of the after sail, the gap is measured from the clew of the forward sail along a line perpendicular to the luff of the after sail (GA and GB, Fig. 7.1).

For a single-sheet system the minimum gap is defined as being $(\sqrt{SA})/5$, where SA is the area of the sail *ahead* of the gap. The answer will be in feet if the SA is in square feet, or in metres if it is in square metres.

As an aid to positioning a foresail, the trace of a mainsail may show a minimum-clearance line, (A in Fig. 7.1) parallel to its luff and with the gap calculated from the area of the *foresail*. Similarly, the trace of a mizzen may include a minimum-clearance line (B in Fig. 7.1) parallel to its luff but with a wider gap based on the

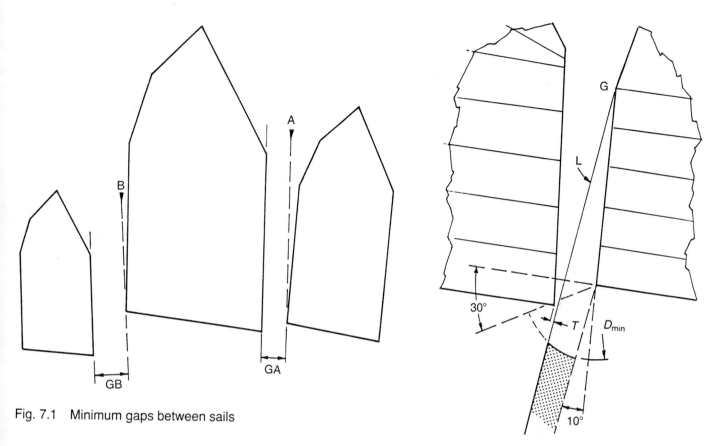

Fig. 7.1   Minimum gaps between sails

Fig. 7.2   Reduced 'shaded area' between two sails

mainsail area. These gaps may with advantage be increased if other considerations permit.

If the minimum gap cannot be achieved, it may be necessary to use double sheets on the sail that is forward of the gap, as on the foresail of *Batwing* (Fig. 16.9). In this case the minimum gap may be reduced to about $(\sqrt{SA})/$ 13. There is nothing precise about these formulae. They are intended only as a guide, but if you use smaller gaps you may expect to have to cope with sheets getting foul.

Having arranged the foresail with its clew on the clearance line, adjust its height to obtain the minimum boom clearance (see p 114) and check the roll angle (see p 40) whilst keeping its mast line (M_1) vertical. Tape it temporarily to the *mainsail* trace in this position. For a three-master, follow the same process with the trace of the mizzen, then tape it to the mainsail trace.

Multiple rigs using single sheets now require a further clearance line (L) in each gap (Fig. 7.2). This is drawn from the highest sheet point (G) and passes forward of the tack of the next sail by a distance (T) equal to $(\sqrt{SA})/30$ where *SA* is the area of the sail forward of the gap. As before, the answer will emerge in feet or metres to correspond with the units of the sail area. The shaded area for the deck blocks must lie forward of line L and is therefore severely reduced, as shown, in order to keep the sheets clear of the tack of the aftermost sail when under full sail.

Having now tentatively arranged all the sails in a multiple rig in their relative positions and taped them together, tape yet another piece of tracing paper over the whole lot and on it work out the combined CE of the rig (see p 107). Compare this with the desired position of the CE on the master trace and move the sailplan, gaps and all, forward or aft until the two coincide, if necessary readjusting the clearances below the booms in the process.

Now examine the result. For each sail, look at the implications of its mast position and sheeting, as set out below, and note any problems. If there are none, the sail plan may be accepted as it stands.

Unacceptable mast positions

The tentative mast position may be unacceptable for one or more reasons:

1. Insufficient bury. 'Bury' is defined as the distance between the heel of the mast and the top of its support at the partners. The recommended minimum bury is 9 per

cent of the overall length of the mast, or roughly 10 per cent of the LAP (length above partners), but the larger the bury the better. Remember that the mast step has appreciable width and must be looked at in relation to the section of the hull. Before rejecting a mast position for insufficient bury, consider whether the partners can be built up higher, as discussed on p 144.

2. Mast too near the bow. A heavy mast that is very near the bow will act like a piledriver when she is pitching, and make her pitch more heavily. As a general rule, the step of a foremast should not be ahead of the forward end of the waterline, and the step of a mainmast should be at least 0.15 of the waterline length abaft its forward end.

3. Mast position incompatible with boat's construction. It must be possible to provide strong support at both partners and step, as discussed in Chapter 9. It will be necessary to consider the diameter of the mast (see p 129) and of the mast hole at the partners, to see what clearances there will be from coamings, bulkheads, etc. If the mast step would be over a tank, centreboard case, engine or keel bolt it may be difficult to provide a strong enough step without interfering with access.

4. Mast position incompatible with accommodation or deck layout. If the boat's accommodation or deck layout is already decided and cannot be altered, the proposed mast position, considered in conjunction with its diameter, may not be acceptable.

Unacceptable sheet positions

The lower sheet blocks will be anchored a few inches to port of the centreline (Fig. 4.44), and require a reasonably strong mounting within the shaded area. When the sheet is hauled flat amidships it should clear all fixed obstructions, including any vane steering gear regardless of the angle of the vane. It is, however, acceptable for the lower sheets to lie across the guardrail when running, as with most conventional rigs. When gybing with the sheets off (see p 208) the slack sheets will drag across the boat and it is best to have nothing that they can catch on, although this is not always possible to achieve. If they sweep across the cockpit, anyone in it is expected to duck.

Suggested solutions

If the position of any mast is unacceptable, it will have to be moved forward or aft. The Chinese are also prepared to move some masts of a multi-masted rig athwartships off the centreline, a move that is facilitated by the absence of standing rigging, but we cannot predict the aerodynamic effects of this. In Western practice there are five options:

1. The simplest way of altering a mast position is to stretch the rule for the position of the sailplan's CE, since the rule itself is very inexact (see p 93). The boat's balance should remain acceptable if the whole sailplan is moved forward or aft by a distance of not more than about 3 per cent of the waterline length in relation to the CE position that you have marked on your master trace.

2. If this would not solve the problem, and if the total sail area falls within one of the 'optional' zones defined on p 94, you may consider changing the number of masts in the rig.

3. With a multiple rig you may consider changing the relative areas of the different sails. There are no hard and fast reasons for the proportions suggested on p 95, other than a wish to keep the largest mast and sail somewhere near the middle of the boat. If the first drawing, say, of a schooner rig had areas of 33 and 67 per cent as recommended, you could try altering it to 25 and 75 per cent, or 40 and 60 per cent, without altering the aspect ratios. Increasing the relative size of the foresail will have the effect of moving both masts aft in order to maintain the same lead, even though the minimum width of the gap will increase in proportion to the square root of the foresail's area (see p 114). Decreasing the relative size of the foresail will move both masts further forward and decrease the minimum gap.

4. It is possible to increase the gap between two sails above the minimum distance, if the length of the hull permits. It will involve moving both masts. For example, in a two-masted schooner with foresail half the size of the main, to increase the gap by x feet while retaining the same 'lead' would involve moving the mainmast aft $x/3$ feet and the foremast forward $2x/3$ feet. Decreasing the gap would involve moving both masts towards each other, although the distance is unlikely to be significant unless you change to using double sheets on the foresail (see p 115).

5. Another way of altering mast position is to change the aspect ratio of the sail. Fig. 7.3 shows how the aspect ratio of the sail affects the position of the mast in relation to the CE of the sail. It shows the three sails from Fig. 6.8, 6.9, and 6.10, all of approximately the same area, superimposed with their CEs all in the same vertical line and their tacks at the same level. They are set on vertical masts using the normal mast lines (M_1) (Fig. 6.28).

If the mast line of the normal sail (2) is a distance V ahead of the CE, then that of the high sail (1) is $0.79V$ ahead and of the low sail (3) is $1.22V$ ahead. Increasing the aspect ratio therefore brings the mast closer to the CE, and vice versa. It is normal to draw all sails of a multi-master to similar aspect ratios but there is no compelling reason for this. Nevertheless, there are usually good reasons for avoiding the extremes of aspect ratio in any sail.

There are three other ways of altering the mast

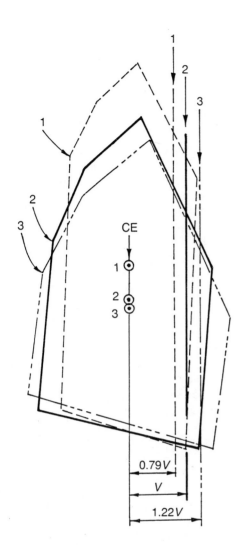

Fig. 7.3   Change of mast position
with aspect ratio

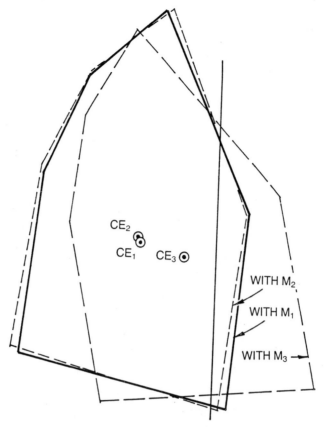

Fig. 7.4   Canting the sail on the mast

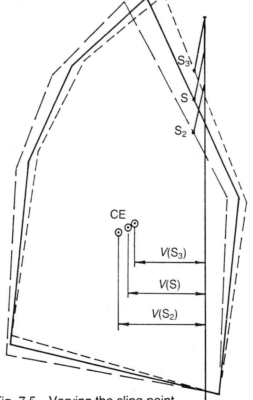

Fig. 7.5   Varying the sling point

position in relation to the CE of the sail: raking the mast forward or aft in the boat, altering the cant of the sail on the mast, and changing the sling point on the yard. Each can be employed by itself, or in conjunction with either or both of the others.

1. Raking the mast. Mast rake has been discussed on p 40, where it was suggested that a rake of 3° aft or 10° forward should be regarded as the extreme limits. It is preferable for a mainmast to be plumb, or to be raked forward not more than 2°. When the sail is set and close-hauled, it tends to bend the mast slightly aft, as it does also when furled unless the bundle is supported on a gallows or crutch. Up to 10° of forward rake can be tolerated on a foremast and up to 3° of aft rake on a mizzen mast. Raking the masts of a multi-masted rig in these directions will often facilitate getting a good sail area onto a short hull although the appearance may cause comment from the ill-informed.

A forward-raking foremast is a potent means of altering the position of the step and partners in the hull, and of increasing the bury, without altering the CE of the foresail or, conversely, of getting the CE of the foresail further forward without stepping the mast too far forward.

2. Canting the sail on the mast. Fig. 6.28 shows that the line of the mast across the sail may be varied between the extremes of M_2 and M_3. If these extreme positions were used with a vertical mast, the relationship between CE and mast line would alter as shown in Fig. 7.4, i.e. very little between M_1 and M_2 but a lot between M_1 and M_3. Using line M_2 would give minimum aerodynamic balance and the shaded area for the sheet anchorage would be further aft, but the tack would have to be allowed to move forward quite a bit when close-reefed or furled (see p 42) in order to keep the upper battens and yard with enough overlap on the mast. Using line M_3 would enable the mast to be much further aft in relation to the CE, but the sail looks awkward with the tack cocked up and its clew drooping, and there are other strong disadvantages. The bottom part of the sail is almost fully balanced aerodynamically and will have little, if any, tendency to weathercock. It may try to snatch one way or the other when head to wind, and be restrained only by the upper part of the sail, which has just enough positive balance to keep it weathercocking. (It has been emphasised on p 106 that the CE is not the same as the centre of pressure. When nearly head-to-wind the sail's CP is well forward of the CE, and it is of course the CP that controls weathercocking.) A sail that will not weathercock freely is an unpleasant shipmate, and could be dangerous. As with all heavily-balanced sails, the sheet loading would be very light but the mast and batten loading would be greater than usual.

The second adverse effect is that the boom and lower battens cannot take up a concave curvature when on the windward side of the mast, but will be trying to bend the other way, so that the sail develops convex arching when viewed from the windward side. This is very poor aerodynamically and will tend to make the luff snatch on and off when going to windward, as described on p 16, giving unstable steering. Convex curvature may be countered only to a limited extent by making the boom and lower battens so stiff that they remain in effect straight.

The mast line M_1 gives the best setting sail, with a mild anti-twist effect through having more balance at the throat than at the tack. It is best not to use any mast line between M_1 and M_3 except for certain foresails whose masts have to be raked forward, and perhaps for a few sails where it is imperative to bring the shaded area for the sheet anchorage further forward. *Batwing* (Fig. 16.9) carries a relatively large (37 per cent) foresail on a mast that is raked 8° forward, and with a mast line that is about halfway between M_1 and M_3. *Yeong* (Fig. 16.5) has a foremast raked 10° forward, giving adequate bury and keeping its lower end clear abaft a self-draining cable locker. In spite of this strong rake, the mast line on her 33 per cent foresail (which is of non-standard shape) is nearer to M_1 than to M_3.

3. Varying the sling point on the yard. The general assumption throughout this book is that the yard will be slung from a point (S) that is at the centre of the head of the sail. This seems to be the best position, but it is not an inflexible rule. Many junk sails have been slung from a point such as S_2 (Fig. 7.5) which is further towards the throat. This permits a shorter mast but increases the twist of the head of the sail, the loading of the yard, the loading of the halyard and the compression on the mast. It also makes for a taut luff and a slack leech, and it is more difficult for the luff parrels to peak the sail up properly so that it sets without creases.

Slinging from a point such as S_3 (Fig. 7.5) which is between S and the peak, is also possible but rather pointless, except as a last resort to reduce twist or sail creasing. It requires a longer mast.

When using one of these unorthodox sling points, the normal mast line (M_1) and the height of the mast head are defined by the same rules as before (Fig. 6.28). On a plumb mast, the distance V between the CE and the mast line would vary a certain amount, as shown. Moving the sling point towards the peak will shorten the distance V and vice versa, but the effect is not very marked and this is not recommended as a means of altering the mast position or the position of the CE. Varying the sling point will also cant the sail slightly as shown, and will therefore slightly alter the position of the shaded area for the sheet block anchorage (Fig. 6.29).

Positioning the lower sheet blocks

These should be offset a few inches to port (Fig. 4.44). In order to keep within the shaded area in profile, it may be necessary to mount them on a bumkin over the stern, or on a strengthened stern pulpit, or on a horse erected on deck or coach roof for that purpose. A sheet horse will commonly have fixed positions for the blocks, but it is possible to experiment with tricing the blocks along the horse on a traveller, as discussed on p 72. If the lower sheet blocks are raised above the deck it may be necessary to raise the sail on the mast correspondingly, in order to maintain the D_{min}.

Summary: designing a sailplan (2)

Prepare the individual sail trace(s) as in the summary at the end of Chapter 6, then:

SINGLE-SAILED RIG

1. Place the sail trace on the profile trace and adjust it until its CE is on the correct vertical line and its mast line M_1 is vertical.
2. Raise or lower it until there is adequate clearance under the boom, adequate roll angle, and adequate all-round visibility for the watchkeeper (p 114).
3. Check the position of the shaded area for the sheet block anchorage and if necessary raise the sail further.
4. Tape the trace to the profile and proceed to stage 12 below.

MULTIPLE-SAILED RIG

1. Place the trace of the mainsail on the profile trace and adjust it with the mast line M_1 vertical and cutting the centre of the waterline.
2. Raise or lower it until there is adequate clearance under the boom, adequate roll angle, and adequate all-round visibility for the watchkeeper (p 114).
3. Check the position of the shaded area for the sheet block anchorage and if necessary raise the sail further.
4. Tape the mainsail trace to the profile.
5. Work out the minimum gap between foresail and mainsail for single sheets and mark the clearance line on the mainsail trace (p 114).
6. Offer up the trace of the foresail with its clew on the clearance line and its mast line M_1 vertical.
7. Raise or lower it until there is adequate clearance under the boom, adequate roll angle, and adequate all-round visibility for the watchkeeper.
8. Sketch in clearance line (L) (p 115) to restrict the shaded area for the foresheets. If necessary, raise the sail further.
9. Tape the foresail to the mainsail trace.
10. Repeat sequence 5–9 for the mizzen, if any, but with a different minimum gap (p 114).
11. Work out the combined CE of the sailplan (p 107). Move the whole sailplan forward or aft until the combined CE is on the correct vertical line on the master trace.
12. Check the position of each mast for
     insufficient bury (p 115)
     being too near the bow (p 116)
     incompatibility with boat's structure,
     accommodation, or deck layout (p 116)
13. If any mast position is unacceptable, consider stretching the rule for position of CE (p 116), or failing that:
     changing the number of masts (p 116)
     in a multiple rig, changing the relative areas of sails (p 116)
     in a multiple rig, increasing the gap(s) (p 116)
     in a multiple rig, decreasing the gap(s) and
        changing to double sheets if necessary (p 115)
     altering the aspect ratio of the sail(s) (p 116)
     raking the mast(s) (p 118) and altering the mast line
        on any sail with a forward-raking mast (p 118)
14. Check what, if any, structures will be necessary to carry the lower sheet blocks.
15. If you are still left with an insoluble problem, it may be necessary as a last resort to reduce the total sail area. The smaller the sail area the easier it will be to position the rig acceptably.
16. When all is approved, either prick through the sail positions on to the master trace, or take a fresh sheet of tracing paper and trace the sail(s) and hull profile on to it. This may then be referred to as the sailplan.

8 Masts

For reasons set out on p 13, we are considering only unstayed (cantilever) masts that stand up without any shrouds, forestays, or backstays. They are supported laterally at the partners (where the mast emerges from the deck or coachroof) and the step (where the heel of the mast is held fixed, usually to the keelson).

The main stresses in these masts are bending loads, made up of the largely static forces induced by the wind in the sail and the dynamic forces induced by the rolling and pitching of the boat.

When the sail is on the lee side of the mast the wind forces act as in Fig. 8.1, which shows the sail in section. The parrels distribute the load fairly evenly up the mast. On the other tack the yard, battens, and boom will press against the mast and the parrels will be slack, but the distribution of forces will be similar.

Considering only the loading of the mast, if the sum of the sail forces is taken as F, and if P and S are taken as the lateral forces induced in the partners and step respectively, then the partners may be regarded as a fulcrum and force S will be such that the moment $S \times B$ (B is the bury) equals $F \times H$. The greater the bury (B) the less the forces of P and S. Force P is the sum of F and S.

In strong winds, most boats can carry more sail when running than when on the wind, and this may be the point of sailing that develops maximum mast loading. It also develops maximum batten loadings (see p 14).

The dynamic forces induced by the weight of the mast when the boat is rolling or pitching are similar. If no sail is set, reversing forces at P and S are induced when the movement of the hull waggles the mast about. If sail is set, its weight increases these forces and its air resistance, even in a flat calm, can set up additional loadings. Every seaman knows the severe forces set up in a rig when the boat rolls heavily in a swell and the sail snatches against the sheets, first one way and then the other. For these reasons the partners and step should be designed to take lateral loads in any direction.

The mast is also subject to compression loads imposed by the halyard (particularly when under full sail) and by the topping-lifts and mast lift (particularly when reefed), but these forces are relatively light, and bear no resemb-

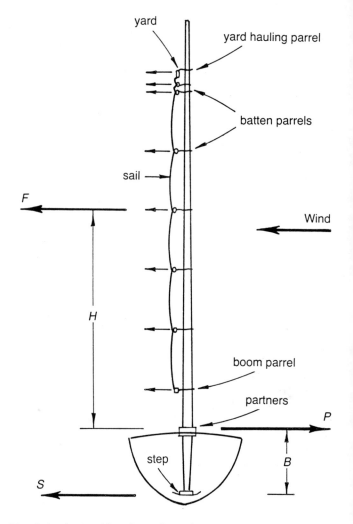

Fig. 8.1 Lateral loading of mast

lance to the huge compression loads imposed by the standing rigging of a conventional rig such as a Bermudian sloop. In fact it is necessary to hold a Chinese mast *down* at the partners or step, to avoid the risk of its jumping upwards under certain extreme conditions, such as when pitching in steep seas in a tide race or when the rig gets foul of an upstanding obstruction when sailing heeled.

Since the main stresses are bending loads it is desirable for the mast to be well tapered above the partners. It needs a lot of strength at the partners and very little at the masthead. If it is untapered it will still need at least as much diameter at the partners but will have quite unnecessary weight, strength, stiffness and windage in its upper part. Nearly all the bending will occur just above the partners, which is unattractive. When sailing the mast should take up a smooth curve all the way from partners to masthead, indicating that there are no stress concentration areas. An untapered Chinese mast could, at a pinch, be accepted for a dinghy, but cannot be recommended for any sail of more than about 100 sq ft (9 m²).

Ideally the mast will have its maximum diameter at the partners and will taper down to the step, as in Fig. 8.1, as well as upwards to the masthead, thereby reducing unnecessary weight and causing less obstruction below decks, but this lower taper is unimportant.

The design and construction of the cantilever mast is of prime importance. A qualified designer approaching the subject from scratch would need to make assumptions about the maximum stresses that the mast would have to bear in the worst foreseeable sailing conditions. Alas! such assumptions are unlikely to be realistic. We can calculate the static loading on the mast that would be required to lay the boat on her beam ends under full sail, but what extra loading would be imposed if she were to be *suddenly* knocked down by a 'williwaw', i.e. a fierce whirlwind squall off the hills? Everything would depend on how suddenly it happened, or in scientific terms what accelerations were involved. A quick recovery to the upright position would also induce severe stresses in the mast.

Again, when running before the wind in smooth water it would be too optimistic to expect the mast to be strong enough to make her pitchpole (somersault) when struck by a stupendous squall from astern.

The best we can do is to state rules for the design of timber masts that have evolved empirically over many years' experience with junk-rigged boats in the open sea. Masts designed to these rules have survived all normal sailing conditions, including severe gales at sea, but cannot be guaranteed to withstand grossly abnormal conditions, such as being hit by a williwaw when under full sail or being dumped upside-down by a rogue wave. Any mast, whether stayed or unstayed, would be likely to carry away under such treatment. The prudent skipper will keep this possibility in the back of his mind, and do what he can to protect the mast when such risks are foreseen.

Most Chinese-rigged boats will be sailed in the open sea, sometimes with a family crew, and their masts therefore need a higher safety factor than that of a dayboat racing round the buoys with a rescue launch in the offing. Mast failure on a cruising boat while trying to claw to windward off a lee shore can lead to shipwreck with loss of life.

The authors of this book are not qualified stressmen and are not going to deal with mast design in a way that would satisfy a mechanical engineer. We simply give our rules for wooden masts, both solid and hollow. If a mast is to be built of some other material, such as aluminium alloy, it should be produced by a designer or sparmaker who is experienced with that material. He should be given a drawing of the recommended timber mast and asked to design one that will have at least as much strength, stiffness, and resistance to fatigue.

Strength and stiffness are two quite different properties that sometimes conflict with each other. Strength is the resistance to breaking or taking on a permanent set (bend), whereas stiffness is resistance to bending. An unstayed mast of small diameter and of suitable material could be like a fishing rod, capable of being bent double and then springing back to its original straightness. It would have great strength but would be useless for sailing because it would not be stiff enough to hold the sail up to the wind. Conversely, a hollow mast could be made with large diameter and very thin walls, for example by wrapping a thin sheet of plywood around diaphragms. This would have great stiffness because of the large diameter, but little strength because of the thin walls. Being unable to bend, it would break or buckle when heavily loaded.

The ideal Chinese mast will be somewhere between these extremes. It will not bend far enough to harm the set of the sail or the skipper's nerve, but will be sufficiently flexible to absorb shock loads from squalls, pitching, rolling, and minor collisions. From the point of view of the set of the sail it would be better for the mast not to bend at all, but an appreciable degree of bending must be accepted in order to combine lightness with strength.

All normal Chinese masts are of circular section, at least above the partners. Where tapered, the sides of the taper are normally straight, so that the tapered part of the mast forms a truncated cone, but there is no objection to the taper being barrelled if this is better suited to the system of construction. The slight difference in bending characteristics is unimportant. Fig. 8.2 shows, exaggerated, the two types of taper.

We do not ever lead halyards or other running ropes inside a hollow mast, but electric cables and lightning conductors may be so led. Similarly, we do not fit any sheaves into the mast, but hang masthead blocks from tangs on the masthead fitting and sometimes fit cheek blocks on the side of the mast just above the partners. The mast itself is thereby kept simple in design.

When stepped, the mast must be prevented from twisting in its step and from lifting upwards. Both can be

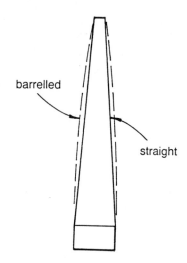

Fig. 8.2 Types of mast taper

achieved by fitting a heavy bolt through the mast, preferably near its heel, and through a heavy bracket on either side that is firmly fastened to the hull. On most wooden masts we also square the heel so that it fits into a square step, sitting down on a flat bottom surface without any tenon.

Timber masts

Timber masts are made of softwood rather than hardwood because this enables them to be lighter, and the softwoods tend to grow taller and straighter. The names used for different species of softwood are often confusing, since different names are often used for the same species while different species are sometimes given the same name. Here we tend to use the terms that are common in Britain, together with the scientific name. In other parts of the world other suitable timbers, unknown to us, will be available. Two trees of the same species may be of quite different quality depending on where, and how fast, they have grown.

GROWN MASTS. In most parts of the world a solid mast made from a single pole will provide the simplest and cheapest Chinese mast. This is known as a grown mast. Such masts may be increasingly used as it becomes more difficult to find a sparmaker with the skill and experience to make a hollow wooden mast. Pole masts can be as satisfactory for junk-rigged yachts as they were for lug-rigged fishing boats in the last century, although the probability of knots and shakes on the surface may make them less elegant than a hollow spar.

In general, any tree that will make a first-class telegraph pole or flagpole will also make a good Chinese mast. Obviously it must be a species that grows tall and straight and is reasonably durable (i.e. resistant to rot)

when seasoned. Knots are acceptable if they are small and not loose. It is worth making contact with the local office of the Forestry Commission, or other forestry organisation. If they can find you a suitable tree that has already been thinned out for their own purposes, it may be cheap and partly seasoned.

A solid mast is normally shaped from a pole (i.e. a tree trunk) that is only just large enough to provide the required diameters after removal of the bark. There is no need to remove all the sapwood, which is the living wood that lies immediately beneath the bark and surrounds the dead heartwood (Fig. 8.3). Commercial poles will have had the bark and knobs removed by a skinning machine, but this cannot be used for shaping the taper.

The grain should be straight. Some trees grow with a spiral twist that can be seen in the bark, or later in the skinned pole. These suffer from short-grain effects and should not be used. The strength of a pole may be partly assessed by measuring, at the sawn butt and halfway out from the centre, the number of growth rings per inch of radius. Poles with less than nine rings per inch (seven rings per 2 cm) should not be used for masts. Nine per inch is permissible, but full strength is not reached until the count is twelve rings per inch (say nine rings per 2 cm). Imported poles from Scandinavia, widely used for telegraph poles, average twenty-five rings per inch (ten rings per cm), but this offers little or no increase in strength.

All mast timbers should be seasoned, that is to say the natural sap should have been dried out of them. Seasoning is a process that demands experience and may take several years. Whole tree trunks are seasoned slowly and kept moist while the sap finds its way out. After removing the bark they may be stacked in the shade but with plenty of ventilation (air seasoning), or may be moored in salt water (often over drying mud in salt ponds), or immersed in a fresh-water stream. In China

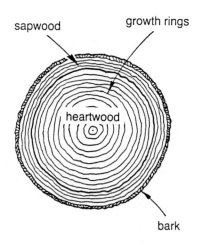

Fig. 8.3 Section of pole

they are said to be seasoned by burying them in the earth for two years. Kiln-drying is the modern and rapid method of seasoning, used particularly for smaller sizes of timber. A good timber merchant will take care of all aspects of selection and seasoning before offering a prime quality pole 'fit for use'.

Having said all this, it must be admitted that serviceable masts have been made from green poles freshly felled, but this is not the right way of doing it. A tree that is to be converted immediately into a mast should if possible be felled in the late autumn, when the sap is down. If it has to be felled in full summer leaf it is advisable to leave all the foliage on it until it has completely dried up. This is said to suck the sap out of the trunk. The disadvantage of using a pole that is not seasoned is that it is more likely to develop shakes, and will not readily absorb any dressing, but may absorb water instead.

As the sap dries out the timber shrinks. In section, it shrinks more along the growth rings than across them, and the sapwood shrinks more than the heartwood. This sets up stresses in the wood that may cause it to warp or to develop checks or shakes (i.e. splits along the grain in the outer surface). A round log (Fig. 8.4) tends to develop radial shakes as it dries out because the outer sapwood is trying to shrink around a fairly incompressible heart. These shakes are very commonly seen in grown masts, even after seasoning, and are not regarded as weakening the spar to any material extent, although they form a route by which rain water can enter and start rot. Some users fill the shakes with a stopping compound to prevent this, but it must be a compound that remains permanently soft because the shakes need to open and close slightly under normal conditions of service. The stopping should be finished 'under flush' so that it is not squeezed out on to the sail, battens, or parrels. Other authorities believe that to put any stopping into a shake

merely encourages rot, and prefer to leave them open, perhaps squirting in some wood preservative or linseed oil.

BUILT MASTS are those which are glued up from a number of pieces of timber. They may be either solid or hollow. The former could be indicated where no suitable pole is available. The latter offers a lighter mast, but at the cost of more skilled work.

Fig. 8.5 shows sections of two planks of wood with the grain running in different directions. Plank a is 'rift sawn', or 'quarter sawn', with the grain running across the thickness of the plank, whereas b is 'slash sawn' with the grain running substantially across the width of the plank. The latter is inferior because the plank tends to warp in such a direction that the grain becomes straighter, as shown. It will also show 'shell grain' (very wide growth rings) on both its flat surfaces, and this is liable to splinter and lift. Many planks will of course show grain that is halfway between the two.

If a pole of the right size is not available, a solid built mast may be glued up from baulks of timber, for example as in Fig. 8.6a, but it would then be preferable to make it slightly hollow, at least by planing off the inside corners as in b, thereby making it lighter and reducing the internal stresses set up when the moisture content of the timber changes.

We have asked various sparmakers which way round they would arrange the grain when fabricating a glued mast, and have received evasive or non-committal answers. Clearly it is not considered important, but Francis Herreshoff in *The Common Sense of Yacht Design* states that a glued-up solid mast will be appreciably stiffer if arranged with the grain radial, as in Fig. 8.6. This would also avoid shell grain on the outside, and we have shown radial grain, as far as possible, in the built mast sections in this book.

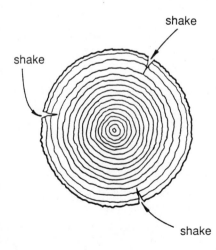

Fig. 8.4   Typical shakes

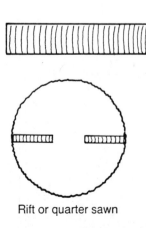

Rift or quarter sawn

Fig. 8.5   Warping of planks

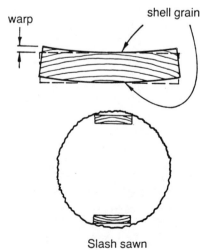

Slash sawn

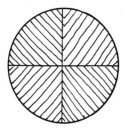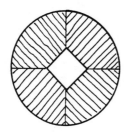

Fig. 8.6   Built mast sections

The baulks used for a built mast will seldom be long enough to run the full length, so that end-to-end joints will have to be made in the pieces by means of glued scarphs whose length should be at least seven times the thickness of the piece. Twelve or thirteen times would be more normal. The position of each scarph should be staggered in relation to the scarphs on adjacent pieces.

Species of timber

The preferred timber for a built mast is Sitka spruce, (*Picea sitchensis*), alias Silver spruce, Tideland spruce, Menzies spruce, or Western spruce, which weighs about 28 lb per cu ft (449 kg/m^3). It is classed as 'moderately durable' but is difficult to impregnate with preservatives. It grows mainly in the western coastal regions of Canada and the USA and is obtainable in Britain only in baulks, not poles. The highest grade is 'aircraft' quality, which has been graded by an inspector, but this puts the price up and the timber may sometimes be less good than some which has been selected by a sparmaker from 'finest' quality. It has good gluing properties.

The next choice is Douglas fir (*Pseudotsuga taxifolia* or *Pseudotsuga douglasii*), alias British Columbian pine, Oregon pine, Idaho pine, Red pine, Red fir, or Yellow fir, which weighs about 33 lb per cu ft (529 kg/m^3) but is harder and stiffer than spruce. It glues well and is classed as 'moderately durable'. It grows on the Pacific coasts of the USA and Canada. In Britain the best quality is called 'prime clear' while lesser grades are known as 'select merchantable' and 'merchantable'. The flagpole at Kew Gardens is, or was, a single pole of Douglas fir 214 ft (65 m) long. Nevertheless, this imported timber is not normally available in pole form in Britain, but only in baulks. Douglas fir is grown to a limited extent in Britain but we have no report on its quality.

For a grown mast the preferred timber, available in pole form, is Scots pine (*Pinus sylvestris*), also called European redwood, Northern pine, Red pine, Redwood, Scots fir, Norway fir, Swedish fir, Finnish fir, and other names, whose density ranges between 26 and 38 lb per cu ft (416 and 609 kg/m^3). This tree is indigenous to Scotland, but the trees grown there are often of inferior quality through having grown too fast. The best poles are imported from northern Europe. The sapwood is very perishable unless well impregnated with preservative, when it becomes very durable. Telegraph poles impregnated with creosote last for 40 years or more in wet ground. The timber glues well.

Another possible timber for a pole mast is common spruce (*Picea abies*), alias European whitewood, White deal, White fir, White pine, Norway spruce, or Spruce fir, and familiar to everyone as the Christmas tree. Weighing about 28 lb per cu ft (449 kg/m^3) it is widely grown in forestry plantations in Britain, but the timber is not durable without preservatives and its mechanical strength is dubious (see 'embrittlement' on p 127). It would be wise to get an expert to select any tree to be used as a mast.

A better possibility for a mast pole is Lawson's cypress (*Cupressus lawsoniana* or *Chamaecyparis lawsoniana*), alias Port Orford cedar, Oregon cedar, White cedar, or Ginger pine, a strong, light, and durable wood that has not yet been grown in any quantity in Britain, being a native of the western coast of the USA. Weight about 33 lb per cu ft (529 kg/m^3).

Another possible timber, which does not seem to have been used for masts, is European larch (*Larix decidua* or *Larix europaea*). Different authorities give its weight as 37 lb per cu ft (593 kg/m^3) and 47 lb per cu ft (753 kg/m^3). The latter density would make it pretty heavy for a mast, but it is much stronger and harder than any of the timbers above and it should be possible to reduce the scantlings of the mast accordingly. It is available in pole form, has good gluing properties and is very durable, being used without preservative as the first choice for farm gateposts and fence posts. For well over a century it has been a favourite timber in Britain for the planking and frames of wooden fishing boats, and here again has been found to be more durable than any other native timber.

Hollow timber masts

These are built masts which are considerably less solid than the section shown in Fig. 8.6b. It can be argued that the wood in the centre of a solid mast does nothing useful, being too near the neutral axis to experience either tension or compression as the mast bends. If this were entirely true a hollow mast could have the same outside diameter as a solid mast. In practice, we give tables for hollow masts and suggest that solid masts can have these diameters reduced by 10 per cent. With timbers of similar density the solid mast will then be about 25 per cent heavier than the hollow mast, a difference that is unlikely to be significant in a cruising boat.

Building a hollow mast is obviously more difficult than shaping a solid pole. Success will depend on good timber, good workmanship, good glue, and good gluing technique.

There are various ways of arranging the pieces of a hollow mast, and the sparmaker will no doubt have his own preference, influenced partly by the timber stock available to him. The simplest method (Fig. 8.7) is to hollow out two halves (each of them scarphed as necessary to get the total length) and then to glue the two halves together before shaping the outside. Some sparmakers prefer to start by shaping the outside of each half before hollowing them out, but either way it is notoriously difficult to hollow the halves out accurately, and templates must be used at frequent intervals to check the section. It is not usual to provide the two halves by sawing down the middle of a pole, but to work from baulks of timber. Fig. 8.8 shows a variation in which each half is built of two square-sectioned pieces glued together. With either of these 'dug-out' systems it is easy for the mast to have a straight taper and for the wall thickness to be varied in proportion to the outside diameter, but because of the large amount of taper they waste a great deal of wood in the upper part.

Less wood is wasted if the mast is fabricated from staves or planks that have been planed to a constant thickness, the taper being formed by reducing the width of the staves and bending them inwards, as in a barrel. Fig. 8.9 shows two sections used for the masts of Bermudian rigs, but these cannot be fully rounded without more internal structure or very thick walls. System b is designed to be assembled in one gluing operation.

A Chinese mast with round sections and the recommended amount of taper and wall thickness (see p 129) cannot be built up of four planks in this way without either (a) using very thick planks as in Fig. 8.10, in which case the thickness as well as the width of the planks may be reduced near the masthead, or (b) fitting substantial corner fillets as in Fig. 8.11. The fillets can be smaller if the mast is designed with radiused-corner square sections in its lower parts, becoming fully circular only near the masthead. Fig. 8.12 shows the sections of a four-plank mast of the latter type built for *Sumner* (Fig. 16.6). The wall thickness is 1½ in (38 mm) throughout, which gives less than the normal wall thickness on the lower mast. The section remains constant between partners and step, and is stiffened by a diaphragm of ½ in (13 mm) plywood at the partners and a spruce plug at the heel. This mast has given satisfactory service for 12 years, cruising between Scotland and Spain, but it was

Sumner in 1972, reaching with three panels reefed. Note the three-panel head portion. (Photo: H. G. Hasler)

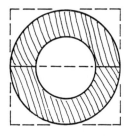

Fig. 8.7   Dug-out mast (1)

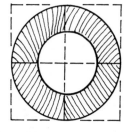

Fig. 8.8   Dug-out mast (2)

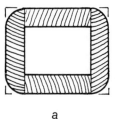

a

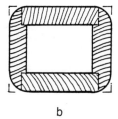

b

Fig. 8.9   Conventional hollow mast sections

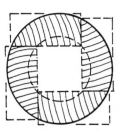

Fig. 8.10   Four-plank circular section (1)

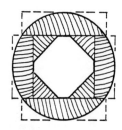

Fig. 8.11   Four-plank circular section (2)

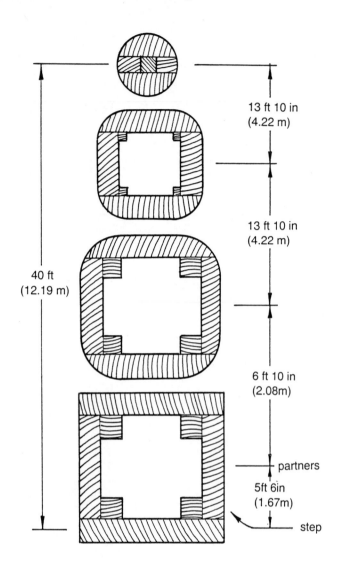

13 ft 10 in
(4.22 m)

13 ft 10 in
(4.22 m)

40 ft
(12.19 m)

6 ft 10 in
(2.08m)

partners

5ft 6in
(1.67m)

step

Fig. 8.12 *Sumner's* four-plank mast

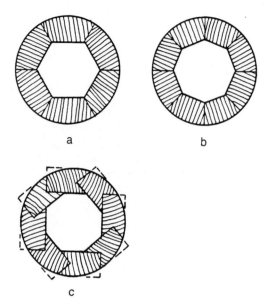

Fig. 8.13   Staved mast sections

not particularly easy to build and would perhaps be better with circular sections from the boom upwards.

All stave or plank masts should have barrel tapering (Fig. 8.2) in the vicinity of the partners in order to give the staves an easy bend. The sophisticated staved sections shown in Fig. 8.13 offer the best mechanical properties. Fig. 8.13a shows the 'Noble' system, invented by Barry Noble, patented by R. Mason & Son of Bristol. This arrangement offers wide gluing surfaces and is self-jigging. The whole mast is assembled and glued in one operation, using giant hose clips that pass right round the spar. Tapering is achieved by adjusting the width of the staves. It is possible, but not usual, to vary the thickness of the staves as well as their width. This may well be the best system yet devised for building a hollow timber mast, but calls for specialist skills and experience.

For a simple job we must revert to one of the dug-out sections shown in Figs. 8.7 and 8.8, and this is assumed from now on.

Gluing

Built masts have relatively large gluing areas. This means that the glued joints are not very heavily stressed, but it does not mean that any old gluing job will do. Badly glued joints may fail without warning, and this has happened even on masts that were professionally built.

The two surfaces to be joined must obviously mate exactly, but their final finish should be with sandpaper rather than the plane. Cramping-up requires a great number of cramps but not too much pressure, in order to avoid squeezing too much glue out of the joint.

The choice of glue is not easy. New resin glues appear on the market with remarkable claims about their strength, resistance to water and fungus, ability to endure boiling for three hours, and so on. Relatively few yachtsmen boil their masts, and no timber mast should get saturated with water unless the boat sinks, but it does have to endure continual flexing, calling for a glue that remains at least as flexible as the timber. Also, depending on where you are, it may have to suffer tropical heat or arctic frost, or both.

There is a difference between gluing up test samples in a dry, warm laboratory and gluing up a 50 ft (15 m) mast in mid-winter in a damp building shed. If a glue requires a certain temperature and dryness in order to cure properly, don't choose that glue without making sure that these conditions can be provided.

There are various aspects of timing. A glue may have a shelf life (maximum time from factory to use), and is certain to have a pot life (maximum time between mixing it and use) and a cramp-up time (maximum time between spreading and cramping-up). The two latter times will be affected by ambient temperature, but don't assume that by choosing a cold day you will give yourself plenty of time: the glue may not cure at all.

In 1953, when *Jester*'s hollow spruce mast was ordered from Camper & Nicholson's, we asked what they were going to glue it with, as there were already several powerful resin glues on the market. They replied that they had been gluing up hollow spars for 50 years with casein (a glue derived from milk), and as they had never yet had a glue failure they were going to go on using what they knew would work. It did. Five years later the mast was lengthened at another yard by scarphing a length on to the top, this time with a modern resin glue. This worked too. It seems that what matters is not so much the type of glue as the knowledge and skill of the person who is using it. Epoxy resin glues are now said to give the most reliable joints.

One or two built masts to our design have carried away when very heavily stressed, and on these it has sometimes been found that part of a glued joint has separated. This should be impossible. A properly glued joint should never separate along the glue line, but should tear the fibres of the wood away first. These faulty joints were probably due to exceeding either the pot life or the cramp-up time, or to gluing in conditions that were too cold and damp.

Preservation of a timber mast

When the wood is fully seasoned it has reached its prime condition, and we want to keep it that way. The things that may defeat us are embrittlement, rot, and chafe.

EMBRITTLEMENT is a subject rarely discussed. If, after years of service, a timber mast should begin to suffer from embrittlement, the symptoms are that the wood, although quite free from rot, loses its fibre strength and becomes brittle and easily broken. This is said to be due to the flexing action forcing all the resin out of the grain of the wood. We do not know of any way of detecting it, short of breaking the mast.

Some species suffer from embrittlement more than others, the worst being Common Spruce. Douglas fir is good, having a high resin content, and Scots pine is average. (See p 124.)

For a grown mast, the recommended treatment is to brush plenty of raw linseed oil into it after it has been shaped. This reduces the risk of shakes and of embrittlement. Good results have also been obtained by periodically rubbing in a 50 per cent mixture of raw linseed oil and vaseline with no other treatment given. It is doubtful whether any treatment is necessary for a built mast, but brushing linseed oil into the outer surface could do no harm, once the glue had cured. After the linseed oil is dry any oil-based paint or varnish may be applied, but it would be necessary to check the compatibility of any synthetic paint or varnish, or of any resin to be used for sheathing.

We have never in fact heard of a Chinese mast that suffered from embrittlement and it may not be a serious risk, except perhaps for a grown mast of Common Spruce.

ROT. Experts define many different kinds of rot that can attack timber, but for our purposes rot can be regarded as the result of the wood remaining saturated with rainwater, particularly in an unventilated crevice such as a shake, and at the partners or step.

The raw linseed oil treatment is said to give no direct protection against rot, but will give indirect protection by inhibiting the absorption of rainwater. Other fluids are available which give direct protection. Tar-based liquids such as creosote are effective but usually ruled out because of their colour and messiness, and because any paint applied over them, even years later, will quickly discolour.

Other preservatives are available, but it would again be necessary to check their compatibility with any proposed painting, gluing, or sheathing specifications. In fact very few of our masts have had any preservative treatment, and it cannot be regarded as normal.

Paint or varnish applied to dry wood will inhibit the entry of moisture but if it does enter, either through local surface damage or from the other side of the wood, it may encourage rot by preventing the wood from drying out. In the case of a hollow mast there can be little objection to treating the inner surfaces with a preservative which can be poured in after gluing-up, rotating and tilting the mast over a period of days so as to get all the inner surfaces properly impregnated.

CHAFE. The heaviest lateral forces on the mast occur at the partners, where it is normally held fixed by softwood wedges. With a softwood mast we recommend gluing a sheath of marine-grade plywood ⅛ in (3 mm) thick round the mast in way of the wedges, of course with its major grain vertical, as in Fig. 8.18. This prevents bruising of the mast by the wedges, and gives it a little bit of extra strength at the fulcrum. It is given the same coating as the rest of the mast.

A more potent source of chafe is the abrasion of the mast by the yard, battens, boom, rope parrels and mast lift. When the boat is pitching heavily, or rolling on a run, or slatting in a calm, each of these tends to chafe the mast in some place. The paint or varnish may eventually get rubbed away, allowing the wood underneath to get chafed in its turn. There is no way of completely preventing such chafe, but various expedients to reduce it are suggested in the sections on yard, battens, boom, and parrels, and on the technique of sailing with the rig. These measures are palliatives rather than cures. The main insurance against chafe can be to give the mast a good coat of paint or varnish, or rather several coats built up according to the makers' instructions and given plenty of time to harden, subsequently touched up from time to time in the chafed areas. We have used synthetic paints and varnishes on masts but have reverted to traditional oil-based yacht enamels and varnishes, which seem to perform better and to be easier to touch up. White paint is the best colour for a mast, particularly in hot climates, because it reduces the heat absorption in sunlight.

SHEATHING. A much better anti-chafe protection for a wooden mast, which also reduces or eliminates maintenance, is to sheathe the whole thing in reinforced plastic. We have done this with glass cloth and polyester resin, but with indifferent results. Sometimes the sheathing has developed cracks and begun to separate, allowing rainwater to enter, and on more than one mast we have subsequently stripped off all the sheathing and reverted to a painted surface. Sheathing that can crack and separate from the timber is a serious danger when sailing, since the rope parrels could jam in it and prevent the sail from being reefed or furled.

Epoxy resin should be used in preference to polyester, and synthetic cloth may be better than glass cloth. Obviously the sheathing must adhere very strongly to the wood, must tolerate indefinite flexing, and must have a reasonably smooth outer surface. Any seams should be kept to a minimum and should be vertical. As with all synthetic resins, it is vital to provide correct conditions of temperature and humidity when laying-up, and expert advice should be sought. Sheathing is more suited to a built mast than a grown one. It is not regarded as adding appreciably to the strength of the mast.

Cable fastening

In addition to the lightning conductor discussed in Chapter 5, most owners will want to run one or more lengths of insulated flex to the masthead for lights and possibly instruments. With grown masts these may be fitted as in Fig. 5.11, preferably on the opposite side to the lightning conductor. With hollow masts the cables should be secured at frequent intervals with saddles and small brass screws to the inside surface before gluing up, as in Fig. 5.12 except that they may emerge through the mast wall at right angles rather than at a gentle slope.

The disadvantage of this system is that the cables cannot be inspected or replaced. If a new or additional

flex is subsequently needed it may be necessary to leave it loose inside the mast, or to spline it into the outer surface as in Fig. 5.11.

Designing and drawing a hollow mast

With the 'dug-out' system the walls may be thickened locally as desired, but no part of a hollow mast is left completely solid. The 'solid' parts at the masthead and at the bottom of the mast have sizeable holes right through the centre. Fig. 8.14 shows in longitudinal section the recommended design for a mast to be built by one of the systems shown in Fig. 8.7 or 8.8.

For convenience, masts are drawn to two different scales on the same drawing: a small scale for all longitudinal measurements and a larger scale (usually full size or half size) for all transverse measurements. Any diagonal line on the drawing will appear distorted in slope. For example, in Fig. 8.14 the curves at the top and bottom of the hollowed part appear to be sharp, but in fact are very gentle.

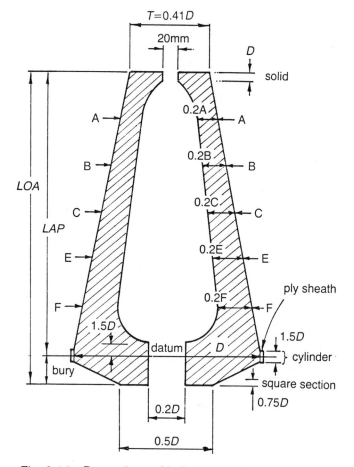

Fig. 8.14   Proportions of hollow dug-out mast

The drawing starts from a datum line at right angles to the mast and passing through the point at which the centreline of the mast intersects the plane of the top of the deck or coachroof. From the profile drawing of the rig you can measure the length of the mast above this line, and we call this the 'LAP' (length above partners).

From the boat, or from her construction drawings, you next measure the bury, the distance from the datum to the heel of the mast, allowing for the structure of the mast step which is normally built up above the boat's keelson (see p 145). The mast's LOA (length overall) will be LAP plus bury, and a suitable longitudinal scale may now be chosen to suit your tracing paper.

The datum line will normally be at the centre of the sheathing for the mast wedges, as in Fig. 8.14. If the mast is to be supported at an appreciable height above the deck, for example by raised partners (see p 144) or a tabernacle (see p 148) a raised datum line should be defined thereby reducing the LAP and increasing the bury. In order not to overstress the mast and the partners, we stipulate that the bury should be at least 10 per cent of the LAP or (say) at least 9 per cent of the LOA, but the more bury the better. If it would be less than this minimum, then some form of raised partners should be used to increase it and reduce the LAP. The mast shown in Fig. 8.14 has nearly the minimum permissible bury.

DIAMETER OF MAST. The maximum diameter D of the mast is at the datum line (or raised datum line), and this diameter remains constant for a distance of $0.75D$ above and below it, so that this part of the mast is cylindrical over a total length of $1.5D$, as in Fig. 8.14. The whole of this cylinder is sheathed with $\frac{1}{8}$ in (3 mm) marine plywood, glued on with its major grain vertical.

The measurement D is obtained either by calculation or from a graph, by entering with LAP and sail area, but it has been found in practice that a foremast has to withstand relatively heavier loading than a mainmast or mizzen. Given the same LAP and sail area, D for a foremast should be about 1.13 times that of a mainmast or mizzen, and this is reflected in the following formulae.

(a) Imperial units:

mainmast or mizzen $D = (LAP + 2\sqrt{SA})/7.1$

foremast $\qquad D = (LAP + 2\sqrt{SA})/6.3$

where D is in inches, LAP in feet, and SA (sail area) in square feet

(b) Metric units:

mainmast or mizzen $D = (LAP + 2\sqrt{SA})/0.85$

foremast $\qquad D = (LAP + 2\sqrt{SA})/0.75$

where D is in centimetres, LAP in metres, and SA in square metres

For the sizes of mast most frequently used in small cruising boats, Fig. 8.15 and 8.16 (imperial and metric respectively) enable D to be derived graphically, either as an alternative method or as a check on calculated results. Note that the figure at the top of each curve is different from that at the bottom, and that the former refers to a mainmast or mizzen while the latter refers to a foremast. A single mast counts as a mainmast. Where necessary D should be rationalised to the nearest $\frac{1}{4}$ in or 5 mm. For example, from Fig. 8.15, a mainmast whose LAP is 36 ft and SA 400 sq ft would have a D of approx. 10.7 in, rationalised to $10\frac{3}{4}$ in. From Fig. 8.16, a foremast whose LAP is 9.3 m and SA 24 m² would have a D of approx. 25.35 cm, rationalised to 25.5 cm.

DIAMETER OF MAST AT MASTHEAD (T). This is $0.41D$. For example, if D is 28 cm, $T = 28 \times 0.41 = 11.48$, rationalised to 11.5 cm.

DIMENSIONS OF MAST AT HEEL. The heel of the mast is made square in section for a distance of about $0.75D$ up from the bottom, after which it blends rapidly into a circular section. The sides of the square at the heel measure $0.5D$, as shown in Fig. 8.14, and the bottom surface is flat, with no tenon.

It is now possible to draw the straight tapers that join the partners to the masthead and the heel, thus defining all the outside dimensions of the mast, as in Fig. 8.14.

STATIONS. The mast should now be divided into the stations (lines at right angles to the long axis) at which the transverse measurements are to be taken. Stations are drawn at the masthead, datum line, and heel. The part between datum and masthead should be divided by four or five stations whose spacing is roughly equal but which has been chosen so as to avoid fractional measurements. Fig. 8.17 shows a dimensioned mast drawing in which five stations have been arranged at intervals of 1.7 m, 1.6 m, 1.5 m, 1.5 m, 1.5 m, and 1.5 m, to make up a total LAP of 9.3 m. The outside diameters and wall thicknesses at these stations will inevitably be fractional; work to the nearest $\frac{1}{16}$ in or 2 mm.

WALL THICKNESS. On the hollow part of the mast the wall thickness is drawn at 20 per cent of the outside diameter at any particular station, therefore becoming less as the outside diameter decreases, as in Fig. 8.14. At each station, measure the outside diameter, divide it by 5 to get the wall thickness, and mark both measurements in figures at each station, as in Fig. 8.17. If working in inches it is easier to use decimals of an inch for the calculation, converting to and from decimals with the table given in Appendix B.

SOLID PORTIONS. The top of the mast is made solid for a length equal to D, with a hole of about $\frac{3}{4}$ in (20 mm) diameter right through the centre for electric cables and lightning conductor. The bottom of the mast is made

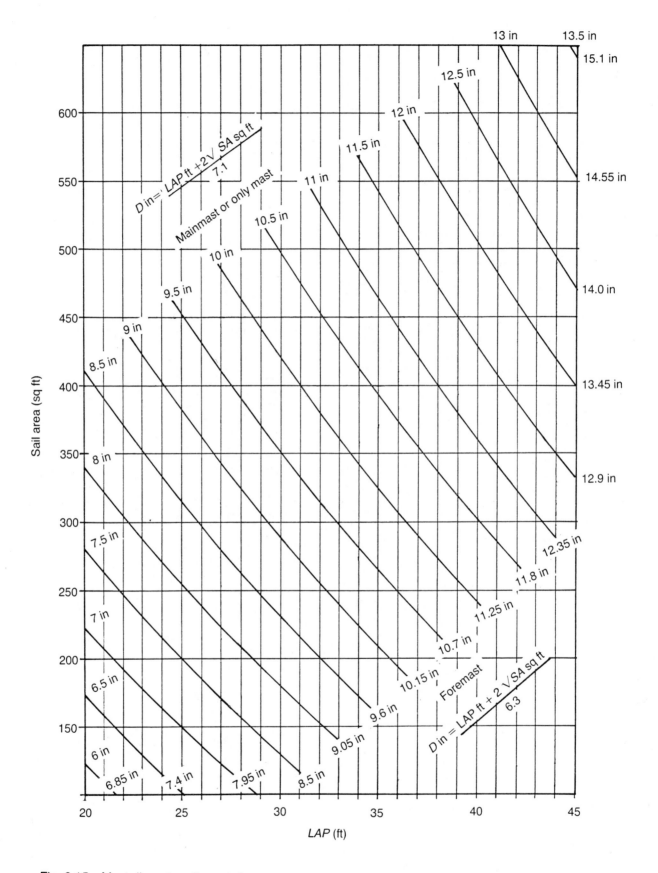

Fig. 8.15   Mast diameters (imperial)

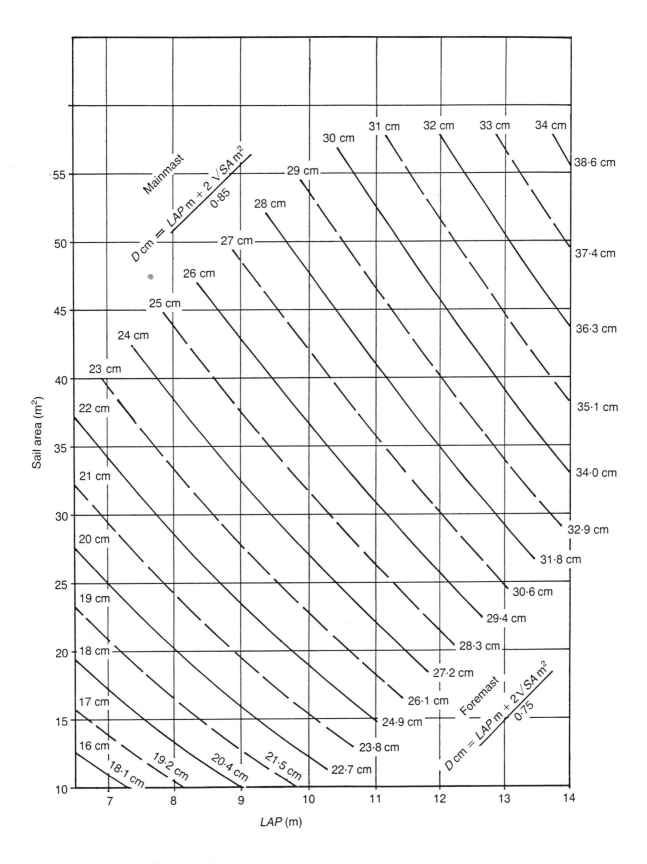

Fig. 8.16   Mast diameters (metric)

solid from the heel to a point that is about 1.5D above the datum line, and has a hole of diameter about 0.2D right through the centre. At each end of the hollow part of the mast the wall thickness is graded into a gentle curve to pick up the wall thickness of the solid parts, as shown in Fig. 8.17. This can safely be left to the sparmaker to do by eye, and does not need dimensioned plotting.

SECTION. A specimen circular section should be superimposed on one of the middle stations, as shown in Fig. 8.17.

CABLES. All cables that are to be fitted inside the mast must be specified and positioned on the drawing. At their lower exit holes either permanent vertical battens, thicker than the cable, should be pinned and glued to the mast to prevent the cables from being damaged against the partners when stepping or unstepping the mast, or the loose cable should be tightly strapped or taped to the mast. Obviously, it is the first few inches of cable emerging from the mast that need positive protection. If the cable gets damaged lower down it can be repaired by joining on a new piece.

The lightning conductor will probably leave the forward or after side of the mast low down and at 30° to the vertical (Fig. 5.12). Any remaining cables for lights, instruments, or radio transmitter may emerge from the mast horizontally just below the ply sheath, but well clear of the bottom ends of any mast wedges. From here they may be led up to junction boxes on the deckhead.

An aerial for a wireless receiver may also be fitted inside the mast.

SPECIMEN MAST DRAWINGS. Fig. 8.17 shows a specimen drawing of a foremast whose LAP is 9.3 m, bury 1.2 m, and sail area 24 m^2. The reader may work out from the preceding pages how the dimensions on the drawing were derived.

Fig. 8.18 shows the lower part of this mast redrawn with its vertical and horizontal scales the same, to enable the cable exits and other detail to be shown more clearly. This could be added as an inset to the mast drawing, or as a separate drawing. Each drawing should show its scale(s), its title or number, and the date. Each mast should be named, and the drawing marked 'FWD' and 'AFT', and in due course the mast itself should be marked in this way at the heel. If you need two masts they may be shown side by side on one drawing, or on separate sheets, but in either case they should be drawn to the same scales.

Designing a hollow staved timber mast

A staved mast (see p 125) should be designed in collaboration with the sparmaker, who will have experi-

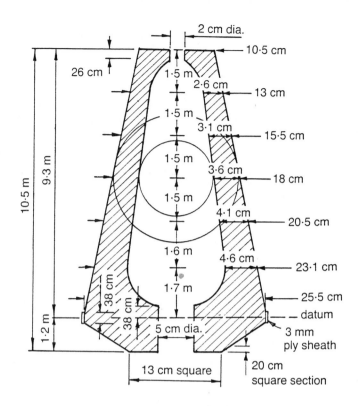

Fig. 8.17   Dimensioned mast drawing

ence of the system to be used. The maximum diameter D and the masthead diameter T may be calculated as for a dug-out mast, and the wall thickness should be based on the dug-out figures even though it may have to be constant throughout. In place of the solid portions, short plugs should be glued into the masthead and heel, and a strong diaphragm with a central hole in it glued in at datum level to take the fulcrum loads at the partners.

The taper in the vicinity of the partners will have to be barrelled rather than straight (see p 126), and it may be advisable to reduce or eliminate the taper between partners and heel in order to avoid too sharp a bend below the partners. The heel may have a circular rather than a square section, relying on the holding-down bolt to prevent the mast from turning.

A ply sheath should be fitted at the partners, as before, but may require tailoring to fit the barrel taper. Internal cables and lightning conductor should again be fastened to the inside of the mast before gluing-up.

Designing a grown mast

As suggested on p 124, a grown mast of good quality timber may have diameters that are 90 per cent of those of a hollow mast. The grown mast may therefore be drawn to these corrected figures, with straight tapers,

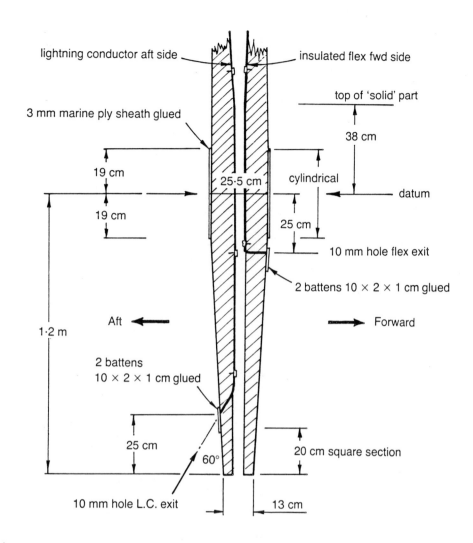

lightning conductor aft side

insulated flex fwd side

3 mm marine ply sheath glued

top of 'solid' part

38 cm

19 cm

25·5 cm

cylindrical

datum

19 cm

25 cm

10 mm hole flex exit

2 battens 10 × 2 × 1 cm glued

Aft

Forward

1·2 m

2 battens
10 × 2 × 1 cm glued

25 cm

60°

20 cm square section

10 mm hole L.C. exit

13 cm

Fig. 8.18   Lower part of mast from Fig. 8.17

squared heel, and ply sheath all as in Fig. 8.14. The cables and lightning conductor will be sunk into the outer surfaces as in Fig. 5.11, with the ply sheath glued over them.

Mast fittings

All mast fittings must be either above the yard or below the boom when under full sail. The length of mast in between must be clear and smooth so as to allow the battens and parrels to slide freely up and down. With a timber mast of anything over dinghy size it is usual to combine all the upper fittings into a single masthead fitting as in Fig. 8.19, which shows a fitting suitable for a sail of 150–300 sq ft (14–28 m²). Fig. 8.20 (a and b) shows a stronger fitting suitable for a sail of 300–600 sq ft (28–56 m²). Each is built up on a watertight cap of

10-gauge (⅛ in or 3 mm) metal designed to fit tightly over the individual masthead and held fixed by four wood screws (W) arranged radially near its lower edge. The heavier design has an internal anti-twist web (J) that fits into a slot in the top of the wooden mast and is offset so as to clear the exit hole. These fittings may be fabricated out of stainless steel or, more reliably, out of mild steel hot-dip galvanised.

Each of these fittings provides one halyard crane (H), two tangs for topping lifts (T), and one for the mast lift (M). The topping-lift tangs in Fig. 8.19 point 45° forward of the beam on either side, whereas those in Fig. 8.20 point athwartships. The former is preferable if the lifts are to be crossed over on the forward side of the mast as in Fig. 3.58a.

In order to lie clear of the topping-lifts, the mast lift tang (M) points athwartships in Fig. 8.19 and 45° forward in Fig. 8.20.

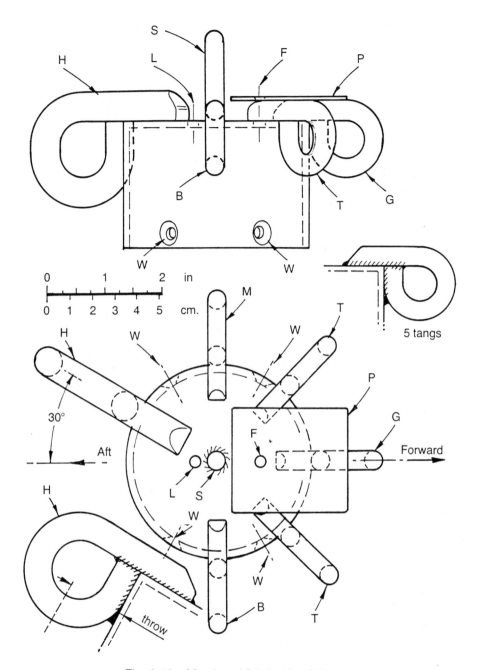

Fig. 8.19   Masthead fabrication (1)

In plan view the halyard, topping-lifts, and mast lift have to twist 90° either way round the mast as the sail swings from amidships to the squared-off position to port or starboard. In order to cope fairly with this twist, the crane and tangs at the masthead should be formed of vertical loops of round-sectioned bar, the loops having sufficient internal diameter to pass the bosses of the shackles so that the shackle pins hang downwards as in Fig. 8.21. The boss of an ordinary screw shackle is roughly twice the diameter of the metal forming the bow of the shackle, and these tangs will permit the shackles to have a small amount of twist, as shown, as well as unlimited swing in any direction. The bar from which the tangs are made should have a diameter of at least 1.1D, to allow for some wear in old age.

Masthead shackles should be of either stainless or galvanised steel. Bronze shackles have been found to show too much wear in this position. It is advisable to design the masthead fitting around the shackles and blocks that you intend to use.

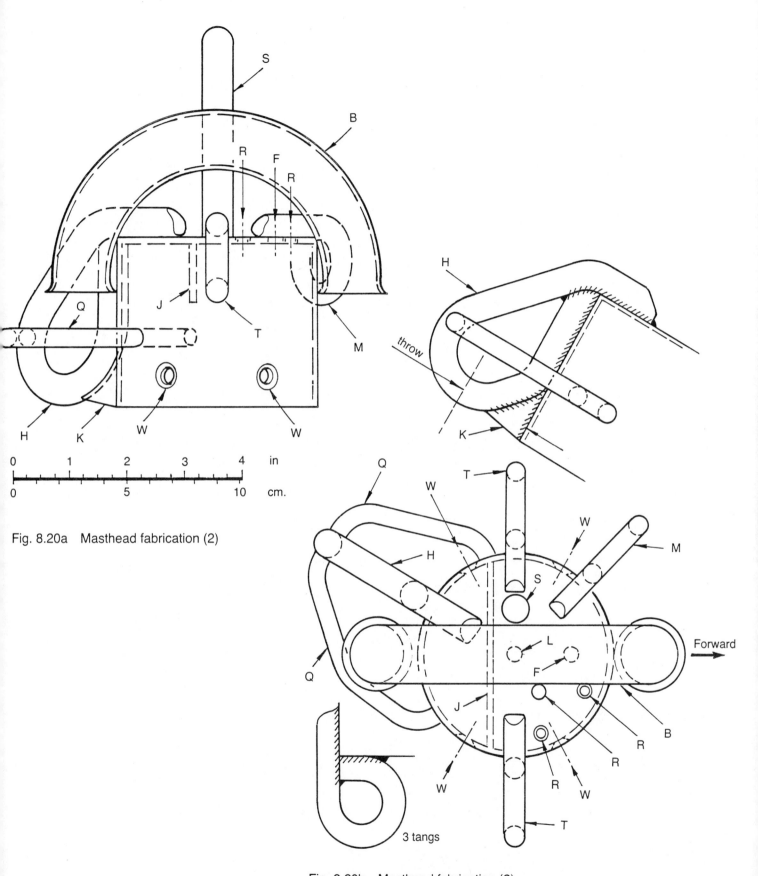

Fig. 8.20a   Masthead fabrication (2)

Fig. 8.20b   Masthead fabrication (2)

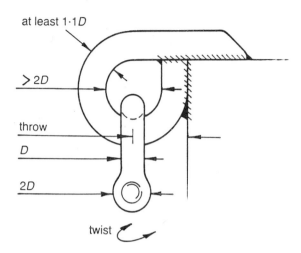

Fig. 8.21 Masthead shackle

In Fig. 8.19 a tang (B) for the burgee halyard points abeam to starboard and is made strong enough to carry a jury halyard if necessary. Shackled to it will be a relatively large block through which the small burgee halyard is rove. If a jury halyard or gantline is needed, the burgee halyard may be used to pull a sizeable rope through this block.

In Fig. 8.20 the burgee halyard is led through a large-bore bell-mouthed tube (B) arching over the top of the fitting, and may be used to pull a jury halyard or gantline through this tube from either direction.

In Fig. 8.19 an additional tang (G) is provided pointing forward, to carry a block for a ghoster halyard (see Chapter 5).

HALYARD CRANE. As discussed on p 32, the crane points towards the port quarter rather than straight aft, and the 'throw' of the crane (i.e. the distance it stands off the mast) should be enough to allow the upper halyard block to hang vertically with its *cheek* against the mast, or just clear of the mast, as in Figs. 3.10 and 3.12. The crane in Fig. 8.20 has a metal web (K) supporting its under side and two bent rods (Q) giving additional support against lateral loads, with the starboard rod embracing the burgee halyard.

LIGHTS, INSTRUMENTS, AND LIGHTNING CONDUCTOR. Lights and instruments may be mounted on a horizontal plate attached to the masthead fitting. In Fig. 8.19 this is shown (P) welded to the three forward tangs. In Fig. 8.20 it is a separate plate (not shown) on the starboard side of the fitting, designed *ad hoc* and held to the fitting by machine screws entering the three tapped holes (R).

Both fittings show cable exits (F) for lights or instruments and exits (L) for the lightning conductor. After the fitting is fully assembled on the mast, these should be made watertight with a soft sealing compound.

A stub rod (S) with a rounded end, designed so as not to catch the burgee, is shown as the terminal of the lightning conductor. If no burgee is to be flown, this rod could be longer and pointed, but this is not of great importance. The copper wire of the conductor should be electrically bonded to this rod, perhaps with two hose clips. If a permanent wind sock or wind vane is to be carried in place of a burgee, S may take the form of a tube whose internal diameter will suit the metal upright of the sock.

A scale is given on each drawing, but the diameter of the cap should be adjusted to suit the diameter of the masthead.

For a Chinese-rigged dinghy with a grown mast it is possible to use a dumb hole for the halyard as in Fig. 3.1b, and to shoulder the mast above this so that the lifts may be carried on strops, which should be stapled to the mast to prevent them from coming off when the mast is unstepped.

MAST FITTINGS BETWEEN BOOM AND PARTNERS. Some Chinese sails will be hoisted and lowered from the foot of the mast. With a dinghy sail it is usually convenient to take halyard, yard hauling parrel, and luff hauling parrel (if any) to small jam cleats mounted on

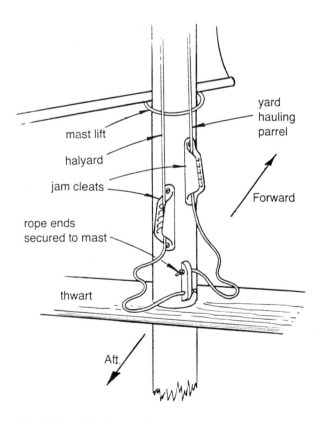

Fig. 8.22 *Hum*'s mast

the mast, or on the boat very close to the mast. Fig. 8.22 shows the arrangement used on *Hum* (Fig. 16.8), where no luff hauling parrel is fitted.

At the other end of the scale, very large Chinese sails (say of more than 700 sq ft, or 65 m²) may use a single-part wire halyard led to a drum or crab winch mounted near the mast, as in Fig. 3.3. In this case provision should also be made for handling the hauling parrels from the same position. A good arrangement would be to have a crab winch on deck for the wire halyard and self-tailing winches mounted on the mast for the hauling parrels. All three should of course lead down through the so-called 'chimney' (Fig. 3.6) on the starboard side of the mast.

On small cruising yachts it is normal to lead all running ropes (except burgee halyards) from a mainmast or a foremast aft to the cockpit, and this involves using turning blocks on or near the mast. These may be either cheek blocks secured flat against the starboard side of the mast, or ordinary blocks mounted on deck eyes positioned near the mast. Deck blocks make it easier to lead the ropes close along the deck on their way aft, whereas cheek blocks make it possible to lead the ropes much higher. Cheek blocks cannot be placed very low on the mast without interfering with the mast coat (see p 142). Fig. 8.23 shows how the ropes may thus be led either over or under an obstruction such as a dinghy stowed on deck.

If deck blocks are used there may be no fittings on the lower part of the mast. The deck layout is discussed in Chapter 13.

If cheek blocks are used they must be carefully positioned so as to give the rope a fair lead, and this is best achieved by aligning them after the mast has been stepped. It should be possible to place your eye close to the after end of the taut rope, near the cleat, and to see the

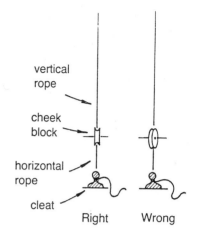

Fig. 8.24 Alignment of cheek block (1)

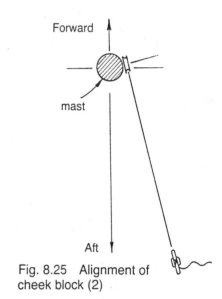

Fig. 8.25 Alignment of cheek block (2)

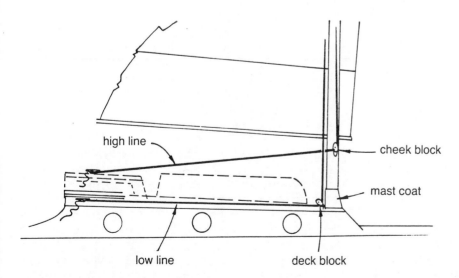

Fig. 8.23 High and low rope lines

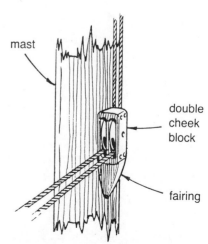

Fig. 8.26 Double cheek block with fairing piece

sheave exactly end-on and appearing to be in a straight line with the upper part of the rope, as in Fig. 8.24. Usually the ropes will be led to one side of the cockpit, in which case the cheek blocks cannot be aligned fore-and-aft on the side of the mast, but will have to be canted so as to point at the rope's destination, as shown exaggerated in Fig. 8.25.

Proprietary turning blocks, commonly used for leading conventional headsail sheets to a winch, may be used for the cheek blocks. Some are available in double form while others may be assembled in stacks of two or three sheaves if required. If two or three single cheek blocks are used it may be difficult to get a clear lead for all the ropes, and a stack may be preferable. A shaped wooden pad may be used to provide a flat mounting at the required angle on the side of a round mast. With a dug-out mast a flat may be left standing proud, to be finished later at the required angle.

It is seamanlike to fit an anti-snarl fairing (Fig. 8.26) to prevent a slack rope from getting a turn under the cheek block, and this may be a wooden pad, as shown.

SPARE CLEAT. When working on a sail whose halyard is led aft, for example when bending or unbending the sail or adjusting the batten parrels, it is convenient to be able to hoist and lower the sail progressively while standing by the mast, without having to go aft to belay the halyard and yard hauling parrel. Some users fit a spare cleat on the mast for this purpose, large enough to take both the halyard and the yard hauling parrel. If it is placed low down and towards the starboard bow it can lie clear of the normal rope leads, but it should have anti-snarl fairings when not in use. Fig. 8.27 shows a form of quick-release fairing consisting of two loose wooden blocks held together by a double length of shock cord.

NAVIGATION LIGHTS. On some boats it has been found convenient to fit a combined port-and-starboard light on the forward side of the mast a short way below the furled position of the boom. This may be the best position for a boat with no pulpit or guardrails and a high boom.

Masts of other materials

Wooden masts seem unattractive to many boat owners because of difficulties in manufacture, uncertainty about the quality of the timber and the gluing, the relatively large diameter and windage, the soft surface which is vulnerable to chafe, and the need for annual maintenance.

Unstayed Chinese masts may be built from other materials, but should be designed by someone with full experience of the material and its limitations. Their

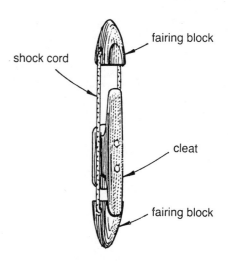

Fig. 8.27   Anti-snarl fairing for cleat

design should be related to the design of the equivalent timber mast and must not have any less strength or stiffness. Other points to be considered are diameter, weight, height of CG, fatigue, chafe, and corrosion.

LIGHT-ALLOY MASTS. Extruded light-alloy tube is the commonest mast material for conventional yachts, and is used successfully on many junk rigs. Lengths of alloy extrusion may be joined end-to-end with internal sleeves located by pop rivets. Different grades of alloy have different tensile strengths and different corrosion resistance, and the mast design must specify the grade required. For a one-off job it is often difficult to obtain the required extrusions in the small quantities needed. Alloy lamp-posts and flagpoles have been used successfully as masts, but it is important to ensure that the alloy is suitable for marine use and the construction is suitable for an unstayed mast.

Some alloy masts of high-tensile material have a maximum diameter that is not much more than half that of the equivalent hollow spruce mast. This has appeared to give an improved performance to windward, particularly on the port tack when the mast is to leeward of the sail, but these trial results are tentative.

The practical advantages of alloy masts include freedom from maintenance, better radar reflection, elimination of mast chafe, and reduction of chafe on sails, battens, spars, and parrels. No separate lightning conductor is needed (see p 82).

Tapered alloy tubes may be fabricated by cutting and welding a cylindrical tube, but only at the expense of reduced strength. Welded tapers are normally used only in the upper part of a mast. Extruded tapered tubes are inherently stronger, being extruded in one seamless piece. They have a straight taper and may be used on the highly-stressed part of the mast if the material has adequate tensile strength. If obtainable in long enough lengths they may be used in one piece, with the penalty of having to accommodate the large butt end at the mast step and making provision for passing it through the partners.

In a more usual arrangement, the mast consists of a parallel cylindrical tube from the step to a point about halfway up, and is then jointed to a tapered extrusion, or alternatively is tapered at the top by cutting and welding.

It will not usually be necessary to make up a multiple masthead fitting as shown in Fig. 8.19 and 8.20. If standard eyeplates are available with their bases radiused to suit the mast diameter they may be riveted directly to the mast. The eyeplate for the halyard will commonly need to be larger than the others in order to get enough throw (see p 136). Alternatively, it may be necessary to fabricate a separate halyard crane based on those shown in Fig. 8.19 and 8.20.

If you are forced to accept an eye with inadequate throw, an extra shackle should be inserted as in Fig. 8.28. This of course requires a block capable of taking the pin of the shackle across rather than in line with the plane of the sheaves. The alternative would be to use two extra shackles (total: three shackles) if the amount of drift permitted it. Do not on any account use swivel blocks at the masthead or on the yard; they will invariably twist up and jam the purchase. Note again the correct attitude of the upper halyard block, with its *pin* pointing towards the centre of the mast.

Where the width of their baseplates would prevent all the eyeplates from being at the same level, one or more may be put at a lower level. Fig. 8.29 shows a masthead for a 22 ft (6.7 m) cruising boat, in which the eye for the mast lift (M) has been lowered for this reason. The single topping-lift eye (T) carries both lifts on a single shackle and is placed well down the forward side of the mast as in Fig. 3.58b, thus bringing the line of the lifts further forward in relation to the peak of the close-reefed sail. Eyeplate G is for a ghoster halyard, H for the main halyard, and B for the burgee/jury halyard. The top of the mast is plugged with a light-alloy casting (C) carrying the lightning-conductor rod (S) and the platform (P) for a masthead light, whose cable emerges through the hole (A).

The heel of the mast tube may be plugged with an alloy casting located by self-tapping screws unless the form of step shown in Fig. 9.14 is to be used, in which case it should preferably be fitted with an external strengthening sleeve.

Insulated cables leading to the masthead for lights or instruments cannot be fastened to the inside walls of the tube, and if left loose will make an intolerable noise when the boat is at anchor by tapping against the mast as she rolls. They may be restrained by hauling bundles of,

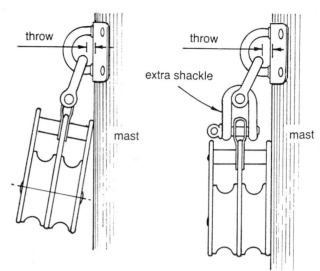

Fig. 8.28 Extra shackle on masthead block

for instance, plastic sacking up inside the mast to press the cables against the walls at intervals of about 3 ft (1 m).

Tubular masts may be strengthened locally, e.g. at the partners, by sleeving a larger-diameter tube over them or a smaller diameter tube inside them. Such sleeves should be a good fit and located by pop rivets.

COMPOSITE MASTS. Satisfactory masts have been built by fitting a tapered timber top portion into an untapered tubular bottom portion. The inside diameter of the tube should be as great as the diameter of a standard solid timber mast at the height of the joint. The larger the internal diameter of the tube the lower the joint may be. The timber 'topmast' should then have enough extra diameter to enable it to be shouldered out to the outside diameter of the tube, and it should extend down inside the tube for a distance of at least four times the diameter. This part should be treated with wood preservative, and although it will probably swell and become immovable it should be located by a couple of wood screws countersunk flush in the wall of the tube. The timber upper part should be tapered in the usual way. Larch would be the preferred timber for this topmast.

STEEL MASTS. If the corrosion problem can be overcome, it is believed that steel tube masts are very suitable for junk rig, particularly in the larger sizes. Tapering the upper part of the mast by cutting and welding may be done with less loss of strength than with a light-alloy mast, and fittings may be attached by either riveting or welding. Other details would be similar to those of light-alloy masts.

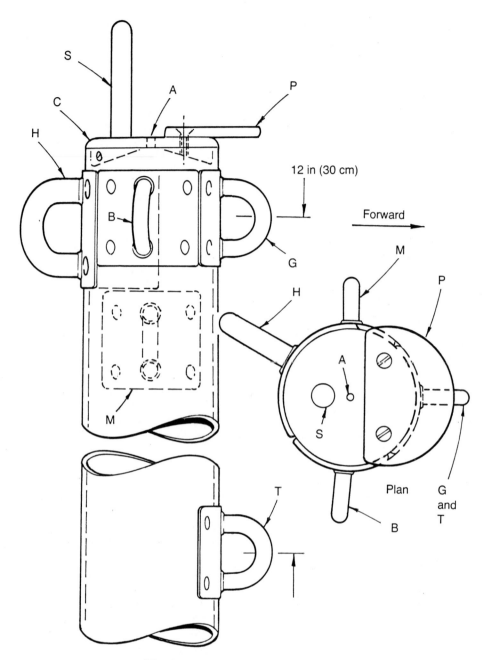

Fig. 8.29   Head of light-alloy mast

REINFORCED-PLASTIC MASTS. Reinforced plastics offer a wide range of possibilities in mast construction. They may be built with any desired taper by laying up on a tapered mandrel.

Normal GRP (glass cloth and polyester resin) does not seem to produce a stiff enough mast without excessive diameter and weight, but various builders are experimenting with variations, particularly the use of carbon fibre. Such masts will require full-length lightning conductors (see p 82) which may be loose inside the mast but restrained, together with other masthead

cables, by some such system as that suggested above.

A multiple masthead fabrication similar to those in Fig. 8.19 and 8.20 will probably be preferred, but cheek blocks and cleats may be secured with self-tapping screws.

Whatever material or type of construction is being considered there must be a mast drawing (if only a rough sketch) to show for each mast the vital dimensions of length (LAP and bury), diameters and thickness to indicate the stiffness and strength required, and the fittings required, before discussions with a sparmaker.

9 Partners and Mast Step

The partners

Although 'partners' has a precise meaning in wooden boat construction, it is used here in a broader sense to mean that part of the hull's structure that supports the mast in the vicinity of its datum line, i.e. at or above the level of the deck. The major horizontal stresses (the fulcrum loads) are sustained here, but even so the loading is relatively light. The junk rig with unstayed mast does not impose heavy loads on the hull.

In a wooden boat with a round-sectioned timber mast the partners may take the form suggested in Fig. 9.1, in which a heavy horizontal piece, the chock (C), forms a round 'mast hole' of larger diameter than the mast. The gap between mast and chock is filled with a ring of mast wedges (W) driven, or rather tapped, down from the top.

The chock should be strongly held between two mast beams (B) and two carlines or partners (U) joining them, the whole being properly assembled with morticed or dovetailed joints, lodging knees, and tie rods as in ordinary shipwright's practice. Some of these features are suggested in Fig. 9.1. The ends of the mast beams must be firmly braced to the deck and hull framing with hanging knees, bulkheads, or partial bulkheads. An elegant method with any form of construction is to provide one or two all-round frames adjacent to each mast, although these may not be necessary in a small boat if the hull is heavily-built. *Pilmer* (Fig. 16.10) has no reinforcement of the deck or coachroof apart from a suitable chock which fills what used to be the forehatch opening.

Most masts will not be exactly square to the plane of the deck: for example, a vertical mainmast stepped through a coachroof that runs down towards the bow, or a forward-raked foremast stepped through a deck that sheers up towards the bow. In all cases the mast hole must of course be parallel to the mast and the line of the top of the wedges should be square to the mast. If the difference in angle is slight it may be accommodated by a slight alteration to the layout shown in Fig. 9.1, but if it is greater the partners may have to be built up as in Fig. 9.2, which shows an arrangement for a forward-raked fore-

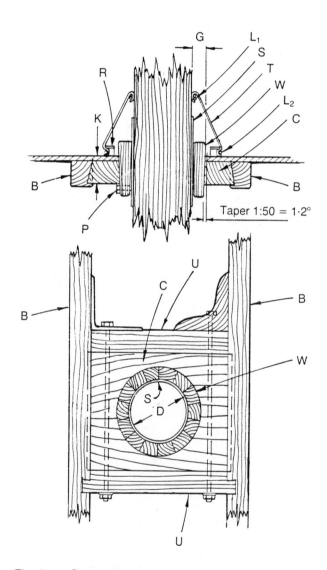

Taper 1:50 = 1·2°

Fig. 9.1   Conventional partners

mast. A substantial pad (Q) takes the main side loads of the wedges (W). The wedges are longer so as to give enough spare length over the maximum depth of bearing

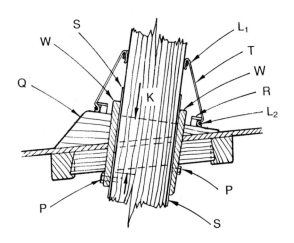

Fig. 9.2   Angled partners

surface (K). Being of equal length they protrude by differing amounts below deck. The length of the ply sheath (S) should also be greater than the standard 1.5D, as shown.

MAST WEDGES. The taper on a mast wedge may be about 1 in 50, a slope of just over 1°, and this is normally all on the outside face as shown in Fig. 9.1. The inside surface of the mast hole should be given the same taper, so that the wedge bears evenly against it. In plan view, the inner face of the wedge should be radiused to fit the curvature of the ply sheath (S), and the outer face to fit the curvature of the mast hole. The side faces of the wedges should be angled radially from the centre of the mast, as shown. The depth (K) of the bearing surface of the chock and decking may vary from about 1 in (25 mm) in a dinghy to about 0.25 of the mast diameter on larger vessels. The gap (G) between mast and bottom of chock should be at least 0.1D all round. When tapped into place the wedges should project by at least 0.5K both above and below the mast hole, i.e. the total length of the finished mast wedges should be at least 2K. Owing to the difficulty of achieving a precise fit with such a slow taper it is preferable to make them longer than this and then to cut off either the top or the bottom, or both, after stepping the mast for trial. This also facilitates making small corrections to the attitude of the mast if the step is not accurately aligned below the partners. After cutting to the finished length all top and bottom edges of the wedges should be chamfered as shown, to reduce the risk of 'mushrooming' and of chafing the mast coat.

The wedges should be of clean-grained softwood, such as spruce, and should of course be seasoned and dry when fitted. Once the mast has been stepped and the boat sailed for some days, the wedges being tapped down periodically, they should be lightly fastened down to avoid any possibility of their working upwards at sea. The simplest way is to nail a small square of

plywood (P) with two brass brads on to the toe of each wedge and bearing against the underside of the chock.

DECK RING. A flanged deck ring (R) is permanently fastened and bedded to the deck, and may be built up of a flat ring of plywood or metal fastened down on top of a thicker ring of plywood. Its internal diameter should be at least 1 in (25 mm) larger than the top of the mast hole so that the wedges cannot touch it, and the groove under the outside of the flange should be of ample size to enable the bottom edge of the mast coat (T) to be pulled in by its lashing L_2.

MAST COAT. A fabric mast coat as shown (T) is the traditional way of waterproofing the partners against the entry of rain and spray. It is normally slid over the heel or the head of the mast before stepping, but if this is impossible its vertical seam may be sewn up *in situ*. Its upper end is seized tightly to the mast by a lashing L_1 which is put on with the mast coat upside-down. The coat is then folded down over L_1 and its lower edge tightly seized into the groove under the flange of the deck ring (R) by means of another lashing L_2. If necessary a little non-hardening sealing compound may then be knifed into the joint between mast and mast coat. The finished coat should not be stretched bar taut, if only because it is bound to get trodden on.

An alternative system would be to caulk or seal all the mating surfaces of the mast wedges, but this is less likely to be effective and may interfere with adjustment of the wedges.

A mast coat should be made of strong material that is waterproof and not subject to ultra-violet degradation. Proofed acrylic cloth is recommended, or traditional flax canvas painted with an oil-based paint. For a neat job, the coat will be made up of three separate pieces of cloth sewn together, as in Fig. 9.3. The top and bottom collars are cylindrical and the middle piece is conical.

The conical piece is designed first, and calls for 'lampshade geometry' as shown in the drawing.

1. Decide on the height (H) of the mast coat above the top of the deck ring. Mark the mast at this chosen line (E). If the mast is not stepped, measure height (H) off your scale drawings so that the top of the coat will lie well above any ply sheath and wedges and well below any mast fittings. The height should be such that the sides of the coat have a steep slope, preferably about 60° to the horizontal or steeper.
2. Measure length X from line E to the outer edge of the deck ring flange. Add about 10 per cent to this measurement to produce a slightly slack coat, and rationalise it to the nearest ¼ in (1 cm).
3. Measure the *circumference* of the mast at E.
4. Measure the *circumference* of the outside edge of the deck ring flange at F.

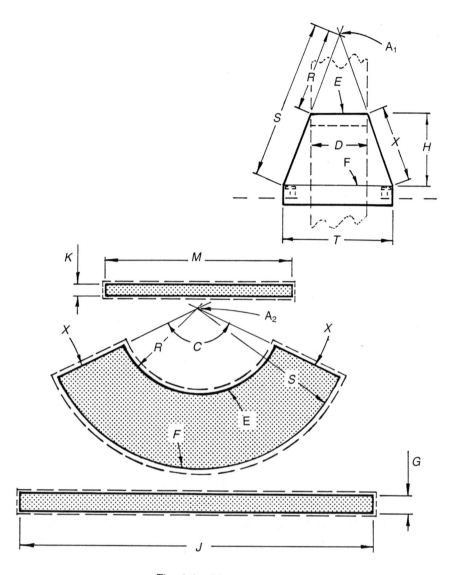

Fig. 9.3   Mast coat

5. To allow for the double thickness of material when the top and bottom collars are sewn on, E and F should be increased by ¾ in (2 cm) and (if using imperial units) converted to inches and decimals of an inch (Appendix B).

6. Calculate R from the formula $R = (X \times E)/(F - E)$. Rationalise R *upwards* to the nearest ⅛ in (3 mm).

7. Calculate S from the formula $S = R + X$.

8. Draw the flat shape of the cloth for the cone, as shown shaded, by striking arcs of radius R and S from a common centre A_2. This defines the top edge E and the bottom edge F of the cone, and the sides X which, if extended, would meet at A_2. The arc required (C) is found from the formula $C° = 180\ F/\pi\ S = 180\ E\ /\pi\ R$ (take π as 3.14). These two results should agree exactly, but are unlikely

to do so because of the rationalisation of measurements and π. If the difference is more than 1° the figures should be checked, particularly the rationalisation of R. If the difference is less than 1°, draw the arc (C) to the nearest whole degree above the largest figure. This will lengthen E and F slightly.

9. The lower cylindrical part may have a depth (G) equal to about 1.5 times the height of the deck ring above the deck, and its length (J) will of course be equal to F as increased in steps 5 and 8. The upper cylindrical part may have a depth (K) equal to about 0.08E and its length (M) will be equal to E as increased in steps 5 and 8.

10. Having marked the cloth to the correct dimensions it remains to allow extra cloth (dotted) along all the

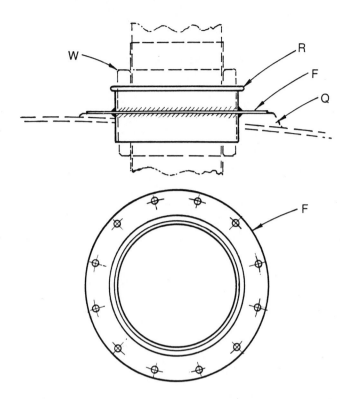

Fig. 9.4   Metal partners

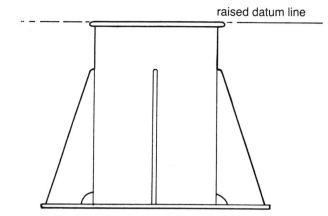

Fig. 9.5   Raised metal partners

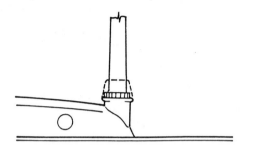

Fig. 9.6   Moulded partners

edges for seaming. You are then strongly recommended to cut the shapes out of paper and glue them together for a check fitting, remembering that the cloth will be thicker.

As an alternative to a fabric mast coat, flexible neoprene mast coats are obtainable.

ALTERNATIVE CONSTRUCTIONS FOR THE PART-NERS. Another good arrangement at the partners is to fabricate a metal cylinder, e.g. from hot-dip galvanised mild steel, as in Fig. 9.4, with a flange (F) for bolting through the strengthened deck. In this example half the cylinder is below the flange, but it may be wholly above it. The flange may be angled to suit the deck, or may be square to the cylinder and mounted on a shaped timber pad (Q), as shown. If the mast is to be stepped close to an obstruction, or to the end of a coachroof, the flange can be shaped to suit it.

A rod (R) welded round its top edge enables a mast coat to be seized underneath, and also strengthens the top edge so that it is capable of taking most of the lateral mast loads. This makes it possible to avoid the complica-tion of tapering the cylinder to match the wedges (W). It may have parallel sides and the wedges will then be compressed mainly at the top, unless the mast is a single tapered extrusion widest at the step, in which case the wedges may have almost the same taper as the mast.

For masts that require raised partners in order to get

enough bury (see p 116) a higher cylindrical fabrication may be used, with a wider deck flange braced by plate webs as suggested in Fig. 9.5.

With a GRP deck or coachroof a cylinder may be moulded *in situ* with or without metal reinforcement. Fig. 9.6 shows such a cylinder moulded into the forward end of a coachroof, whose internal structure will no doubt need reinforcement. Provided that the mast has enough bury, it is desirable to keep the height of any cylinder down to a minimum in order to reduce the wringing loads on the deck or coachroof to which it is attached.

Another treatment of the partners is to fabricate a heavy collar or flange as an integral part of the mast. This collar is then bolted down to the strengthened deck, a system that was first used in *Yeong* (see p 222), where it was built up as shown in Fig. 9.7.

1. The hollow spruce mast (M) was sheathed in GRP by the sparmaker.
2. An oversize mast hole was cut in the deck or coachroof, with a diameter (B) about 1¼ in (32 mm) greater than the diameter (D) of the mast, and so capable of passing any protective battens attached to the lower mast.
3. The heel of the mast was fitted with a detachable GRP cup, as in Fig. 9.12.
4. The mast was lowered through the mast hole and

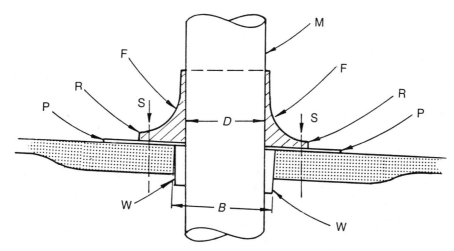

Fig. 9.7 *Yeong*'s partners

held in its correct attitude with its heel cup resting against the inside of the GRP hull. A few temporary wedges (W) were driven in tightly at the partners and then cut off flush with the deck.

5. The heel cup was glassed strongly to the hull as in Fig. 9.12.

6. A plywood spacer (P) (Fig. 9.7), ³⁄₁₆ in (5 mm) thick and in two halves, was placed on the deck and over the wedges, following whatever deck slope and curvature there might be and with its top surface coated with a parting agent.

7. A GRP collar (F) was moulded as shown in Fig. 9.7, adhering to the mast sheathing and conforming exactly to the top surface of the spacer (P). Its flange (R) was about ¾ in (19 mm) thick and 3 in (76 mm) wide, and the collar reached 9–12 in (230–300 mm) up the mast. This collar then became a permanent part of the mast.

8. Twelve bolt holes (S) were drilled through the flange, spacer, and deck.

9. The mast was lifted a few inches out of its step. The spacer and wedges were removed and discarded and a little soft bedding compound spread under the collar.

10. The mast was then lowered and bolted down, straining the deck upwards ³⁄₁₆ in (5 mm) and so holding the mast firmly down into its step. Alignment marks were made on the flange and the deck to ensure correct realignment after any future unstepping.

This system provides a strong and watertight job and eliminates mast coat, wedges, and deck ring or cylinder. The disadvantage is that it requires careful fabrication in a building shed tall enough to enable the masts to be stepped indoors – a process that would have to be repeated if it were ever necessary to provide a replacement mast.

On a junk-rigged dinghy the unstayed mast is simply stepped through a hole in the thwart as in Fig. 8.22, and

any slight amount of play is tolerated. With a timber mast it is necessary to leave some slop, otherwise the mast may swell when damp and jam in the hole. It should have a square heel fitting into a squared step, but no holding-down bolt is normally fitted.

The mast step

There is no point in trying to calculate the loading of a mast step. Just make it capable of taking a heavy load in any direction, including a vertical pile-driving load, and make it much stronger than the mast.

Fig. 9.8 shows a fairly standard form of mast step for timber construction. Two fore-and-afters (A) are set up on a levelling pad (L) and strongly tied to the adjacent floor timbers (F) and to the fillers (G). The depth of cup (Z) should be at least 0.75 of the width of heel (H). The step forms a square-sectioned cup that exactly fits the tapered square heel of the wooden mast. This calls for accurate alignment with the partners, and should be checked with a plank template representing a vertical section of the mast from the heel to a point above the deck. This template is turned athwartships or fore-and-aft as required. A metal angle bracket (B) on either side, bolted down to the top of the fore-and-afters, carries the holding-down bolt (J).

The taper of the heel of the mast is usually very slow, and there is a strong possibility that a wooden mast will swell through dampness and be found to be jammed in the step when the time comes to unstep it. The heel of the mast in Fig 8.18 has a taper of about 3° on each side. This is rather marginal for jamming, although probably permissible if the surfaces are greased before stepping, as they should always be.

The taper at the heel may be increased to (say) 6° on each side as shown on Fig. 9.9, and the step built to

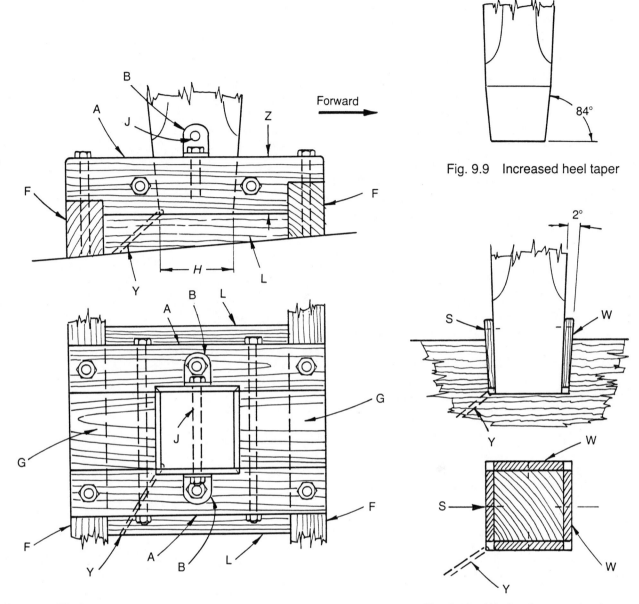

Fig. 9.8   Timber mast step

Fig. 9.9   Increased heel taper

Fig. 9.10   Wedged square heel

match it. Alternatively, the step may be made larger so that step wedges can be used, as at (W) in Fig. 9.10. This shows four wide wedges that bear on the full surface of the mast but leave a space inside the step at each corner. This space, combined with the fact that the wedges protrude at least 2 in (50 mm) above the top of the step, enables the top of the wedge to be tapped from side to side to get it partly withdrawn before unstepping. All edges of the wedge should be chamfered to facilitate this. When in place each wedge should be held down, e.g. by a single wood screw (S) whose point enters the mast.

All masts should, if possible, be drained as shown (Y) in Fig. 9.8, 9.10, and 9.11.

As an alternative to a timber mast step, a metal or GRP fabrication may be used. Fig. 9.11 shows a metal fabrication bolted down to a level pad (L) built between floor timbers (F). The tapered cup (C) is supported by webs (E) and bored for the holding-down bolt (B). Metal mast steps may of course be made larger for use with wedges, if required.

Fig. 9.12 shows the method used in *Yeong* (p 222) for building up a mast step in a GRP hull. A GRP cup (C) is first moulded, with a parting agent, over the heel of the mast, whose taper has been increased as in Fig. 9.9. The mast is then lowered into the boat and held in its correct attitude, with the cup in place on it and resting against

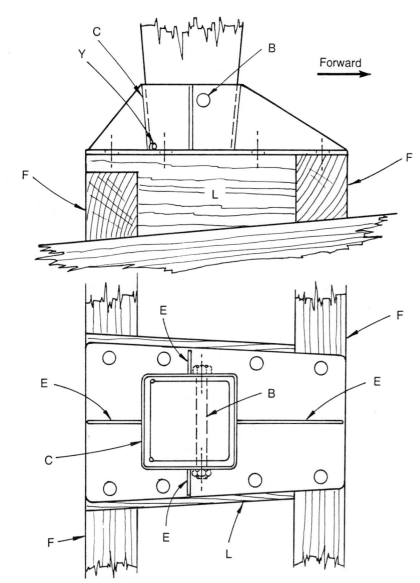

Fig. 9.11   Metal mast step

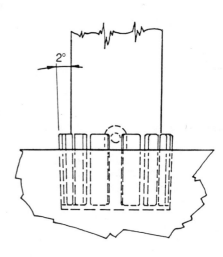

Fig. 9.13   Wedged circular heel

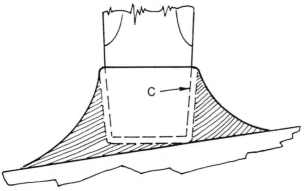

Fig. 9.12   *Yeong*'s mast step

the inside of the hull. The cup is then glassed heavily to the hull as shown, with the reinforcement extending well out to either side. In *Yeong*'s case no holding-down bolt was needed since the mast is held down at the partners (Fig. 9.7).

Many masts will have a circular section at the heel and may use similar forms of mast step but with round-sectioned cups. The holding-down bolt will then perform the additional duty of preventing the mast from turning in its step.

Round-sectioned wooden masts with no heel taper should preferably be wedged into a tapered cup as in Fig. 9.13, leaving gaps between the wedges to enable them to

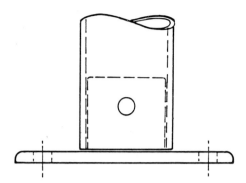

Fig. 9.14   Spigot mast step

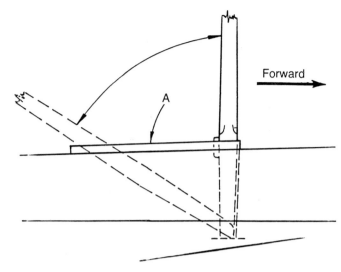

Fig. 9.15   Lowering mast (1)

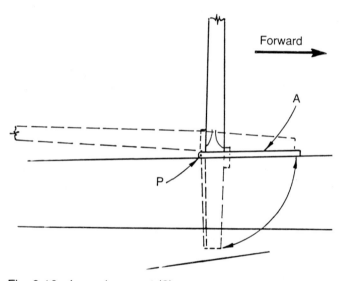

Fig. 9.16   Lowering mast (2)

be worked from side to side for withdrawing. The holding-down bolt can pass through two of these gaps, as shown. Each wedge may be held down by a small wood screw into the mast.

Metal masts with no taper at the heel will not swell and should not jam if stepped, with some grease, into a parallel-sided cup that is a neat fit. Some light-alloy masts have been left open at the heel and stepped over a spigot, as in Fig. 9.14, but this seems to make extra demands on the quality of the mast extrusion. A larger tube sleeved over the heel of the mast would reinforce it.

Tabernacles

Normally a mast will be stepped and unstepped by crane if of any size, but methods of doing it with the boat's own resources are discussed in Chapter 14. If a mast has to be raised and lowered frequently it is best to step it in some form of tabernacle, as is often done in river junks in China. The word 'tabernacle' is used here in a broad sense to mean any kind of strong trunk which is designed to enable a mast to be lowered without first being hoisted bodily. An unstayed mast in a good tabernacle should be just as seaworthy as with normal stepping, but there are penalties to pay in below-decks layout and above-decks appearance. With all forms of tabernacle, timber masts normally have square sections from the top of the tabernacle to the heel.

A tabernacle should provide at least the minimum bury (see p 129) between the heel of the mast and the highest point of support. It is necessary to plan what to do with the furled sail bundle before the mast is lowered. In the case of a mainmast, the masthead often swings down to a point a long way over the stern, and it may then be necessary to hump the mast forward to a better stowage position.

In commercial vessels, a lowering mast commonly makes use of a slot in the deck so that either it pivots about the heel (Fig. 9.15) or about the partners (Fig. 9.16). In either case there is provision for wedging or locking it securely at the partners and step when erected.

The first method does not get the mast right out on deck, but usually only down to about 30° from the horizontal, as shown, with the mast guided between heavy 'skegs' (coamings) (A) on either side of the slot. The head of the mast falls a long way aft, and this system was used mainly by fishing luggers, who had to bring the windage of their big unstayed foremasts further aft in order to lie quietly to nets or an anchor.

The system shown in Fig. 9.16, which seems to be the one mainly used in China, would be quite a good way of lowering a yacht's mast if the accommodation could be designed to clear the heel of the mast and if a really watertight cover were provided for the slot (A). Placing a pivot bolt (P) above deck on the after side of a mast collar would lift the mast a few inches at this point as it was

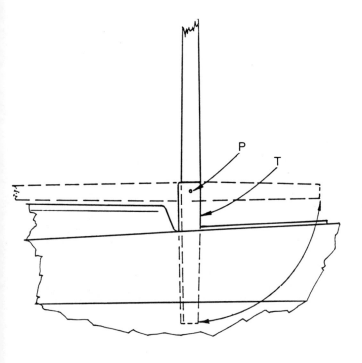

Fig. 9.17   Tabernacle (1)

lowered, but it would often land on a coachroof or doghouse long before it had been lowered far enough. To obviate this, the pivot bolt (P) may be raised as in Fig. 9.17 with a tabernacle (T) in the form of a strong three-sided box heavily built into the boat at deck and heel.

From here it is a short step to the normal higher tabernacle (Fig. 9.18) in which the heel of the mast remains above deck and the bury (*B*) is not less than 0.1 of the overall length of the mast. This removes the previous difficulties of swinging the heel of the mast through the deck. The bottom of the tabernacle will still be built into the keelson and the middle part built strongly into the deck or coachroof.

The part below the heel of the mast may be four-sided and either solid or hollow. Above this, the three-sided box is inherently a weak structural form and will need heavy scantlings. If of timber, it should be held together by tie-rods and strengthened by removable clamps (C) and (E) across the open faces at the top of the box and at the mast heel. If the holes in the mast for the pivot bolt (P) and the heel bolt (H) are slightly oversize, these clamps will grip the mast firmly against the box. Note the timber pad (A) on the upper clamp (C) to fill the gap at the top of the after side of the box. Clamp (E) is similar but without the pad.

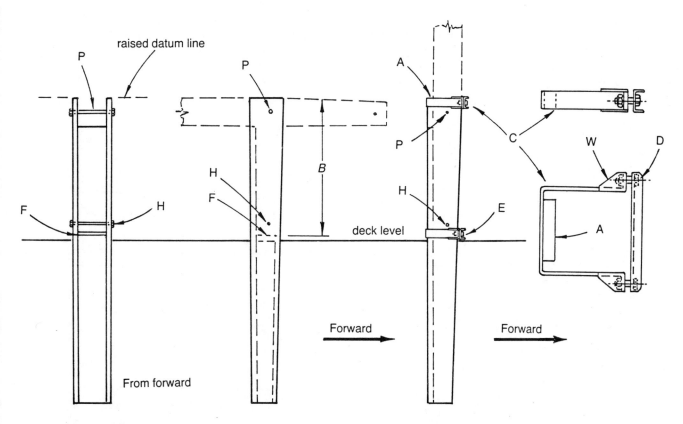

Fig. 9.18   Tabernacle (2)

The heads and nuts of the clamping bolts are shown shrouded to discourage ropes from catching round them, and two box spanners will be needed to operate them. A fixed wedge piece (F) at deck level makes the box watertight and takes the weight of the mast as it comes upright, the heel of the mast being angled to fit it.

Alternatively, a tabernacle may be made up as a steel fabrication, preferably in hot-dip galvanised mild steel, but clamps may still be required as above. Cheek blocks and cleats may be fastened to the starboard side of the tabernacle if required, angled on suitable pads (see p 137).

One other way of lowering a Chinese mast has been used in small cabin boats: a light-alloy mast is built with a hinged joint at a point about 2 ft 6 in (0.8 m) above the deck, enabling the upper part of the mast to be lowered down aft to the horizontal. When upright, a long tubular sleeve covers the joint and supports the mast firmly. Before lowering, this sleeve is slid up the mast and held clear of the joint. There may be difficulty in preventing the sleeve from seizing up if used in salt water.

It is possible to lower a Chinese mast without removing the furled sail from it, as discussed on p 198. Alternatively, with quick-release batten parrels and mast lift, the bundle may be stowed to one side before lowering the mast.

With a mast weighing more than (say) 100 lb (45 kg), all these methods call for a running foreguy to control the mast when partly lowered (Fig. 9.19). If, as here, the distance between mast and stemhead is small in relation to the height of mast, the foreguy should be taken to an improvised traveller (R) hoisted by the halyard to a point above the centre of gravity of the mast. The reason for this is that the guy becomes ineffective when the angle A

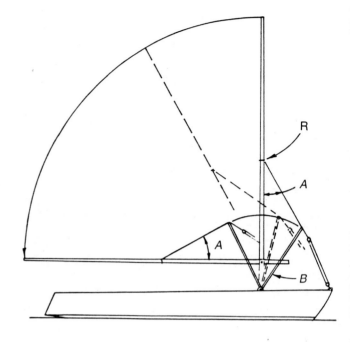

Fig. 9.19   Running foreguy

is less than about 20°. In a smallish vessel the mast may be manhandled below this point, but for larger masts it will be necessary to spread the foreguy upwards with a light bipod (B) whose feet are pivoted on deck and whose head is seized to the foreguy. This enables the mast to be lowered safely right down to the horizontal. Such a bipod will be much smaller than the sheer-legs shown in Fig. 14.4, and may be kept permanently on deck and form part of the pulpit.

10 Yard, Battens, and Boom

It is a disadvantage of the junk rig that the weight of the sail complete with its yard, battens, and boom is greater than that of a conventional Bermudian sail assembly, and this in spite of the fact that the junk's sailcloth and boom are considerably lighter. Further development is needed to reduce the weight of the yard and battens. However a yard that is too light does not facilitate speedy reefing.

The yard

The yard should taper each way from its sling point. It appears to take nearly as much loading sideways as downwards. Experimental 'plank' yards have shown too much lateral bending and have had to be stiffened sideways. The scantlings given here for timber yards may be unnecessarily heavy, but have so far proved safe. As with the mast and battens, the yard takes its highest loading when running before the wind under a press of sail, especially if the boat then runs head-on into the wash of a ship. When close-reefed it gets a small amount of lateral support from the lee topping-lift.

The recommended cross-sectional dimensions of the yard are related only to its length, and not to the area of the sail. A low-aspect-ratio sail therefore has a heavier-sectioned yard than that of a high-aspect-ratio sail of the same area, although its mast is lighter. It has not normally seemed worth while to build a hollow timber yard, although this would be quite a simple job.

Fig. 10.1 shows the dimensions of a solid spruce yard whose underside is straight and whose depth and thickness are tapered from the sling plate towards either end, the section at the throat being the same as that at the peak. The tapers are straight and there is a short parallel length in way of the sling plate.

The dimensions are all related to the length H, which is the designed overall length of the head of the sail *when fully stretched*, and which should be expressed in decimal units to facilitate calculation. It should be taken to the nearest inch or nearest 25 mm. All the other dimensions of the yard should be rationalised as

appropriate, to avoid finicky measurements. If an unorthodox sling plate position is used (see p 118), the maximum section of the yard should be in that position rather than in the middle.

All edges of the yard should be rounded as shown. At the peak and throat it is shaped as shown enlarged in Fig. 10.1, so that the cringle of the sail may be hauled well out with a lanyard arranged as in Fig. 12.3.

There are three ways of securing the head of the sail to the yard:

1. The sail may be laced with a long lanyard that passes round the yard and through eyelets spaced along the head of the sail as in Fig. 10.2. For serious cruising it is safer to use a separate stop of smaller cord through each eyelet, finished with frapping turns and a reef knot as in Fig. 10.3. With either of these methods the yard may be of circular section if desired, keeping equivalent cross-sectional areas, but it is quite feasible to lace around the standard sections shown in Fig. 10.1. With laced heads it takes some time to bend or unbend the sail, and the fitting of a yard fender (see below) is more complicated.

2. The head of the sail may be roped, and this rope fed into a groove on the underside of the yard. With a built timber spar, whether hollow or not, it is easy to make the groove in the spar as in Fig. 10.4, having first agreed with the sailmaker the *minimum* acceptable dimensions for D and G. With this system the depth of the yard should be increased to the figures shown; the thickness can remain unchanged. A simpler way of providing the groove is to screw a length of suitable track, either metal or plastic, to the underside of the yard as in Fig. 10.5. In this case the depth of the yard may remain as in Fig. 10.1, and the length of the track should be the same as dimension H. In both these forms the ends of the yard should be fashioned as in Fig. 10.1. With all grooved yards it is wise to fit emergency lacing eyelets to the sail (see Fig. 11.2) for use if the headrope of the sail should for any reason start pulling out of the groove. Grooved yards are considered to be suitable for sails in the range 150–350 sq ft (14–33 m^2).

3. As a third choice, the head of the sail may be fitted

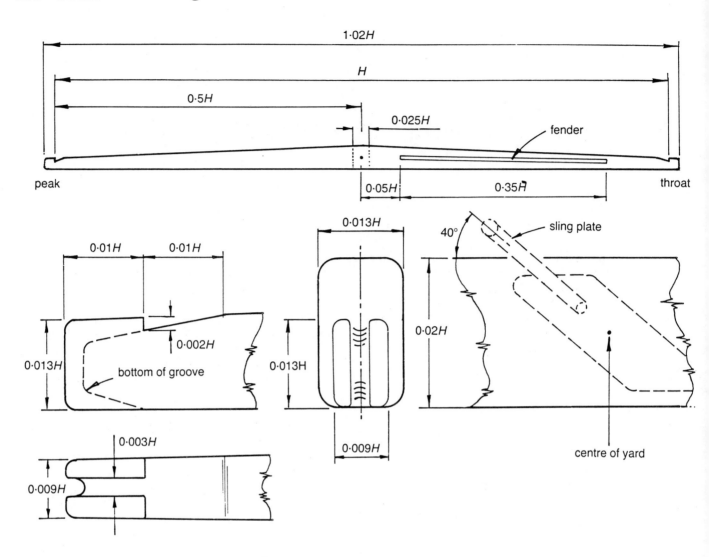

Fig. 10.1   Yard

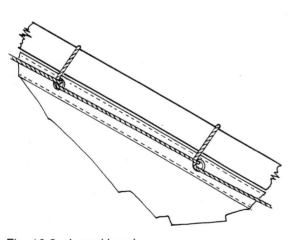

Fig. 10.2   Laced head

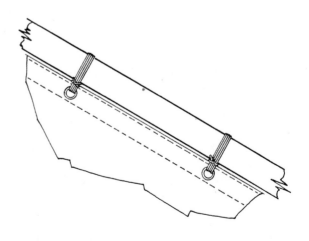

Fig. 10.3   Separate stops

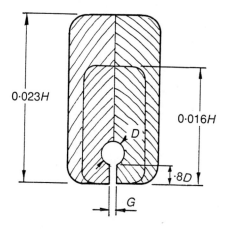

0·023H

0·016H

D

·8D

G

Fig. 10.4   Integral groove

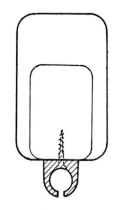

Fig. 10.5   Grooved extrusion

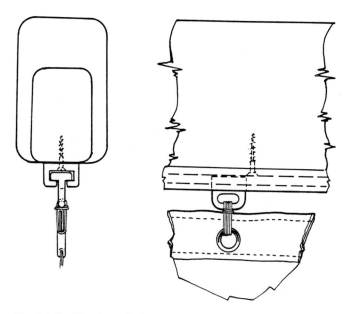

Fig. 10.6   Track and slides

slightly less than the flat side of the yard after rounding its edges, and may be taken as 0.016H where H is the length of the head of the sail. The minimum clearance C between the top of the yard and the inside of the rod loop should range from about ⅝ in (16 mm) on a dinghy to about 1 in (25 mm) for a 20 ft (6 m) yard. Dimension Z must be more than the inside radius R of the loop, and may be taken as 0.01H. The remaining dimensions may be arranged to suit the yard.

YARD FENDER. A length of fendering material should be fitted to the starboard side of the yard to reduce the noise and chafe when it hits or rubs against the mast. To be effective this has to extend over a considerable length, as shown in Fig. 10.1, to allow for the movement of the yard in reefing and furling. Small-sectioned plastic dinghy fendering is suitable, or a rawhide strip glued on. If the head of the sail is laced, the fendering should be put on over the lacing, and be easily removable.

LIGHT-ALLOY YARDS. As an alternative to timber, a good yard may be built of light-alloy tube, preferably of two tapered extrusions sleeved together butt-to-butt at the sling plate. The design should be left to an experienced sparmaker, who should be given a drawing of the equivalent solid spruce yard and asked to meet the same strength and stiffness. The alloy yard should turn out to be somewhat lighter.

  The two ends of the yard should be plugged, and bored with a transverse hole very close to the end to take the lashings that haul out the throat and peak cringles. Light-alloy yards may be designed to suit any one of the three methods of attaching the head of the sail described

with slides to suit a length of track screwed to the underside of the yard, preferably 'internal' track as shown in Fig. 10.6. This is a stronger variation of (2) above, and is recommended for sails of more than about 350 sq ft (33m²). Again, the ends of the yard should be fashioned as in Fig. 10.1.

SLING PLATE. It is possible to sling a yard by means of a rope or wire strop located by thumb cleats, but better to fit a metal sling plate designed so as to take the pull of the halyard at roughly the correct angle, and fastened either by wood screws or by copper rivets. Fig. 10.7 shows a suitable design that may be welded up, preferably in galvanised mild steel. If wood screws are to be used the holes in the opposite plates should be staggered so that the length of screws may be more than half the thickness of the yard. Fig. 10.1 shows how the plate fits on the yard, just clear of the rounded edges.

  The diameter D of the rod may vary from about ⁵⁄₁₆ in (8 mm) for a sail of 100 sq ft (9 m²) to about ⅝ in (16 mm) for a sail of 600 sq ft (56 m²). Dimension Y should be

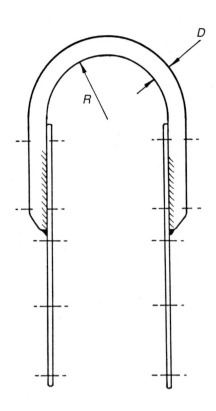

Fig. 10.7   Yard sling plate

on p 151–2, i.e. laced head, roped head, or slides. A sling plate designed to fit the yard should be riveted (not welded) on.

The battens

The loading and bending of battens has been discussed in Chapter 1. The batten lies between the sail and the mast. When the sail is to leeward of the mast the batten is held close to the mast by the batten parrel, and the sail is held close to the batten either by fitting the batten into a pocket on the sail or by seizing the sail to the batten at frequent intervals. The former is normal Western practice whereas the latter is universal in China. When the sail is to windward of the mast the batten parrel is slack and the batten pocket does nothing except support the weight of the batten.

The ideal batten would take on a good bend in ghosting weather and get progressively straighter as the wind speed increases, but there is as yet no practical way of achieving this. The best that can be hoped for is a batten that is very stiff, light, unbreakable, and cheap. It should take on a moderate bend when hard pressed under full sail, and will become virtually straight in ghosting weather. As the sail is progressively reefed, the exposed battens will gain appreciable support against

bending by leaning against the lee topping-lifts.

The different battens in a sail are not all subjected to the same loading. The greatest load is taken by the top sheeted batten, i.e. the highest batten that is connected to the sheeting system. In the standard form of sail it is not usually possible to sheet the top batten without using double sheets. An unsheeted top batten takes less bending load than the sheeted batten below it, except possibly when running close-reefed (Fig. 1.8) when it tries to bend the wrong way round the lee lifts. However, the top batten takes more compression from leech tension (Fig. 1.7) and plays a vital role under gale conditions. It is therefore made as strong as the top sheeted batten.

The loads on the sheeted battens decrease steadily from the uppermost to the lowest, and a set of battens could be made lighter if this fact were reflected in their scantlings by progressively reducing their sectional dimensions in the same way. The problem here is that ordinary battens cannot be guaranteed against breakage. Long-distance cruising boats should therefore carry spare battens, and these should be ready for fitting to the sail. It is therefore standard practice to have only one size of batten for each sail, although a few boats have had two sizes, with the three lower battens lighter than the upper three.

If further development should ever produce a satisfactory batten that is unbreakable, it will be feasible to grade the scantlings of individual battens more scientifically, and they may well all be different. There would then be no particular reason for designing a sail with all its battens of the same length, and it might be profitable to re-examine the geometry of the sail as discussed in Chapter 2.

The standard batten is made slightly longer than the overall width of the sail as measured along the line of the batten after the sail has been fully stretched. The extra length is needed to enable the sail to be stretched quite taut along the batten by means of lacing at one or both ends, but it is undesirable for the batten to protrude substantially beyond either the luff or the leech. If it protrudes at the leech it may tend to catch the upper sheet spans when tacking or gybing, and it will also make it difficult to clear any 'fan-up' (see p 208) in which the upper battens may have got the wrong side of the topping-lifts. Protruding at the luff is less harmful, but in single-masters the ends of the battens may get foul of the burgee halyard or ghoster halyard, and in multi-masters they may get foul of the sheets of the next sail forward.

The Chinese often solve this problem in an efficient but rather untidy way by making each batten in two parts, usually of two bamboos with the butts outwards and their thin ends overlapping and fished (seized) together as in Fig. 10.8. Where necessary for strength, the overlap may be made longer, so that only the ends are single. Such battens are adjustable for length and can finish dead flush at luff and leech. Other advantages would be that spare battens can more easily be stowed in two parts, and that the batten can be expanded to suit any excessive stretching of the sailcloth. The arrangement could be used with materials other than bamboo, but the authors have no experience of it.

A possible variation on this two-part batten would be to connect two parts together by a sleeve. Fig. 10.9 shows timber half-battens joined by a tubular metal sleeve, and Fig. 10.10 shows light-alloy tubular half-battens connected by an internal alloy spigot. In either case the overall length of the batten could be made adjustable by flush-pinning the sleeve to the half-battens, leaving an adjustable gap in the middle. The length of the sleeve would be increased for this purpose. Battens of this sort would be easy to make, repair, and stow.

The standard one-piece batten is cut from solid timber of square section as shown in Fig. 10.11. The shape involves a fair amount of wastage in the tapering, which can be avoided by laminating two thicknesses together as shown by the dotted line at G. For large battens it may be convenient to laminate up from a number of thinner strips, following the usual rules for gluing and scarphing (Chapter 8).

Being asymmetrical, it is necessary to prevent these

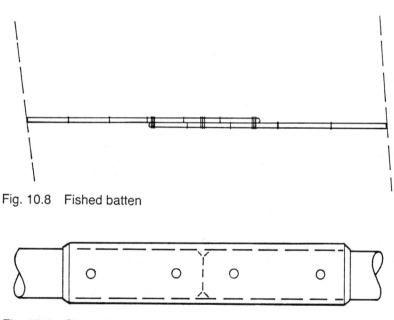

Fig. 10.8   Fished batten

Fig. 10.9   Sleeved batten

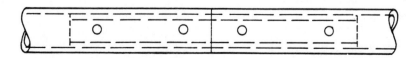

Fig. 10.10   Spigoted batten

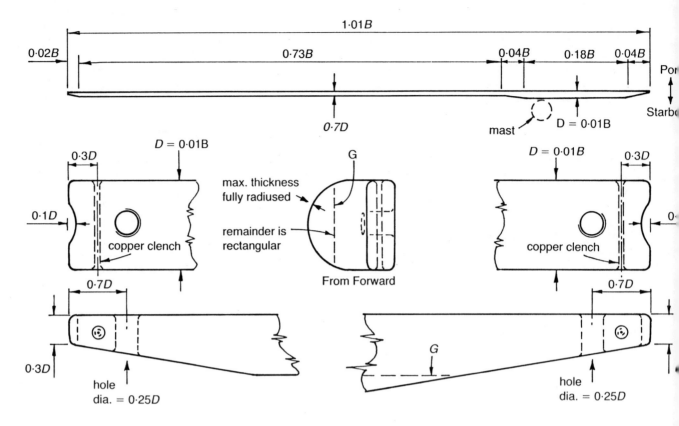

Fig. 10.11   Ash batten for medium-sized sail

timber battens from twisting round in the batten pocket. This is achieved by seizing them to the sail at one or both ends. The batten shown in Fig. 10.11 is laced to eyelets in the sail at the luff and leech. Its dimensions are specified in relation to the width (B) of the fully-stretched sail measured along the line of the batten, and of the depth (D) of the batten which remains constant throughout its length. D is equal to $0.01B$ (i.e. $B/100$), but should be rationalised to a workable unit in the usual way.

At either end the thickness is tapered down for neatness. All tapering is on the starboard (mast) side of the batten, the side against the sail being flat.

The maximum thickness is equal to the depth D and remains constant from the fore taper to a point close abaft the mast, this point being taken from the top batten which has more slope than the others. Over the full length of its maximum thickness the starboard side of the batten is fully radiused to reduce chafe against the mast. On the port tack, with the sail to windward of the mast, this extra thickness helps to stand the sail off the mast, but this effect is not thought to be important. With battens of bamboo, and most other materials, there is no extra thickness in way of the mast.

Abaft the mast the thickness tapers down to the minimum thickness of $0.7D$ which remains constant all the way to the aft taper. Its section is rectangular with the corners rounded.

Each end is strengthened against splitting by a thin copper boat nail clenched vertically through it, and is then bored for the lacing hole. The extreme end is shaped into a shallow fork to retain the lacing.

For sails of over about 300 sq ft (28 m^2) the after end of the batten is left plain as in Fig. 10.12 so as to fit into a closed pocket (see p 163), which is a stronger arrangement and positively prevents the batten from protruding at the leech. Furthermore, when a large sail is furled and lying in the lifts or on a boom gallows, its leech is often out of reach from the deck and it would be inconvenient to have to lower it further in order to put a seizing on the end of a batten. This difficulty seldom arises at the luff, where the furled sail is much nearer the deck.

EXTREME SHAPES OF SAIL. If the parallelogram panels are unusually narrow, i.e. if P/B is less than about 0.15, dimension D may be reduced to about $0.009B$, and all other measurements that are based on D will be reduced accordingly. If this is done, however, the top sheeted batten and any unsheeted batten(s) in the head should remain at the standard scantlings. If the paral-

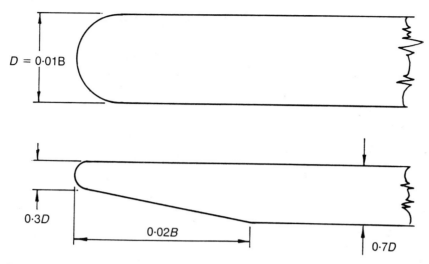

Fig. 10.12   Leech end of ash batten for larger sails

lelogram panels are unusually wide, i.e. if P/B is more than about 0.3, dimension D may be increased to about $0.011B$, again with its related measurements increased accordingly. In this case the top battens should follow suit.

VARIETIES OF TIMBER FOR BATTENS. The scantlings given so far are suitable for battens of straight-grained English ash (*Froximus excelsior*). In different parts of the world different timbers will be available. Any straight-grained wood that is suitable for making an oar, or the shaft of a pitchfork, and can be got in long enough lengths, will be suitable for battens.

Of the timbers available in Britain, if native English ash is unobtainable it is possible to use imported Sitka spruce (see p 124). Spruce battens should be of slightly larger section than ash, e.g. by making D equal to about $0.011B$. Other imported timbers which may be suitable are Douglas fir and European redwood, which should be given the same enlarged sections as spruce.

The strongest battens in our experience were of imported Hickory (*Hickoria glabra*, etc.). These gave excellent service but were heavy and liable to warp. Hickory is difficult to obtain in Britain in long enough lengths, and is said to have only moderate gluing properties and to be only moderately durable.

All timber battens should be protected by at least three coats of paint or varnish, or a coat of epoxy resin, in order to prevent them from soaking up water when left for long periods in a sail pocket that is often saturated. Saturated wood (particularly spruce) is considerably weaker as well as being heavier.

SHEATHED TIMBER BATTENS. Good results have been achieved by sheathing a solid timber batten with woven glass tape or glass rovings laid along the length of the batten, mainly on each side, and epoxy resin. In this case the thickness, but not the depth, of the timber may be reduced to about 0.8 of the figures given in Fig. 10.11.

BAMBOO. Bamboo is now little used in Britain as a structural material, and it is not easy to find good poles, nor any expertise in their selection and use. This is a pity, because bamboo can show qualities unmatched by any other material and can make very good lightweight battens if some untidiness can be tolerated.

For sails of dinghy size, say up to about 80 sq ft ($7m^2$), ordinary garden canes serve excellently, either in single lengths or fished as in Fig. 10.8. If used in single lengths they should have as little taper as possible and the thicker (butt) ends should be at the luff.

For larger sizes, female bamboo should be used, which is hollow except for the knuckles. The strength may be improved by serving with synthetic twine or adhesive tape midway between the knuckles, and the whole should then be given three coats of varnish or similar protection to keep the moisture out.

The treatment of the ends should aim at producing shapes similar to those in Fig. 10.11 or 10.12, either by gluing in timber plugs or by moulding epoxy paste into the hollow ends.

As a tentative guide to the section of bamboo needed for a batten made of a single pole, the mean circumference, taken midway between the knuckles, should be about $0.033B$, equal to a diameter of about $0.011B$. The knuckles should not be planed off, and it may be better to seize the battens to the sail than to fit them into sail pockets, particularly if the batten is fished.

LIGHT ALLOY TUBE. Good battens can be made of light-alloy tube, using material that has a high enough tensile strength and sufficient resistance to seawater

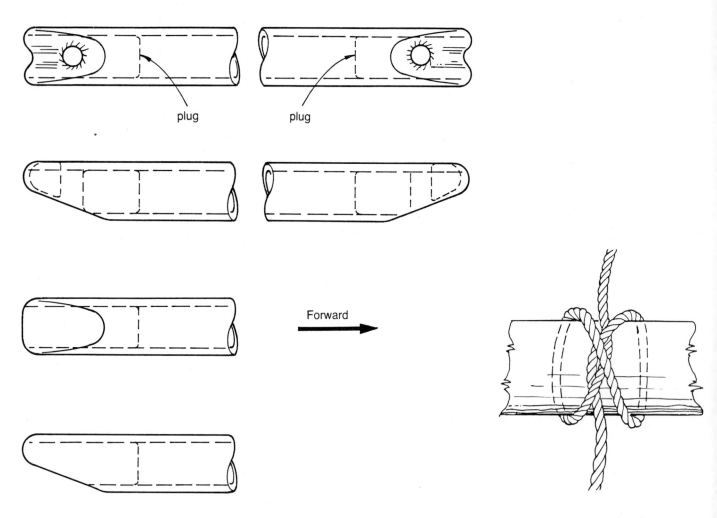

Fig. 10.13   Ends of tubular battens

Fig. 10.14   Constrictor hitch

corrosion. The layman should take advice on these points, and on the outside diameter and wall thickness that will produce a stiffness and strength similar to that of the standard ash batten. Successful alloy battens have tended to have thick walls and a smallish outside diameter. If overloaded, an alloy batten will either buckle or take a set (permanent bend), whereas an ash batten will fracture and splinter.

Light-alloy battens will be considerably smaller in section than ash battens. Those supplied for *Pilmer* (Fig. 16.10) were 12 ft 9 in (3.8 m) long with an outside diameter of ⅞ in (22 mm) and ⅛ in (3.2 mm) thick walls, as compared with the 1½ in (38 mm) diameter of her ash battens. They do not therefore hold the sail as far off the mast when on the port tack. This does not seem to be important, but could if required be corrected by sleeving the tube with plastic hose in way of the mast.

The ends of the tubes should be plugged, either with alloy rod or with epoxy paste, and then finished as in Fig. 10.13, in which a shows an arrangement for sails of

less than about 300 sq ft (28 m²) and b shows the plain after end for a larger sail. The ends need not necessarily be tapered.

GRP TUBE. Attempts to use stock sizes of GRP tube for battens have not been very successful, mainly because the tube was too flexible unless used in large diameters, when it became heavier than ash or light alloy. GRP spigots to fit into the tube were used at the butt joints, which were needed to get the required length, and also for repairing broken battens at sea. These repairs were temporarily reinforced by binding with adhesive tape, and later permanently strengthened with glass tape and resin. The batten ends were treated as in Fig. 10.13.

PLASTIC TUBE. Experiments so far have found stock plastic tubes to be too flexible for their diameter and weight, but further development in plastics may improve this.

SQUARE-SECTIONED TUBES. Since all the bending loads are in one plane it may be argued that tubular battens, of whatever material, could well be of square section. For practical reasons the edges should be rounded.

FITTINGS FOR BATTENS. The after ends of the batten parrels must be firmly secured to the batten so that they cannot slide forward and slacken the parrel. A good seaman can achieve this with a rolling hitch, or, better, a constrictor knot (Fig. 10.14). A clove hitch may also be used but will require some kind of positive stop. An alternative way is to fit a pair of eyelets in the sail at this point and to take the parrel hitch through them, but this tends to pull the sail forward and form a crease.

Fendering is usually required between each batten and the mast in order to reduce the mutual chafe and to deaden the noise made by the batten striking the mast when the sail is slatting in a lop. On dinghy-sized sails there is no need to use any batten fendering, but for sails of over (say) 100 sq ft (9 m^2) some fendering is desirable.

If the mast is of very smooth light alloy it is only necessary to have a layer of sailcloth between batten and mast, provided by extending the batten pocket of the sail through this area as in Fig. 11.1. For sails of more than about 250 sq ft (23 m^2) it is best to double this with another layer of sailcloth that can easily be replaced if it chafes through.

With timber masts, whether sheathed or not, it is necessary to leave a window or gap in the batten pocket in way of the mast (Fig. 11.7) and to fit a plastic tube or rawhide sheath over the batten. The plastic tube may be either thick-walled and rigid or thin-walled and flexible, but should be a neat fit over the batten. Its position and length must be such that it will be effective through all stages of reefing, and when the sail is furled. Its length should be made slightly less than the length of the fender window in the sail, and Fig. 11.7 shows that these lengths will increase progressively from no. 1 batten to the top batten.

The boom

The boom takes very little loading and is of similar section to the battens but without any tapering. It is pleasing if it takes up a mild curve when under full sail in a fresh breeze, but this is not regarded as important. When reefed, the boom and the battens lying on it remain straight for all practical purposes.

The lowest part of the sheet system is attached to the after end of the boom and the topping-lifts are located in their correct positions along it by means of eyeplates or comb-cleats attached to its underside, through which the lifts either render freely or are hitched. Fig. 10.15 shows three suitable forms of eye: small metal eyeplates

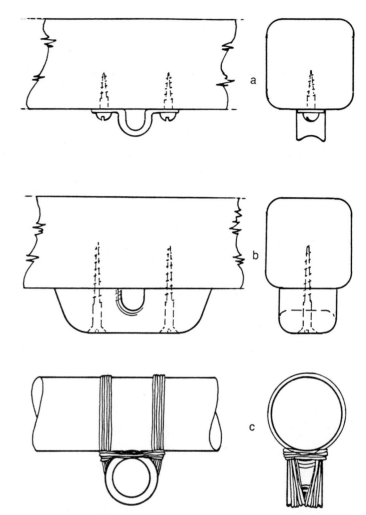

Fig. 10.15   Eye fittings for boom

(a) or hardwood comb-cleats (b) may be screwed to the boom, or round thimbles (c) may be seized to a round-sectioned boom. The latter is suitable for a dinghy, where small round thimbles may be seized to a boom made of garden cane. When bending or unbending the topping-lifts, or when removing the whole sail bundle from the mast, it is convenient with eyes (a) and (b) to be able to slip the bights of the topping-lifts out of the eyes by removing one screw and partly unscrewing the other.

The tackline is hitched to the boom immediately abaft the mast. The forward end of the boom is held aft towards the mast by a tack parrel or the lower end of a fixed luff parrel. Both these exert a slight force, holding the boom in towards the mast when on the starboard tack under full sail, but if this is felt to be insufficient the boom may be given a boom parrel similar to the batten parrels. As soon as the sail is reefed, the mast lift holds the boom tightly against the mast on both tacks.

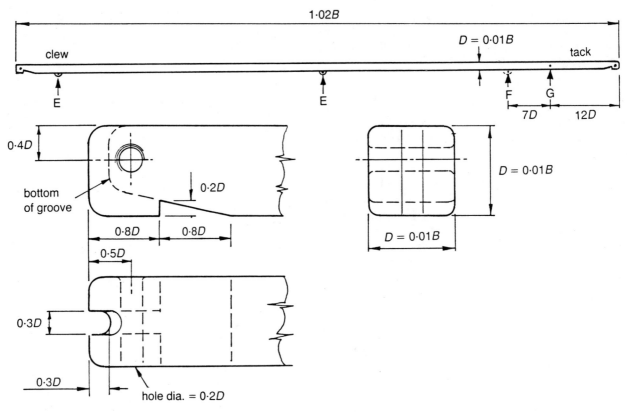

Fig. 10.16   Timber boom

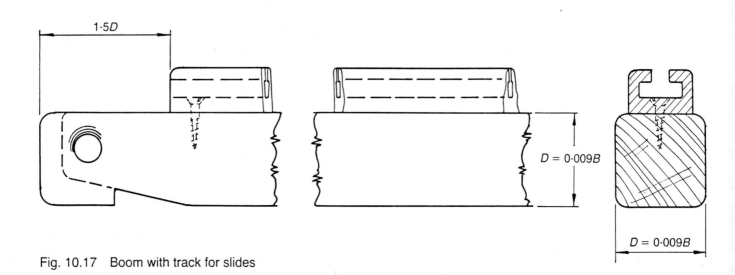

Fig. 10.17   Boom with track for slides

The foot of the sail is attached to the boom by any one of the three methods described for the head of the sail on p 151. A laced foot can be used for sails of all sizes but is recommended for sails of up to about 150 sq ft (14m²). A grooved boom is suitable for sails in the range 150–350 sq ft (14–33 m²), with the foot of the sail roped to suit it. Sails of over about 350 sq ft (33 m²) are best fitted with 'internal' slides along the foot, to run in a metal track along the top of the boom.

With a sail of more than (say) 150 sq ft (14 m²) set on a wooden mast, a boom fender should be fitted to reduce the chafe between boom and mast. This may be similar to the yard fender described on p 153, or to the batten fender described on p 159. The fore-and-aft movement of

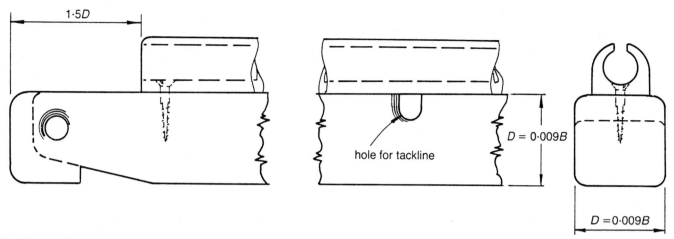

Fig. 10.18   Boom with grooved extrusion

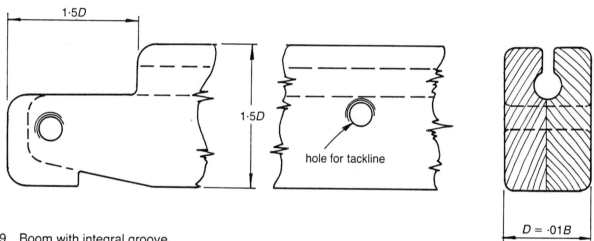

Fig. 10.19   Boom with integral groove

the boom is not great and the fender will be correspondingly short. With a laced foot, either the lacing must be arranged to miss the fender, or the fender must be fitted on top of the lacing. With a smooth light-alloy mast and a wooden boom, a boom fender is not really necessary.

Fig. 10.16 shows the standard design of boom, cut out of solid spruce or ash. Its dimensions are related to length B, which is the length of the foot of the sail when fully stretched, and to D which equals $0.01B$. Both ends of the boom are shaped as shown, the grooves being similar to those at the ends of the yard and enabling the tack and clew to be hauled well out, as shown in Fig. 12.3. The hole in the after end of the boom is for the sheet span, and the hole at the forward end is for the tack parrel or luff parrel.

The exact positions of the two topping-lift eyes (E) will be determined later (p 178). Shown dotted is an

additional eye (F), which must be large enough to take two parts of the rope, for use with a standing topping-lift as in Fig. 3.47.

The position of the tackline is shown at G. If the sail is to have a laced foot, or a sail track with slides (Fig. 10.17), an eye or comb-cleat on the port side of the boom at this point will locate the hitch of the tackline, which will pass right round the boom. If there is to be a grooved extrusion along the top of the boom no eye is required but a groove is cut across the top of the boom as shown in Fig. 10.18.

Fig. 10.19 shows a wooden boom with an integral groove, the boom being glued together in two halves. The tackline passes through a hole below the groove. A disadvantage of this form is the risk of rot being started by rainwater collecting in the groove, and it is preferable to use an extrusion as in Fig. 10.18. It will be seen that in

Fig. 10.17 and 10.18 the cross-sectional dimensions of the boom have been reduced by about 10 per cent, i.e. $D = 0.009B$.

NON-TIMBER BOOMS. A boom may be made of any other material that would have made a serviceable batten, for example light-alloy tube. In this case the eyes may be attached with self-tapping screws, but unless the tube is of square section any track fastened to it should have its base radiused to fit the tube. Alternatively it may be possible to find a standard mast section that incorporates a suitable luffrope groove or track.

11 The Sail

The geometry of the sail has been discussed in Chapter 2. Instructions for drawing to scale the bare outline of the sail with any desired area and aspect ratio are given in Chapter 6.

For each sail the sailmaker should be given (1) a dimensioned scale drawing of the outline of the sail with the batten pockets, (2) a drawing showing sail details to a larger scale, and (3) a sheet of specifications.

The scale outline

This shows the size and shape of the sail when fully stretched, and is marked with all the measurements needed to lay it off on the loft floor. The sailmaker should not have to measure anything off the drawing. He will make his own allowances for stretch by making the sail somewhat smaller than the dimensions given, and this point is emphasised in the specification sheet.

Most of the dimensions on the drawing, including sail area, will already have been established when drawing the sail traces for the sail plan (Chapter 6), but rise is not now shown. Instead, the slope of the battens is defined by the master diagonal, which must be measured off the sail trace for this purpose. Note that it runs to the throat, not to the top corner of the parallelogram.

The mast line, which has already been drawn on the original trace, is defined here by measurements along the head and foot. The drawing also shows, diagrammatically, how the cloths change direction twice in order to remain parallel to the leech.

Fig. 11.1 is a specimen drawing of a sail of 227 sq ft (21 m²) in which the after ends of the battens will be seized through grommets on the leech (see p 156) and the batten pockets are taken through the mast line to act as fendering against a smooth light-alloy mast (p 159). It will also have a roped head and foot to fit grooves or extrusions on its yard and boom, but it could equally well have grommets for lacing at the head and foot or sail slides to fit tracks on yard and boom (see pp 151 and 160).

Fig. 11.6 shows a sail of 508 sq ft (47 m²) in which each batten pocket is closed at the leech (see p 156) and has a 'fender window' in way of the mast to allow for fendering on the batten (see p 159). It is shown as having sail slides to fit tracks in its yard and boom, but the alternatives of lacing or roping could be considered.

On both sails the leech of the two top panels is shown very slightly hollowed (reverse roach). This is to ensure that they remain taut and do not develop flutter which has occurred on some sails in the past.

Detail drawing and specification

It is not necessary to specify the sailmaking technique, which will be decided by the sailmaker, but only the colour, weight, and type of sailcloth and the size, shape, and position of pockets, eyes, beckets, etc whose function is the responsibility of the designer.

Fig. 11.2 shows the detail for the sail in Fig. 11.1. Fig. 11.3 gives the specification for this sail, and includes a key to the letters used in Fig. 11.1 and 11.2. In practice, Fig. 11.2 will probably be drawn to a scale large enough for full details to be written on it, in which case the letters and key will not be needed.

The line of the forward ends of the batten pockets is parallel to the luff and about $0.03B$ from it. The line of the after ends of the pockets is parallel to the leech and a similar distance from it. All such measurements are of course rationalised to remove unnecessary fractions.

The line (J) of the centres of the parrel windows in the pockets is parallel to the mast line and about $0.12B$ abaft it. The windows extend for about $0.02B$ either way from this point and are in the pocket only, not in the sail. All the pockets are open right through from one end to the other.

It is recommended that all sails should be made of woven polyester sailcloth, such as Terylene or Dacron. This will not rot when stowed wet but is liable to deteriorate slowly in sunlight (ultraviolet degradation), particularly in the tropics and if it is lightweight sailcloth. As it is seldom practicable to unbend Chinese sails and stow them below decks, there is a good case for using sail covers in harbour (see p 211).

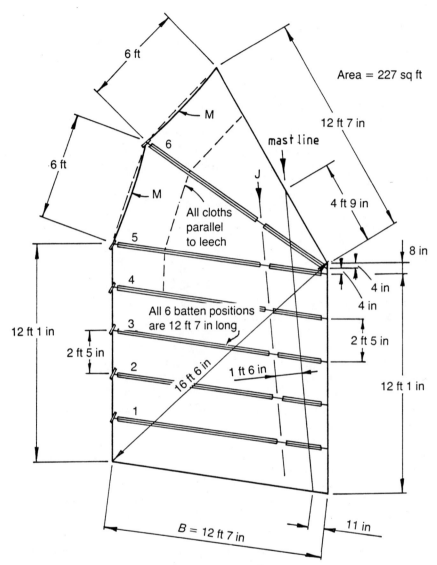

Fig. 11.1   Sail of less than 300 sq ft (28 m²)

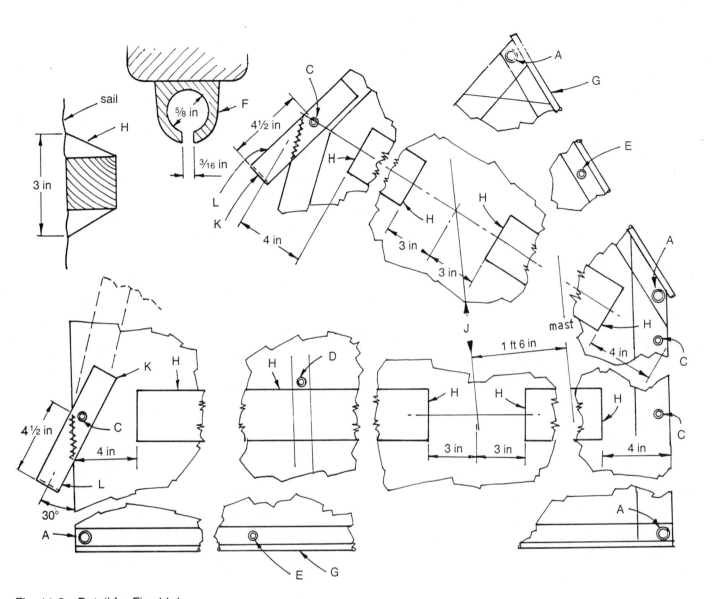

Fig. 11.2   Detail for Fig. 11.1

Fig. 11.3   Specification for sail shown in Fig. 11.1 and
11.2

Key
A   Hand-worked grommets or hydraulic-pressed rings
    approx. 5/8 in (16 mm) i.d.
B   Length of head, foot, and batten positions when fully
    stretched
C   Spurtooth grommets approx. 3/8 in (10 mm) i.d. at each
    end of each batten position
D   Emergency reefing grommets approx. 5/16 in (8 mm) i.d.
    on each seam immediately above each batten pocket
E   Emergency lacing grommets approx. 5/16 in (8 mm) i.d.
    spaced approx. 18 in (0.5 m) along head and foot. To lie
    clear of F
F   Full-sized section of track on yard and boom
G   Head and foot roped to suit F
H   Pockets to take square batten 1 1/2 in × 1 1/2 in (38 × 38
    mm) with sail flat
J   Centres of parrel windows
K   Loop of 1 1/2 in (38 mm) polyester webbing stitched to
    both sides of sail
L   Leave loop open
M   Slight reverse roach in leech

1. Material: 5 1/2 oz polyester, tan. The part of each batten
    pocket forward of the parrel window takes chafe against
    the mast and should preferably be made of heavier
    sailcloth.
2. All measurements to edge of sail when fully stretched. Its
    stretched measurements when new along head, foot,
    and batten positions should be at least 1 in (25 mm)
    short.
3. Sail to be cut absolutely flat. The master diagonal
    measurement is critical. Please note that its upper end
    runs to the throat, not to the top of the parallelogram.
4. Luff to be cut straight between battens, head and foot cut
    straight. Leech to be straight between lower battens but
    slightly hollowed on two top panels at M.
5. Full-width cloths parallel to leech, changing direction at
    nos. 5 and 6 battens.
6. Luff and leech to be slightly taped with same material as
    sail. No patches required for batten pockets.
7. Battens lie on starboard side of sail.
8. Sailmaker, please mark cloth on starboard side of sail at
    head and foot and immediately above each batten
    pocket (e.g. by a short line with dye pen) to show mast
    line.

Coloured sails can give less glare in bright sunlight
and yet may be more visible in daylight conditions,
although less visible at night. They are also somewhat
less liable to ultraviolet degradation. Many owners feel
that tan is the most attractive colour.

Sailcloth is manufactured in different weights, and
the figure describes its weight per specific area. Under
the British system a 5 oz cloth will weigh 5 oz per square
yard, whereas under the American system it will weigh
5 oz per yard length of a cloth that is 28 1/2 in wide. Under
the metric system its weight will be expressed in grams
per square metre. Table 5 gives recommended sailcloth
weights for Chinese sails, showing the equivalents
under all three systems.

Table 5. Recommended weights of sailcloth for sails of different areas

| Sail area (sq ft) | Recommended cloth weight | | | Sail area (m²) |
	British (oz per sq yard)	American (oz per yard 28½ in wide)	Metric (g/m²)	
100–175	5.2	4.1	117	9–16
175–250	5.5	4.4	187	16–23
250–325	6.0	4.8	204	23–30
325–400	6.5	5.1	221	30–37
400–475	7.0	5.5	238	37–44
475–550	7.5	5.9	255	44–51
550–625	8.0	6.3	272	51–58

In Fig. 11.2 a full-sized section is given of the track to
be fitted to the yard and boom, to enable the sailmaker to
plan the roping and the grommets. A scale section of the
batten pocket is given, to show how much slack it should
have when the sail is flat. The gauge here is a square-
sectioned piece of timber whose sides measure $0.01\,B$,
and the width of the pocket on the sail is twice this
measurement. Even if it is intended to use battens of
small section, such as of light-alloy tube, it is advisable
to make the pockets up to this size in order to allow for a
possible jury repair at sea. There is no particular
disadvantage in having the pockets too large for the
batten section.

At the leech end of each batten a becket of strong
polyester tape, or webbing, is sewn to both sides of the
sail as the attachment point of the sheet span. The
grommet (C) is clenched through both parts of the tape,
and the batten lies wholly to starboard of the becket. An
identical becket on the top (unsheeted) batten enables it
to be lashed down to the furled sail bundle on the rare
occasions when one panel only is to be set.

These beckets provide a reliable means of securing the
sheet spans so that they can easily be bent, unbent, or

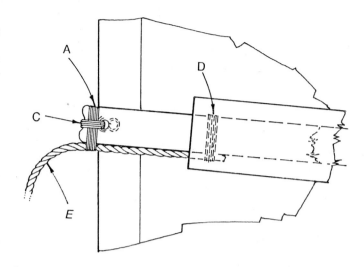

Fig. 11.4   Sheet span seized to batten

With a tubular batten it would be tempting to modify the design shown in Fig. 10.13 so as to permit the sheet span to enter a bell-mouthed hole at the end of the tube, possibly re-emerging a few inches further forward to be seized to the outside of the tube, but it would be necessary to devise a simple way of hauling out the leech of the sail.

With spans seized to the battens it would be doubly necessary for an ocean voyager to provide enough adjustment on the topping-lifts to enable the furled sail bundle to be lowered until the after batten ends could be worked on in safety. Closed-end pockets (Fig. 11.7) could not of course be used with these systems.

If the sail is to have double sheets (Fig. 4.47) no beckets are needed but the battens will require 'sheet windows' which are open right through the sail, to enable the sheet spans to be hitched to the batten from both sides. The positioning of these windows will be a compromise between sheeting efficiency, which would put them close to the leech, and freedom from fouling of the spans (Fig. 4.53) which would put them further forward. Fig. 11.5 shows the suggested position and size of the sheet windows, but this is not based on much experience of double sheets.

With double sheets the top batten may be sheeted, and being further forward it is logical to do this either with a sheet window very close to the leech or with a normal becket fitted to this batten only, as in *Batwing* (Fig. 16.9).

All lacing eyes on the sail, except for those on its four corners, are spurtooth brass grommets punched through the cloth. The worked cringles in the four corners are lightly loaded and need not be heavily reinforced. The emergency reefing grommets (D) are for use if the topping-lifts should carry away. The sail would then be reefed by passing a lacing, or individual stops, round the furled sail-bundle and through these grommets. The emergency lacing grommets (E) in Fig. 11.2 are for use only if the roping of the sail should start to pull out of the track on the yard or boom.

It is suggested that the luff and leech should be lightly

adjusted (see Fig. 12.2), but it is possible for a span to get temporarily caught behind the hitch on a becket below it. Such fouling is not serious, and will automatically free itself if the sail is allowed to weathercock, but it is worth noting that the Chinese commonly seize the sheet span to the end of the batten so that it tends to stand out from the leech and there is nothing to get foul.

Fig. 11.4 shows a possible starting point for developing such a system for Western rigs. The webbing becket has now been omitted and the sheet span (E) secured to the underside of the batten by two seizings, both of which are put on before the sail is stretched out along the batten. A shallow recess (A) on the upper side of the batten helps to locate the after seizing, which is made still more secure by the haul-out seizing (C) that lies on top of it. The second span seizing (D) may finish inside the batten pocket, as shown, and the length of the span (E) would be adjusted by varying the length that lies along the batten.

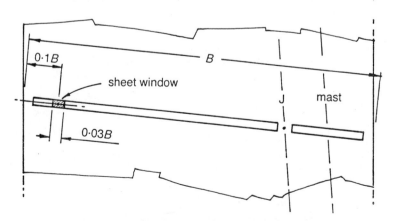

Fig. 11.5   Sheet windows for double sheets

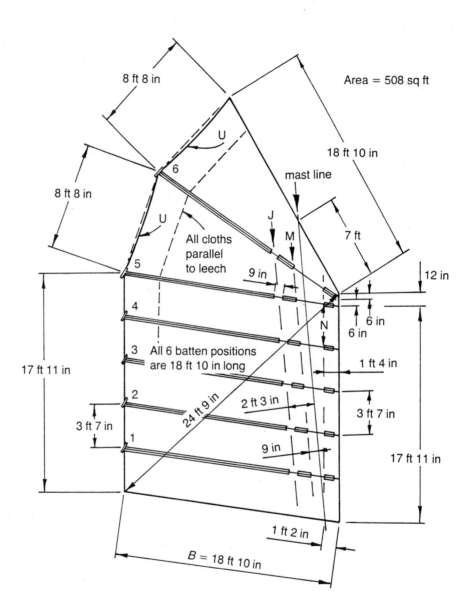

Fig. 11.6   Sail of more than 300 sq ft (28 m²)

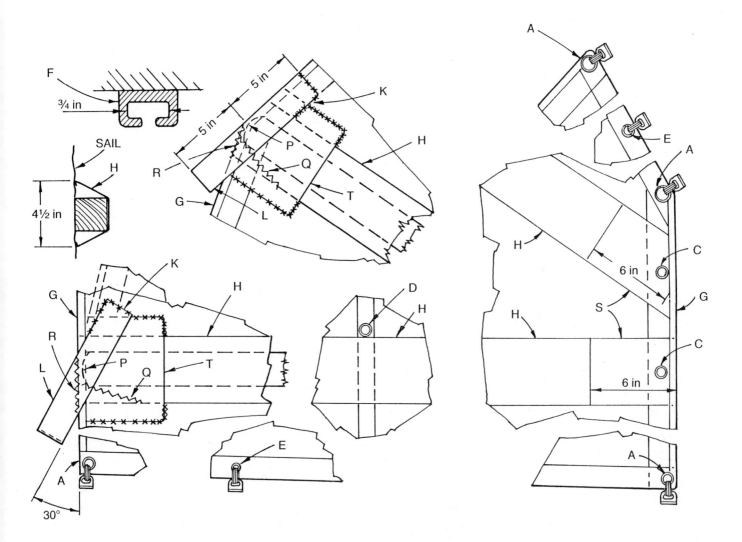

Fig. 11.7   Detail for Fig. 11.6

Fig. 11.8   Specification for sail shown in Fig. 11.6 and 11.7

Key

A   Hand-worked grommets or hydraulic-pressed rings approx. ¾ in (19 mm) i.d.

B   Length of head, foot, and batten positions when fully stretched

C   Spurtooth grommets approx. ½ in (13 mm) i.d. at forward ends of battens

D   Emergency reefing grommets approx. ⅜ in (10 mm) i.d. on each seam immediately above each batten pocket

E   Spurtooth grommets approx. ½ in (13 mm) i.d. for slides, spaced approx. 18 in (0.5 m) along head and foot.

F   Full-sized section of track on yard and boom. Slides to suit this

G   Folded polyester tape along luff and leech, of same cloth as sail

H   Pockets to take square batten 2¼ in × 2¼ in (57 × 57 mm) *with sail flat*, but tapered down to enter under patch T

J   Centres of parrel windows

K   Loop of 2 in (50 mm) polyester webbing sewn to both sides of sail above pocket

L   Leave loop open

M   After ends of fender windows

N   Forward ends of fender windows

P   End of batten enters folded patch T

Q   Extra stitching keeps end of batten on centreline

R   Webbing sewn together close abaft leech tape

S   Batten patches run full length

T   Patch of heavy cloth folded round leech to close pocket. Sewn through sail on top and bottom edges

U   Slight reverse roach in leech of top panels

1. Material: 7½ oz polyester, tan.
2. All measurements to edge of sail *when fully stretched*. When new, its stretched measurements along head, foot, and batten positions should be at least 1½ in (38 mm) short.
3. Sail to be cut absolutely flat. The master diagonal measurement is critical. Please note that its upper end runs to the throat, not to the top of the parallelogram.
4. Luff to be cut straight between battens, head and foot to be cut straight. Leech to be straight between lower battens but slightly hollowed in the two top panels at U.
5. Full-width cloths parallel to leech, changing direction at nos. 5 and 6 battens.
6. Battens lie on starboard side of sail.
7. Sailmaker, please mark cloth on starboard side of sail at head and foot and immediately above each batten pocket (e.g. by a short line with dye pen) to show mast line.

taped with polyester cloth of the same weight as the sail, on sails of about 200 sq ft (19 m²) and over.

Each drawing should be completed by giving it a reference number and marking it with its scale or scales, date, designer's name and address, name of sail, and references to the other two sheets relating to that sail.

LARGER SAILS. Fig. 11.6 shows a specimen sail of 508 sq ft (47 m²), with Fig. 11.7 showing its detail and Fig. 11.8 its specifications. It is similar to the previous example except as follows:

1. The sizes of the grommets have been increased.
2. The batten pockets are now mounted on full-length 'batten patches'. (This is recommended for sails of about 300 sq ft (28 m²) and over.)
3. The leech ends of the batten pockets are closed, with no grommets. The batten is prevented from twisting by being seized to the grommet at the luff. Sails of over about 550 sq ft (51 m²) may need extra reinforcement at these luff grommets, which have to sustain a heavy thrust from the battens. At the leech, the closed end of the pockets is reinforced by a patch (T), by the leech tape (G), and by the becket (K) which now embraces the pocket so that the end of the batten passes between the two sides of the becket.
4. The head and foot are fitted with slides to suit the track shown in Fig. 11.7. This is not as neat as the system used on the smaller sail but is stronger, and makes it easier to run the sail on and off the spars.
5. Emergency lacing grommets are no longer required on the head and foot, since the grommets through which the slides are seized could be used for this purpose.
6. The line (M) of the after ends of the fender windows is parallel to the mast line and about 0.04B abaft it.
7. The line (N) of the forward ends of the fender windows is parallel to the *luff* and about 0.07B from it, so that the windows get progressively longer as you move up the sail. This caters for the fact that the upper battens drift further aft when the sail is reefed (Fig. 2.26). It might be thought that the two short lengths of pocket on each batten are not worth while, but in fact they play an important part in reducing the amount by which the sail can sag away from the batten on the starboard tack.

12 The Rigging

The rigging of a Chinese sail, at least of sizes below about 700 sq ft (65 m²), will use no wire rope but only cordage, preferably of synthetic polyester. This may be of the traditional three-strand lay-up, or one of the many different braided or braided-sheath lay-ups produced by different manufacturers. Three-strand rope is resistant to chafe and convenient to splice, but some types of braided rope are more flexible, less liable to take a twist, and easier on the hands. Pre-stretched rope is not recommended, being less flexible and liable to shrink in service.

The rigging may be divided into standing and running rigging. The former comprises the ropes that are not normally readjusted for any reason other than rope stretch.

The rigging arrangements of all types of Chinese sail have been discussed in Chapters 3 and 4. This chapter gives detailed instructions for rigging the recommended form of sail, whose standing rigging consists of the mast lift, upper topping-lifts, sheet spans, batten parrels, tack parrel or standing lower luff parrel, and tackline. The running rigging consists of halyard, sheet, yard hauling parrel, luff hauling parrel, and burgee halyard, plus ghoster halyard, batten downhauls, yard downhaul, and running tack parrel. The lower part of the topping-lift is also a running rope on all but the smallest sails.

The size of a rope may be expressed either in circumference or diameter, but the latter is universally used with metric measurements. Table 6 gives equivalent rope sizes.

The Chinese sail, with its very light loadings, can be rigged with much smaller rope than an equivalent conventional sail. When used for running rigging, this can be rather hard on the hands. The recommended sizes for the smaller sails are tolerable if the watchkeeper's hands are in good seagoing condition, or if gloves are worn. Alternatively, it is reasonable to increase the rope sizes for the halyard and sheet of a small sail to 1 in (8 mm dia.) simply in order to be kind to the hands, and this has been done in the example given in the Rigging Warrant.

When specifying blocks, excessive friction is avoided

Table 6. Equivalent rope sizes

Circumference (in)	Diameter (in)	Diameter (mm)
¼	0.08	2
⅜	0.12	3
½	0.16	4
⅝	0.20	5
¾	0.24	6
⅞	0.28	7
1	0.32	8
1⅛	0.36	9
1¼	0.40	10
1⅜	0.44	11
1½	0.48	12
1⅝	0.52	13
1¾	0.56	14
2	0.64	16
2¼	0.72	18
2½	0.80	20
2¾	0.88	22
3	0.95	24

by ensuring (a) that the diameter of the sheave is at least twice the circumference of the rope or six times its diameter (preferably more), and (b) that the 'swallow' of the block is substantially wider than the diameter of the rope, to avoid rubbing against the inside of the cheeks. It should not then be necessary to specify roller bearings if the sheaves are free-running.

Blocks with fixed eyes may be either 'eye across' (eye at right angles to the sheave) or 'eye in line' (eye parallel to the sheave). We specify which is required in order to avoid having to use a twist shackle, or two straight shackles. If the eye of the block is to be shackled to another eye, or to the yard sling plate, the two eyes will of course lie in the same direction, with the shackle at right angles to them. A more convenient type of block has its own reversible shackle which may be assembled either in line or across, and this removes the problem.

Swivel blocks must never be used in any position where the ropes that pass through them are substantially parallel, because they will twist up and jam. They may be used as lead blocks if the ropes have an included angle of at least 80°.

The theory of sheet layouts has been discussed at length in Chapter 4. Figs. 6.30 to 6.33 give the recommended forms of sheet, in each case with the option of using either a euphroe or ordinary blocks and thimbles that can be bought off the shelf. The latter systems are perfectly satisfactory and have been chosen for the example in this chapter, but the euphroe systems offer slightly more elegant geometry at the expense of having to make up euphroes to suit the job.

Where winches are recommended they may be of the smallest size that suits the rope, again observing that the working loads are lighter than those of a comparable jib sheet. Self-tailing winches offer the convenience of being able to grind in with one hand while hanging on to the ship with the other.

Steel thimbles, either stainless or galvanised, are recommended at the masthead, while nylon thimbles are suitable for the sheet spans and for the parts of the topping-lifts that rub against the sail, but make sure that there is not a raised seam on the inside of the thimble.

In order to be able to list the rope, blocks, shackles, thimbles, and other fittings needed for the rig it is necessary to produce a scale rigging diagram as in Fig. 12.1. From this a rigging warrant may be made up, as in Table 7, which includes all the rigging components right through to the cockpit. An explanation of items which fall under the heading 'deck layout' will be found in Chapter 13.

Fig. 12.1 shows the rigging diagram for the single-sailed rig on *Pilmer* (Fig. 16.10). (The rigging diagram for other boats will differ in detail, as will the corresponding detail drawings and rigging warrants.) The profile shows all the rigging as far down as the deck, except for a few ropes cut away for clarity, and the deck layout is shown in plan below it. This design uses the 'low line' for the fall of the halyard and yard hauling parrel (see Fig. 8.23), and therefore requires deck blocks rather than cheek blocks on the mast. The key includes notes on how to reeve certain ropes, but these could be different on another boat. The best leads should be worked out on the actual boat with the sail first hoisted and then lowered.

Table 7 shows the corresponding rigging warrant, and Fig. 12.2 is an additional drawing showing details of rigging, which will be needed if the rigger is unfamiliar with the junk rig. The rigging warrant for a particular boat would normally specify the make and catalogue number of the hardware listed. For a multi-masted rig

the gear for each sail would be shown separately, either on a single large warrant or on separate warrants.

The rigging diagram (Fig. 12.1) may be started by tracing off the scale sail plan that has already been produced as described in Chapter 7. It shows the sail(s) fully hoisted and sheeted flat, plus the deck in plan and profile. The lengths of rope measured off it will need allowances for other attitudes of the sail, for the parts that pass around the mast, for the parts that lead along the deck to the cockpit, for the amount of rope used in splices, hitches, stopper knots and for passing round winches and cleats, plus a few feet for the spare ends of the running ropes.

Some of these allowances are larger than might be expected. For example,

> Splice (three-strand rope): rope circumference × 6, diameter × 19
> Splice (braided rope): see makers' instructions for splicing
> Clove hitch (around batten): depth of batten × 10
> Double becket hitch (on sheet spans): rope circumference × 9, diameter × 28
> Stopper knot: rope circumference × 9, diameter × 28
> Bowline (with small bight): rope circumference × 12, diameter × 38
> Cleat or winch: rope circumference × 36, diameter × 113

The alternative to working out these rather precise measurements is simply to order ample rope of the required sizes and to cut off and fuse each length *ad hoc* as you rig the boat. The choice may depend on the circumstances under which the boat is to be rigged, but preparing everything in advance of rigging the boat saves time on the day.

The ends of all synthetic ropes should be fused into a hard cone, except for those that are to be spliced round a thimble, which should be lightly fused before splicing. By heating the end of the rope gently over a blue flame, such as a small spirit stove or gas burner, and working it with a knife blade or a flat metal surface, or between moistened fingers, it is possible to produce hard, transparent, tapered ends that are better than any whipping and will pass through any hole that will accept the rope itself. Similarly, before cutting synthetic rope it should be partially fused at that point, to prevent it from unlaying.

The halyard

Different layouts of halyard, and the correct way of reeving them, have been described in Chapter 3. Of these, Table 8 shows those now recommended.

The number of purchases may be varied to suit the

Table 7. Example of a rigging warrant

Rope lengths are in feet.
Rope sizes are in inches circumference.

	No. off	Length of each	Total lengths				Blocks incl. reversible shackles				Other shackles		Thimbles		Bullseye fairleads	Cleats	Deck eyes	Saddle eyes	
							For 1 in circ. rope			For ¾ in rope									
			1 in circ.	¾ in circ.	½ in circ.	cord	Double	Single and becket	Single	Single	Straight	Bow	Steel	Nylon					
Main halyard	1	99	99				1	1	1						1	1	1		Spliced into becket of block
Burgee halyard	1	50			50				1								1		
Main sheet	1	60	60						2					1	2	1			Thimble spliced in one end
Upper sheet spans	2	7		14					1					2					Thimble spliced in one end
Lower sheet spans	2	6		12															
Topping-lift upper spans	2	12		24								1	2	2					Thimbles spliced in each end, 11 ft 6 in between eyes
Topping-lift after span	1	27		27										2				1	Rove through top spans before splicing thimble in each end
Topping-lift hauling part	1	52		52						2					2	2	2	1	
Mast lift	1	24		24							1		1						Thimble spliced in one end
Yard hauling parrel	1	35		35						2					1	1	1		
Luff hauling parrel	1	30		30						3					1	1	1		
Standing lower luff parrel	1	5		5															
Battens 1 and 2 parrels	2	5		10							2								
Battens 3, 4, 5 parrels	3	5.5		16.5							3								
Batten 6 parrel	1	6.5		6.5							1								
Tackline	1	3.5		3.5													1		
Batten lacings	12	2.5				30													
Yard and boom end lacings	4	4				16													
Totals			159	259.5	50	46	1	1	5	7	7	1	3	7	7	6	7	2	

A – Halyard. Fall passes down inside E, outside C and N.
B – Sheet.
C – Yard hauling parrel. Fall passes down inside E and G, outside N
D – Luff hauling parrel. Fall passes down inside N_1 and N_2.
E – Topping-lift upper spans.*
F – Topping-lift after spans.*
G – Topping-lift hauling part, outside everything except H.*
H – Burgee halyard, outside everything.
J – Upper sheet spans.
K – Lower sheet spans.
L – Mast lift.
M – Standing lower luff parrel.
N – Batten parrels.
P – Tackline.
Q – Boom gallows
R – Furled sail lowered on to gallows.
S – Bullseye leads.
T – Lowest position of yard sling plate.
V – Deck blocks
W – Cleats.
Y – Yard sling plate.
* – Duplicated on port side of sail.
Z – Saddle eyes.

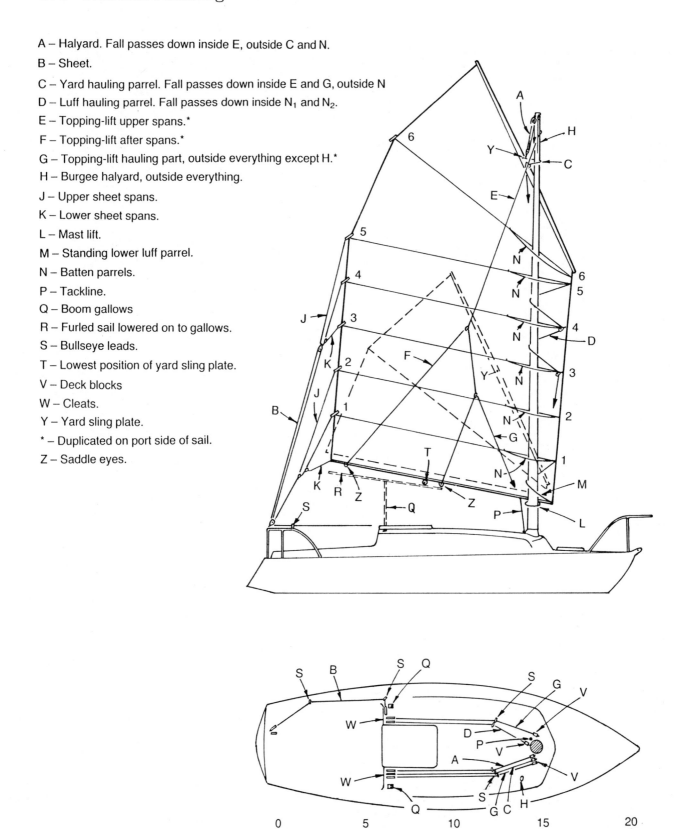

Fig. 12.1   Scale rigging diagram

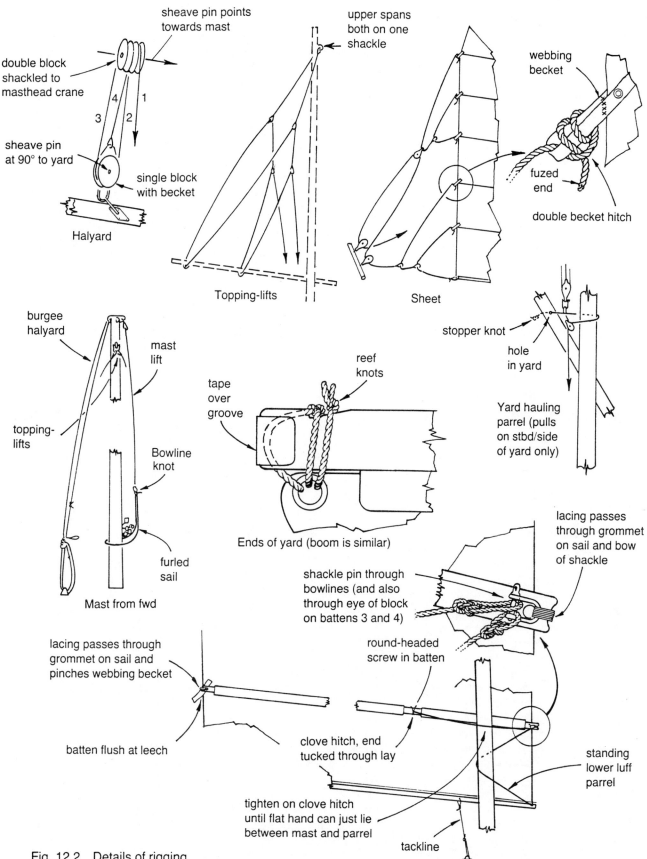

sheave pin points towards mast

double block shackled to masthead crane

sheave pin at 90° to yard

4 1
3 2

single block with becket

Halyard

upper spans both on one shackle

Topping-lifts

webbing becket

fuzed end

double becket hitch

Sheet

stopper knot

hole in yard

Yard hauling parrel (pulls on stbd/side of yard only)

burgee halyard

mast lift

topping-lifts

Bowline knot

furled sail

Mast from fwd

tape over groove

reef knots

Ends of yard (boom is similar)

shackle pin through bowlines (and also through eye of block on battens 3 and 4)

lacing passes through grommet on sail and bow of shackle

round-headed screw in batten

lacing passes through grommet on sail and pinches webbing becket

batten flush at leech

clove hitch, end tucked through lay

standing lower luff parrel

tighten on clove hitch until flat hand can just lie between mast and parrel

tackline

Fig. 12.2   Details of rigging

Table 8. Recommended rope sizes for halyards

Sail area (sq ft)	(m²)	Halyard (no. of parts)	Rope size* (in circ.)	(mm dia)
up to 100	up to 9	1 (Fig. 3.1)	¾	6
100–180	9–17	2 (Fig. 3.9)	¾	6
180–250	17–23	3 (Fig. 3.11) or 2 and winch	¾	6
250–400	23–37	4 (Fig. 3.13) or 3 and winch	1	8
400–700	37–65	5 (Fig. 3.14) or 4 and winch	1¼	10
over 700	over 65	5 and winch or single wire whip and drum winch (Fig. 3.3)	over 1¼	over 10

*¾ in (6 mm) ropes may be increased to 1 in (8 mm) in order to be kind to the hands.

user. For a given area of sail, a strong young man could choose to use fewer parts in the halyard, or an old-age pensioner could choose to use more, but it is not recommended that any tackle should have more than five parts. With practice, it is possible to use the motion of the boat in a seaway to assist in 'snatching' the halyard up, as discussed in Chapter 15.

The upper halyard block is difficult to reach at sea, and not all that easy in harbour. The two-part and four-part halyards have the becket on this upper block, which makes it impossible to reeve new rope for the halyard without climbing to the top of the mast. Fortunately, Chinese halyards usually last a long time: at least four years of normal use, or 20,000 miles of ocean cruising.

The length of the halyard is normally measured with the sail fully lowered on to its gallows, or into its standing topping-lifts. If there is an occasional need to lower the bundle further than this, e.g. down to the deck for repairs, a temporary rope tail will be bent on to the halyard, or a strop rigged between the sail bundle and the lower halyard block. Serious oceangoing yachtsmen may prefer to have enough spare length on the halyard for this purpose and to solve the problem of stowing it (see p 185), but this would be unusual. In either case, mark the rigging plan with the lowest position of the yard sling plate (T in Fig. 12.1) and take your measurements to this point.

The length of the halyard in feet in Fig. 12.1 and 12.2 is found as in the following example:

Splice at becket	1 ft
Three parts between blocks	63 ft
Upper block to deck	22 ft
Deck block to cleat	8 ft
Cleat	3 ft
Spare end	2 ft
Total	99 ft

The maximum length of halyard that will have to be stowed in the cockpit may be worked out by repeating these measurements with the sail fully hoisted, and subtracting the second total from the first.

BURGEE HALYARD. On a keel boat this is normally of three-strand polyester rope of ½ in circ. (4 mm dia.), with its two ends knotted to make an endless loop. It is long enough to allow the bight to be passed through a deck eye or under a grabrail (Fig. 12.2) and then secured to itself some distance above the deck with a rolling hitch on the bight, as shown. This allows plenty of spare cord for throwing hitches around the burgee stick without having to untie the ends of the halyard.

A multi-masted boat should have a burgee halyard on each mast, if only for passing an emergency halyard through the masthead as described on p 136. The rigging warrant allows a large masthead block on the burgee halyard for this purpose, although on the production boats of this class the halyard simply passes through the smooth eye (B in Fig. 8.29) on the stainless masthead fitting.

The Sheets

The recommended sheet systems are given in Chapter 6 (p 110ff). Single blocks rather than multiple blocks are preferred for the lower sheet blocks, because they line up more accurately with the sheet parts.

Before measuring the length of the sheet it is necessary to draw the sheet spans to their correct lengths on the rigging diagram. The instructions in Chapter 6 give the minimum drift (D_{min}) between clew and deck blocks for the sheet layout selected. Pages 62ff give the *net* lengths of the spans themselves to suit these values of D_{min}. If the available drift is more than D_{min}, the spans should be lengthened accordingly in order (a) to reduce the tendency for each span to pull its ends closer together, and (b) to reduce the length of the sheet.

To draw each span in its correct attitude, draw a line (A in Fig. 12.3) from the deck block to bisect the length of leech which that part of the sheet is controlling. The sheet is drawn along this line, as shown, and the lengths of the spans applied by trial and error to give the point of connection with the sheet.

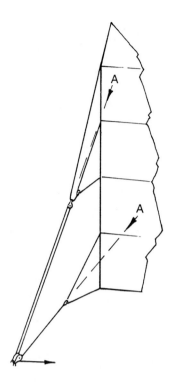

Fig. 12.3   Drawing sheet spans and sheets

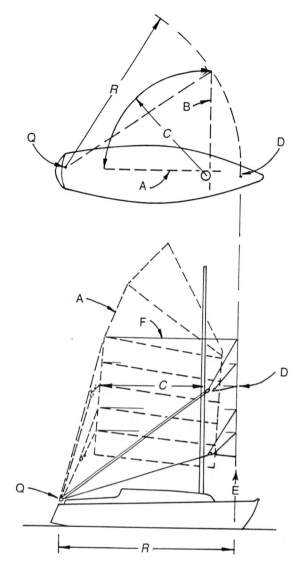

Fig. 12.4   Measuring maximum sheet length

The diagram now shows the sheets with the sail hauled flat amidships, but in order to measure the maximum length of sheet required it is necessary to simulate the condition of running before the wind with the full sail lying dead athwartships. A diagrammatic way of doing this is shown in Fig. 12.4. Use tracing paper over your scale drawings to save redrawing the profile and plan, the steps being as follows:

1. Draw the sail and sheet system hauled flat amidships (A), as described above.
2. In plan view, draw the sail (B) square athwartships to port, taking a point halfway up the leech and measuring its radius (C) from the centre of the mast.
3. To project the angled sheets on to the profile, strike an arc on the plan view with centre at the deck blocks (Q) and radius (R), cutting the boat's centreline at (D).
4. On the profile, draw a line (E) through (D) and parallel to the mast. (This is purely a construction line to enable you to measure the length of sheet when the sail is squared off.)
5. On the profile, strike each sheet point across to (E) by drawing lines (F) at right angles to the mast. Draw in the complete sheeting system as if it led to these points directly from (Q), as shown.

6. Measure each part of the sheet down to the deck blocks and add allowances for leading to the cockpit plus any splice, winch, or cleat, and for the spare end. This is now the length of rope that should be cut.

To find the maximum length of sheet that will have to be stowed in the cockpit, subtract the length of sheet needed when the sail is furled and stowed amidships.

For a multi-masted rig, repeat the procedure for each sail in relation to its own deck blocks.

The recommended rope sizes for sheets are the same as those for halyards, and may be taken from Table 8.

SHEET SPANS. The rope sizes for all these may be taken from List B in Table 9, but if desired the lower spans may

Table 9. Recommended rope sizes for different applications and sail areas

| Sail area | | List A | | List B | | List C | |
(sq ft)	(m²)	(in circ.)	(mm dia)	(in circ.)	(mm dia)	(in circ.)	(mm dia)
up to 180	up to 17	¾	6	⅝	5	½	4
180–250	17–23	1	8	¾	6	⅝	5
250–400	23–37	1¼	10	1	8	¾	6
400–700	37–65	1½	12	1¼	10	1	8
over 700	over 65	over 1½	over 12	over 1¼	over 10	over 1	over 8

Rope size heading spans List A/B/C columns.

Select rope size according to purpose from List A, B, or C as indicated in the text.

be taken from List C. The net lengths of the spans have already been established before drawing the sheet system on the rigging diagram (see above). To these net lengths must be added allowances for any splices and for the double becket hitches on the sail beckets (see p 172 and Fig. 12. 2). (N.B. For most of the remaining ropes in this chapter, the rope sizes may be taken from Table 9, using List A, B, or C as suggested in each case, but for a seagoing cruising boat it is reasonable to use ropes no smaller than ¾ in (6 mm dia.) except for the burgee halyard. This has been done in the rigging warrant.)

Topping-lifts

These are made of ample strength, for three reasons:

1. The weight of the furled sail bundle is considerable, and it is sometimes convenient to be able to add much more weight by using it as a derrick.
2. Small ropes are more liable than larger ropes to catch and chafe the folded sailcloth, and also to stretch too much under the weight of the sail bundle.
3. If a topping-lift should part at sea, the reefing facility is lost and any reefed panels will fall to the deck. It then becomes necessary to crawl round the deck tying lacings through the emergency reefing grommets. Meanwhile it is very likely that the loose end aloft will have snarled round the halyard and jammed it!

Some users have fitted plastic hose over the full length of the upper topping-lift spans, to prevent chafe on the ropes and on a wooden yard.

The size of rope for the upper topping-lift spans should be taken from List A in Table 9. The lower spans may be taken from List B.

Topping-lifts should be designed in relation to the position of the close-reefed sail, which should be drawn

with two panels set as shown by the dotted outline in Fig. 12.1 and 12.5. To do this, make a separate trace of the yard and two top panels and adjust it underneath the trace of the full sail so that it sits slightly above the line of the boom and is staggered aft so that its luff is about halfway between the tack and the mast. This will be accurate enough for our purposes.

A good way of drawing the lifts is shown in Fig. 12.5. This shows the starboard side of the system only, the port side being identical. The spans run freely through to the other side of the boom at A and K.

Mark the point A on the underside of the boom, so that its distance from the clew is about 0.04B, where B is the length of the boom. This will be the position of the aftermost eye fitting on the underside of the boom. Mark a construction point (C) on the underside of boom, whose distance from the tack is about 0.33B. Halfway between A and C mark another construction point (D).

On the forward side of the masthead mark point E, which is either a mast eyeplate as in Fig. 8.29 or the point at which the lifts cross over and are seized together as in Fig. 3.58a. This point must be well above the yard: say about halfway between the masthead and the level of the yard sling plate.

Join DE and mark on it a point (F) which is below the reefed yard and in the middle of a panel when under full sail. EF is then the starboard upper topping-lift span, whose lower end finishes in a nylon thimble, or in a small block in the case of a sail of more than about 300 sq ft (28 m²).

Join AF and FC. On FC mark point G, which is normally towards the bottom of the next sail panel below F. AFG is then the starboard side of the after topping-lift span, finishing in a nylon thimble at its forward end, or a small block if a block is fitted at F. Connect G to the deck block (H) for the hauling span, or in the case of standing lifts to an eye fitting (J) on the underside of boom that will be on a similar line. Mark the position (K) of the remaining eye fitting on the underside of the boom so that CJ and CK are equal

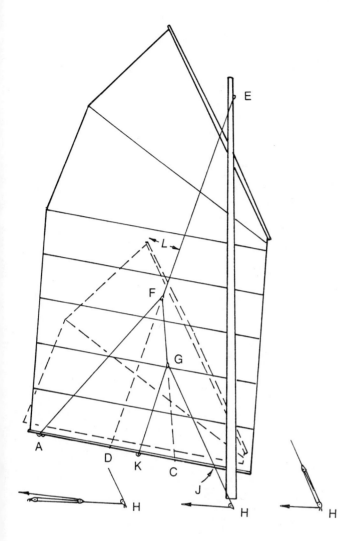

Fig. 12.5   Drawing the topping-lifts

If it is found from experience that a sail-gatherer (Fig. 3.53) is desirable, the form shown at a is preferred.

The final layout of the topping-lifts should be checked as follows:

1. The distance L (Fig. 12.5) between the reefed peak and the upper topping-lift span should be at least $B/7$ $(0.14B)$, where B is the length of the head of the sail. This is necessary in order to discourage the reefed peak from getting the wrong side of the lifts, as discussed on p 53. If it is necessary to increase L, point A may be moved slightly forward, possibly using the form of sail-gatherer shown in Fig. 3.53b.
2. The drift (FG) must be enough to allow the furled sail bundle to be lowered as far as will be needed, usually only on to a gallows or crutch but in some cases (see p 176) right down to the deck. Enough spare rope must be allowed on the two hauling ends, including any tackles, to permit this amount of lowering. If necessary, the fully lowered position may be drawn and the parts measured. If planning to lower the whole bundle to the deck, the mast lift will also have to be let go as discussed below.

The length of each part of the topping-lifts may now be taken off the rigging diagram, with the usual allowances, and entered in the rigging warrant, not forgetting to allow as much again for the port side. Note on the rigging warrant that the after span must be rove through the thimbles or blocks on the top spans before splicing.

Mast lift

Different forms of mast lift have been discussed on p 51. In the current example, Figs. 12.1 and 12.2 show the normal form, as in Fig. 3.49.

If there is a requirement for lowering the whole furled sail bundle to the deck, it will be necessary to provide for lengthening or letting go the mast lift. On a sail of up to about 350 sq ft (33 m²) it may be possible for one man to hold up the forward end of the bundle while he unties the bowline, but for larger sails it would be better to provide a running mast lift as shown in Fig. 3.50b. Rope size: List B.

Parrels

YARD HAULING PARREL. For a discussion of the theory and practice of yard hauling parrels see p 38. The recommended form is shown in Fig. 3.19, although an alternative form is used in this example. Rope size: List B.

LUFF HAULING PARREL. See p 47 and Fig. 3.42 which shows the recommended system used in Fig. 12.1. A

distances. KGH is then the starboard side of the hauling span, and is extended aft to the cockpit with as much spare rope as is needed.

For sails of more than about 300 sq ft (28 m²) it is necessary to fit purchases on the falls of the topping-lifts, either above the deck blocks or along the deck, as shown in alternative forms in Fig. 12.5. The blocks and ropes for these should of course be added to the rigging warrant.

There are a number of possible variations to this topping-lift layout, all of which have been discussed and illustrated in Chapter 3 (pp 50–55). If no boom crutch or gallows is to be fitted, standing lifts may be used such as those in Fig. 3.47, of which a is suitable only for a small sail with narrow panels.

For running topping-lifts, Fig. 3.51 a or c provide alternatives, the latter being associated with purchases (Fig. 3.52) for a sail of more than about 200 sq ft (19 m²).

detail in Fig. 12.2 shows the shackle and grommet at the forward ends of battens 3 and 4 which also carry the two blocks needed. Rope size: List B or C.

STANDING LOWER LUFF PARREL OR STANDING TACK PARREL. See p 42 and Fig. 3.25 and 3.26. The arrangement of a standing lower luff parrel is shown in Fig. 12.1 and 12.2. Rope size: List C.

BATTEN PARRELS. Normal (long) batten parrels are shown, as in Fig. 3.32, but it will be seen from Fig. 12.2 that their forward ends finish in a bowline passing round the pin of a shackle which is held by the luff lacing of the batten. These shackles also carry the components of the luff hauling parrel and the standing lower luff parrel, an arrangement that facilitates bending and unbending the sail from the mast. Alternatively, rope grommets or small strops made up from several turns of polyester cord may be used instead of these shackles.

The after ends of the batten parrels are in the centre of the windows in the batten pockets, on a line (J in Fig. 11.1) parallel to the mast line and, in this case, 1 ft 6 in (0.46 m) abaft it, following the rule given on p 163. At this point a small round-headed screw is shown standing proud from the top of the batten to prevent the clove hitch from sliding forward. Alternatively, a well-tied rolling hitch or constrictor knot may stay in place without the screw.

It will be seen from Fig. 12.1 that the batten parrels get longer as you go up the sail, and this is reflected in the lengths listed in Table 7. Rope size: List C.

Tackline

The upper end of the tackline is located on the boom by an eye, groove, or hole as described in Chapter 10, and may be rigged as shown in Fig. 12.2, its length being adjustable by means of a bowline or rolling hitch. This length controls the height of the sail on the mast when under full sail, and hence the adjustment of the topping-lifts, which should then be just slack. Rope size: List C.

Lacings

BATTEN LACINGS. These are shown in Fig. 12.2. Note that any excess batten length should protrude at the luff and not at the leech, as indicated. The size of the polyester cord may be selected so that at least four turns of it will pass through the sail grommet and the hole in the batten.

YARD AND BOOM LACINGS. In this example the yard and boom are of the grooved type shown in Fig. 10.5 and 10.18, and these lacings simply haul out the peak, throat, tack, and clew. The method of reeving them is shown in Fig. 12.2. The size of polyester cord can be the same as that of the batten lacings. For a laced yard and boom as in Fig. 10.2 a larger size of cord or small rope will be needed, but the separate stops shown in Fig. 10.3 may be of the same cord as the yard and boom lacings shown above.

Optional rigging items

If they are to be fitted, the following ropes should also be included in the scale rigging diagram, details of rigging, and rigging warrant (the suggested rope sizes are taken from Table 9):

Rope	Size
Ghoster halyard (see p 136)	List A
Batten downhauls (see p 48)	List C
Yard downhaul (see p 49)	List C

WINCHES. If winches are to be fitted, these should be added to the rigging warrant. Rigs which require halyard winches are indicated in Table 8. For sheets, winches are suggested (see p 110) for sails of more than about 250 sq ft (23 m²) with three-part sheets, for sails of more than about 300 sq ft (28 m²) with four-part sheets, and for sails of more than about 350 sq ft (33 m²) with five or six part sheets.

It is now possible to obtain and prepare all the items of the rig.

13 Cockpit and Deck Layout

The layout of the deck and cockpit is a separate subject not directly related to the rigging of the sail. For example, a sail of 500 sq ft (46 m^2) may be arranged, as in China, so that the ropes are handled by a crew who move around the deck for the purpose. The deck layout is then simple and obvious.

At the other extreme, the deck may be arranged as in *Ròn Glas* (Fig. 16.4), with all running ropes leading into an enclosable wheelhouse, so that the watchkeeper can perform all sail handling operations without even putting his head out.

Somewhere in between these extremes lie most yacht layouts, in which all running ropes are brought to within reach of a normal cockpit, which may or may not be protected by a folding spray hood or doghouse at its forward end.

The purpose of this chapter is to enable a deck plan to be produced – equivalent to the plans in Fig. 12.1 or Fig. 13.24 – and also detailed plans and drawings of gallows or crutches, a specialised control position, circular hatches, rope stowage reels, etc, if required.

Boom gallows

Before planning the deck layout it is necessary to decide on how the furled sail bundle(s) will be secured, both at sea and in harbour.

At sea, the sail may be fully furled either when reduced to bare pole in a gale, or when motoring, or when becalmed in a left-over lop or swell. With sails of less than (say) 300 sq ft (28 m^2) it is normal practice to leave the furled sail hanging in the lifts at such times, with the addition of a yard lashing (Fig. 15.6) if there is a risk of the head of the sail fanning up (see p 208). If the boat is rolling the sheet will be set up taut, but this puts quite a load on the topping-lifts and bends the mast aft as the bundle snatches from side to side.

Larger furled sails should be lowered and secured into a strong gallows at such times, to avoid the snatching and to prevent the furled sail from chafing against the mast.

In harbour, it is recommended that all mainsails of more than about 150 sq ft (14 m^2) should be stowed on a gallows or boom crutch. On junk schooners, foresails up to about 300 sq ft (28 m^2) may be left hanging in the lifts in harbour, but any hanging sail bundle should be steadied by a guy either side from the after end of the sail bundle down to widely-spaced points on deck.

A gallows must be strong enough to support the full weight of the furled bundle and to cope with severe side loading when rolling, or when hove-to and hit by a sea. It may be a fixed structure (Fig. 13.1), folding (Fig. 13.2), or a dismountable crutch (Fig. 13.3). It is possible for the legs of a fixed gallows to be telescopic, but almost impossible to prevent such an arrangement from jamming. The traditional scissors crutch has little to recommend it, but if used its two feet must be firmly pinned or bolted into fixed sockets on deck.

If the boat has a high doghouse or wheelhouse the gallows may be a low structure on top of it. Looked at in profile it should support the bundle at a point within $0.25B$ of the clew, where B is the length of the boom. If it is necessary to mount it further forward than this in order to land on a high part of the boat's structure,

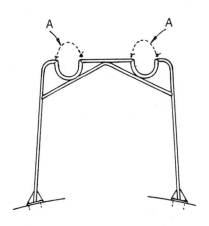

Fig. 13.1 Standing gallows

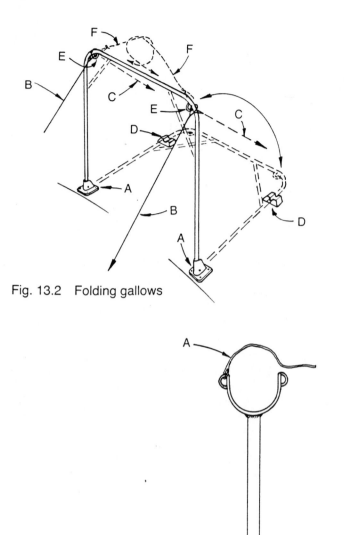

Fig. 13.2   Folding gallows

Fig. 13.3   Dismountable crutch

beware of bending the boom and battens by bowsing down the sheet too hard.

A gallows can provide a useful handhold and support at sea, particularly when standing up to use binoculars or sextant, and a radar-reflector may be carried beneath it if no higher position is feasible. A fixed gallows may need struts or stays in a fore-and-aft direction, and these can often be arranged so as to serve as useful grabrails. The final position of any gallows must be compatible with the layout of cleats, winches, and rope leads.

A fixed gallows should have its upper edge at least $B/20$ (0.05B) below the boom when under full sail. This will allow the reefed sail to settle somewhat into the topping-lifts while still swinging clear over the gallows. For stowing, the bundle is then lowered on to the gallows by paying out the topping-lifts.

The gallows may be lower than this, i.e. may have more than the minimum clearance below the boom, provided that the sheets can take up the slack without becoming 'two blocks', but to most eyes it would be unattractive for the after end of the stowed bundle to droop below the horizontal, although this is common in China.

A hinged gallows or dismountable crutch should preferably have a similar clearance under the boom so that it may be erected before handing the sail, but with a sail of less than about 200 sq ft (19 m²) and standing topping-lifts it is possible for the furled bundle to hang below crutch level. When the gallows or crutch is erected the bundle is then lifted by hand into it and the sheet set up, but this is a dubious operation at sea in heavy weather.

It may be necessary to work on the furled sail at sea, perhaps for repairing stitching or replacing a broken batten. It is not convenient to work at more than chest height, and if the gallows holds the bundle higher than this it is wise to provide for lowering the bundle alongside the gallows for sail repairs.

The top of a gallows, whether fixed or folding, may be formed into one or more 'U-sockets' as in Fig. 13.1, but the main tube will then probably need bracing, as shown. It is easier to fabricate a U-socket on a tubular metal crutch, as in Fig. 13.3. The deeper the 'U' the better it will hold the bundle, at the expense of more travel on the topping-lifts, but it is not strictly necessary for a socket to accommodate more than about three-quarters of the bundle. It will in any case be necessary to pass a tyer or lashing (A in Fig. 13.1 and 13.3) to prevent the unsheeted top panels from fanning up in gale force winds from aft.

Fig. 13.1 shows a U-socket on either side of the gallows. This makes it easy to lower the furled sail into the leeward socket when hulling at sea in a strong wind. In harbour the sail is stowed in the port socket so that the bundle lies roughly fore-and-aft and clear of a centreline companionway.

The folding gallows shown in Fig. 13.2 may be designed to fold either forward or aft, but not both. Its baseplates (A) incorporate stops to prevent it from pivoting past the vertical. It then has wire or rope stays (B) to hold it vertical. Additional stays (C) on the other side may be needed if it is to be left erected at sea. If straddling a companionway hatch, deck chocks (D) may be needed to prevent it from fouling the sliding hatch when lowered. This example has a straight top tube without any U-sockets. Eyes (E) under the top corners are large enough to take both the guys and two separate tyers (F) which hold the furled bundle firmly in any desired position. If necessary, diagonal struts (shown by dotted lines) may be fitted to stiffen the gallows sideways.

The simple dismountable crutch (Fig. 13.3) is suitable for some small boats. It is preferably a steel fabrication and has eyes to facilitate passing the lashing (A) over the top of the bundle. A pin (P) prevents the crutch from turning or jumping.

On all types of gallows leather or plastic may be fitted to reduce chafe on the sail, but this is not entirely necessary if the sail lies against a rounded surface of polished stainless steel, although even this may bruise a timber boom.

Lower sheet blocks

The position of the lower sheet blocks in profile will have been decided when drawing the sail plan (see Chapter 7). In plan view, they should be offset a little to port as shown in Fig. 4.44. It is possible to take all the running parts of the sheet through a multi-sheaved block at this point, but the sheaves will align themselves more accurately if separate single blocks are used. Although shown on the sheet diagrams, for clarity, as being spaced well apart, these blocks should be mounted as close together as is practicable, each supported by the anti-snarl hose shown in Fig. 14.1.

If the blocks are mounted on an existing stern pulpit it will need extra bracing to take the side loads. If they are mounted down on the deck it is probable that the sheets will lie across the guardrails when running. This is normally acceptable, particularly if a piece of plastic hose is fitted over the top wire in that area.

Rope leads

The ropes that come down at or near the foot of the mast are commonly the halyard, yard hauling parrel, luff hauling parrel, burgee halyard, and the two falls of the running topping-lifts. The latter may come down to deck blocks spaced well away from the mast and more or less abreast of it, since the lead of the lifts ensures that they will not get foul of the luff when sailing. The four remaining ropes will come down close to the starboard side of the mast, in the 'chimney' (see Fig. 3.6). Unless they are kept close to the mast they may get foul of the luff of the sail when running on the starboard gybe with the sail fully squared-off to port.

If required, the halyard and yard hauling parrel may be led through a double cheek block on the mast and brought aft along a 'high line' as in Fig. 8.23. This will be almost essential if the mast is stepped just forward of a

coach roof rather than through it; the high line will then follow close along the top of the coach roof. The cheek blocks must be given an anti-snarl fairing as in Fig. 8.26.

If the running ropes are to be led aft to a cockpit it is logical to take them all to the starboard side except for the port topping-lift. This may produce a congestion of cleats on the starboard side, especially if there is a companionway slide occupying the centreline. To reduce this congestion, the luff hauling parrel may be allowed to rub partly round the mast and be led across to the port side, as in Fig. 12.1.

With a two-master the positioning of the cleats calls for more thought, in order to avoid greater congestion and to provide a logical layout that is easy for the watchkeeper to remember. It is often possible to lead all or most of the foresail's running ropes past the port side of the mainmast and so aft to the port side of the cockpit, but this depends on being able to find tolerable rope leads without too many changes of direction.

Ideally, every change of direction in a hauling rope would be achieved with a turning block whose sheave was exactly aligned with the two parts of the rope, but this would be rather clumsy and expensive on a small yacht. It is suggested that sheaves should be used only for changes of direction of more than 40°. A single change of less than 40° can be made with a proprietary bullseye lead, or more compactly with a hardwood B-block, or bee-block, (Fig. 13.4) designed *ad hoc* to carry any required number of ropes. Never lead more than one rope through each hole, even if there is plenty of clearance, as the ropes will develop great friction against each other.

If two or more dumb leads of this sort are to be used on a single hauling rope, the total rope deflection of all these leads should not exceed 40°, e.g. two of 20° each or three of 13° each.

When positioning the fairleads and cleats it may be worth making provision for 'swigging' the rope, particularly for a sheet or halyard where no winch is fitted. This is achieved as shown in Fig. 13.5, by arranging for the cleat (A) to be distant between 4 and 8 ft (1.2–2.4 m) from a rope lead (B), and with provision for the watchkeeper to stand alongside the rope in between the two. For those

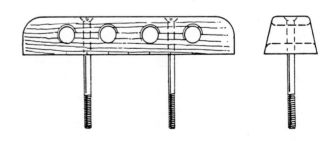

Fig. 13.4 Hardwood B-block

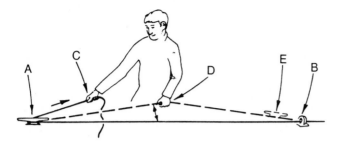

Fig. 13.5   Swigging a rope

Fig. 13.6   Correct alignment of cleat

unfamiliar with the art, swigging consists in holding on with hand C while pulling the rope sideways (as shown by the dotted line) with hand D. The rope is then gently allowed to resume its straight line at D while hand C pulls in the slack. It is a method of harnessing friction, and can provide a safe and powerful way of inching in a rope under load.

The kind of swigging position shown in Fig. 13.5 may well obstruct other cockpit activities. In this case a second cleat (E) may be provided, to which the rope may be transferred after it has been swigged fully home, leaving cleat A vacant. It may then be possible for cleat A to serve as a swigging base for more than one rope, but only if the transfers can be made without losing anything on the fully-loaded ropes.

Cleats, hitches, and jammers

For halyards and sheets where no winch is fitted, use ordinary two-horned cleats of ample size, capable of taking one round turn plus two figure-of-eight turns, and fully radiused for surging the rope under load. Ideally they should be positioned looking about 10° to the left of the line of the taut rope (Fig. 13.6), but this refinement is seldom practised.

If self-tailing winches are fitted and the turns of rope are to be left on the winch while sailing, no cleat is needed. With ordinary winches a small cleat or jam cleat may be used to hold the back-up part. An alternative and very good way of belaying a winch without any cleat is with a bollard hitch (Fig. 13.7), which is made by passing a bight of the back-up part under the taut hauling part, taking it once anticlockwise round the upper part of the drum and then pulling hand-taut on the back-up end. This hitch cannot possibly jam and was used in *Jester* (Fig. 16.1) on a pair of halyard and sheet winches that were commonly used without their handles, simply for snubbing and swigging.

If more than one rope is to be worked on a single winch the tensioned parts may be rove through lever-type rope jammers (A in Fig. 13.8). All forms of jam cleat can

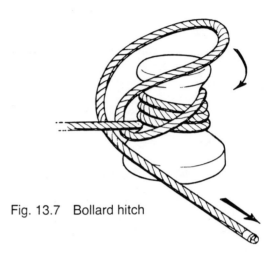

Fig. 13.7   Bollard hitch

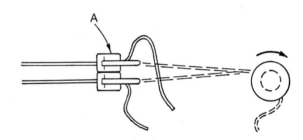

Fig. 13.8   Lever jammers on tensioned ropes

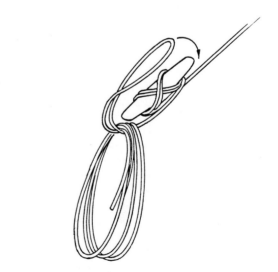

Fig. 13.9   Coil hitch

become difficult or impossible to free when the rope is very heavily tensioned. They are only completely safe when, as in Fig. 13.8, the weight can be taken off them by heaving in on a winch.

Stowage of spare rope

Whether sailing or at anchor considerable lengths of running rigging have to be stowed, notably the end of the halyard when under full sail and of the sheet when the sail is furled. All spare ends should be out of the way but ready for letting go at very short notice without snarling up.

The simplest method of stowage is to coil the rope in the hand, clockwise and *starting from the cleat*, and then to hang the coil on its own cleat. The right way of doing this is to pass the hand through the coil, grab the short length of rope between coil and cleat, twist it once, pull it back through the coil and hang it over the far horn of the cleat. This final stage is shown in Fig. 13.9. Before paying out the rope the whole coil should be unhitched and laid carefully on the deck, right way up, but there is still a risk that it will not run out cleanly.

By far the best way of stowing the end of a halyard or sheet is on a stowage reel (Fig. 13.10) that has been designed to take the amount of rope needed. This is not a drum winch and is not intended for heaving in under load. After the rope has been hove in either by hand or with a winch, it is cleated and the stowage reel is turned by hand to wind on the slack.

The advantages are that the rope is stowed more compactly and is instantly ready to pay out without snarling, if necessary at high speed. If paying out or heaving in only a small amount of rope it is not necessary to disturb the remainder, and the act of reeling in or out does not put any turns in the rope. Nevertheless, the rope will sometimes develop its own tendency to kink, and the bitter end is secured in such a way that it can be revolved in its hole in order to take out any such turns. (A more elegant way, for the expert, is to take out any turns by coiling a few turns on or off the stationary reel.)

Reels may be mounted either vertically or horizontally and the latter, at least, should have a fixed baffle (F) to avoid any risk of the rope jamming between the reel and its supporting surface, or riding on the rim. If mounted horizontally, the lower flange should be of slightly larger diameter than the upper flange.

The reel should be as light as possible to reduce the tendency to over-run, and it is no bad thing to have a little friction on the spindle. Otherwise, use the hand on the rim as a brake.

Fig. 13.10 shows the type of stowage reel mounted vertically in *Ròn Glas* (Fig. 13.24). A brass spool (A) with brazed flanges (B) revolves on a brass spindle (C) whose

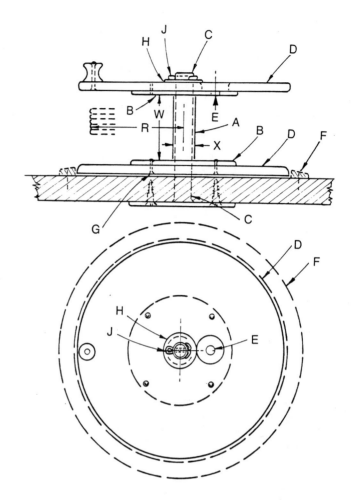

Fig. 13.10   Rope-stowage reel

baseplate is fastened to the far side of the bulkhead. Plywood flanges (D) are riveted to the spool. The bitter end of the rope passes out through a small hole (E) in the spool and its stopper knot sits partly shrouded in the larger hole in the plywood flange. Washers at G and H and a split pin J complete the assembly.

The recommended diameter of the spool (A) is 1 in (25 mm), and the recommended width (W) between the flanges is 3 in (76 mm). The radius (R) of a rope of given length when wound neatly on such a reel may be derived from Fig. 13.11, which gives curves for the four sizes of rope most commonly used. The radius of the plywood flanges must be greater than radius R: add twice the diameter of the rope, or four times the diameter of the rope for the lower flange of a reel that is to be mounted horizontally.

There are other ways of stowing the spare ends of rope. Some users have fitted fabric bags secured to a bulkhead, with a separate bag for each rope. In this case the rope should not be coiled but should be flaked in, starting with the hauling end, each layer forming a figure-of-

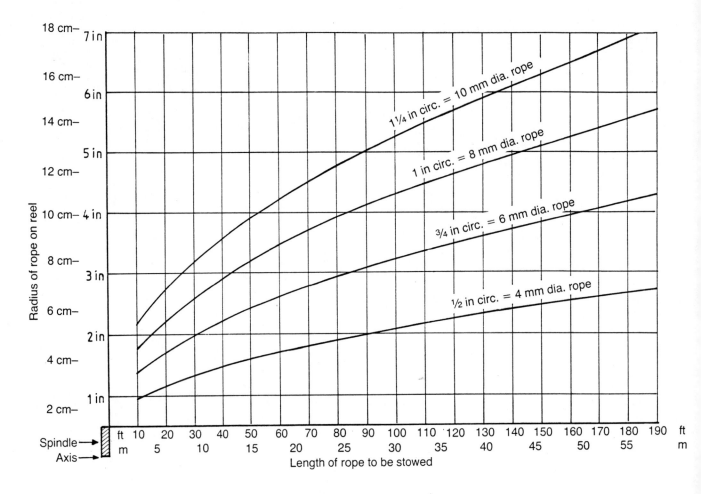

Fig. 13.11 Stowage of rope on standard reel with spindle 1 in. OD × 3 in

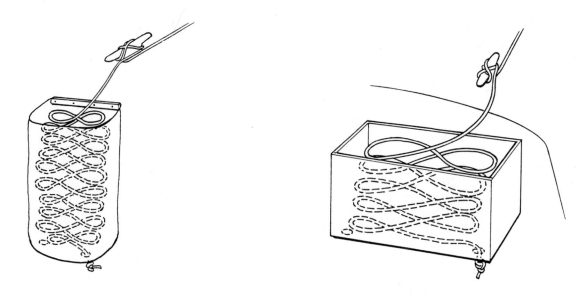

Fig. 13.12 Rope flaked into bag   Fig. 13.13 Rope flaked into box

eight as shown diagrammatically in Fig. 13.12. This prevents the rope from forming kinks and, with luck, enables it to pull straight out of the bag without fouling. Stowing the rope in the bag takes rather a long time. Drain holes will be needed in the bottom, one of which may take the bitter end with a stopper knot outside. A bag may also be mounted horizontally on the deck or coachroof, but this is less convenient to stow.

Boxes may be used instead of bags (Fig. 13.13) and are a bit easier to use. At least one boat has fitted wooden drawers under the side deck of the cockpit. If these are shallow and broad the rope may be coiled in the hand, again starting from the cleat end, and then placed carefully in the drawer the right way up for paying out. Alternatively the rope may be flaked in as above, starting from the hauling end. The drawer should be opened before paying out.

Another method of stowage was used in *Yeong* (Fig. 16.5), but this requires at least 2 ft 6 in (0.8 m) of vertical bulkhead (Fig. 13.14). On the bulkhead are mounted a broad upper hook (A) and a lower hook (B) which is similar except that its hook end can be turned upwards. The rope is stowed starting from the cleat and winding it clockwise round the hooks, finishing with a hitch to look after the free end. To pay out rope the end is unhitched, the lower hook turned to disengage, and the coil lifted off and laid the right way up on deck. With this system the rope may be stowed very quickly – perhaps faster than with any other method described here. The hooks could be mounted sideways on a vertical surface, or perhaps mounted on a horizontal surface.

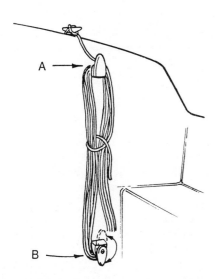

Fig. 13.14   The *Yeong* coil

Integrated deck layouts

It remains to plan an assembly of the features that will suit your boat and your purposes. A singlehanded sailor who is planning a circumnavigation by way of Cape Horn may aim at maximum simplicity of handling and complete weather-protection for the watchkeeper, together with putting a very high priority on his self-steering gear. A family man who wants to cruise across the English Channel in summer with teenage children may feel that they need a fair amount of deck work in the open air to keep them interested and feeling useful. He will still appreciate the junk rig for the safety value of instant reefing and the excellent performance when close-reefed in heavy weather, but extreme ease of handling and weather-protection may not be a requirement.

It is partly a question of how long you expect to stay at sea. In the last days of commercial sail in Britain, small coasting vessels were busily sprouting wheelhouses, but the idea of protecting the watchkeeper seems to be a difficult one for many amateur yachtsmen to swallow. In this they are being unseamanlike. Unnecessary exposure can bring on stupidity and fatigue that will sap the ability of the best of seamen, and 'exposure' in this sense means not only cold and wetness but also the tropical sun, which can be remarkably enervating. In a boat like *Ròn Glas* or *Jester* it is found that the cool shade in the tropics, with plenty of fresh air circulating under the overhead cover, is almost as valuable as the snug enclosure achieved when going to windward in the North Atlantic with most of that fresh air excluded.

Various small-boat sailors in pursuit of protection have put their heads into plastic domes or behind glass windows, but this is not recommended. Vision is cut down to a dangerous extent, particularly when salt spray is drying on the surface and also at night, with reflections from inside confusing the images outside. Equally impeded are the senses of hearing and smell, both frequently valuable to the watchkeeper in a small sailing boat. It is impossible to keep a good watch without having your face out in the open air, but it is still possible to protect your head from wind, rain, and driving spray.

ROTATABLE PRAM HOOD. This is the recommended system, first used in *Jester* and shown in Fig. 13.15. It consists of a hood of waterproof fabric attached to the outside of three hinged hoops (A, B, and C), which are located in pockets that stop well short of the hinges. When erected, the hood forms three-quarters of a hemisphere and is held up by a piece of shock cord (D) permanently attached to the middle of A. When folded the three hoops lie on top of each other, with C resting on the deck as shown.

The whole assembly is mounted on a captive half-ring

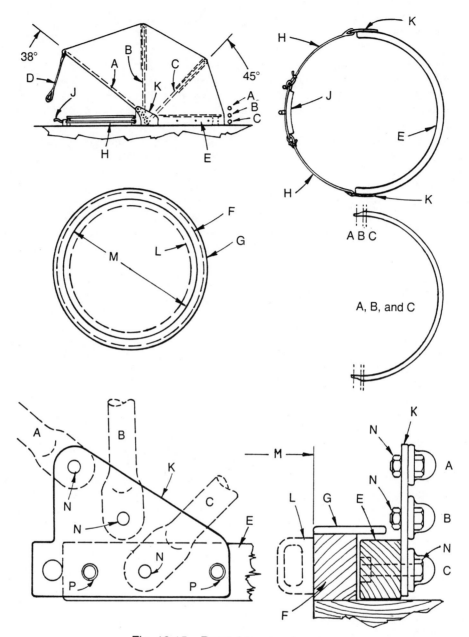

Fig. 13.15   Rotatable pram hood

(E) to which the bottom edge of the hood is attached. E can be rotated through 360° around a circular hatch whose coaming (F) has a projecting flange (G). The normal inside diameter (M) of the hatch proper is 19 in (48 cm), which is enough to permit a grown man wearing oilskins to climb in or out. E is made captive by two polyester cords (H) that connect it to a short curved section (J) carrying a hook for the loop at the bottom of D. One of the cords H is attached to J by a small shackle, for easy removal of the hood assembly.

A, B, and C are permanently pivoted by bolts or rivets (N) to hinge plates (K) which are riveted to E at P. The hoops are of brass tube with flattened ends and are all bent to the same radius but with differing lengths of straight tube at the ends. It is not within the scope of this book to give a dimensioned design; simply to indicate the design features. E and J are usually made of square-sectioned ash steamed to the required radius. Some users have dispensed with the shock cord (D) since the hood will stay up by itself if there is a little friction in the pivots and if turned with its back to the wind, which is of course its normal attitude. All metal parts of the pram hood assembly must be non-magnetic.

If the deck is heavily cambered it is advisable to

provide a flat surface immediately round the hatch, but this need not be horizontal. When erected the hood may easily be rotated with one hand so that its back is facing the wind on any point of sailing. When close-hauled with the back of the hood turned towards the weather bow, there is still a good view ahead through the V-shaped end of the opening. For a quick glance to windward, a push with one hand will partially fold it against the pull of the shock cord. To climb in or out, the shock cord is unhooked and the hood folded.

When folded, the doubled part of the fabric tends to hang inwards over the flange (G) and may get worn by people passing through the hatch. These folds may be held back clear of the hatch by a small fabric tab attached to the inside of the fabric just above the half-ring (E) and buttoned to a stud on the outside.

The inside of the hatch may be fitted with a ring of plastic dinghy fender (L) about ⅝ in (16 mm) thick, to protect your face and teeth when she pitches unexpectedly.

When erected the hood also provides a powerful ventilator, either inlet or exhaust depending upon which way it is facing. The circular hatch may itself be part of a larger sliding hatch cover, as in *Ròn Glas* (Fig. 13.24), but this makes it more difficult to cleat ropes on deck within reach of the circular hatch.

The area immediately below the hatch should be regarded as potentially damp, since it is impossible to prevent a few drops from getting below from time to time at sea. In harbour it is often convenient to have the hood erected and it is possible to keep rain out when the wind changes by providing a shaped piece of fabric (Fig. 13.16) with shock cord in its hems. This can be snapped on to the erected hood so as to cover the opening, with its ends hooked over projecting studs near the hingeplates. It may incorporate a flexible transparent window, as shown.

Under gale conditions at sea it is normal to keep this circular hatch open and the hood erected, whether sailing or hove-to. In more severe conditions it becomes necessary to batten-down with the hood folded and the hatch closed by a strong and reasonably watertight 'hurricane cover'. If there is enough room on deck this can be a rigid circular hatch cover (B in Fig. 13.17) that is captive on two hinged arms (C) pivoting in deck plates (D). It may have catches (A) to prevent it from lifting when stowed.

When in use the cover must be held down very strongly in case the boat gets rolled. One simple way is shown in Fig. 13.18, in which a rope loop hangs from the centre of the cover and a separate round-sectioned strongback (D) is made slightly longer than the hatch diameter. By passing the strongback through the rope loop and winding it up like a Spanish windlass against the underside of the hatch opening, the cover is pulled down with great force and the strongback may be held in place by a pin or catch against the end.

It is essential for a hurricane cover to be operable from below decks, but if this captive cover is not acceptable another good system is to hinge a disc-shaped cover in

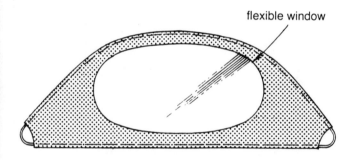
flexible window

Fig. 13.16   Fabric closure panel

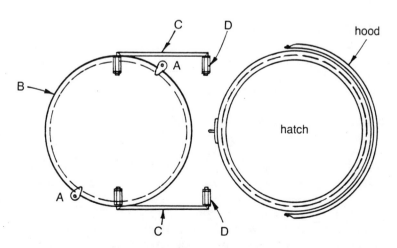

Fig. 13.17   Captive hurricane cover

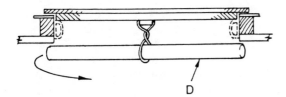

Fig. 13.18   Closing hurricane cover from inside

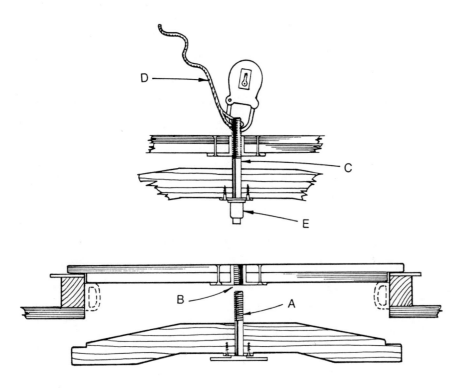

Fig. 13.19   Lockable hurricane cover

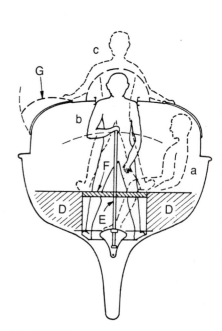

Fig. 13.20   *Jester*'s control position

half so that it can be passed down through the hatch to a stowage below decks. It should be hinged so that the joint folds upwards and may be held down by the strongback described above. It must of course have a good lanyard on it before poking it out through the hatch in Force 10!

Often there will be some other hatch to provide the lockable means of exit in harbour. If not, a means of locking the hurricane cover from the outside will be needed. Fig. 13.19 shows the system used on *Ròn Glas*. When operated from the inside, the cover is held down to the strongback by a T-bolt (A) in the threaded bush (B). To lock the cover from the outside, a wire strop (C) is pulled through the strongback and the threaded bush by a lanyard (D) and then padlocked. The wire strop is made with a swaged collar (E) with a washer above it.

Several boats have been fitted with two rotatable pram hoods, one to port and one to starboard. This permits the watchkeeper to be on the windward side, giving better all-round vision when heeled and better weight distribution in a small boat. It also permits a second crew member (perhaps feeling queasy) to get some fresh air without getting wet, and leaves the centreline of the boat clear. With two hoods the hauling ropes and manual steering are arranged so that they can be handled from whichever is the windward side.

When planning a rotatable pram hood it is useful to study the positions of the watchkeeper who will use it, by drawing a figure to scale on a section of the control position. His positions must be tolerable with the boat heeled either way, or rolling heavily. The maximum angles of heel and roll will depend on the boat, but for mono-hulls a planning figure of 30° either way is one that will seldom be exceeded when cruising.

Fig. 13.20 shows a cross-section of *Jester*'s control position, which is near the centre of the waterline of her 25 ft (8 m) hull. When not in his bunk the watchkeeper is nearly always in one of the three positions shown: (a) sitting below decks on one of the seats (D) when resting, reading, cooking, eating, and so on; (b) standing with his head under the pram hood and his shoulders against the inside of the circular hatch, for keeping a lookout and for manual steering by means of the whipstaff (E); (c) with the pram hood wholly or partly folded, standing waist-high out of the hatch for handling the hauling ropes of the sail and for using binoculars or sextant. The beam (F) provides a foothold between the seats but he is more secure against rolling with a foot on either seat, as shown. The same footholds are used when climbing in or out. The side hatches (G) are opened only in fine weather, or in harbour.

Fig. 13.21 shows the same three positions modified to accommodate 30° of heel. When standing under the pram hood the watchkeeper has to put one foot a very long way to leeward before he can feel comfortable. In a slightly larger boat it would be ideal to provide him with a radiused walkway as at (H).

Jester's enclosure is only partial, in that the watchkeeper is exposed to rain and spray when standing waist-high out of the hatch to work the rig, but these operations take very little time and call for a lightweight waterproof anorak rather than proper oilskins. The latter are needed only when going ashore in harbour in the rain.

Jester steers herself on all points of sailing with a wind-vane steering gear and this layout has proved satisfactory, but the watchkeeper cannot sit down when steering manually or on lookout. On the odd occasions when these jobs have to be done for long periods, such as when sailing through fog in the iceberg zone, he feels the need of a seat, but it would have to be a seat that enabled him to keep his head stationary under the pram hood when heeled or rolling. This could be achieved in one of three ways:

1. A fixed chair facing forwards having padded side rests for his shoulders, hips, and knees, so that when the boat was heeled he lay partly against the side rests. Experiments with this system have so far been unconvincing; the seat becomes very bulky and the heeled position seems uncomfortable.

2. (Fig. 13.22) A small seat (A) that can be clamped anywhere along a curved beam (B) forming an arc whose centre (C) is in the centre of the circular hatch. The beam may be either rigidly suspended from the deckhead or attached to the structure lower down. It would be necessary to have a few widely spaced footholds on the fixed structure. The curved beam could be unshipped, or

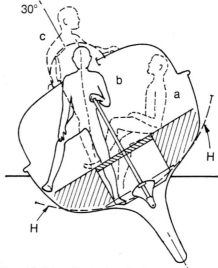

Fig. 13.21 *Jester* heeled

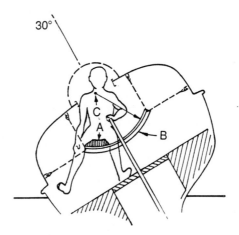

Fig. 13.22 Radiused beam and seat

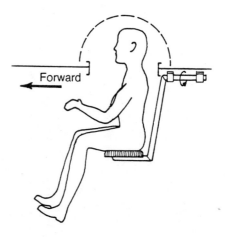

Fig. 13.23 Swinging seat, single pivot

made to hinge up to the deckhead, when not in use. The simplest support would be by four ropes with snap shackles, as shown by dotted lines in Fig. 13.22.

3. A sideways-swinging seat whose axis is close to the underside of the circular hatch. Fig. 13.23 shows such a seat with the helmsman facing forwards, but most people find it more comfortable to face to leeward and the seat could be arranged so that the watchkeeper could face either forwards or athwartships. Swinging seats can be made easy to unship and/or to be stowed swung back against the ship's side or the deckhead. Footholds need to be provided so that the swing of the seat can be controlled by the legs. If there are twin pram hoods the twin swinging seats do not need full swinging ability outwards, but only towards the centreline.

More development work is needed on these systems. The more comfortable the seat, the longer a watchkeeper can remain efficient.

FULLY ENCLOSED SYSTEMS. If planning a fuller degree of enclosure, the rotatable pram hood and any associated seat will still be ideal for a lookout and manual steering, but all hauling ropes will be brought

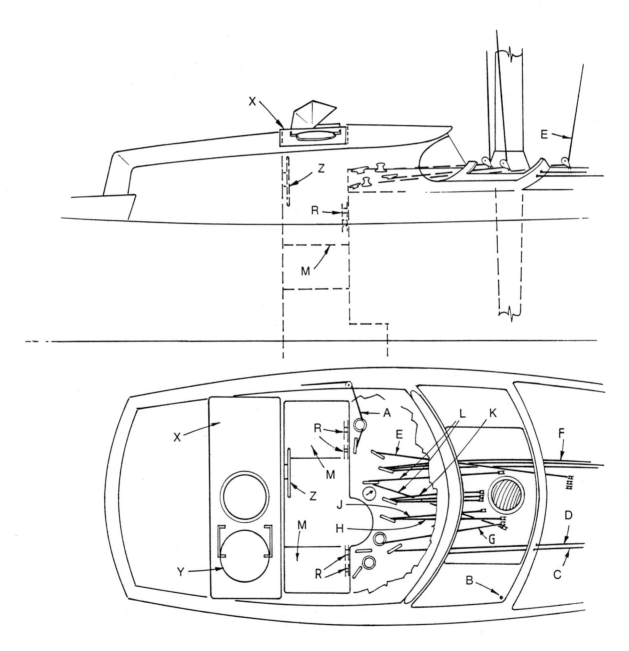

Fig. 13.24   *Ròn Glas*'s fully enclosed control position

into the enclosed control position. To do this they must pass through small carefully-aligned holes in the ends or sides of a doghouse or wheelhouse. If these holes are only slightly larger than the rope very little water will get in and this can be caught by a draining arrangement.

Fig. 13.24 shows the control position in *Ròn Glas*, with all ropes from forward leading through holes below the wheelhouse 'windscreen' and on to a large shelf inside (shown exposed in the plan view), which is an extension of the cambered coach roof and carries the cleats and winches. A small part of this shelf is cut away to give headroom on the companionway ladder to the saloon.

Four rope stowage reels (R) are mounted on the vertical bulkhead below the shelf and have arm rests (not shown) above them for use when sitting on the seats. The large hatch-cover (X) carries a rotatable pram hood with its captive hurricane cover (Y), and slides aft to open the whole of the control position. It is shown closed in profile and open in plan view. The steering wheel (Z) may be disconnected from the rudder when the boat is on vane steering. There is a seat (M) on each side and the watchkeeper adopts the same positions as in *Jester* (see Fig. 13.20 and 13.21) when the large hatch cover is closed.

The mainsheet (A) enters through a hole in the coaming on the port side and its tail stows on a rope reel. The ropes shown in Fig. 13.24 are as follows:

A mainsheet
B burgee halyard (belayed outside)
C fore halyard (tail stows on reel)
D foreyard hauling parrel
E foresheet (tail stows on reel)
F three foresail downhauls (share one cleat)
G main halyard (tail stows on reel)
H mainyard hauling parrel
J main luff hauling parrel
K three mainsail downhauls (share one cleat)
L main topping-lifts (brought together to one cleat)

The foresail has standing luff parrels and standing topping-lifts, having no gallows.

At the time of writing, *Ròn Glas* has made six crossings of the North Atlantic, two of them singlehanded, and it has only rarely been necessary to put on oilskins and go out on deck at sea.

When planning a system of full enclosure such as this it is essential to make a mock-up of the control position in order to test all the working attitudes before starting the final construction. The design has to be tailored to suit your height and reach and to give room to haul ropes and turn winch handles.

There is scope for further thought and development of this concept of a sheltered control position, in order to adapt it for more than two people.

PART III

USING THE RIG

14 Setting Up the Rig

If the boat is to be rigged by someone unfamiliar with Chinese rig, he or she should be provided with a rigging diagram (Fig. 12.1), details of rigging (Fig. 12.2), and, preferably, a rigging warrant (Table 7) – also a deck layout (see Chapter 13) if this is not adequately shown on the rigging diagram. It may be possible to dispense with some of this paperwork if the rig's designer is on hand to advise, but the purpose of the rigging warrant is to enable everything to be made up in advance, working in comfort under cover.

General points

The ends of all synthetic cordage, whether three-strand or braided, should be fused to a hard, blunt point without any increase in diameter. It is not necessary to whip the ends if this is done properly (see p 172).

Splices should be used only where a thimble is called for. All soft eyes should be formed with a bowline knot, and other ends secured with any suitable knot, thus making it easier to replace or adjust the ropes.

Mast wedges of the partners (and step, if any) should be shaped, arranged, and held down as specified in Chapter 9. The mast itself must also be strongly held down (see Chapter 9) so that it is impossible for it to jump upwards or twist.

The extreme running ends of all running ropes should be finished with a figure-of-eight knot to prevent them from running back through the fairlead or block if accidentally let go.

If a detailed rigging warrant has not been made out, the various ropes will have to be cut and fused *in situ* as the sail is rigged, remembering to allow for the full up-and-down movement of the furled sail bundle (see pp 176, 179). If the sheet is to be cut to length it will be necessary to hoist full sail and then persuade it to lie out at right angles to the boat on the port side.

Any chafing gear should be fitted as the boat is rigged. See p 153 for the yard, p 159 for the battens, and p 160 for the boom. Anti-chafe precautions may also be desirable where tensioned parrels bear heavily against a wooden mast, but experiments so far have failed to find a system that will slide easily as the sail is hoisted or lowered. Parrel balls, whether of wood or plastic, tend to chafe both the mast and themselves. On one boat plastic parrel balls wore themselves down, unbelievably, into cubes.

It is possible to use pieces of semi-rigid plastic hose threaded over the parrels and located on them by polyester twine taken through the rope and through a hole in the hose. This will certainly do something to protect both the rope and a wooden mast from chafe, but will run up the mast less smoothly than plain rope when hoisting sail. The most usual place to fit such hose is at the top of the yard hauling parrel, between the sling plate and the block. The length will have to be very short as it cannot pass through the block (see Fig. 3.19) and may come right off the mast when close-reefed. It will not interfere with hoisting and lowering because the yard hauling parrel will be slack at such times.

Tallowed leather or rawhide makes the best traditional chafing gear, or the relevant part of the parrel itself may be rubbed with tallow or water-pump grease on a warm day. This makes it slide easily on the mast, but collects dirt and spreads some of it up the mast and so on to the sail.

Any cheek blocks or cleats on the lower mast should have fairings as in Fig. 8.26 and 8.27. All loose blocks that have to work upside-down, such as the lower sheet blocks and any deck blocks at the foot of the mast, should be held flexibly upright by a short length of plastic hose as in Fig. 14.1. This prevents a slack rope from getting foul under the cheeks of the block. The alignment of each block must be checked to ensure that the part of the rope on either side of it can lie in exactly the same plane as its sheave.

Stepping and unstepping the mast

One person can step or unstep the mast of a junk-rigged dinghy by hand, and this can be done with the sail assembly already bent to the mast. Before unstepping, lift the furled sail bundle on to your shoulder at an angle

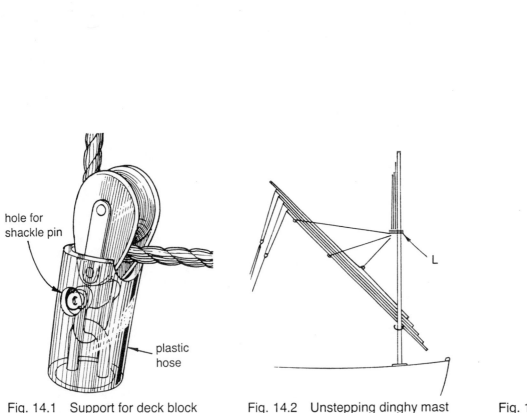

Fig. 14.1   Support for deck block

Fig. 14.2   Unstepping dinghy mast

Fig. 14.3
Sail bundle stowed along mast

hole for
shackle pin

plastic
hose

L

of about 45° (Fig. 14.2) and pass a tight lashing (L) as low as possible round the topping-lifts, the mast, and all ropes leading down the mast. This prevents these ropes from throwing turns round the masthead or round the bundle. The mast may then be lifted out by the roots and laid down with its sail bundle lying almost parallel to it. Fig. 14.3 shows, diagrammatically, that this is possible if the batten parrels are long and if the battens can stagger aft more than their normal amount, as they invariably can (p 21). Turning the diagram on its side shows how a larger mast could be lowered in a tabernacle with the sail bundle still parrelled to it, particularly if the bundle were twisted through 90° round the mast, but the process would have to be worked out to suit the individual boat's layout. Probably a better way would be to fit quick-release snap shackles on all the parrels and the mast lift, so that the furled bundle could be taken sideways off the mast and stowed on deck before lowering the mast.

Normal masts are stepped through the deck or coachroof without a tabernacle. If less than about 30 lb (14 kg) in weight, a mast may be stepped or unstepped in calm weather by one man standing up and using his bare hands. With two strong people, masts of about 80 lb (36 kg) may be handled in this way, and with three people

you can perhaps go up to 100 lb (45 kg) if they are practised in the job. The problem is not the weight but the difficulty of getting a grip on the mast, the height of the centre of gravity, the windage on a breezy day, and the movement of a boat afloat. An unpractised team will invariably be found to be working madly against each other, either all pulling or all pushing, an exhausting activity that is both comic and dangerous. The remedy (as always) is for one person to be in charge and for him to keep the mast upright by a continual stream of instructions such as 'Towards me', 'Towards Henry', and so on. Stepping the mast will require an extra person to guide it into its step and shout instructions to the deck squad. If you like working by 'brute force and bloody ignorance' you will have a field day, but this is not the recommended method for any mast of over about 30 lb (14 kg).

In the absence of any adjacent crane or mast derrick, larger masts may be stepped or unstepped safely by means of sheer-legs or a derrick mounted on the boat's deck. Fig. 14.4 shows the type of sheer-legs used in *Sumner* (Fig. 16.6), which make it possible for three men to step or unstep her mast, 40 ft (12.2 m) long and weighing 300 lb (136 kg), with the boat on moorings in calm water.

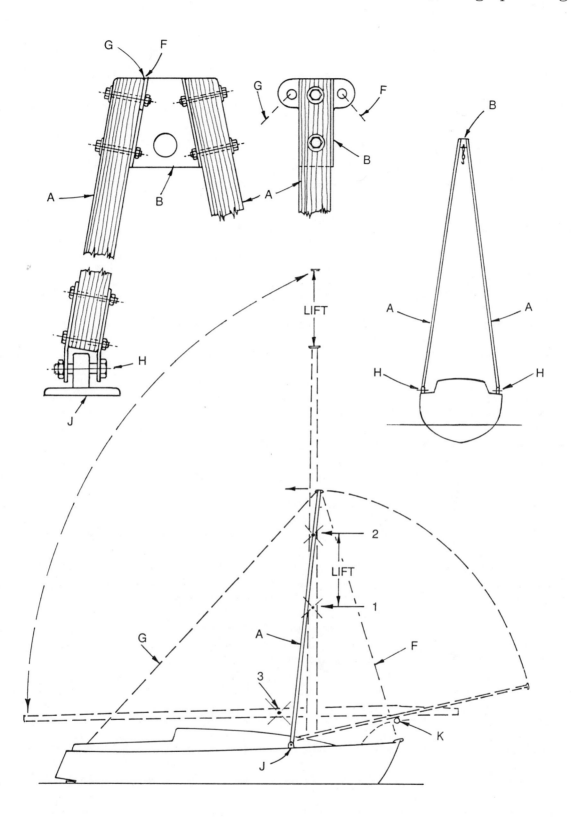

Fig. 14.4   Sheer-legs

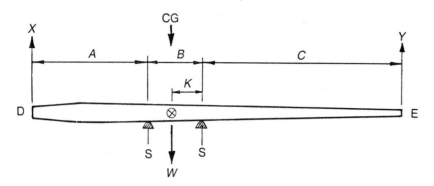

Fig. 14.5   Mast weight and CG

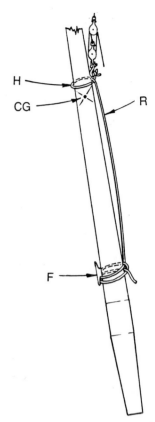

Fig. 14.6   Slinging a mast

When planning such a system, first establish the position of the mast's centre of gravity (CG). If it is light enough to lift by the middle, this presents no problem. Otherwise, use the method shown in Fig. 14.5, which also enables the weight of the mast to be measured with a spring balance whose maximum capacity is much less than half the weight of the mast. Arrange the mast horizontally on two *small* supports (S), that are positioned by trial and error so as to straddle the CG and to be close enough together to enable either D or E to be lifted by your spring balance. Measure distances A, B, and C in decimal units. Again using decimal units, measure the lift (X) needed to raise that end off its support, then lower it and measure the lift (Y) needed to raise the other end off its support. Then the total weight (W) is found from the formula, $W = [Y(B + C) + X(A + B)]/B$, and the distance $K = X(A + B)/W$.

The mast is slung as in Fig. 14.6, with a rope (R) hitched to the lower block of the purchase, hitched *once* round the mast at H, which is as far as possible above the CG, then brought down and hitched firmly round the mast underneath some fixed fitting (F) that is above the partners. If there is no fitting in this position, four or five spaced-out hitches may be thrown around the lower mast with the bottom hitch below the partners and one person can back up on the lower end. The top hitch (H) may be eased up or down the mast with a boathook, which makes it possible to get it very close to the purchase hook before unstepping.

The sheer-legs in Fig. 14.4 consist of two identical spars (A) which may conveniently be of square-sectioned spruce and for extra elegance (not shown) could taper from the middle towards either end, like a spinnaker pole. They are joined rigidly at the head by a galvanised mild-steel fabrication (B) which holds them far enough apart to give room for the upper purchase block. This head fitting includes eyes for the foreguy (F) and after guy (G), and these are offset to one side in order to keep the after guy clear of the mast. The feet of the legs

connect by means of horizontal athwartships pivot bolts (H) to chainplates or deckplates (J).

Having established the position (1) of the CG of the mast when stepped, add the bury to get its position (2) when the heel is just clear above the partners, and make the sheer-legs long enough to give room for the sling and purchase above this point. When lowered to a horizontal attitude near the deck the mast may be swung a good way forward or aft to any desired position, for example with its CG at (3).

The head of the sheer-legs must be forward of the stepped mast so that the mast can be lowered with its heel forward, which is the normal requirement. Assembling and dismantling the sheer-legs may require a temporary cross-bearer (K) fastened to the pulpit, to support them while the pivot bolts (H) are inserted or withdrawn. If they can be carried while cruising, sheer-legs provide an ideal jury mast that can be stepped in fairly rough conditions at sea. This could be worth while on a world cruise, but the means of erecting them at sea would have to be worked out and rehearsed.

A derrick is simpler than sheer-legs, but needs more care with the guys. Fig. 14.7 shows the derrick used in *Pilmer* (Fig. 16.10), which enables one man to step or unstep her light-alloy mast, which is 27 ft (8.4 m) long

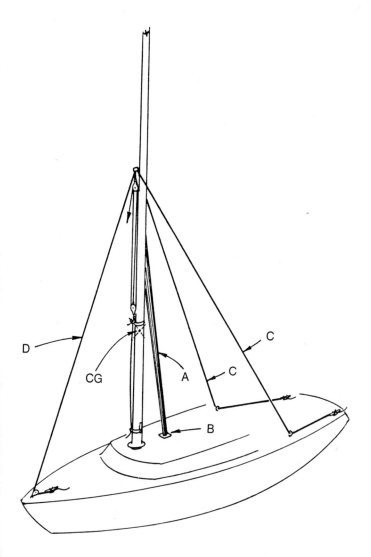

Fig. 14.7   Derrick

after starting to lower, on the other guy, the pinch could be avoided.

With a heavy mast and/or a narrow boat, it is safer to use sheer-legs than a derrick. A derrick may also be adapted to serve as a jury mast, but is less easy to step in a seaway than sheer-legs.

Dressing the mast

Before stepping a mast it should preferably be dressed, i.e. fitted with all the ropes, fittings, and blocks that are attached to its upper part. These may include a lightning conductor, masthead lights, and any masthead instruments. Any shackles with screw pins should have those pins secured by the most appropriate means, either by wiring through the eye of the pin with galvanised or stainless seizing wire, or (if they have slotted heads) by treating the thread with a proprietary semi-locking fluid or paste, or by making three centre-punch indentations into the thread between the small end of the pin and the boss of the shackle.

The insulated cables inside a light-alloy mast should be restrained as described on p 139. If possible the mast coat should be slid on to the mast upside-down and seized to it by means of its upper lashing as described on p 142 It may be necessary to slide it down from the masthead. If it cannot be slid into place it should be stitched *in situ*.

The mast will normally be dressed with the halyard, burgee halyard, topping-lifts, mast lift, and a ghoster halyard if needed. Having secured all these to the masthead they may be laid down the mast and held there temporarily by winding the burgee halyard in a spiral around the lot. After reeving the halyard through its blocks pull them together block-to-block while you check that it is rove correctly and that the *pin* of the upper block points towards the centre of the mast (Fig. 12.2). Then overhaul the purchase so that the lower block is at boom level. If the topping-lifts are to be crossed forward of the mast (Fig. 3.58), do this now and seize them together with polyester twine at a point half-way between the masthead and the level of the yard sling plate when under full sail.

Dressing the mast will raise the height of its CG slightly in addition to increasing its weight. If this is unacceptable it may be dressed with only a gantline through the burgee halyard block or tube. The masthead may then be rigged later from a bosun's chair, but this should be done only as a last resort. The hitches of the mast sling (Fig. 14.6) should be passed underneath all other ropes after dressing the mast.

Before stepping the mast, check that any cables emerging from it below the partners are protected against possible damage.

After the heel of the mast has been lowered below the

and weighs 59 lb (27 kg) stripped or 64 lb (29 kg) dressed. The single spar (A) is in fact a spare yard for the sail, and it may be possible to use the yard of any sail of fairly low aspect ratio for this purpose. It is stepped into a strong cup fitting (B) on the coachroof and held up by two after guys (C) and a foreguy (D). Its stability depends on having a good athwartships spread on the after guys, which should therefore not be taken to the stern.

The derrick is shown stepped on the centreline and raked forward past the starboard side of the mast, which may then conveniently be lowered with its heel forward. When upright the mast is slightly pinched between the head of the derrick and the port after guy. This is tolerable for a small mast, but could be avoided by fitting an additional port after guy with its head to starboard of the mast. By taking the weight first on this guy and then, partners, it should be greased in way of the step and any step wedges before final lowering.

Having stepped the mast, fit the holding-down bolt to prevent it from twisting, then tap in three wedges at the partners, and any that there are at the step. Before fitting the remaining wedges, check that the mast is standing vertically when viewed from forward and at the desired angle (usually vertical) when viewed from athwartships. It is not unknown for the alignment of partners and step to be faulty, in which case the mast alignment can often be corrected by varying the thickness of the wedges or, at the partners, by making the wedges over-length and tapping them in further on one side than the other. They can then be cut off to the same distance above and below the partners, the top and bottom edges chamfered, and the wedges marked so that they can always be put back in the same place. Wedges should not be *driven* home; a tap with a mallet or hammer is usually quite enough.

The holding-down system for any step wedges should be fitted now, as in Fig. 9.10, but the wedges at the partners should be tapped down again after a little sailing before fitting their holding-down arrangement (see p 142).

Rigging the sail

With sails of up to about 300 sq ft (28 m²), the yard, battens, and boom should now be fitted to the sail. This is best done with the starboard side laid face up on a floor of sufficient area or on a grass lawn on a dry day. The lacings and parrels may be cut off and fused *in situ* as you proceed, if not already done from a rigging warrant. For larger sails see below.

The method of lashing the peak, throat, tack, and clew is shown in Fig. 12.2, which also shows the piece of adhesive tape which may be put over the groove to reduce the risk of its catching other ropes. The methods of securing the head and foot of the sail to their spars are shown in Chapter 10.

After bending the sail to its yard and boom each batten should be fitted into its pocket and the sail laced out fairly taut as in Fig. 12.2, remembering to include any batten fender (see p 159) and any shackle or grommet at the luff. Timber battens (Fig. 10.11) should have their flat sides against the sail. Tubular battens (Fig. 10.13) should have the flat side of their end tapers (if any) against the sail. The battens should be as flush as possible at the leech, with any surplus protruding from the luff.

The sail bundle may now be inserted, either from forward or from aft, into the topping-lifts that are already hanging from the mast. Each topping-lift span that passes under the boom should be inserted into its eye fitting on the underside of the boom by removing one

screw and loosening the other, then screwing up again for a full due.

A temporary tack parrel (B in Fig. 3.28) should now be fitted to hold the boom aft, close to its designed position. With the boat lying head to wind the sail is now rigged progressively, starting at the top. Shackle the lower halyard block to the yard sling plate, checking that the sheaves are the right way round relative to the yard and that the parts of the purchase are not crossed. If the shackle has a screw pin, secure it as discussed above. Reeve the yard hauling parrel through the block on the sling plate, then anticlockwise round the mast and secure its standing end as in Fig. 3.19, noting that it pulls on the starboard side of the yard only.

Hoist the top panel of the sail. Fit the batten parrel to the top batten as in Fig. 12.2, tensioning the hitch (Fig. 10.14) until your hand can just lie flat between the parrel and the mast. Tuck the end through the lay, or secure it by some other means.

Hoist another panel and repeat as above, but bending the top of the luff hauling parrel to the shackle pin or grommet (Fig. 12.2). Bend the top of the upper sheet span to the becket on the leech, as in Fig. 12.2. Hoist a third panel and repeat as above, bending the top of the lower sheet span to its leech becket. Continue this procedure, following Fig. 12.1 and 12.2, until full sail is set. Remove the temporary tack parrel. Adjust the standing lower luff parrel (M) until the centreline of the mast crosses the foot of the sail at the correct place, which should have been marked on the sail as called for in Fig. 11.3.

With sails of more than about 300 sq ft (28 m²) the above system becomes difficult, certainly for a single-handed operator, because of the weight of the sail bundle complete with its battens. In that case it is possible to bend the sail to the yard and boom only, before inserting it into the lifts, fitting each batten complete with parrels as the sail is hoisted. For larger sails still, it is best to lay the bare boom into the lifts and locate the topping-lift spans through the eye fittings; then lay the furled sail without any spars attached along the top of the boom, and fit and rig the yard and battens as the sail is hoisted.

Finally, with the sail fully hoisted, adjust the halyard until the boom crosses the mast at the correct height. Fit the tackline and adjust it so that it is taut at this height. Take the mast lift under the boom and round the mast and secure it with a long bowline (Fig. 12.2) adjusted so that the boom can settle by about half the diameter of the mast before the mast lift takes the weight.

The notes in Fig. 12.1 suggest how the falls of the halyard, yard hauling parrel, and luff hauling parrel may be rove in relation to the other ropes in the vicinity of the mast, but the best leads may vary with different layouts. They should be tested both under full sail and close-reefed, and altered if necessary. If a double cheek block is used on the mast, the halyard should use the inner sheave and the yard hauling parrel the outer.

Adjust the topping-lifts so that they are just slack under full sail but support the furled sail bundle as soon as the boom has dropped by a distance equal to about half the diameter of the mast. This may be called the 'first position' and is the normal adjustment when under way, remaining unchanged under all normal sailing conditions. It is the permanent adjustment for standing topping-lifts.

With running topping-lifts, the 'second position' is found with the sail furled by paying out both sides of the topping-lifts equally until the sail bundle is resting in the gallows with the topping-lifts slightly slack.

If there is a requirement for the bundle to be lowered further than this to a 'repair position' as discussed in Chapter 12, check that there is enough spare rope on the halyard and on the falls of the topping-lifts. This would then be the third position.

It is convenient to have the first two positions pre-adjusted or the lifts marked, so that they can be found automatically. Bring the hauling parts to cleats or winches in the ordinary way, then mark the rope at the two or three positions required. With three-strand rope this may be done by tucking small pieces of coloured cloth through the lay.

If not already done, the sheet should now be rove through its upper and lower blocks as the sail is hoisted. Then with the sail furled and stowed on its gallows, or hanging in its lifts if there are no gallows, heave the sheet in taut and examine the positions of the blocks and thimbles.

All sheet spans should be as long as possible, and the sheet blocks should therefore be nearly, but not quite, 'two blocks' in this position. With a simple two-point span this is easily achieved by adjusting the length of the span. With a multiple span it is necessary to study the attitude of the span when the sail is hoisted. For example, Fig. 4.26 shows that the thimbles (U and V) should be close together when close-hauled under full sail, but widely separated when the sail is furled. The three-part euphroe spans as used in China (Fig. 4.16 and 4.27) are easier to adjust, since the thimble, the euphroe, and the lower sheet block should all be close together when the sail is furled.

On some boats, such as *Pilmer*, the drift between lower sheet blocks and clew of sail is barely sufficient for the type of sheet spans chosen. Her sheets (Fig. 12.1) should have a D_{min} of $2P$ (Fig. 4.25), but this is achieved only when the furled sail is lying in the lifts, and not when it is stowed on the gallows. This is made acceptable in practice by tricing the furled sail bundle across to the starboard side of the gallows and holding it there with a separate lashing. This tautens the sheets so that they provide the necessary steadying force, but this expedient would not be acceptable with a sail of more than about 300 sq ft (28 m²), when it would be necessary at sea for the sheets to control the sail bundle right down on to the gallows.

If batten downhauls (see p 48) or a yard downhaul (see p 49) are to be fitted, this can be done now.

When weathercocking, the sail should now drop freely under its own weight when the halyard is let go. If it does not, either the halyard or the parrels have too much friction, and the fault must be diagnosed and corrected.

Finally, when lying in harbour with the sail furled it is probable that (as with conventional rigs) the ropes lying close to the mast will slat against it in the wind. This is annoying to everybody and may cause chafe. It should be avoided by rigging a swifter on each mast. This consists of a piece of line or shock cord that trices the fall of the halyard, and the mast lift, back towards the topping-lifts. It should be rigged as high as you can reach.

15 Handling the Rig

The Chinese rig is at its best in hard weather, when it will often outsail a Bermudian-rigged sister ship on all points of sailing. In light or moderate winds it may outsail the Bermudian sloop when reaching or running, until the sloop sets a spinnaker. Going to windward in moderate weather the rig should perform about as well as a gaff cutter. Its weakest point is going to windward in ghosting weather through a lop or swell, although skilled helmsmen have sometimes been able to fan along in a surprising way. A ghoster (Chapter 5) will help under these conditions.

Sail handling

The sheet, yard hauling parrel, and luff hauling parrel (plus the batten downhauls and yard downhaul, if fitted) all go slack as the sail is lowered, and may be referred to collectively as the 'downward ropes'. The universal rule is that the halyard works against all the downward ropes. If the halyard is let go or eased out the downward ropes will all go slack and may be hauled in either simultaneously or subsequently. Conversely, and more important, when heaving in on the halyard all the downward ropes must be allowed to pay out, otherwise the sail cannot be hoisted.

MAKING FULL SAIL. The sequence of making sail when lying with the wind forward of the beam is as follows:

1. Remove any swifters.
2. Let go all the downward ropes and ensure that they can run out freely.
3. If the sail is stowed on a gallows or crutch, remove any lashings, ease out and overhaul some of the sheet, then either remove or lower the crutch or gallows, or heave in both parts of the topping-lifts to hoist the sail bundle to the correct height for the reefed sail, i.e. to the first position as described on p 203.
4. Alternatively, if the sail is stowed in its lifts rather than on a gallows, remove its steadying lines.

5. Hoist full sail, watching the downward ropes run out and finally watching the tackline. When it goes taut, stop hoisting. With a sail of any size the last part of hoisting can be a hard pull. In a sea or swell it is often possible to snatch in the halyard by hand, a few feet at a time, by catching the moments when the swing of the mast takes some of the weight off it. This can be faster than grinding in continuously with a winch. Belay the halyard.
6. With the sail still weathercocking with slack sheets, haul in the yard hauling parrel as far as it will go, and then ease back a few inches so that the block on the sling plate is not jammed hard against the mast. Then belay it.
7. Set up the luff hauling parrel so as to pull the luff in towards the mast a few inches. For light weather, stop before the boom begins to move aft. For heavy weather, stop when the boom has moved aft several inches; it will move forward again when the sail is full of wind. Another method is to watch any creases that may have formed in the sail after completing 6 above. These may be expected to run in the directions shown in Fig. 3.29. The luff hauling parrel should then be set up until these disappear or (for hard weather) until they begin to reappear sloping in the opposite directions. In addition to controlling the creasing of the sail, the luff hauling parrel helps to put compression into the upper sheeted battens and so encourages them to take a bend, which should be beneficial.
8. Make up and stow the spare ends of all running ropes in whichever manner has been selected from Chapter 13. Note especially that if the rope is to be coiled you must start from the cleat and not from the free end, whereas if it is to be flaked or reeled you naturally start from the free end.
9. Set any second or third sails in the same manner.
10. Let go the mooring, trim the sail(s) as required, and stow the spare end(s) of the sheets.

MAKING A REEFED SAIL. Stop hoisting when the required amount of sail has been spread. In order to get a neat reef the halyard should be belayed when the forward end of the lowest operational batten is a little way above its final position. The yard hauling parrel should then be set up, hauling the yard forward and slightly lowering the luff until this batten lies parallel with, but very slightly above, the boom or the residual furled bundle. Finally, set up the luff hauling parrel (and downhauls if fitted) and adjust the sheet.

WEATHERCOCKING. A sail may be allowed to weathercock when the wind is anywhere from ahead to abeam. The natural tendency of any hull to lie beam-on to the wind suits the junk rig perfectly, since the absence of shrouds enables the sail to swing freely, with slack sheets, at right angles to the hull in a weathercocking attitude. It is quite unlike a conventional western sail in that it does not flap or frog, even in a gale of wind.

This weathercocking ability is a major asset, and if there is any weight in the wind the boat should be brought beam-on and the sheet let go before starting any adjustment of sail area. It is slightly preferable to do this on the starboard tack, so that all the parrels and other ropes are fully visible from aft, while the boat will have right of way over most other vessels.

REEFING AND HANDING SAIL. A sail may be reefed a panel or more at a time, or completely furled. The sequence of reefing, handing, and stowing sail when weathercocking is as follows:

1. In an emergency the whole sail may be crash-furled by simply letting go the halyard and making sure that it runs out freely, but this may cause trouble with two of the downward ropes: a lot of slack sheet may festoon the cockpit or fall over the side near your propeller, while the luff hauling parrel will probably get a turn round the forward end of one of the battens, which will need to be cleared before you can again hoist sail.

A more seamanlike method, if you have time, is to lower more slowly, or in several quick stages, while taking in the slack of the sheet and luff hauling parrel.

2. If reefing, stop lowering when the forward end of the new lowest operational batten is a little higher than its final position, and proceed as described under 'Making a reefed sail' above.

3. In the last stage of furling the yard sling plate has to fall aft a long way from the mast, and the yard hauling parrel needs to take back a good deal of rope to permit this. A well-reefed sail cannot be furled without letting go the yard hauling parrel, and this is the only exception to the 'universal rule' stated on p 204.

4. After the sail has been furled and the bundle hauled amidships by the sheet, it may be lowered into the gallows or crutch by easing out both parts of the topping-lifts, and secured in place by a lashing. The halyard and topping-lifts should now be slightly slack.

Alternatively, if a gallows or crutch is not used the furled bundle may be steadied with either one or two lashings that pass right round the bundle and out to a point near the rail.

The furled sail should be fully stowed, as in 4 above, for motoring at sea in a lop or swell, or when subject to rolling at sea or in harbour, since this reduces wear and chafe. Under gale conditions at sea it may be possible to leave the bundle hanging in the lifts and controlled by the sheet only, but a sail tyer should then be passed round the after end of the bundle to prevent any risk of the head fanning up (see p 208).

ADJUSTMENT OF SHEETS. When close-hauled, the junk sail should be sheeted more like a conventional headsail than a conventional mainsail. The sheet cannot be flattened in without destroying most of the drive. Under full sail there should be little or no twist, and the boom should lie at about 15° to the centreline of the boat, as shown diagrammatically in Fig. 4.44.

Different boats, and different wind strengths, may call for optimum angles that are slightly different from 15°. Because the sail is on the port side of the mast, the boom lies further outboard to port than to starboard for the same angle of incidence. This tends to produce an optical illusion whereby the sail on the port tack *appears* to be hauled flatter than it does on the starboard tack, and it is as well to guard against this illusion. With a single sail on a narrow hull it is often correct for the clew to be outside the rail on the starboard tack when close-hauled.

With a multi-masted rig and the wind on or forward of the beam, the foresail should be sheeted a bit fuller than the main, and the mainsail fuller than the mizzen, in accordance with normal practice.

Having got the sail(s) sheeted at a reasonable angle to the boat, in light or moderate weather she should be sailed to windward appreciably freer than a Bermudian sloop. Getting the best out of her is not easy and demands close attention to the 'feel' of the boat, in the absence of any clear indications from the sail itself. As the breeze hardens it becomes much easier to sail her well, and she can be allowed to claw up closer to the wind with the sail feathering at a fine angle of incidence, but still without flattening the sheets.

TWIST. The recommended sheeting systems give little or no twist under full sail, but develop increasing twist as the sail is reefed. One or two possible ways of reducing reefed twist are discussed in Chapter 4 (p 66 ff) but none of these is standard practice and it is normal for the reefed sail to develop twist. With the wind forward of the beam this means that the boom and furled bundle should be trimmed a bit further inboard, so that the head of the sail is correctly trimmed. With the wind aft, the boom should be kept a bit aft so that the head of the sail is square.

TACKING. It is still open to debate whether the rig sails better to windward on the port tack or on starboard. Some evidence suggests that this may depend on wind strength. Tacking should involve nothing more than putting the helm down. Hulls that are slow in stays may sometimes get themselves in irons through not having a jib that can be backed to help her round. The remedy may be to pay off and get more speed before tacking, then to watch the waves and put her firmly round in a 'smooth'. Depending on the individual boat, it may be better to apply full helm gradually rather than suddenly. In lighter weather it may help to hold the boom aback, i.e. out to its original side, for a few moments as she comes into the wind. In a multi-masted boat this would be done with the foresail. Alternatively, with a two-masted rig it may pay to let go the foresheet and harden the mainsheet immediately after putting the helm down, readjusting to normal sheeting as soon as she is through the wind. A modern yacht hull will not normally get into irons if properly handled, and these expedients will be needed only on rare occasions.

An unusually long, narrow, and light boat such as *Sumner* (Fig. 16.6) may occasionally reach a stage where she cannot be tacked at all when close-reefed under gale conditions in the open sea, because the big breaking seas stop her dead before she can get through the wind, even after going into the tack at her maximum speed. In this rare event *Sumner* used to wear (gybe) round onto the other tack. This could be done painlessly, however strong the wind, by dropping the yard and holding it down with the yard downhaul (Fig. 3.46) fitted for that purpose. She was then gybed under bare poles, treating the furled sail bundle as a sail, before rehoisting two or three panels on the new tack.

REACHING AND RUNNING. When reaching in light airs the sheet may be paid out until the burgee shows about 10° of incidence at the head of the sail, but in fresh winds the sheet may be eased further and the rig will then develop a lot of drive with very little heeling moment. When broad-reaching the sheet may be let right out until the sail is square to the boat or, if reefed, until the head of the sail is square to the boat.

When running, the sail remains trimmed as for broad-reaching. Be careful not to let out more sheet than this, allowing the head of the sail to sag forward of the mast, because this puts a heavy compression load on the sheeted battens (Fig. 1.6) and is a common cause of breakage. If the sheet is accidentally let go too far when running in a hard breeze, do not try to haul it in without first coming up a-hull and weathercocking.

As the sail is squared-off, the tackline, and downhauls if in use, may get too tight. In this case the halyard may be eased a little.

With multi-masted rigs the foresail will of course tend to get blanketed when running. It may then be goose-winged, but there may still be points of sailing close to a dead run where the foresail is restless. This appears to be due to the wind eddies curving round the luff and leech of the mainsail, but a small alteration of course may enable the foresail to settle down goose-winged.

In strong following winds it is normal to reef the mainsail first and to a greater extent than the foresail, even to the point of running under foresail alone with the mainsail furled and stowed.

REEFING AND UNREEFING. Ease of reefing and unreefing is the outstanding advantage of the junk rig. Cruising yachtsmen will alter their sail area very frequently as a means of adjusting speed, avoiding stress, and achieving the right compromise between progress and comfort. It is never necessary to reef in deference to the weather forecast, but only in deference to the wind that you are actually experiencing. This leads to more efficient sailing and less worry.

On a typical non-stop singlehanded seven-day coastal passage made by *Pilmer* (Fig. 16.10), a total of 64 changes of sail area were made, all without leaving the cockpit: an average of one sail change every two-and-a-half hours throughout the day and night.

In fresh winds it is customary to reef for entering and leaving restricted anchorages and for picking up moorings, and no other rig is as handy at these times. Many owners of junk-rigged boats get extra pleasure out of devising ways of manoeuvring in very tight corners under sail alone, and these are skills that may one day be needed urgently.

If it becomes necessary to reef or furl the sail with the wind aft and no sea room to bring her up a-hull, the sheet must be hauled in before, or while, the halyard is paid out, in order to prevent the top panels from sagging forward of the mast.

The processes of reefing and unreefing follow those of furling and setting sail as described above. When close-hauled or reaching it is not necessary to get the sail weathercocking before reefing. As soon as the halyard is started the sheet and other downward ropes go slack, allowing the sail to shake down without being too heavily pressed against the topping-lifts.

The luff hauling parrel has less and less function as the sail is progressively reefed, and when close-reefed it is sufficient merely to keep it hand-taut, to prevent it from getting foul.

The geometry of reefing the standard sail is such that the yard sling plate should lie progressively further away from the mast as the sail is progressively reefed. Fig. 12.1 shows its position when only two panels are set. Some users have preferred to haul in further on the yard hauling parrel so as to bring the sling plate closer to the mast, but this also raises the leech so that the lowest exposed batten is no longer parallel to the furled bundle but is raised at its after end, giving an untidy appearance to the reefed sail and possibly producing a flapping bit of slack leech below the batten. This could be cured by raising the after end of the furled bundle with the topping-lifts, but it is preferable to leave the lifts untouched and to allow whatever drift is required between the yard sling plate and the mast.

When manoeuvring under sail in tight corners it will often be necessary to pause momentarily while hoisting or lowering sail, or to raise the top few panels of a furled sail, in order to sail a few more yards or to tack or gybe. At such times there is no need to set up the yard hauling parrel or luff hauling parrel, but merely to ensure that their slack ends do not get foul. The sail may be controlled by the halyard and sheet only, until there is time to work the parrels.

We rely on the downward pull of the sheet spans, plus the weight of the battens, to hold the leech of the sail down when reefed. The downward component of the sheet is greatest when close-hauled and least when running, and its magnitude depends partly on the position of the lower sheet block anchorage, i.e. whether in the upper or lower part of the shaded area in Fig. 6.29. Unless batten downhauls are fitted (see p 48), the luff of the reefed sail is held down mainly by the weight of the battens, although the luff hauling parrel exerts a slight downward pull on the upper luff.

The reefed sail presses against the lee topping-lifts when full of wind and may be difficult to hoist or lower, but when weathercocking it should shake down automatically as the halyard is paid out. All sheeted battens should then stay down when the sail is full of wind, on all points of sailing.

DEEP REEFING. To reef the sail down to the last panel, if the top batten is unsheeted it is necessary to hold that batten down by a reef gasket or pendant. This can be useful in heavy winds, and the one-panel sail can be surprisingly effective. The reef gasket consists of a small lashing passed through the vacant becket on the top batten and round the gathered sheet spans, as at A in Fig. 15.1. This normally requires the watchkeeper to stand up in an exposed position on deck, but it can be avoided by keeping a reef pendant permanently rove from the top batten, through one or two cringles on the leech, and down through a thimble on the next batten, where it finishes in a soft eye (A in Fig. 15.2). This eye may be hooked and pulled in from a safe position by using a boathook or a specially-made very light hand-hook, (shaped like a crozier), designed for hooking ropes with one hand.

After the reef pendant has been hooked and hauled taut it is transferred to a hook-rope that is kept permanently rove through a block near the mast, as at A in Fig. 15.3. This rather elaborate system is not needed for ordinary cruising, but could be worth its place for anyone tackling the Roaring Forties. There is, however, a

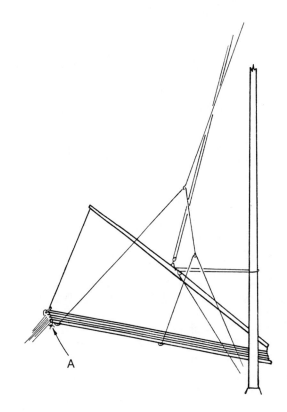

Fig. 15.1   Reef gasket

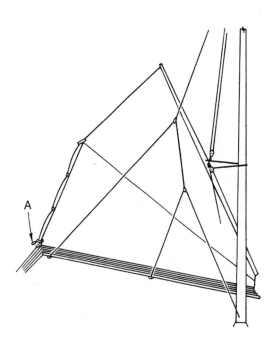

Fig. 15.2   Standing reef pendant

related problem which does apply to ordinary cruising, even in sheltered waters. This is the 'fan-up', as described below.

FAN-UPS. A 'fan-up' is defined as a situation in which the leech of a furled or reefed sail is thrown upwards with the yard and battens pivoting about their forward ends, thereby unreefing the sail into a non-standard and potentially dangerous shape. Fig. 15.4 shows (by dotted lines) the standard sail reefed down to the last two panels and (by solid lines) this same sail suffering a severe fan-up. Note that the whole yard has gone forward of the mast and that the forward ends of the yard and battens have not moved appreciably. The top batten has been arrested by its batten parrel against the mast. The yard is restrained only by the yard hauling parrel, now leading back-to-front, but if it had been fitted with a standing yard parrel (Fig. 3.56) its swing would have been stopped much earlier.

While Fig. 15.4 shows the normal limit of a severe fan-up, it is possible under extreme conditions for the boom and any residual furled battens to be lifted up as well, thereby slackening the topping-lifts and creating even more possibilities of a snarl-up. It might be thought that batten downhauls would prevent a fan-up, but in practice the lifting forces may be too strong and the leverage of the downhauls too slight. Either the downhaul or the batten is liable to break.

Similar fan-ups can happen with the sail fully furled, but severe fan-ups can happen only when the sheets are slack. With the sail furled and the sheets taut, only the two top panels can fan up, and then only as far as their normal position when set.

The usual cause of a severe fan-up is a very strong wind blowing straight at the leech when it is facing into the wind, notably when gybing with slack sheets. A less severe form can be caused at sea by violent rolling while lying a-hull with slack sheets (see Fig. 3.54), in which case the yard may be flung upwards by its own momentum, without any wind effects.

During a severe fan-up the peak of the yard, and possibly the after end of the top batten, may get the wrong side of the topping-lifts so that the sail will not drop back to its previous state, while it is not unknown for the peak or the throat to get foul of the mast lift or the halyard (which will have gone slack in mid-fan-up), thus completing a snarl-up that calls for some difficult deck-work.

Under full sail, or with only one or two panels reefed, the sail cannot fan up to any appreciable extent because the diagonal tension in the sailcloth would have to pull the lower battens a long way aft, and the batten parrels prevent this. Parallelogram panels can only fan up from the furled position.

It is worth avoiding the risk of a fan-up by observing certain rules:

1. When close-reefed but with no reef gasket or pendant rigged, do not gybe with a slack sheet. Either tack her right round, or get the sheet right in before gybing, even though this may be a bit brutal.
2. Alternatively, pass a reef gasket or pendant and gybe as you please. If more than one panel is set the gasket can be passed through the becket of the lowest operative batten.
3. When lying a-hull with a close-reefed sail in a steep sea with the sheet right off, keep the yard hauling parrel set up taut so as to prevent the yard from developing an independent swing.
4. With a sail that is furled, whether in harbour or at sea, before the approach of heavy weather pass a yard lashing or tyer right round the bundle. At sea it is possible to achieve a similar result without climbing out on deck, by throwing a weighted heaving line over the bundle and securing both ends.
5. As an alternative to 4 above, fit a yard downhaul (Fig. 3.46). This can be set up from the cockpit on any point of sailing and will prevent a fan-up in a furled sail.

GYBING. Accidental gybes should be very rare, as the squared-off sail will not gybe until the boat is a very long way by the lee. Under full sail, or with only a few panels reefed, it is normal to gybe without hauling the sheet in, i.e. by putting the helm up and bringing her smartly round until the sail finally gybes. By this time the wind will be almost abeam and the sail will tend to stop swinging before the sheets go taut. The boat is then brought back on course. This method gives a very soft gybe, but some care must be taken to prevent the slack sheets from wrapping around deck fittings, or people's necks. If there is some particularly vulnerable item, such as a wind-vane steering gear, it may be desirable to fit a lightweight arched horse either above or below the sheets, to protect it.

After such a gybe it may sometimes be found that one or more of the sheet spans has fouled under a lower batten. This does no immediate harm, although over the years the leech tape may show chafe under the battens at these points. It is customary to continue sailing downwind with the sheet span foul until it can conveniently be cleared. This will happen automatically if the sheet is pulled in, or when she is next brought up close-hauled, or if she is momentarily brought up beam-on to the wind with the sail weathercocking.

In restricted waters there may not be enough sea room to gybe with the sheets off in this way, in which case the sheet must be got in and the sail gybed heavily, as with a normal gaff or Bermudian sail.

Gybing a close-reefed sail in heavy weather involves the risk of a fan-up which should be avoided by one of the means described above.

HEAVING-TO. There are two ways of heaving-to, i.e. of

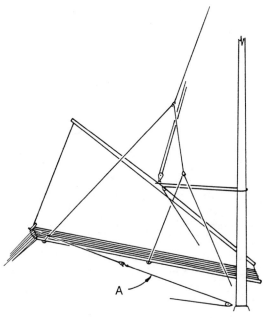

Fig. 15.3   Deep reefing with pendant and hook rope

Wind

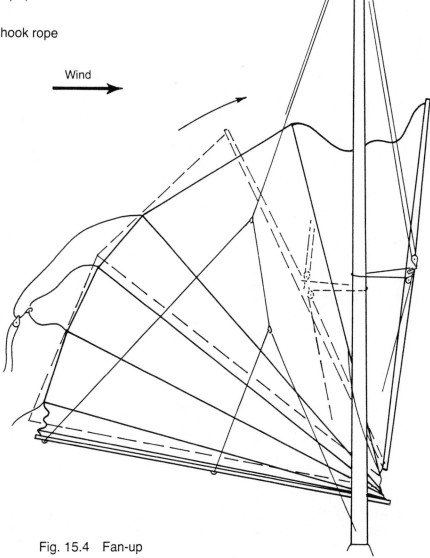

Fig. 15.4   Fan-up

taking most of the way off the boat while getting her to look after herself with lashed helm.

The sail(s) may be well reefed and then sheeted flatter than the close-hauled attitude, with the helm lashed amidships or slightly to weather. She will then jog very slowly to windward, making appreciable leeway.

Alternatively, the boat may lie a-hull with the sheet eased right off and the sail more or less weathercocking, the helm being lashed down as if trying to tack her. Playing with the sheet will alter her heading somewhat in relation to the wind, and vary the amount of headway and leeway she is making.

Do not regard heaving-to as being useful only under gale conditions. It is very often useful in normal sailing breezes, to slow down while taking bearings or checking your navigation, or when giving way to other shipping, or carrying out any job that calls for less motion and dry decks, such as preparing an anchor or fenders before entering harbour.

BARE POLES. Normally used only in a severe gale, there are two basic attitudes under bare poles: lying beam-on a-hull with the helm lashed down, or running before the wind with the boat being steered, whether manually or by a vane steering gear.

The former can in theory be combined with a sea anchor streamed from the bow to keep her head up, but traditional sea anchors seem to be effective only in boats with very little lateral resistance, such as a centre-boarder with centreboard raised. Modern parachute anchors may be more effective.

Running under bare poles may be assisted by towing the bight of a long warp from the boat's two quarters, with the triple purpose of slowing down any surfing, of interfering with the crests of overtaking waves, and of assisting the steering by holding her stern upwind. (Good results have also been reported from towing a small Bruce anchor on a long warp from the stern.) With or without a warp, the boat will sail faster and may be slightly easier to steer if the furled sail bundle, complete with yard lashing, is sheeted out square, acting as a tiny sail, but beware of being pooped if you go too fast in a heavy boat in a steep following sea.

GHOSTERS. The handling of different forms of ghoster has been discussed in Chapter 5. A singlehanded sailor may think it wise to rig some form of overload device that will release the ghoster sheet in a squall, particularly if he intends to carry the ghoster while asleep in his bunk. Taking the weight of the sheet on a piece of twine is a traditional method.

HANDLING ROPES. All ropes in the rig, whether standing or running, are liable to develop twists. If severe, these will cause the rope to kink. Three-strand rope tends to unlay (untwist) slightly when first used

under load. The amount of twist that a rope will accept without kinking varies enormously with the construction of the rope and with the degree of weathering. All synthetic rope, but particularly three-strand polyester, gets permanently harder and less flexible after prolonged weathering. This appears to be mainly due to the ultraviolet component of sunlight and is worst in the tropics, where braided construction is usually preferred.

When a twist becomes evident it must be taken out by going to one end of the rope and putting in the required number of counter-turns. With a purchase, such as the halyard or sheet, the blocks should be pulled together as closely as possible before doing this as the turns will not easily pass around sheaves. With a sheet span, it is obviously necessary to let one end go from the sail before untwisting.

The twisting of running ropes can be largely avoided by following the rules already touched on in Chapter 13, and which may now be restated as follows:

1. Rope reels. If a rope is wound on or off a reel tangentially by rotating the reel, no twist will be put into it. If pulled off or wound on over the flange of a stationary reel, twists will be put in exactly as if it were coiled. As shown in Fig. 13.10, the end of the rope should be attached to the reel in a way that enables any twists to be taken out without letting it go.
2. Flaking. A rope that is flaked down in figure-of-eight turns, as in Fig. 13.12, will not develop any twist.
3. Coils. Right-handed and braided rope is normally coiled clockwise. Only left-handed (hawser-laid) rope is coiled anti-clockwise. Coiling puts in a 360° twist for each turn of the coil, and uncoiling takes this twist out again. If the diameter of the coil is large in relation to the diameter of the rope, the rope may accept this amount of twist without kinking. If it will not, either the free end will start turning to relieve the strain, or if this is not possible the coils will begin to form themselves into figure-of-eight turns exactly as in flaking.

It has already been emphasised that the coiling of a spare end of rope in the hand must start at the cleat and finish at the free end, thus permitting the free end to twist as it pleases in order to take the kinking strains out of the coil before hanging it on the cleat. Before veering the rope the coil is placed down carefully in the cockpit so that the rope comes off the top of the heap.

There remains a risk of the underneath coils getting picked up and jammed against something when veering rope fast. A way of avoiding this is to place the coiled rope on the cockpit seat, work back along it until you reach the free end, and then work back *flaking* it neatly. A flaked rope should run out absolutely clear.

Various users have suffered from twists in the sheets, and it is believed that these are usually due to coiling from the free end and finishing at the cleat. This

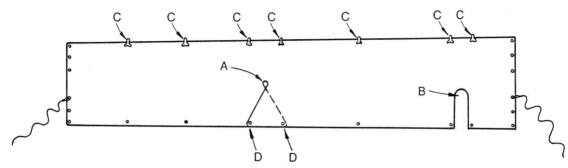

Fig. 15.5   Sail cover

concentrates the accumulated twists next to the cleat, and they will pass up into the purchase when the rope is next veered.

Polyester rope is liable to shrink slightly as it hardens with weathering. Pre-stretched polyester should not be used anywhere, as it shrinks much more and is unpleasantly hard.

Maintenance

Timber masts, spars, and battens should not rot if prevented from remaining sodden with fresh water. This is achieved by periodical varnishing, painting, or oiling, with particular attention to the hidden surfaces at the partners and step, inside the batten pockets, and in the groove of a grooved yard or boom.

Light-alloy spars made of salt-water resistant alloy need no maintenance, and nor do reinforced plastic spars.

SAIL COVERS. Polyester sails do not suffer from being stowed wet, but should be protected as far as possible from daylight, since the ultraviolet component in ordinary daylight is the major cause of degradation of the sailcloth. Protection involves using a sail cover when the sail is furled in harbour, at least if the boat is to be left for more than a day or so. Fig. 15.5 gives a design for a sail cover that fits inside the topping-lifts and round the yard sling plate at A and the mast at B. Each end is secured by a lanyard. Hooks (C) underneath one edge engage with eyelets on the opposite edge. At the sling plate there is an overlapping flap and two pairs of eyelets register with each other at D, with a hook passing through each pair.

When measuring for a cover, get the furled sail and the yard stowed down as neatly as possible and then add a little to the girth measurements because the sail will often be less neatly stowed. The recommended material for a sail cover is woven acrylic cloth.

Everything at the masthead should be inspected at least once a year, or after (say) 3,000 miles of cruising. If the mast is kept permanently stepped and rigged this can be done from a bosun's chair on the halyard, but it is more easily done from an outside position such as a high dock wall or a crane. The boat may be heeled as necessary by a horizontal rope from the masthead.

Blocks with plain bearings will benefit from a drop of oil occasionally, and if it is physically possible for the edges of the sheaves to touch the cheeks a few drops of oil should be put between the two, since this is a potent source of friction when the ropes lie slightly out of line. A sheave is more likely to rock in this way when its bearing becomes worn.

All ropes, whether standing or running, should be end-for-ended when about half-way through their life, in order to shift the points of wear. It is sometimes said that weathered synthetic ropes can be made soft again by soaking in warm fresh water and detergent, but we have not found this to be effective, athough it does make them cleaner.

The batten parrels will get slacker in use and this allows the sail to hang too far from the mast on the starboard tack. When necessary they should be re-adjusted so that it is just possible to get the hand flat between the parrel and the mast when the batten is just above the boom.

The mast lift should be occasionally checked, and if necessary readjusted so as to keep the forward end of the reefed bundle at the designed height.

Repairs and emergency procedures

The most common repair required at sea is the replacement of a broken batten. When overloaded, a timber batten will usually fracture in one place but remain joined by loose wood fibres, looking like two straight lengths hinged together. If you go on sailing with it in this state it will eventually break completely. The broken ends then slide past each other, allowing the leech to sag inwards while a jagged end may poke through the sail or the batten pocket. A broken batten should therefore be removed from its pocket at the first opportunity.

This is normally done by reefing the sail until the

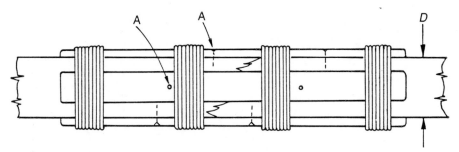

Fig. 15.6   Seized batten

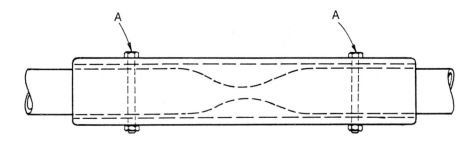

Fig. 15.7   Sleeved repair

Fig. 15.8   Bamboo fracture

broken batten is lying on top of the furled bundle, and then heaving-to with the sheet in. Next, let go the lacing at the leech (if rigged as in Fig. 12.2), but if this cannot be reached from the deck it will be necessary to ease the topping-lifts.

Then let go the aftermost hitch of the batten parrel and the lacing at the luff. The broken batten is then normally withdrawn forwards, but it may be easier to withdraw a foresail batten from the leech end, if the design of batten pocket permits.

If spare battens are carried, as they should be for any long voyage, the replacement may now be inserted and laced in. If not, the broken batten must be fished or

sleeved, taking care to keep it at its original length. The fished batten may be too thick to pass into the batten pocket, in which case either the stitching will have to be cut in that part of the pocket or the fished batten will have to lie partly or wholly outside the pocket.

Fig. 15.6 shows a timber batten repaired with four ash staves and four seizings, but the staves should be relatively longer than shown, say 10 times the depth (D) of the batten. If necessary small nails (A) through drilled holes in the staves may be used to locate them. It is good practice to carry one or two batten-fishing kits ready for use. Light-alloy strips may be used in place of ash staves.

A batten of alloy tube, if overloaded, may first take a

permanent set (bend). If it is then removed from the pocket it is usually possible to bend it more or less straight again by hand, finding a suitable fulcrum and end stop somewhere round the deck and pulling sideways on the other end.

If severely overloaded it may buckle by flattening and taking a sharp bend in one place. After removing from the pocket it can then be straightened, but needs a good splint or sleeve extending well to either side of the crippled part. Fig. 15.7 shows a sleeve made from alloy tube which is a very easy fit over the batten. The buckled part will have bulged out in one plane and might be difficult to flatten back sufficiently to fit into a sleeve, but there is no particular disadvantage in having a bit of play here. It may be located by self-tapping screws, or by two stainless bolts (A) as shown, which should be taped over to avoid chafing the sail. Tubular sleeves of this sort are equally effective for fishing timber battens.

Battens of reinforced plastic tube, such as GRP, have sometimes failed in the manner of a 'bamboo fracture' (Fig. 15.8) in which the longitudinal fibres remain joined but the tube breaks up into flexible strips. This can be repaired by cutting right through the break, inserting a plug or spigot extending either side of it, and then heavily bandaging with glass tape impregnated with resin. Similar fractures in bamboo battens may be repaired in the same way.

If there should be damage to several battens making it impossible to keep a full set of battens in the sail, the remaining battens should be moved upwards and any gaps left at the bottom of the sail, which may then be kept permanently reefed by lacing it down to the boom through the emergency reefing eyelets. The best batten should be put in the position of the top sheeted batten, since this takes the most load.

TROUBLE ALOFT. It is possible, although very unlikely, for something to go wrong aloft while sailing. A pin that is inadequately moused may work out of a masthead shackle, or part of a topping-lift may chafe through unnoticed, or a running rope may lose its stopper knot and finish up streaming in the wind as an 'Irish pennant'.

In such cases it is often necessary to work fast to prevent something that is loose aloft from swinging about with the motion of the boat and winding itself into a cocoon, jamming everything that it embraces. The first action should be to try to grab any loose part from the deck, preferably with a hand-hook, which is shaped to facilitate catching and winding up a single rope's end. If it is not long enough it should be lashed to a boathook or spare batten. The burgee halyard may be used to support its weight.

If this fails it may be possible, if the motion is not too violent, to go aloft and sort things out. Before doing this on a small boat, satisfy yourself that the boat's stability

will permit it. We have watched a man (luckily in harbour) approaching the masthead when the boat slowly heeled over and dumped him in the water.

Going aloft with the junk rig is easiest with the sail set, when a reasonably active sailor can climb up the batten parrels, ideally with the sheet flat in and the boat hove-to on the starboard tack. If the sail cannot be set another crew member can hoist him up in a bosun's chair, but with any motion on the boat the man going aloft will need all his strength and both hands and feet to prevent himself from being swung around, as if by somebody throwing the hammer. While steadying himself in this way he can't help much with the hoisting, so the hard work will have to be done from the deck, preferably with the main halyard.

In a flat calm an active singlehanded sailor can hoist himself in a bosun's chair, preferably on the main halyard, but the long length of halyard descending to the deck as he goes up will easily get foul of something. This risk is reduced by securing the hauling end of the halyard to the chair so that it goes aloft with it, or can be eliminated by flaking the spare rope into a bucket attached to the chair. For safety the man should tie himself into the chair and pass a bosun's chair hitch (Fig. 15.9) round the bridle of the chair before starting to hoist. After every few feet of hoist the slack rope may be worked round the hitch. The hitch may also be passed on the bight of the hauling rope, passing it right round both man and chair after he has hoisted himself.

What is needed at sea is a means by which a

Fig. 15.9   Bosun's chair hitch

singlehanded sailor can easily climb to the masthead without any sail set. If the main halyard cannot be used there may be a ghoster halyard, and in any case there should be provision for passing a gantline as discussed on p 136. It remains to hoist something to the masthead up which he (or she) can climb, again remembering that he will need both hands to climb with and will not be able to reach out sideways to prevent himself from swinging. It is also necessary, at any stage of the climb, to be able to pause with both feet and both hands taking your weight.

A normal rope ladder with wooden rungs swings about far too much at sea, whether triced up taut against the mast or set up taut to the boat's rail. In the latter case it invariably twists round so that the man is clinging to the underside. A workable, but clumsy, solution is to convert the rope ladder into something resembling a ship's ratlines, by setting up an additional rope shroud either side of it and connecting the rope ladder to these by a number of wooden crosspieces (A in Fig. 15.10) held loosely to the ladder ropes. This requires four spaced deck eyes or (preferably) four chainplates along the rail, and it is then possible to climb up and down without capsizing the ladder. If there is any stretch in the ladder it must be heavily bowsed down with tackles, as shown. If it is to be ready for immediate use, the whole assembly will have to be set up and tested in harbour.

A more attractive idea, taken from a yachting magazine, would be to hoist one end of a single stout warp to the masthead. This warp would have small loops of rope projecting from it every 18 in (46 cm) or so, providing both handholds and footholds. After hoisting, the warp would be spiralled round the mast and set up as taut as possible. In order to provide enough handholds and footholds there might be a case for hoisting two such warps simultaneously, and spiralling them round the mast in opposite directions.

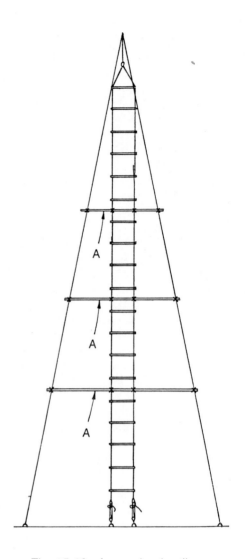

Fig. 15.10   Improvised ratlines

SAIL REPAIRS. Sail damage may be of two sorts: a hole may be chafed or punctured somewhere in the middle of the sail, or a break may occur right through the luff or leech. The former is seldom critical, and it is quite usual to go on sailing for days, or weeks, in this state until it is convenient to make a repair.

A broken luff or leech is more serious, since the sail cannot be used without taking considerable tension all the way up the leech, and lesser tensions up the luff. Damage of this sort can be made good temporarily with a short length of rope or strong cord, bridging the gap between adjacent batten ends and fastened to each. Any loose flaps of sail may then be temporarily laced or stitched to this rope.

Other sail repairs may involve lowering the furled sail bundle to the deck and perhaps taking out one or two battens. Since the sailcloth in the junk rig is not heavily stressed, repairs may be less strong than would be needed in a conventional sail of the same area, and the repair kit should include an adhesive. Proprietary sticky tape for sail repairs may be obtained from sailmakers.

JURY RIG. No designer of any rig can rule out the possibility, however remote, of having to set up a jury rig at sea. Most jury rigs will need stays, usually of rope, and the first requirement is for strong points on each rail to which stays may be set up. It is recommended that the boat should be built with emergency chainplates (shroud plates), preferably two or three well spaced out along each side in way of each mast.

If there are no chain plates or other suitable strong points they will have to be provided at sea either (a) by drilling and bolting through the deck or topsides or (b) by passing ropes or wires right under the hull, strongly-secured on deck on the opposite side.

If an existing mast is sprung but still standing, every

Galway Blazer II *on trials in the solent in 1968. She subsequently made a world circumnavigation. (*Photo: H. G. Hasler*)*

effort should be made to keep it up with jury shrouds and perhaps by fishing over the damaged part as in Fig. 15.6. It may then be possible to set its own Chinese sail, well-reefed, on it. If one strong gantline can be passed through the masthead it may be used to hoist the top ends of two or more jury stays part way up the mast. As discussed on p 13, a mono-hulled boat is seldom beamy enough to provide the 15° minimum shroud angle at the masthead, and these jury shrouds will be effective only if their upper ends are some way down the mast.

At least two junk-rigged boats (*Galway Blazer II* and *Sumner*) have carried on board bipods similar to the sheer-legs shown in Fig. 14.4. These make the most efficient jury masts, since they can be raised and lowered by one man in a seaway using only a rope foreguy and afterguy. A bipod may be used either by itself as a jury mast, or to support a sprung mast that is still standing, or to unstep the lower part of a broken mast and step an undamaged upper part in its place.

As a last resort, a jury mast may have to be a lash-up bundle of any spars or battens available. Even the tiniest jury sail is worth setting if you can't set anything else. If the jury sail is to consist of the normal Chinese sail heavily reefed, it will be best to take out the unused

lower battens and to hold the furled part of the sail down to the boom by lacing through the emergency reefing eyelets. In addition to lightening the sail this would provide battens for jury spars.

Correction of excessive lee/weather helm

Steering problems are nearly always caused by underwater features, such as unbalanced hull shape, excessive beam, faulty rudder or keel configuration, or wrong fore-and-aft trim, and will vary greatly with wind strength and angle of heel. If the underwater faults cannot be corrected, some improvement can often be made through the rig, as suggested below.

Lee helm is very rarely experienced with Chinese rig, except sometimes to a modest degree when close-hauled in ghosting weather, when it does no particular harm.

Excessive weather helm is much commoner, either when close-hauled or (more frequently) when broad-reaching or running, particularly with a single low-aspect-ratio sail. There are a number of possible ways of reducing it:

Hull
1. Trim her more by the stern, e.g. by transferring weight from the bow further aft.
2. Close or reduce any aperture in the rudder.
3. Increase the size of the rudder, or mount it further aft.
4. Reduce the angle of heel by shortening sail.

Rig
1. If the battens are bending a lot, particularly near the leech, fit stiffer ones.
2. With a multi-masted rig, reduce sail on the aftermost mast(s) only.
3. With a multi-masted rig and the wind on or forward of the beam, ease the sheets of the aftermost sail(s).
4. With a single-masted rig, bring the CE closer to the mast by increasing the sail balance, using such means as
   (a) lengthening the tack parrel or standing lower luff parrel, or fitting a running tack parrel.
   (b) shifting the yard sling plate further up the yard, if sufficient drift can be retained on the halyard.
   (c) if all else fails, cutting a strip off the whole leech of the sail.
   (a) and (b) above could also be tried with a multi-masted rig.
5. If you are in despair, the rig may have to be re-designed with its CE further forward and with higher-aspect-ratio sails.

16 Some Specimen Chinese-Rigged Vessels

These examples of rigs designed by the authors have been chosen to illustrate steps in development, and some experimental designs. The original owners are named, but some boats have subsequently changed hands.

Jester (1960)

Owner: H. G. Hasler. Carvel wooden Folkboat hull built in 1953 specifically for the development of ideas for singlehanded ocean passage-making. LOA 25 ft (7.6 m), LWL 20 ft (6.1 m), beam 7 ft (2.1 m), draught 4 ft (1.2 m).

Originally rigged with experimental 'Lapwing' (modified Ljungstrom) rig. Converted 1960 to single Chinese lug designed by Hasler. Tapered hollow spruce mast (1987 new hollow Douglas fir mast built by Noble process).

SAIL. 240 sq ft (22 m²). Aspect ratio 2.2. Yard angle 40°. Six panels. Fanned battens of unequal length with longest in the middle. Convex luff and leech. Balance 22 per cent at batten 3. Yard protrudes at throat, with standing yard parrel. Single sheets, all battens sheeted. Six-part sheet with three two-point spans. Short batten parrels. Batten downhauls. No luff parrels.

No cockpit. Enclosed control position amidships with manual steering by whipstaff. Single pram hood and hinged side hatches. Working ropes belayed on coachroof within reach. Portable boom crutch. Various successive Hasler vane gears controlled from amidships. No auxiliary engine.

OCEAN PASSAGES

1960	Plymouth–New York	singlehanded
	New York–Solent	singlehanded
1964	Plymouth–Newport RI	singlehanded
	Newport RI–Solent	singlehanded

Under the ownership of Michael Richey from 1964 onwards:

1966	Portsmouth–Horta (Azores)	singlehanded
	Horta–Newhaven	singlehanded
1968	Plymouth–Newport RI	singlehanded
1972	Plymouth–Newport RI	singlehanded
	Newport RI–Dartmouth	singlehanded
1975	Falmouth–Ponta Delgada	singlehanded
	Ponta Delgada–Falmouth	singlehanded
1977	Cowes–Faial (Azores)	two-handed
	Faial–Newport RI	two-handed
	Newport RI–Bermuda	singlehanded
	Bermuda–Plymouth	singlehanded
1979	Falmouth–Ponta Delgada	singlehanded
	Ponta Delgada–Cork	singlehanded
1980	Plymouth–Newport RI	singlehanded
1981	Newport RI–Bermuda	singlehanded
	Bermuda–Plymouth	singlehanded
1983	Falmouth–Ponta Delgada	singlehanded
	Ponta Delgada–Plymouth	singlehanded
1984	Plymouth–Halifax NS	singlehanded
1986	Halifax NS–Western Approaches	singlehanded
1987	Plymouth–Nazaré–Ponta Delgada–Plymouth	singlehanded

Redlapper (1962)

Owner: Major-General W. H. Lambert. Hard-chine plywood Waterwitch hull designed by Maurice Griffiths but built with junk rig in 1962. Hull LOA 30 ft (9 m), LWL 26 ft (8 m), beam 8 ft 6 in (2.6 m), draught 3 ft (0.9 m). Bilge keels, transom-hung rudder.

Square-headed Chinese schooner rig designed by Hasler. Tapered light-alloy masts fabricated from different sizes of cylindrical tube with lapped joints. Total sail area 477 sq ft (44 m²).

MAINSAIL. 322 sq ft (30 m²) Aspect ratio 1.96. Yard angle 14°. Seven panels. Slightly fanned battens of unequal length, longest at the top. Balance 16 per cent at batten 4. Single sheets, all battens sheeted. Five-part

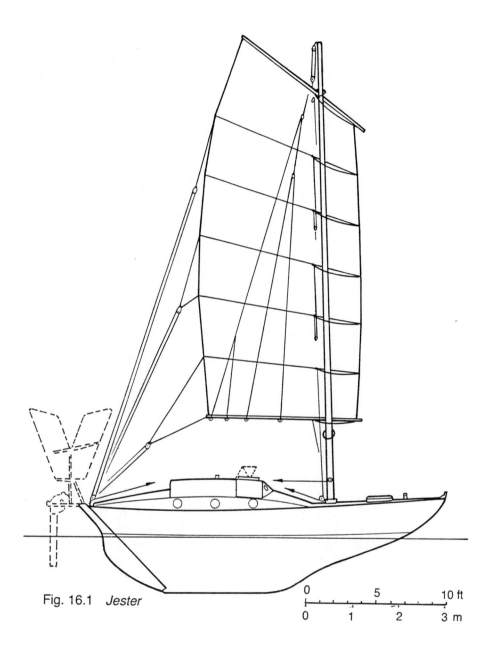

Fig. 16.1   *Jester*

0   5   10 ft

0   1   2   3 m

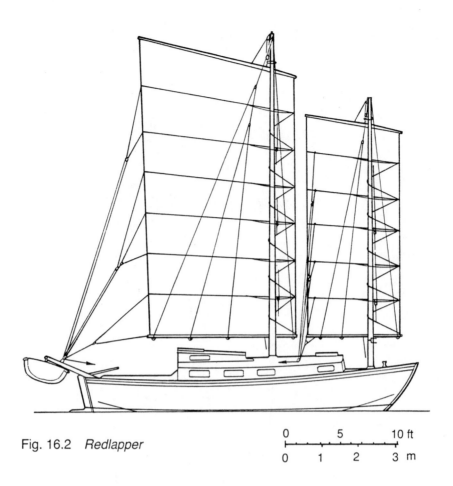

Fig. 16.2 *Redlapper*

0   5   10 ft

0 1 2 3 m

sheet with two two-point spans and one three-point span. Metal traveller instead of yard hauling parrel. Long batten parrels. Standing luff parrels. Batten downhauls forward of mast.

FORESAIL. 155 sq ft (14 m²). Aspect ratio 2.29. Yard angle 10°. Six panels. Slightly fanned battens of equal length. Balance 31 per cent at batten 3. Double sheets to each edge of coachroof. All battens sheeted. Five-part sheets with three two-point spans. Mast traveller. Long batten parrels. Standing luff parrels. Batten downhauls forward of mast. Both sails with twin lifts to forward ends of booms instead of mast lifts.

Normal cockpit with all working ropes belayed at its forward end. Drawers for rope stowage. Diesel auxiliary engine.

Sling plates are well forward on both yards. Standing ends of halyards taken to yard well abaft sling plates, necessitating upper halyard block with plane of sheaves pointing at centre of mast and long masthead cranes.

PASSAGES. Used for cruising in English Channel.

Galway Blazer II (1968)

Owner: Bill King. Designed specifically for a single-handed non-stop circumnavigation. Light-displacement cold-moulded timber hull designed by Angus Primrose and built by Souters. Single keel, skeg rudder, whaleback deck, no cockpit. LOA 42 ft (12.8 m), LWL 30 ft (9.1 m), beam 10 ft 6 in (3.2 m), draught 6 ft (1.8 m).

Two-masted Chinese schooner rig designed by Hasler and McLeod. Tapered hollow timber masts sheathed with polyester cloth and resin, later replaced by masts of Noble staved construction (see Fig. 8.13c). Total sail area 522 sq ft (48.5 m²).

MAINSAIL. 348 sq ft (32.3 m²). Aspect ratio 2.1. Yard angle 60°. Four-panel parallelogram with two-panel fanned head, total six panels. All battens the same length. Balance 11 per cent at batten 3. Six-part single sheets with two two-point spans. Top batten not sheeted. Long batten parrels. Standing luff parrels. Batten downhauls.

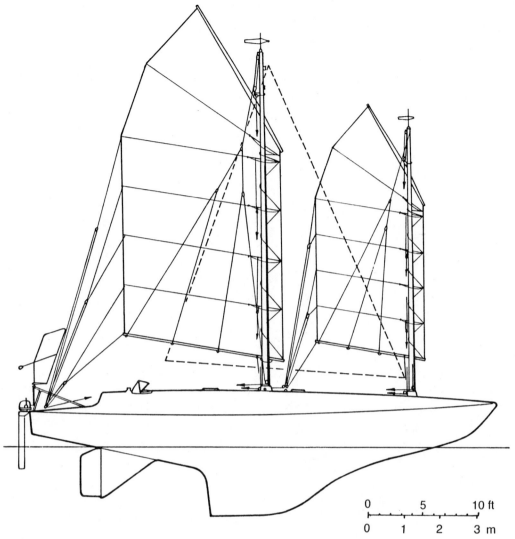

Fig. 16.3 *Galway Blazer II*

FORESAIL. 174 sq ft (16.2 m²). Aspect ratio 2.2. Yard angle 60°. Four-panel parallelogram with two-panel fanned head, total six panels. All battens the same length. Balance 12 per cent at batten 3. Five-part single sheets with two two-point spans. Top batten not sheeted. Long batten parrels. Standing luff parrels. Batten downhauls.

GHOSTING GENOA. Set to main masthead as shown dotted.

Enclosed control position aft with manual steering by tiller. Two pram hoods abreast, with working ropes belayed on deck within reach. Hasler vane gear adjusted from inside control position. No auxiliary engine.

OCEAN PASSAGES

1973   Completed solo circumnavigation, Plymouth–Plymouth via Cape Horn with a stop in Western Australia. Believed to have been the first Chinese-rigged vessel in history to have sailed round the world and round the Horn. Sailed a total of 40,000 miles of ocean under Bill King's command.

Under the ownership of Peter Crowther from 1974 onwards:

1976	Plymouth–Newport RI	singlehanded
	Newport RI–Dartmouth	singlehanded
1979	UK–Cape Town	singlehanded
	Cape Town–UK	singlehanded

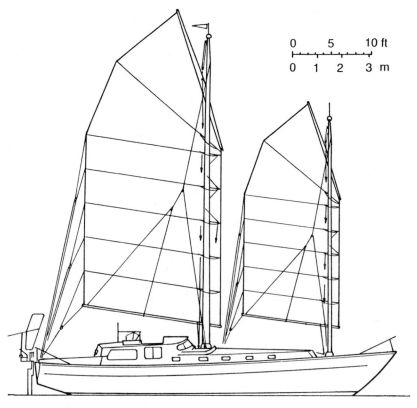

Fig. 16.4 *Ròn Glas*

Ròn Glas (1970)

Owner: J. K. McLeod. Designed for serious cruising with a minimum of deck work and exposure. Cold-moulded timber hull sheathed with polyester cloth and resin, designed by Angus Primrose, built by Souter's and Emsworth Yacht Harbour. LOA 47 ft (14 m), LWL 36 ft (11 m), beam 12 ft 6 in (3.8 m), draught 6 ft 6 in (2 m). Single keel, skeg rudder.

Two-masted Chinese schooner rig designed by McLeod. Tapered hollow timber masts. Total sail area 810 sq ft (75 m²).

MAINSAIL. 540 sq ft (50 m²). Aspect ratio 2.2. Yard angle 70°. Five-panel parallelogram with two-panel fanned head, total seven panels. All battens the same length. Balance 10 per cent at batten 3. Six-part single sheets with three two-point spans. Top batten not sheeted. Long batten parrels. Luff hauling parrel. Batten downhauls. Fixed gallows.

FORESAIL. 270 sq ft (25 m²). Aspect ratio 2.2. Yard angle 70°. Five-panel parallelogram with two-panel fanned head, total seven panels. All battens the same length. Balance 10 per cent at batten 3. Six-part single sheets with three two-point spans. Top batten not sheeted. Long batten parrels. Partial standing luff parrels. Batten downhauls.

*Ròn Glas sailing close-hauled at the start of the 1972 singlehanded transatlantic race. The co-author is keeping watch from under the shelter of the pram-hood. Note the early GRP battens siezed to the sails and fully exposed. Pockets were fitted later. (*Photo: John Etches of Bournemouth*)*

Central enclosable control position with full-width sliding hatch carrying a single pram hood (see Fig. 13.24). All hauling ropes are led inside the control position. Manual steering by wheel. Hasler vane gear adjusted from control position. Aft cockpit is not used for handling the ship. 36 hp auxiliary diesel engine.

OCEAN PASSAGES

1972	Plymouth–Newport RI	singlehanded
	Newport RI–St John's (Newfoundland)–Oban (Scotland)	two-handed
1976	Plymouth–Newport RI	singlehanded
	Newport RI–St John's–Oban	three-handed
1982	Oban–St John's–Newport RI	two-handed
	Newport RI–Azores	two-handed
	Azores–Oban	three-handed

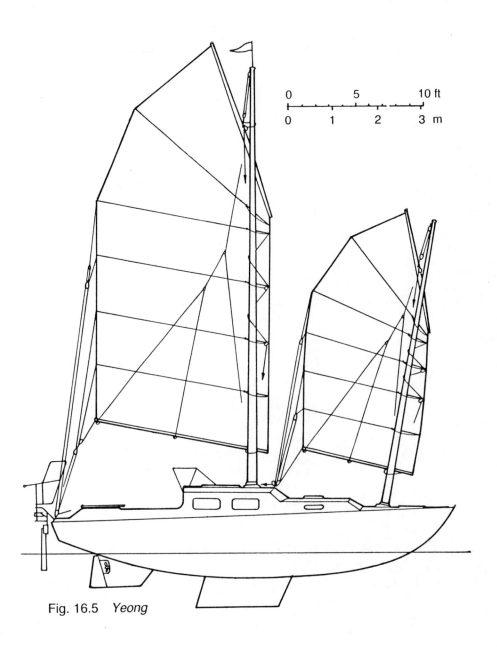

Fig. 16.5 *Yeong*

Yeong (1972)

Owner: Rear Admiral R. L. Fisher. Standard GRP Kingfisher 30 hull, designed by R. A. G. Nierop. Twin keels with 1 cwt (51 kg) of extra lead in each to compensate for heavy mainmast. Skeg rudder. Centre cockpit. LOA 30 ft (9.1 m), LWL 25 ft (7.6 m), beam 9 ft (2.7 m), draught 3 ft 9 in (1.1 m).

Hull modified by builder while under construction to carry two-masted Chinese schooner rig designed by J. K. McLeod and R. L. Fisher. Foremast raked 10° forward to keep its heel far enough aft to give adequate bury. Tapered hollow timber masts, originally sheathed in GRP but latterly stripped and coated with polyurethane enamel. All hauling ropes led to cockpit. Total sail area 443 sq ft (41 m²).

Hasler vane steering gear type SP. 25 hp diesel auxiliary engine.

MAINSAIL. 303 sq ft (28 m²). Aspect ratio 2.2. Yard angle 70°. Four-panel parallelogram with two-panel fanned head, total six panels. All battens of same length. Balance 10 per cent at batten 3. Four-part single sheets with one three-point span and one two-point anti-twist span (see Fig. 4.12). Top batten not sheeted. Short batten parrels. Luff hauling parrel. No batten downhauls.

FORESAIL. 140 sq ft (13 m²). Aspect ratio 2.0. Yard angle

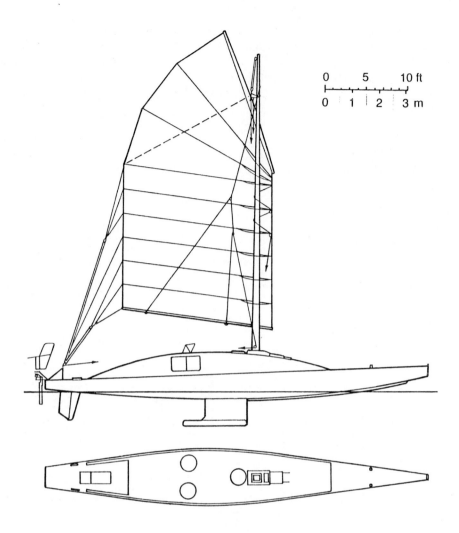

Fig. 16.6 *Sumner*

76°. Battens of different lengths. Six fanned panels. Convex luff and leech. Balance 17 per cent at batten 2. Five-part single sheets with two two-point spans. Top batten not sheeted. Short batten parrels. Luff hauling parrel. No batten downhauls.

PASSAGES

1976 Clyde – North coast of Spain – Clyde
1979 Clyde – circuit of Ireland – Clyde

both crewed by husband and wife only, combined ages 150 in 1979

Sumner (1972)

Owner: H. G. Hasler. Designed by Hasler to compete in the first two-man Round Britain Race in 1966. Experimental light-displacement plywood hull inspired by the American 110 dayboat, with flat bottom and rectangular sections throughout. Vertical twin keels, skeg rudder. LOA 46 ft (14 m), LWL 32.5 ft (9.9 m), beam 6.75 ft (2 m), draught 4 ft (1.2 m).

Originally rigged as a Bermudian sloop, converted to single Chinese lug in 1972, with tapered hollow spruce mast of four-plank construction as in Fig. 8.12.

Enclosed control position amidships with two side-by-side pram hoods and sliding side hatches. Cockpit aft is not used for sailing. Manual steering by a fore-and-aft whipstaff each side inside the side hatch. Hasler vane gear type SP. 4 hp outboard auxiliary engine.

All hauling ropes are led to within reach of the pram hood hatches, with reel stowage below decks for the ends of the halyard and sheet.

SAIL. 480 sq ft (45 m²). Aspect ratio 1.9. Yard angle 70°. All battens the same length. Six-panel parallelogram with three-panel fanned head, total nine panels. Balance 11 per cent at batten 3. Five-part single sheets with two three-point spans. Top two battens not sheeted. Long batten parrels. Luff hauling parrel. Yard downhaul. No batten downhauls. Portable boom crutch.

PASSAGES. Bought in 1974 by paraplegic French yachtsman Bernard Brécy, who has since cruised between Scotland and Spain in her with his wife and young family.

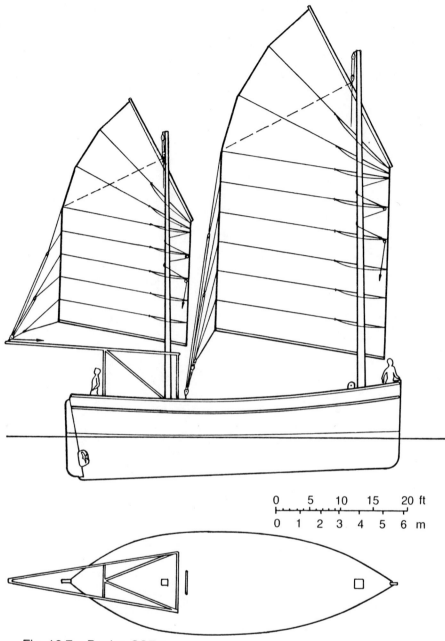

Fig. 16.7   *Design SSF/1*

Design SSF/1 (1973)

Designed by Hasler for Ian Major, but not built. Intended for commercial fishing and sport fishing. Deck layout designed to give a clear passage right round the boat inside the bulwarks, with no obstructions to sport fishing or working nets. Hull is based on that of a traditional Scottish Fifie lugger, LOA 50 ft (15.2 m), LWL 48 ft (14.6 m), beam 15 ft (4.6 m), draught 6 ft 9 in (2 m).

Chinese ketch rig with fixed mizzen and lowering foremast (mainmast). The latter lowers between skegs as in Fig. 9.15 to an angle of 47° above the horizontal, as shown by dotted line, thus helping the boat to lie quietly to drift nets or an anchor. Total sail area 1,530 sq ft (142 m²).

FORELUG SAIL (MAINSAIL). 1020 sq ft (95 m²). Aspect ratio 1.9. Yard angle 60°. All battens the same length. Six-panel parallelogram with three-panel fanned head, total nine panels. Balance 16 per cent at batten 4.

Six-part single sheet with two two-point spans and one three-point span. Top two battens not sheeted. Long batten parrels. Luff hauling parrel. Yard downhaul. No batten downhauls. Halyard led to crab winch near foot of mast, which is also used for raising and lowering mast. Other hauling ropes led to foot of mast.

MIZZEN. 510 sq ft (95 m^2). Aspect ratio 1.7. Yard angle 60°. All battens the same length. Five-panel parallelogram with three-panel fanned head, total eight panels.

Balance 17 per cent at batten 3. Five-part single sheet with three two-point spans, led to high bumpkin supported from triangulated tubular frame which could itself support an awning in the tropics, or a deckhouse. Top two battens not sheeted. Long batten parrels. Luff hauling parrel. Yard downhaul. No batten downhauls. Hauling ropes led to foot of mast.

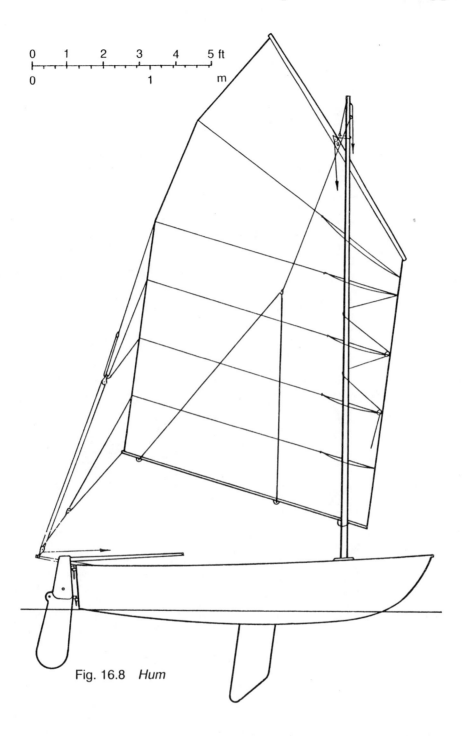

Fig. 16.8 *Hum*

Hum (1974)

Owner: H. G. Hasler. Standard Scandinavian dinghy of hot-moulded veneers, used for rig experiments and as a yacht's tender. LOA 10 ft (3 m), LWL 8 ft 6 in (2.6 m), beam 4 ft (1.2 m). Wooden daggerboard, metal drop-rudder. Tapered solid spruce mast.

SAIL. Single Chinese lug designed to have small head

panels. Area 66 sq ft (6.13 m²). Aspect ratio 1.74. Yard angle 50°. Four-panel parallelogram with two-panel fanned head, total six panels. All battens the same length, and made of garden cane. Balance 18 per cent at batten 3. Three-part single sheets led to bumkin. One two-point span, one three-point span. Top batten not sheeted. Single-part halyard through dumb hole in mast. Yard hauling parrel. Long batten parrels. Luff hauling parrel (dotted line) has been discarded. No downhauls.

Fig. 16.9 *Batwing*

Batwing (1974)

Owner: Timothy Dunn. Designed for man-and-wife ocean cruising. Hull designed by Edwin Monk. LOA 34 ft (10.36 m), LWL 27 ft 6 in (8.38 m), beam 10 ft 10 in (3.32 m), draught 5 ft (1.52 m).

Two-masted Chinese schooner rig designed by Hasler, aimed at getting a relatively large sail area onto a short hull. Tapered solid fir masts. Foremast raked forward 8° in order to get CE of foresail far enough forward. Double sheets on foresail permit minimum gap between sails. Total sail area 768 sq ft (71 m²). Auxiliary engine.

MAINSAIL. 486 sq ft (45 m²). Aspect ratio 1.77. Yard angle 60°. All battens the same length. Five-panel parallelogram with two-panel fanned head, total seven panels. Balance 14 per cent at batten 4. Seven-part double sheets with three two-point spans and all battens sheeted, but these proved too prone to foul (see p 75) and were later replaced by single sheets led to a bumkin. Long batten parrels. Luff hauling parrel. No downhauls.

FORESAIL. 282 sq ft (26 m²). Aspect ratio 1.9. Yard angle 60°. All battens the same length. Five-panel parallelogram with two-panel fanned head, total seven panels. Balance 23 per cent at batten 3. Seven-part double sheets with three two-point spans, all battens sheeted. Long batten parrels. Luff hauling parrel. No downhauls.

OCEAN PASSSAGES. 1977–78 Puget Sound – Los Angeles – Marquesas – Society Islands – Samoa – Fiji – New Zealand, crewed by owner and wife only.

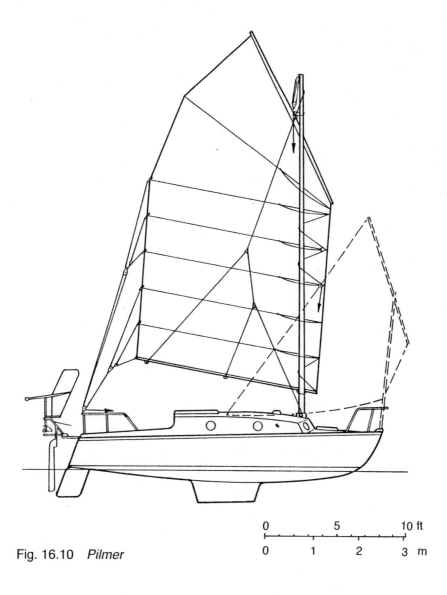

Fig. 16.10   *Pilmer*

Pilmer (1975)

Owner: H. G. Hasler. Believed to be the first GRP production boat to be offered with a standard Chinese rig. Hull and accommodation are the standard Kingfisher 20 Plus, designed by R. A. G. Nierop. LOA 21 ft 7 in (6.58 m), LWL 19 ft 3 in (5.8 m), beam 6 ft 11 in (2.1 m), draught 2 ft 4 in (0.71 m). Twin keels, large spade rudder. Single Chinese lug rig designed by Hasler. Light-alloy mast. Hasler vane gear type SP. 4 hp outboard auxiliary engine mounted in trunk.

SAIL. 227 sq ft (21 m²). Aspect ratio 1.86. Yard angle 60°. All battens the same length. Five-panel parallelogram with two-panel fanned head, total seven panels. Balance 13 per cent at batten 3. Three-part single sheets with two three-point spans. Top batten not sheeted. Long batten parrels. Luff hauling parrel. No downhauls. All hauling ropes led to the cockpit.

GHOSTING FORESAIL (dotted outline) 81 sq ft (7.5 m²) added in 1981 for racing and light-weather cruising, comprising featherweight standing lug set on unstayed dinghy mast supported by pulpit. Increases working sail area by 36 per cent.

OCEAN PASSAGES. *Pilmer* has been used only for coastal cruising, but two of her sister-ships have made a total of at least four singlehanded crossings of the North Atlantic, namely *Griffin* (David Stookey) and *Amethyst* (Kenneth Elliot).

APPENDICES

Appendix A

IMPERIAL/METRIC EQUIVALENTS

Imperial

1 inch	= 25.4000 mm
1 foot	= 0.3048 m
1 square foot	= 0.0929 m²
1 pound	= 0.4536 kg
1 long ton (UK) = 2240 lb	= 1016.047 kg
	= 1.0160 t
1 short ton (US) = 2000 lb	= 907.185 kg
	= 0.9072 t

Metric

1 millimetre	= 0.0394 in
1 metre	= 39.3701 in
	= 3.2808 ft
1 square metre	= 10.6243 sq ft
1 kilogram	= 2.2046 lb
1 tonne	= 2204.6 lb
	= 0.9843 long tons (UK)
	= 1.1023 short tons (US)

Appendix B

Inches and fractions of an inch as decimals of a foot

Inches	\multicolumn{8}{c}{Fractions of an inch}

Inches	0	⅛	¼	⅜	½	⅝	¾	⅞
0	.000	.010	.021	.031	.042	.052	.062	.073
1	.083	.094	.104	.115	.125	.135	.146	.156
2	.167	.177	.187	.198	.208	.219	.229	.240
3	.250	.260	.271	.281	.292	.302	.312	.323
4	.333	.344	.354	.365	.375	.385	.396	.406
5	.417	.427	.437	.448	.458	.469	.479	.490
6	.500	.510	.521	.531	.542	.552	.562	.573
7	.583	.594	.604	.615	.625	.635	.646	.656
8	.667	.677	.687	.698	.708	.719	.729	.740
9	.750	.760	.771	.781	.792	.802	.812	.823
10	.833	.844	.854	.865	.875	.885	.896	.906
11	.917	.927	.937	.948	.958	.969	.979	.990

Fractions of an inch as decimals of an inch

1/16	=	0.062	9/16	=	0.562
⅛	=	0.125	⅝	=	0.625
3/16	=	0.187	11/16	=	0.687
¼	=	0.250	¾	=	0.750
5/16	=	0.312	13/16	=	0.812
⅜	=	0.375	⅞	=	0.875
7/16	=	0.437	15/16	=	0.937
½	=	0.500			

Bibliography

The following books contain interesting material about Chinese rig.

Campbell, John. *Easier Rigs for Safer Cruising*, Hollis & Carter, London, 1985

Colvin, Thomas. *Cruising Designs*, Seven Seas Press, 1977, and other books by same author

Kemp, Dixon. *A Manual of Yacht and Boat Sailing*, 6th edn, Horace Cox, London, 1888

King, Bill. *Capsize*, Nautical Publishing Co, Lymington, 1969

Landström, Björn. *The Ship*, Doubleday & Co, New York, 1961

Needham, Joseph. *Science and Civilisation in China*, vol IV, part 3, Cambridge University Press, 1971

Petersen, E. Allen. *Hummel Hummel*, Vantage Press, New York, 1952

Richey, Michael (ed). *The Shell Encyclopedia of Sailing*, Stanford Maritime, London, 1980

Ronan, Colin A. *The Shorter Science and Civilisation in China*, vol 3, Cambridge University Press, 1968

Slocum, Joshua. *The Voyage of the Liberdade*, Rupert Hart-Davis, London, 1963

Warrington Smyth, Herbert. *Mast and Sail in Europe and Asia*, Wm Blackwood & Sons, London, 1929

Worcester, G. R. G. *Junks and Sampans of the Yangtze*, vols I and II, Inspectorate General of Customs, Shanghai, 1947–48. Reprinted, US Naval Institute Press, 1971

Index

a-hull (lying), 9, 49, 210
  and 'fan-up', 208
  and stowing sail, 182
  to take in sheets, 206
  and weathercocking, 205
aerials, 132
aerodynamics (of sails), 3, 5, 18, 28, 81–2,
    118
aerofoils
  sails, 7
  thin plate, 18
airflow, 16, 28
  slot effect, 17, 18
  tufting for, 16, 18, 28
aloft
  going, 213–14
  trouble, 213
American Boat and Yacht Council (ABYC)
  and lightning conductors, 82
Amethyst, 229
anti-chafe, *see* chafing gear
anti-snarl devices
  for cheek blocks, 138, 183
  for cleats, 138
  for deck blocks, 197
  for ghosters, 81
arching (of sails), 13, 14, 16, 17
  convex, 118
  inducing, 16
aspect ratio
  definition, 97
  diagram for drawing sails, 103
  effects of altering, 97, 116
  recommended, 97
  variation, 97

'B', key letter for batten length and head and
    foot of standard sail
backing sails
  with double sheets, 73
  when tacking, 73, 206
balance (aerodynamic), 10, 27, 30, 39
  and canted sails, 118
  excessive, 118
  and mast loading, 118
  and sheet loading, 118
bamboo (for battens), 155, 156, 157

bare poles
  lying and running under, 210
batten(s)
  affecting reefing, 19, 44–5, 97
  angles of, 22–30 *passim*
  attachment to mast, 10, 24, 159, 202
  attachment to sail, 10, 13, 154, 156, 157,
    163, 166–7, 170, 180, 202
  auxiliary, 17–18
  bamboo, 155, 156, 157, 213
  behaviour on reefing, 19–31, 42, 46, 98–9,
    118, 159, 170
  bending of, 13–14, 16, 48, 118, 154, 159,
    182, 204
  breakage of, 31, 154, 158, 182, 206, 208,
    211–13
  Chinese construction of, 17–18, 155
  compression force on, 13–14, 48, 73, 154,
    204, 206
  dimensions and construction, 154–9
  fendering of, 159, 163, 197, 202
  fittings on, 159, 197
  flexibility of, 13, 14–16, 118, 154
  forward movement of, 21, 42–4
  GRP, 158
  LA, tube, 155, 157–8, 166, 167, 212–13
  laminated, 155
  limitations on, 13
  number in sail, 5, 97, 98
  numbering of, 10, 97
  parallel, 24
  plastic tube, 158, 167, 213
  purpose of, 6, 10, 13
  repair of, 155, 158, 166, 211–13
  requirements for, 13–14, 48, 154
  sheathing of, 157
  and sheet systems, 10, 22, 97, 167
  slope of, 28–9, 98, 102
    effect of heeling on, 28
  square sectioned tubular, 159
  timbers for, 157
  top
    fouling topping lifts, 208
    sheeted, 154, 167, 204, 213
    unsheeted, 14, 31, 56, 73, 76, 97, 154,
    166, 182
  two-part, 155

  uniformity of length, 22, 24, 31, 154–5
  of varying lengths, 22–30 *passim*, 155
batten downhauls, *see* Downhauls
batten hoops, 46
batten lifts, 17
batten parrels, 10, 16, 154, 171, 208
  anti-chafe on, 197
  bamboo, 44
  climbing the, 213
  long (normal), 43–4, 180, 198, 202
  parrel stop, 159, 180
  periodic adjustment, 202, 306
  quick-release, 150, 198
  rope size, 180
  short, 43–4, 48
batten patches, 170
batten pockets, 154, 156, 157, 202
  closed at leech, 156, 163, 167
  drawing and dimensions, 163–70
  and fendering, 159, 170, 202
  open at leech, 156, 163, 167
  width of, 166
Batwing, 228
  and double sheets, 73, 75, 115, 167
  and forward raking mast, 40
  and sail balance, 39, 118
beckets (on sails), 166, 178, 202
  top, and deep reefing, 207
blocks, 171–2, 197
  burgee halyard, 176
  cheek, 121, 137, 138, 150, 183, 197, 202–3
    alignment of, 137–8
  deck, 137, 172, 183, 197
  fixed-eye, 171
  friction in, 36–7, 68, 171, 211
  halyard, 36, 121, 139, 176
    alignment of, 34, 36, 139, 201–2
  luff hauling parrel, 180
  maintenance of, 211
  masthead, 121, 176
  reversible shackle, 172
  sheet, 70–1, 176, 183, 197
  sister, 59, 61
  sizes of, 171
  swivel, 139, 172
  topping lifts, 178, 183
  turning, 137–8, 172, 183

bollard hitch, 184
boltropes, 5, 19
   Chinese use of, 5, 17
   on modern sails, 151, 160, 166
boom, 10, 159–62
   alternative materials, 162
   control of, 42
   dimensions and construction, 161
   fender on, 160, 197
   fittings on, 161, 197
   securing sail to, 160, 180
   topping up, 41, 55
boom clearance, 114, 182
boom guy, 40
boom parrel, 52
bosun's chair, 213
   hitch, 213
Bréçy, Bernard, 224
bruce anchor
   and streaming warps, 210
bullseye fairleads, 183
bumkin
   for sheet anchorage, 119
burgee
   halyard for, 136, 171, 176, 201, 213
   and lightning conductor, 83, 136
bury, of masts, see mast bury

cables (for mast instruments), 128, 132
   exits of, 132, 136
   in LA masts, 139, 201
   protection of, 132, 201
   on solid masts, 133
calculator, requirement for, 89
canting (of sail), 118
capsizing moment, 18, 95
centre of area (of sails), 18, 106
centre of effort (CE)
   with ghosters, 78, 80, 81
   and mast line, 116, 118
   plotting the, 106–7, 109
   positioning the, 93–4, 114–16, 215
centre of gravity (CG)
   of masts, 198, 200
   of sails, 18, 37
centre of lateral resistance (CLR) (of hulls), 92
   finding, 92
centre of pressure
   of hull, 92
   of sail, 106, 118
   of sail plan, effect on heeling, 93
chafing gear
   on battens, 159
   on booms, 160–61
   on gallows, 183
   on parrels, 197
   on topping lifts, 178
   on yards, 153
chain plates
   for jury rig, 214
   for rope ladder, 214
chimney (on mast) (see also mast chimney),
   34, 137, 183

Chinese practices
   battens
      auxiliary, 17–18
      construction, 18, 155
      fitting, 18
      lifts, 17
      parrels, 44
      securing, 154
   boltropes, 5, 17
   cloths in sail, 17
   deckwork, 6, 8, 181
   euphroe, 59
   halyards, 32, 37
   Hong Kong parrel, 46–7
   Junk sails, 13, 14, 24, 26, 29
   luff parrels, 47–8
   mast lifts, running, 52
   mast positions, 116
   reefing, 8, 52–3
   running span-line, 74
   sailcloth, 3, 5
   sails
      construction, 17
      shape, 5, 24, 29
      stowing, 182
   sheets
      blocks, 8
      double, 72
      hauling spans, 8, 10, 61
      lead, 67
      system, 8, 56, 167
      tailed, 72
   shrouds, 13
   tabernacles, 148
   tack parrel, 42
clearances,
   boom, 114
   boom gallows, 114, 182
   for masts, 116
   for sheets, 114–16
   for visibility, 114
cleats
   alignment of, 184
   on deck, 172, 183, 184
   jam, 184–5
   on mast, 138, 197
   rope allowance for, 172
   and swigging rope, 183–4
   on tabernacle, 150
cloths (in sail)
   Chinese system, 17
   direction of, 163
   gaps in, 17
Coastguard, of United States,
   and lightning conductors, 82
coil hitch, 185
coiling of rope, 185, 204, 210
   'Yeong' method, 187
Colvin, Thomas E, 74
comb-cleats, see eye fittings
commercial sail, 7, 8, 187, 225
comparisons
   with conventional rig, 6, 204
   with gaff rig, 3, 204

   between sails, 28
   of sail to windward or leeward, 13, 16
   between single and multi-masts, 18, 94–5
   of stresses, 13
   between winches and purchases, 34
compasses, pair of, for drawing
   extending radius, 89
   requirement, 89
   uses, 20–30 passim
constrictor hitch, 159, 180
control position
   enclosed, 192–3
   on Jester, 9, 191
   on Ròn Glas, 9, 193
   and seats, 191–3
cordage, see ropes
creases, see under sailcloth
Crowther, Peter, 219
crutch, see gallows
Cutty Sark, 3

D_{min}
   definition, 63
   also mentioned, 64–76 passim, 176, 203
deck eyes
   for burgee halyard, 176
   for rope ladder, 214
deck layout, 172, 181 et seq., 197
   affecting gallows, 182
   affecting mast position, 116
   on Pilmer, 172
   on Ròn Glas, 193
deck ring, 142
deckwork
   by Chinese, 6, 8, 181
   for deep reefing, 207
   for downhauls, 49
   for family sailing, 187
   after fan-up, 208
   with ghosters, 78–9
   lack of in Junk rig, 8, 9
   for lowering sail to deck, 51, 176
   for parted topping-lifts, 167, 178, 213
   for replacing battens, 182, 212–13
   for sail repair, 53, 182
   for securing yard, 208
   with sheets, 67, 69, 75, 167
   for trouble aloft, 213–14
   unnecessary, 38
derrick, 200–201
Design SSF/1, 225–6
designers, professional, 87
   of masts, 121, 138
   of spars, 153, 158
design work, 87
diagonals (in sail panel)
   controlling furling, 19–27 passim
dinghies, rig on, 48
   battens for, 157
   booms for, 159
   halyard fitting, 136
   hauling parrels, 137
   Hum, 137, 227
   masts, 121, 145

partners, 142, 145
    stepping mast, 197
    topping lift, 51, 53
    yachts tender, 5, 98
dipping-lug ghoster, 78, 79–80
    action to dip, 79–80
dividers (for drawing), 90
domes, plastic
    not recommended, 187
downhauls
    batten, 16, 48–9, 180, 203, 207
        too taut, 206
    drift, 49, 114
    ineffective in fan-up, 208
    on *Ròn Glas*, 193
    yard, 49, 180, 206
downward ropes, 204
drawing instruments, 88–9
drawing masts, 128 *et seq.*
drawing sails, 20–31 (*see also* scale drawings)
    standard sail, 103, 163–170
    summary, 110–113
drawings, scale (*see also* scale drawings)
    important rule, 89
    masts, 128 *et seq.*
    profile, 90–91, 172
    rigging diagram, 172
    sails, 110–13
    sail plan, 114–19, 172
    topping-lifts, 178–9
dressing a mast, 201
Dunn, Timothy, 75, 228
    and double sheets, 75

Elliot, Kenneth, 229
euphroe, 59, 60, 61
eye fittings, on boom, 50, 51, 52, 159–61, 178
eyeplates, on LA masts, 139, 176

fairleads, 183
fan shaped sails, 24–30
fan-up (of sails), 181, 182, 205, 209
fanning (to windward), 204
fenders (on spars)
    battens, 159
    booms, 160
    yards, 153
Fifie hull, 95, 225
Fisher, Rear Admiral R.L., 60, 222
flaking, of rope, 185, 187, 204
flapping (of sailcloth)
    definition, 6
flogging (of sails)
    in conventional rig, 6
    freedom from in Junk rig, 6, 205
fluttering (of sailcloth), 6
Folkboat, 216
fore-and-aft rig, definition, 3
Freedom rig, 8
friction
    in blocks, 36–7, 68, 171, 203
    in fairleads, 183
    on mast, 34, 36, 44, 47, 48, 49, 197, 203
    in sheet system, 68

fully automatic (of rig and sails), 9, 22, 56
    definition, 8
furling (of sails), *see* reefing

gaff rig, 3, 204
gallows, 51, 53, 118, 156, 181–3
    and anti-chafe, 183
    and boom clearance, 114, 182
    height of, 182
    positioning, 181–2
    types of, 181
Galway Blazer II, 218–19
    and jury mast, 215
    and Yard sling point, 39
genoas, *see under* ghosters
geometry, of sail, 19–31
ghosters, 10, 78–82, 204, 210
    dipping-lug, 78, 79–80
    extra foremast, 78, 80–81
    genoas, 78–9
    halyard for, 136, 180, 201
    pilmer, 80–82
    sheeting angle, 79
    sheet overload device, 210
    topper, 81
ghosting, 3, 10, 40
gluing, of masts, 126–7
goosewinging
    with ghoster, 82
    with multi-masts, 206
greasing mast heel, 201–2
Griffin, 229
Griffiths, Maurice, 216
grommets, in sail
    rope/cord, 180
    spurtooth, 166–70 *passim*
gybing, 8, 208
    when close reefed, 208
    and fan-up, 208
    and sheets, 116, 208
    on *Sumner*, 206

halyard, 10, 32–7, 171, 201
    burgee, 136, 171, 201
    Chinese practice, 32, 37
    for dinghies, 136
    drift in, 32, 37
    double, 37
    always external, 121
    fall of, 34, 136–7, 172, 183, 202, 213
halyard crane, 34, 36, 55, 133–4, 136
    on LA masts, 139
    throw of, 136, 139
hand-hook
    for catching ropes, 213
    for use deep reefing, 207
Harris, Sir William Snow, 82
Hasler, H. G. 216, 223, 225–9 *passim*
hatch, circular, 187–93
    lockable, 190
    twin, 190
headsails, 13
heaving to, 13, 210
    and load on gallows, 181

and pram-hood, 189
    useful practice, 210
heeling, 28, 93, 94
    affecting helm balance, 93, 215
    max probable angle 30°, 190–91
helm, balance of, 215
    Chinese practice, 48
    effect of
        flexible battens, 13, 16, 215
        ghosters, 78, 81–2
        lead and CE, 93, 116
        mast position, 18
Herreshoff, Francis, 123
hitches
    bollard, 184
    bosun's chair, 213
    coil, 185
    constrictor, 159, 180
Hong Kong parrel, 46–7
hook-rope, for deep reefing, 207
Hoyt, Gary, 8
Hum, 137, 227
hurricane cover, 189
    lockable, 190
    on *Ròn Glas*, 190

Jester, 216
    and batten parrels (short), 43
    control position, 191
    convex luff, 27
    mast, 13, 127
    pram hood, 187 *et seq.*
    protection for watchkeeper, 9, 187, 191
    sheet horse, 72
    and winches, 184
    yard, 22, 55
junk
    large, 3, 13, 96
    Foochow Pole, 61
junk rig
    acquiring, 7, 86
    advantages of, 5, 8, 9, 204, 206
    arrangement, choice of, 94–5, 116, 187
    as auxiliary to power vessels, 7
    description, 4–5
    disadvantages, 3, 151, 204
    and shorthanded sailing, 7, 187
junk rigged vessels
    achievements, 6, 8, 216–29 *passim*
    for fishing etc, 8, 98
    history, 3
    large size, 3, 5, 96
junk sail (*see also under* sails)
    Chinese practices, 13, 24, 26, 29, 37, 44, 47, 61
    correct setting of, 205–6
    description, 10
jury mast, 200, 201, 215
jury rig, 214

ketch rig, 129, 151
kicking strap, 45, 49
King, Commander Bill, 218

Kingfisher
    30 hull, 222
    20 plus hull, 229

Lambert, Maj-Gen W. H., 216
lamp posts, for masts, 138
LAP (length above partners) 116, 129–32
    passim
lapwing rig, 216
lateral resistance (see also centre of lateral
    resistance)
    in junk hulls, 6
    and sea anchors, 210
lazy jacks, see topping-lifts
lead (of rig), 93–4
    altering, 116
    and moving masts, 116
    zero, on Sumner, 94
leather (for anti-chafe)
    on gallows, 183
    on ropes, 197
leech
    and batten positions, 156
    forward sloping, 76
    hollowing of, 163
    kinking of, 57, 67, 75
    movement of, 68
    repair of, 214
    scalloping of, 57
    and sheet clearance, 76
    taping of, 16, 167, 170
    tension in, 14, 56, 154, 214
lee helm, 215
leeway, hove-to, 210
Liberdade, 6
lightning conductors, 82–4, 121, 136, 140,
    201
    and LA masts (not required on), 138
    minimum section, 82
    protected area, 83
    temporary, 82–3
    top end, 136
lightning strikes, 82
lights
    masthead, 136, 201
    navigation, 138
Lloyds Register of Shipping
    and lightning conductors, 82
loads (on spars, rig, etc), see stresses
luff
    angle of, 39, 45
    concave, 24, 29
    convex, 27
    dimension L, 103
    dimension U, 98
    fouling rigging, 183
    of ghosters, 79, 80
    repair of, 214
    and sheet clearance, 114–15
    straight, 24–9 passim
    taping of, 16, 167–70
    tension in, 27, 48–9, 214
luff parrels
    anti-chafe on, 197

correct adjustment of, 204, 205, 206, 215
    rope sizes, 180
luff parrels, hauling, 47–8, 171, 179, 202,
    204, 207, 215
    in China, 47–8
    fall of lead, 183, 202
    fouling battens, 205
luff parrels, standing, 42, 44, 55, 161, 171,
    180, 202, 215

McLeod, J. K., 218, 220, 222
maintenance, of the rig, 211
Major, Ian, 225
Marco Polo, 3
Mason, R. and Son, 126
mast, 13, 120–40, 197 et seq.
    ascending the, 213–14
    building systems, 125–6, 132
    built, hollow, 123, 124–5
        solid, 123–4
    bury, see below
    cables in, 128, 132, 133, 139
    centre of gravity, 200
    chafe on, 127–8, 197
    cheek blocks on, 137, 197, 202–3
    chimney, see below
    chock, see below
    cleat, 138, 197
    coat, see below
    composite, 139
    damage to, 215
    diameter, see below
    drawing a, 128 et seq.
    dressing a, 201
    fittings on, 133 et seq.
    for ghosters, 81
    gluing, 126–7
    grown, 122–3, 132
    heel, see below
    hole, see below
    hoops, see below
    ideal, 121
    inertia effect, 7
    Jester's, 13, 127
    jury, 200, 201, 215
    lamp post, 138
    lift, see below
    light alloy (LA), 121, 138–9
    and lightning conductors, 83–4, 128, 132,
        136
    and lightning strikes, 82
    lights and instruments, 136, 138, 139
    line, see below
    lowering, see below
    materials, other than timber, 121, 138–40
    partners, see below
    position, see below
    protection for, 127–8
    raked, see below
    reinforced plastic, 140
    sails embracing the, 8
    scantlings for, 121, 129, 132, 138
    section, 121, 132
    sheathing, 128, 144

sheath, ply, for partners, 127, 129, 142
    solid portions, 129, 132
    steel, 139
    step, see below
    stepping and unstepping, 197 et seq.
    stresses, see below
    Sumner's, 125
    in tabernacles, 148–50
    taper, see below
    timber, 122 et seq.
    traveller, see below
    truck, see below
    wall thickness, 129, 132
    wedges, see below
    weight, calculating the, 200
mast bury
    definition, 115
    determining, 129
    minimum, 115–16, 129
    and raked mast, 118
    in tabernacle, 148, 149
mast chimney, 34, 137, 183
mast chock, 141
    depth of, 142
mast coat, 137, 142–3, 201
mast diameter, 3, 116, 121
    for hollow timber masts, 129
    large, 3, 121
    for LA masts, 138
    small, 121
    for solid masts, 124
mast heel, 122, 147
    dimensions, 129, 132, 145
    greasing, 145, 148, 202
    on LA masts, 139
    with tabernacle, 148
    taper of, 145–8 passim
mast holding-down bolt, 145, 146, 147, 197
    202
mast hole, 141, 142
mast hoops, 46
mast lift, 10, 42, 51–2, 171, 179
    adjustment, periodic, 211
    quick release, 150, 198
    rigging the, 201, 202
    rope size, 179
    running, 52, 179
    tangs for, 55, 133–4, 139
mast-line (on sail), 22, 27, 30, 39, 40, 116,
    118, 202
    and CE, 116, 118
    drawing the, 109, 163–70 passim
masts, lowering (see also tabernacles)
    hinged, 150
    and sail bundle, 197–8
mast partners, 13, 116, 120, 141–5
    for extra foremast ghoster, 81
    in GRP, 144, 145
    for LA masts, 139
    loads on, 120–21, 141
    metal, 144
    on Pilmer, 141
    raised, 144
    for raked masts, 141

for tabernacles, 149
on *Yeong*, 144–5
mast position, 39, 116
    off centre-line, 116
    and choice of rig, 96
    unacceptable, 115–16
mast, raked, 39–41, 118
    partners for, 141
mast step, 13, 116, 120, 129, 145–8
    for extra foremast, 81
    for LA masts, 139, 146
    loads on, 120, 145
    metal and GRP, 146–7
    position for foremast, 116
        for mainmast, 116
    spigot type, 148
    on *Yeong*, 146–7
mast, stresses
    bending, 39, 118, 120, 121
    compression, 27, 32, 34, 36, 118, 120
    with ghosters, 78
    lateral, 5, 120, 121, 141
    at masthead, 5, 27, 37, 120
mast taper, 44, 45, 121, 129, 132, 138–9
mast traveller, 38, 80
    for lowering mast, 150
mast truck
    diameter of, 129, 132
    establishing on drawing, 110, 118
    solid portion, 129
mast wedges
    at partners, 141, 142, 143–5 *passim*, 197,
        202
    at step, 146–8, 197, 202
master diagonal (on sail), 161, 163
masthead crane, *see* halyard crane
masthead fitting, 55, 121, 133–6, 201
    diameter of, 136
    on GRP masts, 140
    inspection of, 211
    on LA masts, 139
    and lightning conductor, 82, 136, 139, 201
minimum gap (for sheets), 114, 166
    with double sheets, 115
    with single sheet system, 114
Monk, Edwin, 228
multi-masted rigs
    advantages, 95
    and burgee halyards, 176
    and deck layout, 183
    and gallows, 181
    and ghosters, 79, 82
    ketches, 95, 114
    and lightning conductors, 83
    5 masts, 3
    positioning on hull, 114–15
    and raked masts, 118
    and recommended aspect ratio, 97, 116
    and rigging warrant, 172
    and sail balance, 39
    and sails on different sides, 13
    and sail setting, 205–6, 215
    and slot effect, 18
    schooners, 95, 114

with double sheets, 73
and weather helm, 215

Nierop, R. A. G., 222, 229
noble mast, 126
nomenclature, of junk sail, 12

panels (in sails)
    creasing in, 42–4, 48, 118, 204
    diagonals in, 19–27 *passim*
    head, 29–30, 31, 97, 98
    narrow, 49, 50, 57, 100–101, 156
        effect on furling, 19–20
    number, recommended, 97–8
    reefing behaviour, 19–28 *passim*, 97
    shape, 19–20, 27, 97
    wide, 20, 27, 53, 97, 100–101, 157
    width of,
        determining, when drawing, 103
        ratio of, 97, 98, 99–102
        recommended, 28
        variety of, 5, 19, 22, 24, 27–8, 97
paper, tracing, 88
parrel balls, 197
Pilmer, 229
    battens, 158
    derrick, 200
    ghoster, 80–82
    lightning conductor, 83–4
    partners, 141
    rigging diagram, 172
        warrant, 173 (Table 7)
    sail area, adjusting, 206
        balance, 39
        recommended, 31
    sheet drift, 203
    topping lifts, 55
planimeter, 103
positioning of rig
    multiple sail, 114–15
    single sail, 114
pram hood (rotatable), 187–91, 192–3 *passim*
Primrose, Angus, 218, 220
printing, of drawings, 88
profile drawing, of hull, 90–91
protractor, 88, 100, 102
purchases,
    in halyards, 34–6
    in topping-lifts, 53, 179

radar reflector, 182
reaching (and running)
    setting of sails, 206
Redlapper, 216–17
    mast traveller, 38
    yard sling plate, 39
reefing (and furling)
    analysis of, 20–31, 62 *et seq.*
    Chinese methods, 8, 53, 61
    crash reefing, 53, 205
    deep, 207
    early, 18, 206
    emergency, 167
    method of, 10, 49, 204, 205, 206–7

moving tack, 118
    with multi-masted rig, 206
    natural tendency of sails to, 6, 8, 9, 203
    restrictions on, 19
    when running, 49, 206
    to slow down, 9, 206
    topping lifts, action of, 51, 62, 114, 207
reef gasket (pendant), 207, 209
reel (for rope stowage), 185, 210
    on *Ròn Glas*, 193
Resistance, H.M.S., 82
Richey, Michael, 216
rigging (running and standing), 32–55,
        171–80
    definitions, 32, 171
    'downward ropes', 204, 205
    layout of, 137, 172, 183, 193
    measuring lengths for, 172–80
    ropes for, 171
    stowing ropes of, 185–7, 210
    twist kinks, removing, 185, 210
    universal rule, 204
        exception to, 205
rigging diagram, 172–180 *passim*, 197
rigging warrant, 172, 197
    sketch drawing, 172
rise, of battens, 101–2
    not on sail drawing, 163
Roaring Forties, sailing in
    aid for deep reefing, 207
    need for downhauls, 49
    need for protection, 187
roll angle, 40, 41, 114
roller furling, for ghosters, 79
Ròn Glas, 220–21
    control position layout, 9, 181, 187, 193
    and hurricane cover, 190
    and pram hood, 189
    and protection for watchkeeper, 9
    rope layout, 181, 193
    and sail balance, 39
    stowage reels, 185, 193
rope, and cordage for rigging, 171, 178, 197,
        210–11
    for batten downhauls, 180
    for batten lacings, 180
    for batten parrels, 180
    for boom lacings, 180
    burgee halyard, 176
    fusing ends, 172, 197
    for ghoster halyards, 180
    for halyards, 176
    length allowances for hitches etc., 172
    for luff parrels, 180
    maintenance of, 211
    for mast lifts, 179
    for sheet spans, 178
    for sheets, 177, 197
    sizes of, 171, 176, 180
    stowing spare ends, 185, 187, 204
    table for sizes, 176
    for tackline, 180
    for topping lifts, 178
    twist kinks, removing, 185, 210

for yard downhaul, 180
for yard lacings, 180
for yard hauling parrel, 179
rope ladder, 214
rot, in timber, 123, 127
rules and formulae
  aspect ratio, of sails, 97
  batten stagger, 99
  boom clearance, 114
  boom gallows clearance, 114
  clearance line, for sheets, 114
  downhaul drift, 49, 114
  lead, of CE, 93
    altering, 116
  lead of sheets, ghosters, 79
  leech kink, 67
  mast
    bury, 115–16, 129
    diameters, 129
    heel dimension, 129
    rake, 40
    solid portions, 129, 132
    truck diameter, 129
    wall thickness, 129
  panels (in sails)
    diagonal, 24
    width, 28, 101
  peak overlap on topping-lifts, 55
  rise, 101–2
  roll angle, 41, 114
  sail area, proportions, 95
  sheets
    anchorages, 71
    D$_{min}$, 63
    gap for, 114
    'shaded area', 63
    span length, 62
  yard overlap on mast, 55
  'universal', for running rigging, 204
running (and reaching)
  bare poles, 210
  reefing, 49, 206
  setting of sails, 206

S bending (of battens), 14–16, 118
saddle eyes, see eye fittings
sail(s)
  assymetry on mast, 34
  balance of, 10, 30, 39
    altering, and weather helm, 215
    causing S bending, 14, 39, 118
  'canting' of, 118
  chafe in, 13, 18, 181
  curvature of, 16
  description, 10
  flatness of, 3, 13
  'fully automatic', 8, 22, 56, 73
  heavy, 6
  in jury rig, 215
  large, 3, 6, 13, 17, 37, 47, 52, 96, 98
  lowering to deck, 34, 51, 53, 167, 176, 179,
    182, 197, 214
  'plywood', 37, 42

position on mast, 13, 22, 34, 37, 39, 53,
  114–19 passim, 202
'pressing', 40
repairs to, 214
rigging on mast, 202–3
setting correctly, 42–4, 48, 68, 205–6
size, maximum, 5, 96
small, 5
stowage of, 181 et seq., 205
weight of, 6, 37, 42, 96, 202
wrap-round, 7
sail area
  adjustable, 9
  adjusting on drawing, 103
  adjusting under way, 204–5, 206
  calculating in conventional rig, 94
  centre of, 18
  checking on drawing, 103
  of Chinese rigs, 94
  and choice of rig, 94
  considerations, 18
  diagram for drawing sails, 103
  large, 73
    drawing, 103
  proportions in sails, 95, 116
    effect of altering, 116
  reduce, need to, 119
  size, maximum, 96
  'working', 94
sailcloth
  chafe in, 6, 73, 214
  colour of, 166
  creases in, 42, 118, 204
  damage to, 5, 7, 166, 214
  folding when furled, 19–21, 53, 97
  loading of, 5, 97
  matting, 3, 5
  modern, 3, 5, 19, 21, 163
  Polyester, 19, 42, 163, 211
  protection of, 211
  repair of, 214
  soft, 42, 50
  stretch in, 16, 155
  tension in, 16, 19, 42, 99, 208
  weights of, 166
sail construction,
  at batten positions, 156, 159, 163–70
  by Chinese, 17
  at head and foot, 151–3, 160, 166, 170
  by sailmaker, 101, 163–70 passim
  at sheet windows, 167
sail cover, 163, 211
sail gatherer, 53, 55, 179
sail plan
  drawing the, 114–19
    summary for, 119
sail, reefed
  drawing, 20–21, 53
  efficiency of, 30, 97
  examination of action, 62 et seq.
  and fan-up, 208
  and gybing, 208
  and reduced clearances, 114
  setting, 204–5

sail shape
  bent parallelogram, 24
  bent rectangle, 24
  broad-headed, 22
  and capsizing moment, 18
  Chinese use of, 8, 24, 29
  extreme shapes, 156–7
  fan-shaped, 18, 24–30
    staggered, 24, 76
  for ghosters, 78–9 passim
  high-peaked, 5, 30
  parallelogram, 24
  recommended form, 30–31, 96–7, 154
  rectangular, 22
  restrictions on, 9, 13, 73, 154
  square-headed, 5, 17, 18, 22, 24, 30
  trapezium, 24
  varieties of, 5, 18, 22 et seq.
  and weather helm, 215
sail track
  on booms, 160, 161
  on yards, 151–3
scale, 88
  'brochure', 90–91
  constructing, 90–91
  lines, 90
  for mast drawings, 128
  rulers, 88
Scale drawings (see also drawings, scale)
  important rule, 89
  masts, 128 et seq.
  profile, 90 et seq.
  rigging diagram, 172
  sail plan, 114–19
  sails, 94–103, 110–13, 163–70
  topping-lifts, 159, 178–9
scalloping (of sails), 16, 28, 42, 45, 97
scarphing, 124
seats for watchkeepers, 191–2
setting sail, 10, 204
shackles, 134, 172
  at batten ends, 180
    alternative to, 180
  at masthead, 134, 136, 139, 201
'shaded area' (for sheet anchorage), 63, 65,
  71, 110, 115, 116, 118, 119
  for double sheets, 73
sheathing
  of battens, 157
  of masts, 128
  for mast wedges, 127, 129
sheer legs, 198, 200, 215
sheet, 56 et seq., 176–7, 204
  adjustment of, 205–6
  blocks for, 176
  danger of easing too much, 206
  definition, 10
  drawing to scale, 176–7
  friction in, 57, 68
  functions of, 56, 207
  for ghosters, 80, 81
  and gybing, 208
  horsed, 72, 110
  loading on, 14

measuring length from drawing, 176–7, 197
minimum gap for, 114–15
overhauling, 57, 74, 204
power of, 56 *et seq.*, 110
reeving, 203
rope for, 177
single, requirement for stagger, 22, 27
split, 69–70
stowing tail, 185–7
sweeping cockpit, 116, 205, 208
tailed, 72
twist kinks in, 210–11
    removing, 185
sheet anchorage (lower blocks), 14, 56, 63
arrangement of, 70, 183
with double sheets, 72–3
on Junks, 8
position and downward component, 207
positioning of, 63–6, 70–76, 110, 115, 116, 119, 183
variable, 72
sheets, double, 10, 69, 72–6 *passim*, 97, 99, 115, 154, 167
fouling, 75, 167
for ghosters, 79, 81
minimum gap, 115
with running span-line, 74–5
and S bending, 14
and sheet windows, 167
sheet hauling spans, 8, 10
sheet spans, 10, 56–62 *passim*, 171, 177, 203
anti-twist, 59, 64, 110
attachment to sail, 166–7, 178, 202
drawing to scale, 176–7
fouling battens, 155, 167, 208
long, 57, 62, 203
measuring length, 176–8
minimum length, 62, 64–6, 203
reefing, action on, 10, 22, 62 *et seq.*
rope for, 177
short, 57
single part, 66
tension in, 57
sheeting angle, 60–61, 63, 72, 110
for ghosters, 79, 80
sheeting systems, recommended, 110
shrouds
disadvantages, 13
jury, 214
minimum angle, 13
on Junks, 13
slatting of ropes, 203
sling point, *see* yard sling point
Slocum, Joshua, 6
Souters, W. H. and Son, 218, 220
span-line, running, 74–5
Spanish burton, in topping-lifts, 53
spinnakers, 5, 13, 18
and rhythmic rolling, 8
sock (for ghosters), 79
splices, 197
length allowance for, 172
stagger (of battens), 17, 22, 27, 31, 44, 48, 62, 73

definition of, 22
desirable degree of, 22, 99
standing rigging, *see* rigging, standing
stepping (and unstepping) masts, 197–201
Stookey, David, 229
stowing rope tails
in bags or boxes, 185, 187
on reels, 185
Yeong coil, 187
straight-edge, requirement, 88
strength and stiffness, definition, 121
stresses
on battens, 13, 14, 30, 97, 120, 154, 182
    excessive, 14, 206
on booms, 159, 182
in halyards, 5, 14, 27, 79, 118
in masts, 5, 13, 27, 78, 79, 118, 120 *et seq.*, 181
in rig, 5, 13, 27
by shrouds, 13
Sumner, 223–4
and head panels, 97
and lead (zero), 94
mast, 125, 198
    jury, 215
sheerlegs, 198, 215
and tacking close reefed, 206
surging (of rope)
axial, on winch, 33
and cleats, 184
swifter, 203
swigging (of rope), 183–4

tabernacles, 129, 148–50
Chinese method, 148
construction, 149–50
in fishing vessels, 148
operation of, 150, 198
tack angle (in sails), 97–101 *passim*
tacking (and gybing)
assymetry of sails when, 34, 205, 206
backing foresail, 73, 206
    mainsail, 206
fully automatic, 8, 292
with ghosters, 79–80
methods of, 206
sheets behaviour, 76
tackline, 16, 42, 45, 49, 171, 180
length, 180, 202
positioning, 45, 159, 161
rope size, 180
and setting sail, 204, 206
tack parrel, 37, 42, 44, 48, 161, 171, 202, 215
tallow, for anti-friction, 197
thimbles (in rigging)
materials, 172
in sheets, 56–7, 59, 60, 172, 203
and splices, 197
in topping-lifts, 51, 53, 172, 178
throat parrels, 46
timber for battens, 157
timber for booms, 161
timber for masts, 122 *et seq.*
    for composite mast, 139

embrittlement, 127
gluing, 126–7
grain alignment, 123
ply sheath at partners, 127, 129
preservation of, 127, 128
rot in, 123, 127
sawing of, 123
scarphing, 124, 125
seasoning of, 122–3
selection of, 122
shakes in, 123
sheathing of, 128
shell grain, 123
strength and growth rings, 122
timber for yards, 151
topmast, timber, on composite mast, 139
'topper' sail, 81
topping-lifts (lazy jacks), 10, 50–51, 178–9, 201
action if broken, 167, 178
anti-chafe gear, 178
and batten support, 13, 14, 154, 207
chafing sail, 18
deck blocks for, 183
designing, 51, 55, 178–9
fouling, battens, 155
    peak, 30, 55, 139, 179
load on, 181
locating on boom, 50, 159–61, 178–9, 202
lower part, 171, 178
and lowering sail to deck, 51, 53, 167, 179, 203
measuring lengths, 179
purchases in, 53, 179
rope sizes for, 178
running, 41, 53, 55, 62, 167, 179, 182, 203, 204
and setting sail, 204
standing, and boom gallows, 182
supporting sailcloth, 20
tangs for (on mast), 55, 133–4, 139
upper part, 171, 178
'topsail', 7
trade-wind sailing, 95
traveller, 38, 80
sheet, 72
tufting, 16, 18, 28
twist (in sail)
anti-twist, 58–60 *passim*, 66, 69
definition, 5
in gaff rig, 5
in junk rig, 5, 39, 68, 70, 76, 118, 205
when reefing, 66, 205

vane steering gear, 7, 16, 187, 210
clearance from sheets, 116, 209
and *Jester*, 191
and *Ròn Glas*, 193

watchkeepers
and control position design, 190–93 *passim*
and deck layout, 187
management by single, 7, 8, 187

protection for, 9, 181, 187, 192–3
and seats, 191–2
and visibility all round, 114, 187, 189, 191
Waterwitch, 216
weathercocking (of sails), 6, 203, 205
and aerodynamic balance, 118
restriction on by shrouds, 13
and sail handling, 204, 207
weather helm, 13, 16, 93, 97, 215
wheelhouse
and commercial vessels, 187
and gallows, 181
on *Ròn Glas*, 181
whipstaff tiller, on *Jester*, 191
winches
and bollard hitch, 184
capstan, 33, 96, 172
crab, 33, 96, 137
drum, 33, 137
for ghosters, 80
for halyards, 176, 180, 204
rope allowance for, 172
self-tailing, 33, 69, 110, 137, 172, 184
for sheets, 69, 110, 180
wind gradient, 5, 18
windsock/vane, 136
windward sailing
with conventional rig, 3
with damaged sails, 7

with dipping lug, 80, 82
ghosting, 3, 16
and high aspect-ratio sail, 97
in junk hulls, 6
and LA masts, 138
normal conditions, 205–6
when reefed, 30
Worcester, G. R. G., 17, 37, 47, 61, 67

yard(s), 10, 30, 151–4
chafe on, 39, 153, 197
dimensions and construction, 151–4
as derrick, 201
fender, 153, 197
fitting sling plate, 153 (*see also* yard sling point)
fouling rigging, 53–5, 208
hollow, 151
LA, 153–4
large, 6
loading on, 118, 151
overlap on mast, 22, 26–7, 29, 30, 53–5, 118
peaking up, 40, 45, 46, 48
pitching of, 53–4
securing sail to, 151–3, 180, 202
timber for, 151

yard angle
recommended, 97
steep, 18
varieties, 5, 30, 97
yard downhaul, 49, 203, 204, 208
on *Sumner*, 206
yard guy, 40
yard hauling parrel, 37–9, 42, 46, 53, 171, 179, 202, 204, 208
adjustment of, 204, 205, 208
anti-chafe on, 197
fall of, 136–7, 172, 183, 202
and reefing, 205, 206–7, 208
rope size, 179
yard lashing, 181, 208
yard parrel, 55, 208
yard sling point (plate), 30, 32, 34, 37, 39–40, 118, 151, 153, 154, 202
best position, 39, 97
construction of plate, 153
for dipping lug, 80
reefed position, 206
varying position of, 118, 151, 215
Yeong, 41, 222–3
anti-twist span, 59–60
mast, forward raking, 40, 118
partners, 144–5
step, 146–7
Yeong coil, 187